Mass Media 12/13
Eighteenth Edition

EDITOR

Joan Gorham
West Virginia University

Joan Gorham completed her undergraduate work at the University of Wisconsin and received master's and doctoral degrees from Northern Illinois University. She is currently associate dean for academic affairs in the Eberly College of Arts and Sciences and a professor of communication studies at West Virginia University. Dr. Gorham is the author of *Commercial Media and Classroom Teaching* and has published numerous articles on communication in instruction. She has taught classes dealing with mass media and media literacy at the high school and college levels, as well as for teachers throughout the state of West Virginia.

Mc Graw Hill

Connect
Learn
Succeed™

ANNUAL EDITIONS: MASS MEDIA, EIGHTEENTH EDITION

Published by McGraw-Hill, a business unit of The McGraw-Hill Companies, Inc., 1221 Avenue of the Americas, New York, NY 10020. Copyright © 2013 by The McGraw-Hill Companies, Inc. All rights reserved. Printed in the United States of America. Previous edition(s) © 2005, 2007, 2008, 2011, and 2013. No part of this publication may be reproduced or distributed in any form or by any means, or stored in a database or retrieval system, without the prior written consent of The McGraw-Hill Companies, Inc., including, but not limited to, in any network or other electronic storage or transmission, or broadcast for distance learning.

Some ancillaries, including electronic and print components, may not be available to customers outside the United States.

This book is printed on acid-free paper.

Annual Editions® is a registered trademark of The McGraw-Hill Companies, Inc.
Annual Editions is published by the **Contemporary Learning Series** group within the McGraw-Hill Higher Education division.

1 2 3 4 5 6 7 8 9 0 QDB/QDB 1 0 9 8 7 6 5 4 3 2

ISBN 978-0-07-805124-1
MHID 0-07-805124-X
ISSN 1092-0439 (print)
ISSN 2159-1083 (online)

Managing Editor: *Larry Loeppke*
Developmental Editor: *Dave Welsh*
Senior Permissions Coordinator: *DeAnna Dausener*
Senior Marketing Communications Specialist: *Mary Klein*
Marketing Specialist: *Alice Link*
Senior Project Manager: *Joyce Watters*
Cover Graphics: *Studio Montage, St. Louis, Missouri*
Design Coordinator: *Margarite Reynolds*
Buyer: *Susan K. Culbertson*
Media Project Manager: *Sridevi Palani*

Compositor: Laserwords Private Limited
Cover Images: PhotoAlto/Frederic Cirou/Getty Images (inset); Digital Vision/SuperStock (background)

www.mhhe.com

Editors/Academic Advisory Board

Members of the Academic Advisory Board are instrumental in the final selection of articles for each edition of ANNUAL EDITIONS. Their review of articles for content, level, and appropriateness provides critical direction to the editors and staff. We think that you will find their careful consideration well reflected in this volume.

ANNUAL EDITIONS: Mass Media 12/13
18th Edition

EDITOR

Joan Gorham
West Virginia University

ACADEMIC ADVISORY BOARD MEMBERS

Editors/Academic Advisory Board continued

Preface

In publishing ANNUAL EDITIONS we recognize the enormous role played by the magazines, newspapers, and journals of the public press in providing current, first-rate educational information in a broad spectrum of interest areas. Many of these articles are appropriate for students, researchers, and professionals seeking accurate, current material to help bridge the gap between principles and theories and the real world. These articles, however, become more useful for study when those of lasting value are carefully collected, organized, indexed, and reproduced in a low-cost format, which provides easy and permanent access when the material is needed. That is the role played by ANNUAL EDITIONS.

The mass media are a part of the fabric of American society. Learning how to evaluate media messages critically—asking, Who created this message? What is its intent? How objective is it? How does what I am seeing or hearing reflect and/or shape real-world realities?—is a part of being literate in today's world. The organization of articles in this collection reflects this media literacy perspective. Unit 1 offers commentary on mass media use and content and its impact on individuals and society. Unit 2 explores media as sources of news, information, and political influence. Unit 3 introduces perspectives on media access, regulation, and ethics. Unit 4 turns attention to business decisions, including relationships between the content and financial sides of media enterprises.

The articles selected for inclusion in this eighteenth edition of *Annual Editions: Mass Media* reflect the firm entrenchment of "new media" into the traditional media landscape. Where the "mass" in mass media was traditionally about selected messages reaching large audiences through few channels—narrow on the head end, wide on the receiving end—it is increasingly about mass channels and messages. Articles reviewed over the past year for inclusion in this edition often analyze changes in business models, the evolving organizational and financial structures within which media messages are produced, as opposed to message effects. Two other hot topics have been effects of media *quantity* on concentration, social interaction, and mental processing, and free speech, from WikiLeaks to political revolution.

The eminent media theorist Marshall McLuhan proposed four questions that help predict how new media invariably affect the form and content of old media: (1) What does a new medium enhance or amplify in the culture? (2) What does it make obsolete or push out of a position of prominence? (3) What does it retrieve from the past? and (4) What does a medium "reverse into" or "flip into" when it reaches the limits of its potential? Early adopters of new media tend to use them like old media. Network television, for example, started out with actors reading scripts. It took a while for producers to fully understand how television could tell stories differently from radio, but once they did, folks who had been listening to

serial dramas, comedies, and soap operas on radio came to prefer watching them on TV. Radio, in turn, flipped into talk and music programming. Post-theatrical distribution options have flipped the way movies are made and marketed. Outtakes and special features such as alternative endings and camera angles became part of the filmmaking craft, saved for the DVD release where "active viewers" can fiddle with them. In return, movie theatres added stadium seating and enhanced sound systems, a return to the grand cinema experience of earlier years, with hopes of making moviegoing a bigger and more sensual, if more passive, experience than watching at home.

Technology is the conduit through which mass media messages move between senders and receivers. Its development is a scientific experiment, but its use is a social endeavor. Mass media shape the form and content of what is communicated, of who communicates with whom, with what intent and to what effect.

Many of the articles in this collection, even those that are primarily descriptive, include an editorial viewpoint and draw conclusions or make recommendations with which you may disagree. These editorial viewpoints are more frequently critical than they are complimentary. They are not necessarily my opinions and should not necessarily become yours. I encourage you to debate these issues, drawing from the information and insights provided in the readings as well as from your own experiences as a media consumer. If you are an "average" American, you have spent a great deal of time with mass media. Your own observations have as much value as those of the writers whose work is included in these pages.

As always, those involved in producing this anthology are sincerely committed to including articles that are timely, informative, and interesting.

Joan Gorham
Editor

The Annual Editions Series

Contents

UNIT 1
Living with Media

Unit Overview   xvi

The concepts in bold italics are developed in the article. For further expansion, please refer to the Topic Guide.

UNIT 2
Telling Stories

The concepts in bold italics are developed in the article. For further expansion, please refer to the Topic Guide.

UNIT 3
Players and Guides

The concepts in bold italics are developed in the article. For further expansion, please refer to the Topic Guide.

UNIT 4
Paying the Bills

The concepts in bold italics are developed in the article. For further expansion, please refer to the Topic Guide.

Correlation Guide

The *Annual Editions* series provides students with convenient, inexpensive access to current, carefully selected articles from the public press. **Annual Editions: Mass Media 12/13** is an easy-to-use reader that presents articles on important topics such as *the coverage of war, catastrophes, advertising, the Internet,* and many more. For more information on *Annual Editions* and other *McGraw-Hill Contemporary Learning Series* titles visit www.mhhe.com/cls.

This convenient guide matches the units in **Annual Editions: Mass Media 12/13** with the corresponding chapters in three of our best-selling McGraw-Hill Mass Communication textbooks by Dominick and Baran.

Annual Editions: Mass Media 12/13	Dynamics of Mass Communication: Media in Transition, 12/e by Dominick	Introduction to Mass Communication: Media Literacy and Culture, 7/e by Baran	Introduction to Mass Communication: Media Literacy and Culture, 7/e Updated Edition by Baran
Unit 1: Living with Media	**Chapter 1:** Communication: Mass and Other Forms **Chapter 2:** Perspectives on Mass Communication **Chapter 3:** Historical and Cultural Context **Chapter 5:** Newspapers **Chapter 9:** Sound Recording **Chapter 10:** Broadcast Television **Chapter 18:** Social Effects of Mass Communication	**Chapter 1:** Mass Communication, Culture, and Media Literacy **Chapter 3:** Books **Chapter 4:** Newspapers **Chapter 5:** Magazines **Chapter 6:** Film **Chapter 7:** Radio, Recording, and Popular Music **Chapter 8:** Television, Cable, and Mobile Video **Chapter 13:** Theories and Effects of Mass Communication	**Chapter 1:** Mass Communication, Culture, and Media Literacy **Chapter 3:** Books **Chapter 4:** Newspapers **Chapter 5:** Magazines **Chapter 6:** Film **Chapter 7:** Radio, Recording, and Popular Music **Chapter 8:** Television, Cable, and Mobile Video **Chapter 13:** Theories and Effects of Mass Communication
Unit 2: Telling Stories	**Chapter 4:** Newspapers **Chapter 10:** Broadcast Television **Chapter 13:** News Gathering and Reporting **Chapter 18:** Social Effects of Mass Communication	**Chapter 4:** Newspapers **Chapter 8:** Television, Cable, and Mobile Video **Chapter 15:** Global Media	**Chapter 4:** Newspapers **Chapter 8:** Television, Cable, and Mobile Video **Chapter 15:** Global Media
Unit 3: Players and Guides	**Chapter 16:** Formal Controls: Laws, Rules, Regulations **Chapter 17:** Ethics and Other Informal Controls **Chapter 18:** Social Effects of Mass Communication	**Chapter 7:** Radio, Recording, and Popular Music **Chapter 14:** Media Freedom, Regulation, and Ethics	**Chapter 7:** Radio, Recording, and Popular Music **Chapter 14:** Media Freedom, Regulation, and Ethics
Unit 4: Paying the Bills	**Chapter 15:** Advertising **Chapter 16:** Formal Controls: Laws, Rules, Regulations	**Chapter 12:** Advertising	**Chapter 12:** Advertising

Topic Guide

This topic guide suggests how the selections in this book relate to the subjects covered in your course. You may want to use the topics listed on these pages to search the Web more easily.

On the following pages a number of websites have been gathered specifically for this book. They are arranged to reflect the units of this Annual Editions reader. You can link to these sites by going to www.mhhe.com/cls

All the articles that relate to each topic are listed below the bold-faced term.

Internet References

The following Internet sites have been selected to support the articles found in this reader. These sites were available at the time of publication. However, because websites often change their structure and content, the information listed may no longer be available. We invite you to visit www.mhhe.com/cls for easy access to these sites.

Annual Editions: Mass Media 12/13

General Sources

Associated Press Managing Editors
www.apme.com/

Allows you to view all the front pages of newspapers across the nation.

The Center for Communication
www.cencom.org

The Center for Communication is an independent nonpartisan media forum that introduces issues, ethics, people and media business. The site provides archived seminars like the panel discussion on Marshall McLuhan entitled "Oracle of the Electronic Age." Students can tap into these seminars via videostreaming. This site also provides links to numerous other sites.

Current.org
www.current.org

This is a newspaper about public broadcasting in the U.S. It is editorially independent and is an affiliate of the Educational Broadcasting Corporation.

Digital Forensics and Tampering
www.cs.dartmouth.edu/farid/research/tampering.html

Dartmouth scientist Hany Farid posts examples of photo editing, and illustrations of his work developing mathematical and computational algorithms to detect tampering in digital media. Links to articles including www.cs.dartmouth.edu/farid/publications/deception07.html "Digital Doctoring: can we trust photographs?" and www.cs.dartmouth.edu/farid/publications/significance06.pdf "Digital Doctoring: How to tell the real from the fake" (pdf files), well-illustrated with examples, historical and current.

Media Awareness Network
www.media-awareness.ca

Media Awareness Network provides resources and support for parents and teachers interested in media and information literacy for kids. Concise, vest-pocket summaries of issues including media stereotyping, media violence, online hate, information privacy. Includes educational games (e.g., *Jo Cool* or *Jo Fool*: Interactive Module and Quiz on Critical Thinking for the Internet). From Canada.

NewsPlace
www.niu.edu/newsplace/

This site of Professor Avi Bass from Northern Illinois University will lead you to a wealth of resources of interest in the study of mass media, such as international perspectives on censorship. Links to government, corporate, and other organizations are provided.

The Web Journal of Mass Communication
www.scripps.ohiou.edu/wjmcr/

This site can also be easily accessed from http://wjmcr.org. The Web Journal of Mass Communication out of Ohio University focuses on articles that relate to how the Web shapes mass communication.

Writers Guild of America
www.wga.org

The Writer's Guild of America is the union for media entertainment writers. The nonmember areas of this site offer useful information for aspiring writers. There is also an excellent links section.

UNIT 1: Living with Media

American Center for Children and Media
www.centerforchildrenandmedia.org

Continually amasses up-to-date research, news and writings about children and media, from which it digests, analyzes and disseminates information on trends and themes.

Children Now
www.childrennow.org

Children Now's site provides access to a variety of views on the impact of media on children. Public opinion surveys of young people, independent research on television and print media, industry conference proceedings, and more are available. An Internet resource list is included.

Freedom Forum
www.freedomforum.org

The Freedom Forum is a nonpartisan, international foundation dedicated to free press, free speech, and free spirit for all people. Its mission is to help the public and the news media understand one another better. The press watch area of this site is intriguing.

Media Literacy Clearing House
www.frankwbaker.com/default1.htm

Frank Baker's Media Literacy Clearing House provides access to a wealth of resources designed for teaching media literacy and of interest to anyone seeking to improve their own media literacy.

UNIT 2: Telling Stories

Fairness and Accuracy in Reporting
www.fair.org

FAIR, a U.S. media watch group, offers well-documented criticism of media bias and censorship. It advocates structural reform to break up the dominant media conglomerates.

Organization of News Ombudsmen (ONO)
www.newsombudsmen.org

This ONO page provides links to journalism websites. ONO works to aid in the wider establishment of the position of news ombudsmen on newspapers and elsewhere in the media and to provide a forum for the interchange of experiences, information, and ideas among news ombudsmen.

Internet References

Television News Archive
http://tvnews.vanderbilt.edu

By browsing through this Vanderbilt University site, you can review national U.S. television news broadcasts from 1968 onward. It will give you insight into how the broadcast news industry has changed over the years and what trends define the industry today.

UNIT 3: Players and Guides

The Electronic Journalist
http://spj.org

This site for The Electronic Journalist, an online service of the Society of Professional Journalists (SPJ), will lead you to a number of articles having to do with journalistic ethics, accuracy, and other topics.

Federal Communications Commission (FCC)
www.fcc.gov

The FCC is an independent U.S. government agency whose mission "is to encourage competition in all communications markets and to protect the public interest." Access to information about such topics as laws regulating the media is possible.

Photo Ethics
www.sree.net/teaching/photoethics.html

Examples of famous digitally altered photographs

Ethics Case Studies
http://journalism.indiana.edu/resources/ethics/#photos

Case studies from Indiana University

Poynter Online: Research Center
www.poynter.org

The Poynter Institute for Media Studies provides extensive links to information and resources on media ethics, media writing and editing, visual journalism, and much more. Many bibliographies and websites are included.

World Intellectual Property Organization (WIPO)
www.wipo.org

Click on the links at WIPO's home page to find general information on WIPO and intellectual property, publications and documents, international classifications, and more.

UNIT 4: Paying the Bills

Advertising Age
http://adage.com

Gain access to articles and features about media advertising, such as a history of television advertising, at this site.

Citizens Internet Empowerment Coalition (CIEC)
www.ciec.org

CIEC is a broad group of Internet users, library groups, publishers, online service providers, and civil liberties groups working to preserve the First Amendment and ensure the future of free expression. Find discussions of the Communications Decency Act and Internet-related topics here.

Media Literacy Clearing House
www.frankwbaker.com/default1.htm

Frank Baker's Media Literacy Clearing House provides access to a wealth of resources designed for teaching media literacy and of interest to anyone seeking to improve their own media literacy. Click "Math in the Media" for links to data on 30 second ad costs, calculating ratings and shares, and Nielsen markets.

Young MediaAustralia
www.youngmedia.org.au/mediachildren/03_advertising.htm

This organization's "members share a strong commitment to the promotion of the healthy development of Australian children. Their particular interest and expertise is in the role that media experiences play in that development."

UNIT 1

Living with Media

Unit Selections

1. **In the Beginning Was the Word,** Christine Rosen
2. **Revolution in a Box,** Charles Kenny
3. **Tele[re]vision,** Jenny Price
4. **Television and the Decline of Deference,** Stuart Clayton
5. **I Can't Think!,** Sharon Begley
6. **The Digital Disruption: Connectivity and the Diffusion of Power,** Eric Schmidt and Jared Cohen
7. **Journalist Bites Reality!,** Steve Salerno
8. **Girls Gone Anti-Feminist,** Susan J. Douglas

Learning Outcomes

After reading this Unit, you should be able to

- Critically evaluate the effects of living with media on how consumers attend to and process information.

- Distinguish between feedback and feedforward relationships between social reality and the media.

- Assess the potential of feedforward effects in terms of desirable and undesirable outcomes.

- Evaluate the relationship between connection technologies and international governance.

- Assess the relationship between gender roles and media images.

Student Website
www.mhhe.com/cls

Internet References

American Center for Children and Media
www.centerforchildrenandmedia.org
Children Now
www.childrennow.org
Freedom Forum
www.freedomforum.org
Media Literacy Clearing House
www.frankwbaker.com/default1.htm

The media have been blamed for just about everything, from a decrease in attention span to an increase in street crime, to undoing our capacity to think. In *Amusing Ourselves to Death* (Penguin, 1986), social critic Neil Postman suggested that the cocktail party, the quiz show, and popular trivia games are reflections of society's trying to find a use for the abundance of superficial information given to us by the media. Peggy Noonan, a former network writer and White House speech writer, has observed that experiences are not "real" unless they are ratified by media (which is why, she says, half the people in a stadium watch the game on monitors rather than the field). Marie Winn's memorable description of a child transfixed by television—slack-jawed, tongue resting on the front teeth, eyes glazed and vacant (*The Plug-In Drug,* Penguin, 1985, 2002)—has become an oftquoted symbol of the passivity encouraged by television viewing.

The average American watched 34 hours 39 minutes of television in the 4th quarter of 2010. Adults over 50 watched about twice as much traditional TV as teens age 12–17. Of 301 million American mobile phone users, 24.7 million watched a video on a mobile phone, a 41 percent increase since the 4th quarter of 2009. Consumers age 12–17 were the heaviest mobile video watchers, watching on average 7 hours 13 minutes a month. A total of 143.9 million Americans viewed video on PCs/laptops in January 2011, on average for 4 hours 39 minutes. In the same month, social networking and blog sites attracted 151.7 million Americans. Forty-seven percent of Internet users ages 50–64 used social networking between April 2009 and May 2010, up 25 percent from the year before.

Of business professionals surveyed by Magnify.net in spring 2011, 50.3 percent reported being connected to the Web from the time they wake up until the time they go to bed; 62.5 percent wished they could filter out the flood of data. We, as a nation, have a distinct love–hate relationship with mass media.

Questions of whether, and to what extent, media influence our behaviors, values, expectations, and ways of thinking are difficult to answer. We don't grow up in bubbles, some with and some without media. We get information about the same topic from multiple sources, some mediated and some not. Isolating media as a causal agent in examining human behavior is a difficult task.

Media messages serve a variety of purposes: They inform, they influence public opinion, they sell, and they entertain— sometimes below the level of consumers' conscious awareness. Children watch *Sesame Street* to be entertained, but they also learn to count, to share, to accept physical differences among individuals, and (perhaps) to desire a Sesame Street lunchbox. Adults watch crime dramas to be entertained, but they also learn that they have the right to remain silent when arrested, how (accurately or inaccurately) the criminal justice system works, and that the world is an unsafe place.

Nicholas Johnson, a former chairman of the Federal Communications Commission, has noted, "Every moment of television programming—commercials, entertainment, news—teaches us something." The same might be said of all mass media. So we ask: who crafted this message? The answer has obvious

© George Doyle/Getty Images

implications for the topics and the spin of the newscast (FOX or CNN?) or the blog or any media content. Below the surface, learning is often indirect or incidental. How incidental learning occurs is most often explained by two theories. Social learning (or modeling) theory suggests that the behavior of media consumers, particularly children, is affected by their imitating role models presented via media. The degree to which modeling occurs depends on the presence of *inhibitors,* lessons learned in real life that discourage imitation, and *disinhibitors,* experiences in real life that reinforce imitation.

Cultivation theory holds that media shape behavior by influencing attitudes. Media provide a "window to the world," exposing consumers to images of reality that may or may not jibe with personal experience. *Mainstreaming* effects occur when media introduce images of things with which the consumer has no personal experience. *Resonance* effects occur when media images echo personal experience. Heavy media consumers are more likely to be affected than light consumers, since they spend more time absorbing information from media. People who have had real-world experiences similar to those in the media they consume may find that the media reinforce their beliefs (resonance). However, consumers who have had personal experiences that differ from the images portrayed in media are not as likely to believe "media reality" over what they have observed in real life.

The readings in this unit examine media use, media content, and media effects. All of them acknowledge the increasingly complex interactions among media producers, technology, forms, formats, and consumers. They share concerns over media influence on daily living and on society. Some take a *feedforward* perspective, holding media accountable for shaping changes in public attitude and behavior. Others argue a *feedback* viewpoint, in which media simply reflect what consumers choose to make popular.

"In the Beginning Was the Word" is about the role of the book in the contemporary media landscape. While the experience of reading (traditional book? Kindle?) and competition for time to read are changing, "our need for stories to translate our experience hasn't changed." The number of books published in 2000 was 282,242; in 2010, 1,052,803.

"Revolution in a Box" and "Tele[re]vision" focus on prosocial feedforward effects of television. "Television and the Decline of Deference" asks whether the mass media have undermined the authority of British politicians and royalty. The conclusion leans toward a feedback perspective: "The changes in the mass media and the changes in the treatment of leading authority figures are themselves the products of broader developments that have affected popular deference in Britain."

"I Can't Think!" is about the volume of media content—not how loud, but how much. Living with media means having access to huge amounts of information, and there's a lot that is good about that. There's also a downside: "Creative decisions are more likely to bubble up from a brain that applies unconscious thought to a problem rather than going at it in a full-frontal, analytical assault. So, while we're likely to think creative thoughts in the shower, it's much harder if we're under a virtual deluge of data."

"The Digital Disruption" discusses the implications of widespread access to connective technology on international governance: "There will be a constant struggle between those striving to promote what United States. Secretary of State Hilary Clinton has called 'the freedom to connect' and those who view that freedom as inimical to their political survival." The argument presented in "Journalist Bites Reality!" is captured in the article's subtitle: "How broadcast journalism is flawed in such a fundamental way that its utility for informing viewers is almost nil." Steve Salerno takes on agenda-setting, feedforward effects of news and information media, including events set in motion by partial truths that become widespread perceptions of reality. "Girls Gone Anti-Feminist" also takes a critical feedforward stance: "This is the mass media—exaggerating certain kinds of stories, certain kinds of people, certain kinds of values and attitudes, while minimizing others or rendering them invisible."

In the Beginning Was the Word

The book, that fusty old technology, seems rigid and passé as we daily consume a diet of information bytes and digital images. The fault, dear reader, lies not in our books but in ourselves.

Christine Rosen

In August, the company that owns *Reader's Digest* filed for bankruptcy protection. The magazine, first cobbled together with scissors and paste in a Greenwich Village basement in 1922 by De Witt Wallace and his wife, Lila, was a novel experiment in abridgement—in 62 pages, it offered Americans condensed versions of current articles from other periodicals. The formula proved wildly successful, and by midcentury *Reader's Digest* was a publishing empire, with millions of subscribers and ventures including Reader's Digest Condensed Books, which sold abridged versions of best-selling works by authors such as Pearl Buck and James Michener. *Reader's Digest* both identified and shaped a peculiarly American approach to reading, one that emphasized convenience, entertainment, and the appearance of breadth. An early issue noted that it was "not a magazine in the usual sense, but rather a co-operative means of rendering a time-saving device."

The fate of *Reader's Digest* would have been of interest to the late historian and Librarian of Congress Daniel Boorstin. In his renowned 1962 book *The Image: A Guide to Pseudo-Events in America,* Boorstin used *Reader's Digest* as an example of what was wrong with a culture that had learned to prefer image to reality, the copy to the original, the part to the whole. Publications such as the *Digest,* produced on the principle that any essay can be boiled down to its essence, encourage readers to see articles as little more than "a whiff of literary ectoplasm exuding from print," he argued, and an author's style as littered with unnecessary "literary embellishments" that waste a reader's time.

Today, of course, abridgement and abbreviation are the norm, and our impatience for information has trained even those of us who never cracked an issue of *Reader's Digest* to prefer 60-second news cycles to 62 condensed pages per month. Free "aggregator" Web sites such as The Huffington Post link to hundreds of articles from other publications every day, and services such as DailyLit deliver snippets of novels directly to our e-mail in-boxes every morning.

Our willingness to follow a writer on a sustained journey that may at times be challenging and frustrating is less compelling than our expectation of being conveniently entertained. Over time, this attitude undermines our commitment to the kind of "deep reading" that researcher Maryanne Wolf, in *Proust and the Squid: The Story and Science of the Reading Brain* (2007), argues is important from an early age, when readers learn to identify with characters and to "expand the boundaries of their lives."

As Boorstin surveyed the terrain nearly half a century ago, his overarching concern was that an image-saturated culture would so distort people's sense of judgment that they would cease to distinguish between the real and the unreal. He criticized the creation of what he called "pseudo-events" such as politicians' staged photo-ops, and he traced the ways in which our pursuit of illusion transforms our experience of travel, clouds our ability to discern the motivations of advertisers, and encourages us to elevate celebrities to the status of heroes. "This is the appealing contradiction at the heart of our passion for pseudo-events: for made news, synthetic heroes, prefabricated tourist attractions, homogenized interchangeable forms of art and literature (where there are no 'originals,' but only the shadows we make of other shadows)," Boorstin wrote. "We believe we can fill our experience with new-fangled content."

Boorstin wrote *The Image* before the digital age, but his book still has a great deal to teach us about the likely future of the printed word. Some of the effects of the Internet appear to undermine Boorstin's occasionally gloomy predictions. For example, an increasing number of us, instead of being passive viewers of images, are active participants in a new culture of online writing and opinion mongering. We comment on newspaper and magazine articles, post our reviews of books and other products online, write about our feelings on personal blogs, and bombard our friends and acquaintances with status updates on Facebook. As the word migrates from printed page to pixilated screen, so too do more of our daily activities. Online we find news, work, love, social interaction, and an array of entertainment. We have embraced new modes of storytelling, such as the interactive, synthetic world of video games, and found new ways to share our quotidian personal experiences, in hyperkinetic bursts, through microblogging services such as Twitter.

Many observers have loudly and frequently praised the new technologies as transformative and democratic, which they undoubtedly are. But their widespread use has sparked broader questions about the relevance and value of the printed word and the traditional book. The book, like the wheel, is merely a technology, these enthusiasts argue, and thus we should welcome improvements to it, even if those improvements eventually lead to the book's obsolescence. After all, the deeply felt human need for storytelling won't fade; it will merely take on new forms, forms we should welcome as signs of progress, not decay. As Boorstin observed in the foreword to the 25th-anniversary edition of *The Image,* "We Americans are sensitive to any suggestion that progress may have its price."

Our screen-intensive culture poses three challenges to traditional reading: distraction, consumerism, and attention-seeking behavior. Screen technologies such as the cell phone and laptop computer that are supposedly revolutionizing reading also potentially offer us greater control over our time. In practice, however, they have increased our anxiety about having too little of it by making us available anytime and anywhere. These technologies have also dramatically increased our opportunities for distraction. It is a rare Web site that presents its material without the clutter of advertisement, and a rare screen reader who isn't lured by the siren song of an incoming e-mail's "ping!" to set aside her work to see who has written. We live in a world of continuous partial attention, one that prizes speed and brandishes the false promise of multitasking as a solution to our time management challenges. The image-driven world of the screen dominates our attention at the same time that it contributes to a kind of experience pollution that is challenging our ability to engage with the printed word.

The digital revolution has also transformed the experience of reading by making it more consumer oriented. With the advent of electronic readers (and cell phones that can double as e-readers), the book is no longer merely a thing you purchase, but a service to which you subscribe. With the purchase of a traditional book, your consumer relationship ends when you walk out of the bookstore. With a wirelessly connected Kindle or iPhone, or your Wi-Fi-enabled computer, you exist in a perpetual state of potential consumerism. To be sure, for most people reading has never been a pure, quasi-monastic activity; everyday life has always presented distractions to the person keen on losing herself in a book. But for the first time, thanks to new technologies, we are making those distractions an integral part of the experience of reading. Embedded in these new versions of the book are the means for constant and elaborate demands on our attention. And as our experience with other screen media, from television to video games to the Internet, suggests, such distractions are difficult to resist.

Finally, the transition from print reading to screen reading has increased our reliance on images and led to a form of "social narcissism" that Boorstin first identified in his book. "We have fallen in love with our own image, with images of our making, which turn out to be images of ourselves," he wrote. We become viewers rather than readers, observers rather than participants. The "common reader" Virginia Woolf prized, who is neither scholar nor critic but "reads for his own pleasure, rather than to impart knowledge or correct the opinions of others," is a vanishing species. Instead, an increasing number of us engage with the written word not to submit ourselves to another's vision or for mere edification, but to have an excuse to share our own opinions.

In August, Stanford University released preliminary results from its Stanford Study of Writing, which examined in-class and out-of-class writing samples from thousands of students over five years. One of the study's lead researchers, Andrea Lunsford, concluded, "We're in the midst of a literacy revolution the likes of which we haven't seen since Greek civilization." The source of this revolution, Lunsford proposed, is the "life writing" students do every day online: The study found that 38 percent of their writing occurred outside the classroom.

But as Emory University English professor Mark Bauerlein pointed out in a blog post on *The Chronicle of Higher Education*'s Web site, this so-called revolution has not translated into concrete improvements in writing skills as measured by standardized tests such as the ACT; nor has it led to a reduction in the number of remedial writing courses necessary to prepare students for the workplace. Of greater concern was the attitude students expressed about the usefulness of writing: Most of them judged the quality of writing by the size of the audience that read it rather than its ability to convey ideas. One of the most prolific contributors to the study, a Stanford undergraduate who submitted more than 700 writing samples ranging from Facebook messages to short stories, told the *Chronicle* that for him a class writing assignment was a "soulless exercise" because it had an audience of one, the professor. He and other students in the study, raised on the Internet, consistently expressed a preference for writing that garnered the most attention from as many people as possible.

Our need for stories to translate our experience hasn't changed. Our ability to be deeply engaged readers of those stories is changing. For at least half a century, the image culture has trained us to expect the easily digestible, the quickly paced, and the uncomplicated. As our tolerance for the inconvenient or complex fades, images achieve even more prominence, displacing the word by appealing powerfully to a different kind of emotional sensibility, one whose vividness and urgency are undeniable but whose ability to explore nuance are not the same as that of the printed word.

What Boorstin feared—that a society beholden to the image would cease to distinguish the real from the unreal—has not come to pass. On the contrary, we acknowledge the unique characteristics of the virtual world and have eagerly embraced them, albeit uncritically. But Boorstin's other concern—that a culture that craves the image will eventually find itself mired in solipsism and satisfied by secondhand experiences—has been borne out. We follow the Twitter feeds of protesting Iranians and watch video of Michael Jackson's funeral and feel connected to the rest of the world, even though we lack context for that feeling and don't make much effort to achieve it beyond logging on. The screen offers us the illusion of participation, and this illusion is becoming our preference. As Boorstin observed, "Every day seeing there and hearing there takes the place of being there."

This secondhand experience is qualitatively different from the empathy we develop as readers. "We read to know we are not alone," C. S. Lewis once observed, and by this he meant that books are a gateway to a better understanding of what it means to be human. Because the pace is slower and the rewards delayed, the exercise of reading on the printed page requires a commitment unlike that demanded by the screen, as anyone who has embarked on the journey of an ambitiously long novel can attest. What the screen gives us is pleasurable, but it is not the same kind of experience as deeply engaged reading; the "screen literacy" praised by techno-enthusiasts should be seen as a complement to, not a replacement of, traditional literacy.

Since the migration of the word from page to screen is still in its early stages, predictions about the future of print are hazardous at best. When *Time* magazine named "YOU!" its person of the year in 2006, the choice was meant as a celebratory recognition of our new digital world and its many opportunities for self-expression. We are all writers now, crafters of our own images and creators of our own online worlds. But so far this power has made us less, not more, willing to submit ourselves to the singular visions of writers and artists and to learn from them difficult truths about the human condition. It has encouraged us to substitute images and simplistic snippets

This Is Your Brain on the Web

As scientists begin to bear down on the cognitive differences between reading online and off, they are discovering that the two activities are not the same at all.

Numerous studies have shown that we don't so much *read* online as *scan*. In a series of studies from the early 1990s until 2006, Jakob Nielsen, a former Sun Microsystems engineer, and Don Norman, a cognitive scientist, tracked the eye movements of Web surfers as they skipped from one page to the next. They found that only 16 percent of subjects read the text on a page in the order in which it appeared. The rest jumped around, picking out individual words and processing them out of sequence. "That's how users read your precious content," Nielsen cautions Web designers in his online column. "In a few seconds, their eyes move at amazing speeds across your Web site's words in a pattern that's very different from what you learned in school."

Nielsen recommends that designers create Web sites that are easy to comprehend by scanning: one idea per paragraph, highlighted keywords, and objective-sounding language so readers don't need to perform the mental heavy-lifting of determining what's fact and what's bias or distortion.

It is particularly hard to hold readers' attention online because of all the temptations dangled before them. Psychologists argue that our brains are naturally inclined to constantly seek new stimuli. Clicking on link after link, always looking for a new bit of information, we are actually revving up our brains with dopamine, the overlord of what psychologist Jaak Panksepp has called the "seeking system."

This system is what drives you to get out of bed each day, and what causes you to check your e-mail every few minutes; it's what keys you up in anticipation of a reward. Most of your e-mail may be junk, but the prospect of receiving a meaningful message—or following a link to a stimulating site—is enough to keep your brain constantly a bit distracted from what you're reading online.

What are the effects on the brain of all this distraction? Scientists are only beginning to answer this question. A recent study by three Stanford researchers found that consummate multitaskers are, in fact, terrible at multitasking. In three experiments, they were worse at paying attention, controlling their memories, and switching between tasks than those who prefer to complete one task at a time. Clifford Nass, one of the researchers, says, "They're suckers for irrelevancy. Everything distracts them." Unable to discriminate between relevant material and junk, multitaskers can get lost in a sea of information.

The things we read on the Web aren't likely to demand intense focus anyway. A survey of 1,300 students at the University of Illinois, Chicago, found that only five percent regularly read a blog or forum on politics, economics, law, or policy. Nearly 80 percent checked Facebook, the social networking site.

Maryanne Wolf, director of the Center for Reading and Language Research at Tufts University, says it's not just what we read that shapes us, but the fact that we read at all. She writes, "With [the invention of reading], we rearranged the very organization of our brain, which in turn expanded the ways we were able to think, which altered the intellectual evolution of our species." When children are just learning to read, their brains show activation in both hemispheres. As word recognition becomes more automatic, this activity is concentrated in the left hemisphere, allowing more of the brain to work on the task of distilling the meaning of the text and less on decoding it. This efficiency is what allows our brains the time to think creatively and analytically. According to Wolf, the question is, "What would be lost to us if we replaced the skills honed by the reading brain with those now being formed in our new generation of 'digital natives'?"

In the end, the most salient difference isn't between a screen and a page but between focused reading and disjointed scanning. Of course, the former doesn't necessarily follow from opening a book and the latter is not inherent to opening a Web browser, but that is the pattern. However, that pattern may not always hold true. Google, for example, recently unveiled Fast Flip, a feature designed to recreate the experience of reading newspapers and magazines offline. Other programs, such as *The New Yorker*'s digital edition or *The New York Times*' Times Reader 2.0, have a similar purpose, allowing readers to see on the screen something much like what they would normally hold between their two hands. And with the Kindle and other e-readers quickly catching on, we may soon find that reading in the future is quite like reading in the past.

Until such innovations move into wider use, the surest bet for undistracted reading continues to be an old-fashioned book. As historian Marshall Poe observes, "A book is a machine for focusing attention; the Internet is [a] machine for diffusing it."

of text for the range, precision, and peculiar beauty of written language, with its unique power to express complex and abstract ideas. Recent surveys by the National Endowment for the Arts reveal that fewer Americans read literature for pleasure than in the past; writers of serious fiction face a daunting publishing market and a reading public that has come to prefer the celebrity memoir to the new literary novel.

There is a reason that the metaphor so often invoked to describe the experience of reading is one of escape: An avid reader can recall the book that first unlocked the door of his imagination or provided a sense of escape from the everyday world. The critic Harold Bloom has written that he was forever changed by his early encounters with books: "My older sisters, when I was very young, took me to the library, and thus transformed my life." As Maryanne Wolf notes, "Biologically and intellectually, reading allows the species to go 'beyond the information given' to create endless thoughts most beautiful and wonderful."

An Avid Reader can recall the book that first unlocked his imagination or provided a sense of escape from the everyday world.

The proliferation of image and text on the Internet has exacerbated the solipsism Boorstin feared, because it allows us to read in a broad but shallow manner. It endorses rather than challenges our sensibilities, and substitutes synthetic images for our own peculiar form of imagination. Over time, the ephemeral, immediate quality of this constant stream of images undermines the self-control required to engage with the written word. And so we find ourselves in the position of living in a highly literate society that chooses not to exercise the privilege of literacy—indeed, it no longer views literacy as a privilege at all.

In *Essays on His Own Times* (1850), Samuel Taylor Coleridge observed, "The great majority of men live like bats, but in twilight, and know and feel the philosophy of their age only by its reflections and refractions." Today we know our age by its tweets and text messages, its never-ending litany of online posts and ripostes. Judging by the evidence so far, the content we find the most compelling is what we produce about ourselves: our tastes, opinions, and habits. This has made us better interpreters of our own experience, but it has not made us better readers or more empathetic human beings.

Critical Thinking

1. Christine Rosen writes, "We live in a world of continuous partial attention, one that prizes speed and brandishes false promise of multitasking as a solution to our time management challenges." If this is accurate, to what is it because of mass media?

2. Summarize Rosen's key differences between the experience of reading words on paper vs. words on screen.

CHRISTINE ROSEN is a senior editor of *The New Atlantis: A Journal of Technology and Society.*

Revolution in a Box

It's not Twitter or Facebook that's reinventing the planet. Eighty years after the first commercial broadcast crackled to life, television still rules our world. And let's hear it for the growing legions of couch potatoes: All those soap operas might be the ticket to a better future after all.

CHARLES KENNY

"The television," science-fiction writer Ray Bradbury lamented in 1953, is "that insidious beast, that Medusa which freezes a billion people to stone every night, staring fixedly, that Siren which called and sang and promised so much and gave, after all, so little." Bradbury wasn't alone in his angst: Television has been as reviled as it has been welcomed since the first broadcasts began in 1928. Critics of television, from disgusted defenders of the politically correct to outraged conservative culture warriors, blame it for poor health, ignorance, and moral decline, among other assorted ills. Some go further: According to a recent *fatwa* in India, television is "nearly impossible to use . . . without a sin." Last year, a top Saudi cleric declared it permissible to kill the executives of television stations for spreading sedition and immorality.

So will the rapid, planetwide proliferation of television sets and digital and satellite channels, to corners of the world where the Internet is yet unheard of, be the cause of global decay such critics fear? Hardly. A world of couch potatoes in front of digital sets will have its downsides—fewer bowling clubs, more Wii bowling. It may or may not be a world of greater obesity, depending on whom you ask. But it could also be a world more equal for women, healthier, better governed, more united in response to global tragedy, and more likely to vote for local versions of *American Idol* than shoot at people.

Indeed, television, that 1920s technology so many of us take for granted, is still coming to tens of millions with a transformative power—for the good—that the world is only now coming to understand. The potential scope of this transformation is enormous: By 2007, there was more than one television set for every four people on the planet, and 1.1 billion households had one. Another 150 million-plus households will be tuned in by 2013.

In our collective enthusiasm for whiz-bang new social-networking tools like Twitter and Facebook, the implications of this next television age—from lower birthrates among poor women to decreased corruption to higher school enrollment rates—have largely gone overlooked despite their much more sweeping impact. And it's not earnest educational programming that's reshaping the world on all those TV sets. The programs that so many dismiss as junk—-from song-and-dance shows to *Desperate Housewives*—are being eagerly consumed by poor people everywhere who are just now getting access to television for the first time. That's a powerful force for spreading glitz and drama—but also social change.

Television, it turns out, is the kudzu of consumer durables. It spreads across communities with incredible speed. Just look at the story of expanding TV access in the rural areas of one poor country, Indonesia: Within two years of village electrification, average television ownership rates reached 30 percent. Within seven years, 60 percent of households had TVs—this in areas where average surveyed incomes were about $2 a day. Fewer than 5 percent of these same households owned refrigerators. Television is so beloved that in the vast swaths of the world where there is still no electricity network, people hook up their TVs to batteries—indeed, in a number of poor countries, such as Peru, more homes have televisions than electricity.

As a result, the television is fast approaching global ubiquity. About half of Indian households have a television, up from less than a third in 2001; the figure for Brazil is more than four-fifths. (In comparison, just 7 percent of Indians use the Internet, and about one-third of Brazilians do.) In places like Europe and North America, 90-plus percent of households have a TV. Even in countries as poor as Vietnam and Algeria, rates are above 80 percent. But the potential for real growth in access (and impact) is in the least/developed countries, like Nigeria and Bangladesh, where penetration rates are still well below 30 percent.

If an explosion of access is the first global television revolution, then an explosion of choice will be the second. By 2013, half of the world's televisions will be receiving digital signals, which means access to many more channels. Digital broadcast builds on considerably expanded viewing options delivered through cable or satellite. Indeed, nearly two-thirds of households in India with a TV already have a cable or satellite connection. And in the United States, a bellwether for global television trends, the spread of cable since 1970 has meant an increasing number of broadcast channels are sharing a declining proportion of the audience-down from 80 percent to 40 percent over the last 35 years. The average American

What they're Watching

Soaps, soaps, and more soaps. But not all of the dramas are created equal. In Colombia, viewers enjoy a hard-bitten saga of gang violence; in Iran, they're tuning into tales of Jewish rescue during World War II.

Noor
Turkey

An Arabic-dubbed version of this popular Turkish soap opera became a bona fide pop-culture phenomenon throughout the Middle East during its 2005-2007 run, attracting millions of fans from Egypt to the Persian Gulf to Gaza and the West Bank. It is also "replete with evil, wickedness, moral collapse, and a war on the virtues," said one Saudi cleric. What's so dangerous about the show? It depicts a young couple as an equal partnership in which the husband supports his wife's career aspirations, and their friends are young cosmopolitan Muslims drinking and flirting on screen. Plenty of Muslim women apparently liked what they saw.

The Cartel of the Snitches
Colombia

Drugs, sex, street fights, and money. No, it's not the latest edition of *Grand Theft Auto;* it's Colombia's most popular soap opera, *El Cartel*. The multiseason series traces the lives of characters who are enthralled by the drug trade's prospect of easy wealth, but who learn that their star-studded hopes will not be met in reality; the cartel life is bloody and thankless. The show, based on the book by Andres Lopez Lopez, who was himself once in the drug business, was Colombia's highest rated last year, attracting more than 1 million viewers ages 18 to 49.

Zero Degree Turn
Iran

While Iranian President Mahmoud Ahmadinejad was busy making international headlines by denying the Holocaust, his fellow Iranians were riveted by a drama depicting the terror faced by Jews in Nazi-occupied France. *Zero Degree Turn* tells the true story of an Oskar Schindler-like Iranian diplomat who helped Jews escape Europe by providing them with false Iranian passports. The show was popular with Iranians, but the show's writer and director says he also meant it to show the world that Iran was not the anti-Semitic caricature often depicted in the international media.

Jewel in the Palace
South Korea

This historical soap opera, following the lives and loves of the Korean royal family during the 15th century, is the flagship product of the so-called Korean wave, the onslaught of South Korean pop culture that has swept through East Asia in recent years. Concerned about the show's "nonsocialist ideas," North Korean authorities have created a special squad of police to crack down on smugglers. Many apparently still try to watch illicit soaps, however, including *Jewel in the Palace* fanboy Kim Jong Il, whom then-South Korean President Roh Moo-hyun presented with a DVD boxed set of the show during negotiations in 2007.

Kwanda
South Africa

It's not every day that a prime-time drama written by a non-profit organization makes it to the top of national ratings. But the Soul City Institute for Health and Development Communication program *Soul City*—with plotlines like a wife presenting her cheating husband with condoms, or a husband's remorse over spousal abuse—has done just that. *Soul City* has been so popular that the NGO is starting a new "community makeover show" this fall. Like *Soul City*, *Kwanda* won't steer clear of controversy. Episode 7, for example, looks at "sugar daddies that are endangering young girls' lives," according to the NGO's promotional materials.

household now has access to 119 channels, and a similar phenomenon is spreading rapidly around the globe.

The explosion of choice is loosening the grip of bureaucrats the world over, who in many countries have either run or controlled programming directly, or heavily regulated the few stations available. A 97-country survey carried out a few years ago found that an average of 60 percent of the top five television stations in each country were owned by the state, with 32 percent in the hands of small family groupings. Programming in developing countries in particular has often been slanted toward decidedly practical topics—rural TV in China, for example, frequently covers the latest advances in pig breeding. And coverage of politics has often strayed from the balanced. Think Hugo Chavez, who refused to renew the license of RCTV, Venezuela's most popular TV network, after it broadcast commentary critical of his government. He regularly appears on the state channel in his own TV show *Aló Presidente*—episodes of which last anywhere from six to a record 96 hours.

But increasingly, the days when presidential speechmaking and pig breeding were must-see TV are behind us. As choices in what to watch expand, people will have access both to a wider range of voices and to a growing number of channels keen to give the audience what it really wants. And what it wants seems to be pretty much the same everywhere—sports, reality shows, and, yes, soap operas. Some 715 million people worldwide watched the finals of the 2006 soccer World Cup, for example. More than a third of Afghanistan's population tunes into that country's version of *American Idol—Afghan Star*. The biggest television series ever worldwide is *Baywatch*, an everyday tale of lifesaving folk based on and around the beaches of Santa Monica, Calif. The show has been broadcast in 142 countries, and at its peak it had an audience estimated north of 1 billion. (Today, the world's most popular TV show is the medical drama *House*, which according to media consulting firm Eurodata TV Worldwide was watched by 82 million people last year in 66 countries, edging out CSI and *Desperate Housewives*.)

Ghulam Nabi Azad, India's health and family welfare minister, has even taken to promoting TV as a form of birth control. "In olden days people had no other entertainment but sex, which is why they produced so many children," he mused publicly in July. "Today, TV is the biggest source of entertainment. Hence, it is important that there is electricity in every village so that people watch TV till late in the night. By the time the serials are over, they'll be too tired to have sex and will fall asleep." Azad is certainly right that television helps slow birthrates, though experience from his own country and elsewhere suggests that it is by example, not exhaustion, that TV programs manage such a dramatic effect.

Since the 1970s, Brazil's Rede Globo network has been providing a steady diet of locally produced soaps, some of which are watched by as many as 80 million people. The programs are no more tales of everyday life in Brazil than *Desperate Housewives* is an accurate representation of a typical U.S. suburb. In a country where divorce was only legalized in 1977, nearly a fifth of the main female characters were divorced (and about a quarter were unfaithful). What's more, 72 percent of the main female characters on the Globo soaps had no kids, and only 7 percent had more than one. In 1970, the average Brazilian woman, in contrast, had given birth nearly six times.

But the soaps clearly resonated with viewers. As the Globo network expanded to new areas in the 1970s and 1980s, according to researchers at the Inter-American Development Bank, parents began naming their kids after soap-opera characters. And women in those parts of the country—especially poor women—started having fewer babies. Being in an area covered by the Globo network had the same effect on a woman's fertility as two additional years of education. This wasn't the result

of what was shown during commercial breaks—for most of the time, contraceptive advertising was banned, and there was no government population-control policy at all. The portrayal of plausible female characters with few children, apparently, was an important social cue.

Cable and satellite television may be having an even bigger impact on fertility in rural India. As in Brazil, popular programming there includes soaps that focus on urban life. Many women on these serials work outside the home, run businesses, and control money. In addition, soap characters are typically well-educated and have few children. And they prove to be extraordinarily powerful role models: Simply giving a village access to cable TV, research by scholars Robert Jensen and Emily Oster has found, has the same effect on fertility rates as increasing by five years the length of time girls stay in school.

The soaps in Brazil and India provided images of women who were empowered to make decisions affecting not only childbirth, but a range of household activities. The introduction of cable or satellite services in a village, Jensen and Oster found, goes along with higher girls' school enrollment rates and increased female autonomy. Within two years of getting cable or satellite, between 45 and 70 percent of the difference between urban and rural areas on these measures disappears. In Brazil, it wasn't just birthrates that changed as Globo's signal spread—divorce rates went up, too. There may be something to the boast of one of the directors of the company that owns *Afghan Star*. When a woman reached the final five this year, the director suggested it would "do more for women's rights than all the millions of dollars we have spent on public service announcements for women's rights on TV."

TV's salutary effects extend far beyond reproduction and gender equality. Kids who watch TV out of school, according to a World Bank survey of young people in the shantytowns of Fortaleza in Brazil, are considerably less likely to consume drugs (or, for that matter, get pregnant). TV's power to reduce youth drug use was two times larger than having a comparatively well-educated mother. And though they might not be as subtly persuasive as *telenovelas* or reality shows, well-designed broadcast campaigns can also make a difference. In Ghana, where as few as 4 percent of mothers were found to wash their hands with soap after defecating and less than 1 percent before feeding their children, reported hand-washing rates shot up in response to a broadcast campaign emphasizing that people eat "more than just rice" if preparers don't wash their hands properly before dinner.

Indeed, TV is its own kind of education—and rather than clash with schooling, as years of parental nagging would suggest, it can even enhance it. U.S. kids with access to a TV signal in the 1950s, for instance—think toddlers watching quality educational programming like *I Love Lucy*—tended to have higher test scores in 1964, according to research by Matthew Gentzkow and Jesse Shapiro of the University of Chicago. Today, more than 700,000 secondary-school students in remote Mexican villages watch the *Telesecundaria* program of televised classes. Although students enter the program with below-average test scores in mathematics and language, by graduation they have caught up in math and halved the language-score deficit.

The World's Most Popular TV Shows

After surveying 66 countries with 1.6 billion viewers between them—from Australia to Japan, Latvia to Venezuela—Eurodata TV Worldwide named the winners for the world's most-watched shows of 2008. What does the world love to watch?

- **Winner:** *House*
- **Category:** Drama
- **Viewers:** 81.8 million worldwide
- **Runners-up:** *CSI: Miami* and *CSI: Las Vegas*

- **Winner:** *Desperate Housewives*
- **Category:** Comedy
- **Viewers:** 56.3 million
- **Runners-up:** *Monk* and *Ugly Betty*

- **Winner:** *The Bold and the Beautiful*
- **Category:** Soap Opera
- **Viewers:** 24.5 million
- **Runners-up:** *Marina* and *The Young and the Restless*

Similarly, evidence that television is responsible for the grim state of civic discourse is mixed, at best. Better television reception in Javanese villages in Indonesia, according to research by Ben Olken, comes with substantially lower levels of participation in social activities and with lower measures of trust in others. Villages with access to an extra TV channel see a decline of about 7 percent in the number of social groups. Similar outcomes have been found in the United States. But improved television reception did not appear to affect the level of discussion in village meetings or levels of corruption in a village road project undertaken during Olken's study. And an examination of the early history of television in the United States by Markus Prior suggests that regions that saw access to more channels in the 1950s and 1960s witnessed increases in political knowledge, interest, and turnout, especially among less-educated TV viewers.

What about television's broader impact on governance? Here, it's the level of competition that seems to matter—a hopeful sign given that the future of global TV is likely to be considerably more competitive. If the only channel that viewers watch is biased in its coverage, then, unsurprisingly, they are likely to be swayed toward that viewpoint. Brazil's Globo channel, for all its positive impact on fertility rates, has played a less positive role in terms of bias-free reporting. It has long had a close relationship with government, as well as a dominant market share. In Brazil's 1989 election—a race in which Globo was squarely behind right-leaning presidential candidate Fernando Collor de Mello—the difference between people who never watched television and those who watched it frequently was a 13 percentage-point increase in the likelihood of voting for Collor, scholar Taylor Boas found. But with channels proliferating nearly everywhere, television controllers may have much less power to sway elections today. In the choice-rich United States, for example, there is no simple relation between hours watched and voting patterns, even if those who watch particular channels are more likely to vote Republican or Democrat.

Then there's corruption. Consider the bribes that Peruvian secret-police chief Vladimiro Montesinos had to pay to subvert competitive newsmaking during the 1990s. It cost only $300,000 per month for Montesinos to bribe most of the congressmen in Peru's government, and about $250,000 a month to bribe the judges—a real bargain. But Montesinos had to spend about $3 million a month to subvert six of the seven available television channels to ensure friendly coverage for the government. The good news here is that competition in the electronic Fourth Estate can apparently make it more expensive to run a country corruptly.

Corruption is one thing, but could television help solve a problem we've had since before Sumer and Elam battled it out around Basra in 2700 B.C.—keeping countries from fighting each other? Maybe.

U.S. researchers who study violence on TV battle viciously themselves over whether it translates into more aggressive behavior in real life. But at least from a broader perspective, television might play a role in stemming the global threat of war. It isn't that TV reporting of death and destruction necessarily reduces support for wars already begun—that's an argument that has raged over conflicts from Vietnam to the Iraq war. It is more that, by fostering a growing global cosmopolitanism, television might make war less attractive to begin with. Indeed, the idea that communications are central to building cross-cultural goodwill is an old one. Karl Marx and Friedrich Engels suggested in the 19th century that railways were vital in rapidly cementing the union of the working class: "that union, to attain which the burghers of the Middle Ages, with their miserable highways, required centuries, the modern proletarians, thanks to railways, achieve in a few years," they wrote in the *Communist Manifesto*. If the Amtraks of the world can have such an impact, surely the Hallmark Channel can do even better.

The fact that Kobe Bryant (born in Philadelphia, plays for the Los Angeles Lakers) sees his basketball shirt considerably outsell those of Yao Ming (born in Shanghai, plays for the Houston Rockets) in China suggests something of that growing global cosmopolitanism at work. The considerable response of

Want to Know More?

- Charles Kenny has written extensively on technology and poverty, beginning with "Development's False Divide" (FOREIGN POLICY, January/February 2003), in which he questions whether the Internet will really be a boon to the world's poor. He elaborates on this idea in his book, *Overselling the Web?: Development and the Internet* (Boulder: Lynne Rienner Publishers, 2006). Kenny looks more broadly at development on his blog, www.charleskenny.blogs.com.
- Matthew Gentzkow and Jesse Shapiro's "Preschool Television Viewing and Adolescent Test Scores: Historical Evidence from the Coleman Study" (*The Quarterly Journal of Economics*, February 2008) finds that childhood TV-viewing improves test scores down the road. In "The Power of TV: Cable Television and Women's Status in India" (*The Quarterly Journal of Economics*, forthcoming), Robert Jensen and Emily Oster find striking correlations between adult TV-watching and lowered fertility rates, among other positive outcomes.
- Steven Johnson agrees that television—even the trashy stuff—can have big social benefits, a theory he details in *Everything Bad Is Good for You: How Today's Popular Culture Is Actually Making Us Smarter* (New York: Riverhead Books, 2005).
- Some skeptics of development include William Easterly, who condemns the whole concept as Western ideology in "The Ideology of Development" (FOREIGN POLICY, July/August 2007). Meanwhile, researchers Dimitri A. Christakis et al. find that television might have its downsides—attentional disorders among children ("Early Television Exposure and Subsequent Attentional Problems in Children," *Pediatrics*, April 2004).

global television viewers to images of famine in Ethiopia, or the tsunami in Asia, also shows how TV is a powerful force for shrinking the emotional distance between peoples within and between countries. In the United States, an additional minute of nightly news coverage of the Asian tsunami increased online donation levels to charities involved in relief efforts by 13 percent, according to research from the William Davidson Institute. And analysis of U.S. public opinion indicates that more coverage of a country on evening news shows is related to increased sympathy and support for that country.

Of course, the extent to which television helps foster cosmopolitanism depends on what people are watching. People in the Middle East who only watched Arab news channels were considerably less likely to agree that the September 11 attacks were carried out by Arab terrorists than those exposed to Western media coverage, researchers Gentzkow and Shapiro found, even after taking into account other characteristics likely to shape their views such as education, language, and age. Similarly, the tone and content of coverage of the ground invasion of Iraq was notably different on Al Jazeera than it was on U.S. and British network broadcasts in the spring of 2003—and surely this helped sustain notably different attitudes toward the war. But with the growing reach of BBC World News and CNN in the Middle East, and the growing reach of Al Jazeera in the West, there is at least a greater potential to understand how the other side thinks.

Just because soap operas and reality shows can help solve real-world problems doesn't mean the world's politicians should now embrace TV as the ultimate policy prescription. There are of course a few things governments could do to harness television's power for good, such as supporting well-designed public service announcements. But for the most part, politicians ought to be paying less attention to TV, not more. They shouldn't be limiting the number of channels or interfering in the news. A vibrant, competitive television market playing *Days of Our Lives or Dias de Nuestras Vidas* on loop might have a bigger impact even than well-meaning educational programs. And competition is critical to ensuring that television helps inform voters, not just indoctrinate them.

In the future, the world will be watching 24 billion hours of TV a day.

In the not-too-distant future, it is quite possible that the world will be watching 24 billion hours of TV a day—an average of close to four hours for each person in the world. Some of those hours could surely be better spent—planting trees, helping old ladies cross the road, or playing cricket, perhaps. But watching TV exposes people to new ideas and different people. With that will come greater opportunity, growing equality, a better understanding of the world, and a new appreciation of the complexities of life for a wannabe Afghan woman pop star. Not bad for a siren Medusa supposedly giving so little.

Critical Thinking

1. Define *feedforward* using examples from this article.
2. Are ethical issues associated with television's feedforward effects different for programs produced in the United States for distribution within the United States than for programs produced for or exported to less developed countries?

CHARLES KENNY, a development economist, is author of the forthcoming book *The Success of Development: Innovation, Ideas and the Global Standard of Living.*

Reprinted in entirety by McGraw-Hill with permission from *Foreign Policy*, November 2009, pp. 70–74. www.foreignpolicy.com. © 2009 Washingtonpost.Newsweek Interactive, LLC.

Tele[re]vision

Researchers are taking a new look at TV. Instead of just filling time or acting as a passive babysitter, can the medium be a good teacher?

JENNY PRICE

Society gives parents plenty of reasons to feel guilty about the time their children spend in front of the television. Nicknames for the medium—boob tube or idiot box, for example—do little to help alleviate their worries.

For years, researchers have shown the negative effects of TV violence and, more recently, they have found links between childhood obesity and too much viewing. President Obama implored parents to "turn off the TV" during a campaign ad pitching his education policy. Still, the average child in the United States spends nearly four hours watching television each day, even though pediatricians recommend no more than two hours of educational programming for kids two years and older.

TV viewing is a given in the average household, but in many cases, parents have no idea what programs their children are watching or whether they understand them at all.

"What we seldom get—and need—is solid, research-based advice about when to turn the TV on," noted Lisa Guernsey, an author and journalist who covers media effects on children, in a column she wrote for the *Washington Post.*

Researchers, including UW-Madison faculty and an alumnus who is behind some groundbreaking work in the field, are working to fill that void, showing that some TV can actually be good for kids.

Their efforts have improved educational programming for children, pinpointing what engages their developing brains and how they learn as they watch. Now the researchers are exploring whether children are really getting the lessons from programs that adults think they are, and how exposure to television might affect children as young as babies and toddlers.

Spoonful of Sugar

Well-crafted shows for children can teach them the alphabet, math, and basic science concepts, as well as manners and social skills. But what really makes for good television when it comes to younger viewers? That's a key question Marie-Louise Mares MA '90, PhD '94, a UW-Madison associate professor of communication arts, is trying to answer.

Much of the educational programming aimed at children falls into the category of "prosocial"—meaning that it's intended to teach lessons, such as healthy eating habits, self-esteem, or how to treat others. The classic example of a prosocial program is *Mister Rogers' Neighborhood.* Mares has shown that a prosocial program's positive influence can be just as strong as a violent program's negative influence.

But good messages can get lost.

"Children's interpretations of what a show is about are very different from what an adult thinks," Mares says. "Some kids take away the completely wrong message."

Mares began studying children's comprehension of prosocial messages after watching the movie *Mary Poppins* with a four-year-old fan. Although the child predicted each scene before it appeared on screen, she had difficulty doing what Mares calls "making sense of the story." The girl did not know why the character Bert, played by Dick Van Dyke, was on the roof dancing or that the "spoonful of sugar" Julie Andrews sings about was a metaphor. As they continued to watch the movie together, Mares learned that what is obvious to an adult doesn't necessarily sink in with children.

She demonstrated that confusion in a study involving a TV episode of *Clifford the Big Red Dog,* in which the cartoon character and friends meet a three-legged dog named K.C. The intent of the program was to teach children to be accepting of those with disabilities. But throughout much of the episode, Clifford and his friends behave badly toward the dog. At one point, one of the dogs expresses fear of catching three-legged dog disease. Sure enough, in follow-up interviews, one-third of the children thought the dogs could catch the disease, and many of them interpreted the lesson of the episode along the lines of this child's comment: "You should be careful . . . not to get sick, not to get germs."

"Showing the fear can actually be more conflicting and more frightening to kids," Mares says.

Her findings are important because much of kids' programming attempts to teach lessons by showing characters behaving badly in some way and then having them learn better behavior. That's confusing for children, Mares says, and could even lead them to focus on the bad behavior.

Her findings are important because much of kids' programming attempts to teach lessons by showing characters behaving badly in some way and then having them learn better behavior. That's confusing for children and could even lead them to focus on the bad behavior.

In the end, 80 percent of the kids in the study said the lesson of the *Clifford* episode was to be nice to dogs with three legs. Although that's a nice sentiment, Mares says, "You don't encounter many [three-legged dogs]."

The producers of prosocial programs also should consider the methods they use to portray the behaviors they're trying to teach kids, Mares says, as well as ensure that the content is relevant and realistic to young viewers. That might be one of the reasons why stories involving dogs or other animal characters don't seem to get the message across to children. One group of youngsters in Mares' study watched a *Clifford* episode that had been edited to remove the dogs showing fear of K.C.—yet the children still interpreted the story as being about dogs, not about inclusiveness and tolerance.

Mares is in new territory; virtually no research has been conducted to identify programming that would effectively foster inclusiveness in children. She has experimented, with mixed results, by embedding some kind of prompt within children's programs that could help young viewers comprehend the intended message, especially since most parents aren't watching along with their kids. Attempts include having the main character start off the show or interrupt mid-lesson to say, "Hey kids, in this story we're going to learn that we shouldn't be afraid of people who are different."

She's still looking for answers on how that practice—which she calls scaffolding—could work effectively. But balance is essential, Mares says, noting that she could create the "ideal" show, but then kids wouldn't want to watch.

Making over *Sesame Street*

The end of the 1960s saw the debut of two landmark educational programs for young people: *Sesame Street* and *Mister Rogers' Neighborhood.* Not long after, Daniel Anderson '66 began trying to discover what exactly was going on with children while they watched TV.

Anderson, a professor at the University of Massachusetts-Amherst who has advised the producers of children's shows including *Sesame Street* and *Captain Kangaroo,* dispelled one of the central myths on the subject—that when the TV is turned on, children's brains turn off. In fact, parents are more likely than their children to become couch potatoes while watching television, says Anderson, who holds a UW bachelor's degree in psychology.

He observed children watching television and witnessed them turning away from the screen several times during a broadcast to play with toys, fight with siblings, or talk to their parents. After they were done watching, he tested their understanding of what they had just seen. Anderson's findings were the exact opposite of what most people thought.

"It was very clear that children were mentally active, that they were constantly posing questions for themselves, [asking], 'What's going to happen next, why are they doing that . . . is this real?' " he says. "And it was also clear that when television invited participation, that kids would become very active—pointing at the screen or talking to the characters on the TV."

This finding ushered in a new era of children's programming, with the cable channel Nickelodeon enlisting Anderson's help to develop a new generation of shows in the late 1990s, most notably *Blue's Clues* and *Dora the Explorer,* that were centered on the concept that children would dance, sing, and follow along with programs they enjoyed rather than sit and stare vacantly at the screen.

Blue's Clues features a mix of animated characters—including a cute blue puppy—and backgrounds, with a live host who invites children who are watching to look for and decipher clues to solve a puzzle, such as, "What does Blue want for her birthday?" Along the way, the show focuses on information such as colors or shapes or numbers.

Anderson pushed producers to make the show visually simple, with very little editing or transitions that require viewers to process jumps in time or location—something young children have a hard time doing, his research showed.

While most researchers "focus on the negative contributions of media," experts such as Anderson and Mares have been "at the forefront of recognizing that television that is designed to be educational really can be beneficial for children," says Amy Jordan, who oversees research on children's media policy for The Annenberg Public Policy Center.

In his best-selling book *The Tipping Point,* which examines how ideas and trends spread, author Malcolm Gladwell labeled *Blue's Clues* as one of the "stickiest"—meaning the most irresistible and involving—television shows ever aired, and noted that its creators "borrowed those parts of *Sesame Street* that did work."

In turn, the success of *Blue's Clues* prompted the producers of *Sesame Street* to seek Anderson's help in giving the long-running staple a makeover. With the new millennium approaching, the show needed to catch up with the way kids watch TV. Rather than the repetitive narrative format children delighted in following as they watched *Blue's Clues, Sesame Street* featured a series of about forty short segments, ranging in length from ten seconds to four minutes.

Even venerable *Sesame Street,* airing since the late 1960s, has evolved, thanks to research about children's TV. The show's original concept assumed short attention spans, cramming as many as forty short segments into each hour.

What Is Educational Television?

POP QUIZ

Is the TV show *Hannah Montana* educational?
If your answer is no, guess again.

The ubiquitous Disney Channel sitcom featuring pop star Miley Cyrus airs during ABC's Saturday morning block of shows aimed at children. And, believe it or not, it helps the network's affiliates fulfill their obligation under federal law to air educational and informational (E/I) programming for kids.

Congress first passed legislation in 1990—the Children's Television Act—requiring broadcast stations to increase E/I programming, but what followed were some laughable claims of compliance. For example, *The Jetsons* was labeled educational because it taught children about the future, and stations were sometimes airing educational shows at times when children weren't likely to be awake and watching. So in 1997, lawmakers revisited the act, putting in place what's known as the "three-hour rule," stipulating that the networks air at least three hours of E/I programming for kids per week. Although the rule isn't enforced unless viewers complain, it is used as a guideline when the Federal Communications Commission reviews a station's license for renewal.

So have things gotten better? The FCC has acted on complaints, such as when it fined Univision affiliates $24 million for claiming that serial melodramas known as telenovelas were educational. But even under the three-hour rule, broadcasters maintain shows featuring professional athletes, such as *NBA Inside Stuff* or *NFL Under the Helmet,* count toward the requirement.

Amy Jordan, who oversees research on children's media policy for The Annenberg Public Policy Center and has studied implementation of the three-hour rule, says most commercial network programs are prosocial in nature, aimed at teaching children lessons. *Hannah Montana* falls into that category.

"We actually don't know the take-away value of those kinds of programming," Jordan acknowledges. "And that's an important question, because it speaks to whether or not the broadcasters are living up to the spirit of the Children's Television Act."

A study released last fall by advocacy organization Children Now found that only one in eight shows labeled E/I meets the standard of "highly educational." The majority of the programs studied—a little more than 60 percent—were deemed "moderately educational." The picture looked better at PBS, where the programming for kids was rated significantly higher than E/I shows on commercial stations.

Another issue is that the E/I label is confusing for many parents, with some mistaking programs such as *The Oprah Winfrey Show* and *Who Wants to Be a Millionaire?* as educational.

"In theory, I think parents believe they have a sense of what their kids are exposed to, but in fact, their knowledge is pretty limited," Jordan says. "So to get parents to direct their children to positive programming . . . it's an uphill battle for broadcasters."

Part of the misunderstanding, she says, results from broadcasters doing little to promote which shows carry the E/I label, thereby keeping parents and their children in the dark about which shows are intended to be educational.

"They have this concern about the spinach syndrome—if children think [a program is] good for them, they won't watch it," she says.

—J.P.

"The original conception was that you needed a lot of novelty and change to hold a preschooler's attention. And so they quite explicitly would put things together in unpredictable orders," Anderson says. "A story that was happening on the street with Big Bird and the human characters might be followed by a film about buffalos, which in turn might be followed by a Muppet piece about the letter *H.*"

Sesame Street offered children no connection or context among the concepts and segments, and, not surprisingly, it lost viewers when shows like *Blue's Clues* began airing. At Anderson's suggestion, producers made the show more storylike and predictable, reducing the number of characters and sets, and connecting more concepts. Now the typical episode features around ten segments per hour.

"You're dealing with children who don't need complexity," Anderson says. "In a sense, a lot of what they were doing was almost for the adults and not so much for their audience."

Research Gap

The notion of children and television as a research prospect first confronted Anderson when he was a young assistant professor. He had just given an undergraduate lecture on child development, in which he said younger children tend to have more trouble sustaining attention than older children, when one of his students asked, "Well, if those things are true, how come my four-year-old brother can just sit and stare [at *Sesame Street*]?"

"I kind of glibly answered him," Anderson recalls, "that 'Oh, it's because television is just being a distractor. It just looks like your brother's sustaining attention, but the picture is constantly changing and so on.' I just made that up—I had no idea."

Feeling guilty, Anderson sent a graduate student to the library with orders to find out everything he could about children's attention to television.

"He kept coming back and saying he couldn't find anything, and that's what got me started," Anderson says.

> **"Television that has a clear curriculum in mind—that studiously avoids problematic content like violence—has been shown in dozens of studies to really enhance the way children think, the kinds of things that they know, and even how they get along with one another."**
>
> —Amy Jordan

Beginning in the 1980s, Anderson and his colleagues followed 570 children from preschool until high school graduation to see what effect watching *Sesame Street* had on their school performance, behavior, and attitudes. They found that children who had watched when they were young earned better grades in high school, read more books, placed more value on achievement, and showed less aggression. Anderson's study included controls for many other factors, including family size, exposure to media in adolescence, and parents' socioeconomic status.

"We think that the effects are really traceable and cumulative all the way, at least, through high school. So television, I think, can be a powerful educator," Anderson says.

Jordan says those findings hold up in other research. "Television that has a clear curriculum in mind—that studiously avoids problematic content like violence—has been shown in dozens of studies to really enhance the way children think, the kinds of things that they know, and even how they get along with one another," she says.

An Uncontrolled Experiment

So where does that leave guilt-ridden parents looking for answers about television? It seems it comes down to what and how much kids are watching, and at what age.

Anderson, who has been working in the field for decades, thinks that despite educational programming, children are growing up within a vast, uncontrolled experiment. And he draws a sharp distinction about TV's potential value for children over age two.

His recent research focuses on how very young children are affected by simply playing or spending time in a room where adult programming, such as news programs or talk shows, is on the television. Anderson's latest study observed what happened when fifty children ages one to three played in a room for an hour. Half of the time, there was no TV in the room; for the last thirty minutes, the game show *Jeopardy!*—not exactly a toddler favorite—was showing.

The conventional wisdom, based on previous research, was that very young children don't pay attention to programs that they can't understand. But Anderson's study found clear signs that when the television was on, children had trouble concentrating, shortened and decreased the intensity of their play, and cut in half the time they focused on a particular toy.

When the TV was on, the children played about ninety seconds less overall. The concern is whether those effects could add up and harm children's playtime in the long term, impairing their ability to develop sustained attention and other key cognitive skills.

The Annenberg center's Jordan says more studies looking at the effects of TV on younger children are essential, in part because surveys have found that as many as two-thirds of children six years and under live in homes where the TV is on at least half the time, regardless of whether anyone is watching.

"Babies today are spending hours in front of screens . . . and we don't really understand how it's affecting their development," she says. "We can no longer assume children are first exposed to TV when they're two years old because it's happening at a much younger age."

Critical Thinking

1. Define *prosocial programming,* adding your own examples to those in this article.

2. Are *prosocial programming* and *educational programming* synonymous? Why or why not?

JENNY PRICE '96 is a writer for *On Wisconsin*.

Television and the Decline of Deference

Stuart Clayton asks whether the mass media have undermined the status of leading authority figures in Britain since 1945.

STUART CLAYTON

Unlike Gladstone and Disraeli, the careers and achievements of David Lloyd George and John Prescott are rarely the subject of fruitful comparative analysis. Yet a glance over their respective biographies does give rise to one interesting comparison: whereas Lloyd George was able to keep his affair with his secretary, Frances Stevenson, hidden from the public for 30 years, Prescott's 'two year fling' with one of his secretaries was splashed all over tabloids in 2006, with headlines such as 'My Affair: By Prezza'. Clearly there has been a great deal of change in the way leading figures of authority are presented to the public via the mass media. The greater scale, intrusiveness and instantaneous-ness of the media have undermined the reserved detachment that was once the privilege of elites. Through the promotion of the cult of 'celebrity', the mass media have also encouraged the British public to hold more democratic criteria for the treatment and judgement of all kinds of public figure, from the Queen to 'reality TV stars'. However, to hold the media solely responsible for a decline in popular deference is unconvincing: in most cases they have simply reflected changes ushered in by other powerful forces, such as the legacy of two World Wars and vastly increased material prosperity.

> **to hold the media solely responsible for a decline in popular deference is unconvincing: in most cases they have simply reflected changes ushered in by other powerful forces**

The Mass Media

Leading figures of authority operate in a much more demanding environment at the start of the twenty-first century than their predecessors in the mid-twentieth century. Briefly put, this is because there is a greater demand for information about them, a greater incentive to sensationalise this information, and a greater acceptability that it is reasonable to treat authority figures in this fashion. Technological and legislative changes affecting the media have brought about a vast increase in demand for news and stories. In 1945, the mass media comprised newspapers, radio and cinema; television was still in its infancy and BBC broadcasts did not resume until 1946. Cinema was still a major source of news as well as entertainment thanks to the newsreels that preceded films. The newsreels (which you can see at www.britishpathe.com and www.bfi.org.uk) were usually less than ten minutes long and were highly deferential towards leading figures of authority. A decline in cinema attendance led to the demise of the newsreel format: after a peak of 1.6 billion admissions in 1945–6, cinema audiences plunged to under a third of this figure by the mid-1950s. This collapse was almost entirely due to the rise of television, which soon emerged as the main provider of news and entertainment.

News was a staple part of early television, and news bulletins became longer and more regular. The legalisation of commercial television in 1955 and commercial radio in 1973, of satellite and cable television in the mid 1980s, and of digital television after 1998, all added to the sheer quantity of news and entertainment broadcast. While newspaper circulation has declined massively since the 1980s, the papers themselves have grown in thickness and hence column inches. In addition, editors now need to find material for their online editions. The rise of the World Wide Web as a popular source of information since the mid 1990s has expanded the amount of information available about an individual or event to a potentially limitless extent. The question for editors and journalists has been, How to fill this huge expanse of air-time?

Paying the Piper

The answer, to a large degree, depends upon who owns the medium in question. In 1945, the BBC was a monopoly broadcaster. Its first Director General, Lord Reith, decided that its purpose was 'to carry into the greatest number of homes everything that was best in every department of human knowledge'. The aim was to edify rather than excite, to promote high standards rather than attract the largest number of listeners and later viewers. The news was read by 'the best of the ruling classes', while entertainment was subject to a strict code of conduct. 'The Green Book' of 1948 did not allow for jokes about 'immorality of any kind', and even banned the 'vulgar use of such words as "basket"'! However, the launch of commercial television and radio meant that broadcasters had to sell advertising space rather than rely on the Licence Fee as the BBC had done. Advertisers naturally pay more for this air-time if audience figures are high; many critics, ranging from the MPs who voted against the 1954 Television Act to many media experts today, have worried about the 'dumbing down' or 'sexing up' of news and entertainment intended to maximise viewing figures. The competition for advertising revenue has substantially increased since 1990, largely due to the free market-inspired legacy of Margaret Thatcher's time as Prime Minister (1979–1990).

> **many critics, ranging from the MPs who voted against the 1954 Television Act to many media experts today, have worried about the 'dumbing down' or 'sexing up' of news and entertainment intended to maximise viewing figures**

The 1990 Broadcasting Act not only led to a large increase in the number of commercial radio stations and satellite TV channels available, but also softened the regulations placed on broadcasters. Crucially, it allowed for the acquisition and merger of media firms; since 1990, commercial broadcasters have had to make enough profit to avoid being taken over by rivals. Competition for advertising was further increased by the rapid rise of the internet in the late 1990s. Newspaper owners and commercial broadcasters have had to adapt to fight for the shrinking amount of potential revenue left after online advertising. Profits for media moguls, rather than the political but class-bound objectives of the pre-war press barons, have become the compelling force in large swathes of mass media; in this environment it is hardly surprising that John Prescott became the subject of such sensationalist headlines in 2006. The internet has also led to the rapid growth of 'social media', with stories, opinions, photos and videos uploaded into the public domain often without any editorial controls whatsoever. In a world where anyone with a mobile phone is a potential journalist and broadcaster, there are even fewer barriers between the public and private sphere for leading authority figures.

> **anyone with a mobile phone is a potential journalist and broadcaster**

Satire

In addition to the changes in scale and control of mass media, the 'satire boom' of the 1960s, investigative journalism and

the cult of celebrity have all affected the depiction of elites and undermined popular deference towards them. Satire has been a prominent feature of British humour for a very long time. The crucial difference between earlier forms of satire and that inspired by a handful of Oxford and Cambridge educated comedians in the early 1960s, was the intended audience: whereas the satirical prints of Hogarth or Gillray were intended for an elite audience, the adaptation of Peter Cook and Dudley Moore's satirical stage shows for television was designed for popular consumption. Although not everyone appreciated the biting personal jokes made about Prime Minister Harold Macmillan or the Queen, regular viewing figures of 12 million point to the huge popularity of *That Was The Week That Was* (BBC 1962–4).

> **whereas the satirical prints of Hogarth or Gillray were intended for an elite audience, the adaptation of Peter Cook and Dudley Moore's satirical stage shows for television was designed for popular consumption**

Around the same time, *Private Eye* began to print satirical stories about public figures, to 'simply poke fun at the powers that be'; the impact of this was far greater than its relatively small circulation of 10,000 would suggest. In March 1963, *Private Eye* exposed the scandalous story of Conservative Minister for War John Profumo's affair with prostitute Christine Keeler. Keeler was having an affair with a Soviet spy at the same time and, as a result, there were serious concerns about national security. Profumo lied to parliament when he denied the allegations the day before he resigned. It was only at this point, over a month after *Private Eye* first ran it, that the story appeared in national newspapers. This can be seen as something of a watershed. Before 1963, politicians like Lloyd George had generally been allowed to keep their private lives out of the public eye; after this, knowledge of private scandals was increasingly deemed to be 'in the public interest'. Only a few months after the Profumo affair, the Denning Report revealed several sleazy stories about politicians. 'The Man in the Mask', about a cabinet minister who served dinner at a party dressed in nothing but a mask and lace apron, and with a sign around his neck that said 'If my services don't please you, whip me', was perhaps the most famous.

Satire became even more personal and biting in the decades that followed, with shows such as *Spitting Image* (ITV 1984–96), *Have I Got News For You* (BBC2 1990–) and *Bremner, Bird and Fortune* (Channel 4 1999–) mercilessly lampooning all sorts of elite figures.

Satirical attacks on leading public figures made more serious forms of investigative journalism increasingly acceptable. A number of enterprising TV and print journalists have exposed a range of serious scandals involving high-ranking politicians, ranging from the 1985 Al Yamamah affair, where ministers were accused of using bribes to secure vast arms deals from the Saudi Royal Family, to the recent exposé of MPs' expense claims by the *Daily Telegraph*. However, rather than merely report such abuses, journalists have increasingly intruded into the private lives of the elite, and in doing so have blurred the boundary between the treatment of figures of authority and mere 'celebrities'. Stories about the relationships and family life of politicians and royals now commonly feature alongside 'news' about the lives of pop, film or even reality TV stars. By placing leading figures of authority on a par with entertainers and ordinary members of the public, the mass media have encouraged a decline in popular deference.

Nevertheless, as with all historical questions about popular attitudes, the historian must consider the extent to which public discourse reflects private sentiment. It is possible to explore this issue, albeit rather imperfectly, in the context of popular attitudes to a range of elite figures: the royal family, high-ranking politicians and leading members of the clergy.

Royalty

Mass media have at times undermined popular deference to the royal family. Yet, despite a dip in respect for the Windsors in the 1990s, their status has been generally held in high regard in a world where monarchs are something of an anachronism. Evidence for this comes in a range of opinion polls and in the way royals continued to be received with great enthusiasm on their tours and visits.

In 1945, the royals still had an aura of mystery or detachment from everyday life. Public contact with the royal family was limited to coverage of important state events and the annual Christmas Day broadcast. The expansion of the media and the growth of 'celebrity' style news have removed this sense of mystique. The private lives of the Princes William and Harry are often splashed in the tabloids despite promises by the paparazzi not to intrude after their role in the death of Diana, Princess of Wales in August 1997. The legacy of the satire boom and investigative journalism mean that mass media are more willing to treat the royal family in a critical fashion. This was most clearly shown in the wake of Diana's death. Several newspapers were critical of the Queen for not mourning in public: the *Independent* went so far as to offer the advice that it 'would be good for the Queen and the Prince of Wales to break down, cry and hug one another'.

However, it is clear that mass media are not entirely at fault for the dip in the popularity of the royal family since the 1980s. To a degree, they have continued to uphold a deferential treatment of the monarchy: critics said that the 2007 BBC documentary *Monarchy: The Royal Family at Work* was overly deferential; a 2008 ITV documentary about the Duke of Edinburgh was similarly respectful in its tone and content; and *The Queen,* a hit film of 2006, was very supportive of the way Elizabeth II dealt with the death of Diana, Princess of Wales. The royals too have invited

greater media scrutiny. The first example of this was the 1969 documentary *The Royal Family,* which attempted to show the royals in an informal setting to boost their popularity with the British public. A further notorious example was *It's A Royal Knockout* in 1987. The show, which involved Prince Edward, Princess Anne and Prince Andrew running around obstacle courses in costumes, was largely designed to help Prince Edward establish a career in television. It was a public relations disaster which lowered the dignity of the royals.

Above all, the divorce and scandals that surrounded Prince Charles and Diana, Princess of Wales, and Prince Andrew and Sarah Ferguson in the mid 1990s, marked a watershed in the treatment of the royal family. The divorce of Charles and Diana followed the 'Squidgy-gate' and 'Camillagate' stories of 1992, embarrassing exposés of conversations they had had with extra-marital partners. Both Charles and Diana subsequently sought to use the media to get their side of their marital breakdown story across to the public: Diana famously remarked on a BBC *Panorama* programme in 1995 that 'there were three of us in this marriage, so it was a bit crowded'. Yet, despite these scandals and the constant celebrity-style coverage of the royals, polls by British Social Attitudes indicate that their popularity has improved since the late 1990s. This strongly implies that it is the behaviour of the members of the royal family, rather than the intrusion of mass media per se, that affects levels of respect for the royals.

Politicians

Similarly, mass media can only be seen to have undermined deference towards politicians to a limited degree. In 1944, the BBC agreed to the '14-Day rule'; this prevented the discussion of a political issue for a fortnight before it was to be debated in Westminster. Although this rule was relaxed in 1956, it was not until 1975 that debates in the House of Commons were broadcast on radio. Several letters in newspapers echoed the views of one listener who wrote that the boisterous nature of the debates was 'an affront to the British electorate, destructive of any lingering respect it might have had for parliamentary procedure'. From 1990 onwards, the proceedings were regularly televised; an Ipsos Mori report from 2001 concluded that 'media, especially television, plays a key role in creating . . . images which gave [British people] their negative perceptions'. Clearly the greater exposure of parliamentary affairs did nothing to encourage deference towards MPs. The rise of satire and investigative journalism also damaged the representation of politicians. (If you are able, do have a look online at the depiction of politicians on *Spitting Image.*) A full list of politicians' extra-marital affairs and other sexual misdemeanours, in addition to the corruption mentioned earlier, would take up too much room here: allegations of 'sleaze' have been a staple of tabloids since the mid 1990s.

Yet in seeking to use mass media for their own ends, MPs have encouraged this greater press intrusion and brought about a decline in deference as a result. A brief selection of the many possible examples will serve to illustrate the point. Harold Wilson was keen to feature prominently in the media in his bid to become Prime Minister in the early 1960s, and only became hostile when the press exposed a number of lies he had made publicly. Conservative MP Edwina Curry went public with the story of her affair with then Prime Minister John Major in a bid to boost sales of her *Diaries (1987–92)*. The use of 'spin doctors' to manage the release of information to the public has also reduced the amount of popular trust since the 1980s. Perhaps the most repellent example of this cynical manipulation of information came shortly after the terrorist attack on the World Trade Centre on 11 September 2001: government press officer Jo Moore wrote that 'It's now a very good day to get out anything we want to bury'. It should be noted, however, that the trust placed in MPs by the British public has been fairly low throughout the post-war years. One typical view from a series of Mass Observation interviews in 1943 came from a tradesman who said, 'I don't trust the government and I don't suppose they're likely to worry much about us'. It would be rather unfair to pin the blame on mass media for a lack of popular deference towards politicians when the bar was this low at the start of the post-war period.

Religion

The well-known atheist Richard Dawkins has complained for many years that religious authorities get too privileged and deferential treatment by mass media. Although ITV cut the air time allocated to religious programming from 104 to 52 hours per year in 2005, religious debate still gets wide coverage on radio and in the press. Certainly it is probably true to say that the mass media have reflected rather than inspired a decline in deference towards religious authorities. There has been no concerted attack from the media against the churches. In soaps and dramas, with the exception of the 1994–2007 BBC comedy *The Vicar of Dibley,* the clergy have not featured prominently; and the few seemingly shocking attacks on religious authority in the media drew very little anger from the British public. There was no scandal in 1967 when anthropologist Desmond Morris said in his book *The Naked Ape* that 'Religion has . . . given rise to a great deal of unnecessary suffering and misery'; indeed, it boosted sales of the *Daily Mirror* when it serialised the book. The blasphemy in Monty Python's film *The Life of Brian* (1979) did cause some outrage: it was banned in Surrey, east Devon, Harrogate and in Swansea. However, many people in those areas simply visited cinemas in areas where they could see the film.

The Anglican Church has often 'played catch-up' with popular morality in a bid to maintain its relevance

Puzzled People, a Mass Observation report in 1947, concluded that 'most people nowadays don't think much about religion [and] don't set much conscious store by it'. Around this time no more than 13 percent regularly attended church once a week. Yet this figure had fallen to just 6 percent in 2007. How do we explain this 'de-churching' (perhaps a better word that secularisation, since in the 2001 census only 15 percent of Britons said they had no religious belief)? Historian Callum Brown has pointed to a growth in permissive values after the 1960s, in particular those fuelled by more liberal girls' and women's magazines, while social historian James Obelkevich sees the rise of urbanisation and industry as far more significant long-term factors. He argues that the traditional rural calendar and holidays were strongly linked to Christian festivals; the introduction of bank holidays in 1871 and the commercialisation of the remaining festivals of Easter and Christmas have severed this link. The process was perhaps completed in 1994 when the Keep Sundays Special campaign failed to stop supermarkets opening on 'the Lord's day'. The Anglican Church has often 'played catch-up' with popular morality in a bid to maintain its relevance: the Anglican ordination of women after 1994 and the acceptance of openly gay clergy both came after the huge strides made by these groups in other social spheres. Yet in doing so, the Church has undermined its authority in the eyes of more conservative church-goers.

Conclusion

The changes in the mass media and the changes in the treatment of leading authority figures are themselves the products of broader developments that have affected popular deference in Britain. For reasons too numerous to go into here, the World Wars brought about a large degree of social levelling which irrevocably changed the social structure of Britain. Owing to their collective sacrifice, ordinary people began to feel entitled to things which had been the preserve of their 'betters' in previous generations. The frustration caused by the gap between expectation and reality drove a good deal of post-war drama and humour, which inevitably was at the expense of the elite. Broadcasters and publishers had no choice but to respond to this shift in attitudes if they were to be commercially successful (or justify the Licence Fee in the case of the BBC). The rapid growth in material wealth since 1945 not only drove advertising (and hence competition for revenue), but also blurred the rigid class identities that had underpinned popular deference. Young workers with disposable income, in a bid to define themselves by what they bought, created classless, popular styles of dress and made stars of classless rock and pop icons. Although class has not disappeared as part of British identity, respect and deference are not rigidly tied to class status as before 1945.

Whereas pre-war generations of leading authority figures could expect deference, their modern equivalents must earn and maintain respect. This is not merely a result of changes in mass media, but a reflection of changes in British attitudes and behaviour more generally. Although authority figures may like to periodically blame the mass media for a range of problems they face, the reality is that TV, radio, the press and new media are obvious scapegoats, either for problems with far deeper roots, or for their own lapses of judgement.

Issues to Debate

- Why were politicians treated with greater deference before 1945?
- Have the mass media merely reflected, rather than promoted, social change in Britain after 1945?
- Was the decade of the 1960s a watershed in the decline of deference?

Further Reading

S. Clayton, *Mass Media, Popular Culture and Social Change in Britain since 1945* (Pearson Education, 2010)

J. Obelkevich and P. Catterall (eds). *Understanding Post-War British Society* (Routledge, 1994)

D. Sandbrook, *Never Had It So Good: 1956–63* (Little, Brown and Company, 2005)

D. Sandbrook. *Whits Heat: 1963–70* (Little, Brown and Company, 2007)

B. Harrison, *Seeking a Role: Britain 1951–1970* (Oxford, 2009)

B. Harrison, *Finding a Role? Britain 1970–1990* (Oxford, 2010

Critical Thinking

1. Prior to 1945, the BBC was a monopoly broadcaster with a philosophy "to edify rather than excite; to promote high standards rather than attract the largest number of listeners and viewers." The BBC product largely adhered to these principles, which have been lost since deregulation. Is this a cogent argument for monopoly?

2. If ratings and sales figures indicate that the public is attracted to "intellectually bare" content, should media owners give media consumers what they want? Why or why not?

STUART CLAYTON is Head of History at Emanuel School, Wandsworth.

I Can't Think!

The twitterization of our culture has revolutionized our lives, but with an unintended consequence—our overloaded brains freeze when we have to make decisions.

SHARON BEGLEY

Imagine the most mind-numbing choice you've faced lately, one in which the possibilities almost paralyzed you: buying a car, choosing a health-care plan, figuring out what to do with your 401(k). The anxiety you felt might have been just the well-known consequence of information overload, but Angelika Dimoka, director of the Center for Neural Decision Making at Temple University, suspects that a more complicated biological phenomenon is at work. To confirm it, she needed to find a problem that overtaxes people's decision-making abilities, so she joined forces with economists and computer scientists who study "combinatorial auctions," bidding wars that bear almost no resemblance to the eBay version. Bidders consider a dizzying number of items that can be bought either alone or bundled, such as airport landing slots. The challenge is to buy the combination you want at the lowest price—a diabolical puzzle if you're considering, say, 100 landing slots at LAX. As the number of items and combinations explodes, so does the quantity of information bidders must juggle: passenger load, weather, connecting flights. Even experts become anxious and mentally exhausted. In fact, the more information they try to absorb, the fewer of the desired items they get and the more they overpay or make critical errors.

This is where Dimoka comes in. She recruited volunteers to try their hand at combinatorial auctions, and as they did she measured their brain activity with fMRI. As the information load increased, she found, so did activity in the dorsolateral prefrontal cortex, a region behind the forehead that is responsible for decision making and control of emotions. But as the researchers gave the bidders more and more information, activity in the dorsolateral PFC suddenly fell off, as if a circuit breaker had popped. "The bidders reach cognitive and information overload," says Dimoka. They start making stupid mistakes and bad choices because the brain region responsible for smart decision making has essentially left the premises. For the same reason, their frustration and

anxiety soar: the brain's emotion regions—previously held in check by the dorsolateral PFC—run as wild as toddlers on a sugar high. The two effects build on one another. "With too much information," says Dimoka, "people's decisions make less and less sense."

So much for the ideal of making well-informed decisions. For earlier generations, that mean simply the due diligence of looking things up in a reference book. Today, with Twitter and Facebook and countless apps fed into our smart phones, the flow of facts and opinion never stops. That can be a good thing, as when information empowers workers and consumers, not to mention whistle-blowers and revolutionaries. You can find out a used car's accident history, a doctor's malpractice record, a restaurant's health-inspection results. Yet research like Dimoka's is showing that a surfeit of information is changing the way we think, not always for the better. Maybe you consulted scores of travel websites to pick a vacation spot—only to be so overwhelmed with information that you opted for a staycation. Maybe you were *this close* to choosing a college, when suddenly older friends swamped your inbox with all the reasons to go somewhere else— which made you completely forget why you'd chosen the other school. Maybe you had the Date From Hell after being so inundated with information on "matches" that you chose at random. If so, then you are a victim of info-paralysis.

The problem has been creeping up on us for a long time. In the 17th century Leibniz bemoaned the "horrible mass of books which keeps on growing," and in 1729 Alexander Pope warned of "a deluge of authors cover[ing] the land," as James Gleick describes in his new book, *The Information*. But the consequences were thought to be emotional and psychological, chiefly anxiety about being unable to absorb even a small fraction of what's out there. Indeed, the Oxford English Dictionary added "information fatigue" in 2009. But as information finds more ways to reach us, more often, more insistently than ever before, another consequence is becoming alarmingly clear: trying to drink from a firehose of information has harmful cognitive effects. And nowhere are those effects clearer, and more worrying, than in our ability to make smart, creative, successful decisions.

The research should give pause to anyone addicted to incoming texts and tweets. The booming science of decision making has shown that more information can lead to objectively poorer choices, and to choices that people come to regret. It has shown that an unconscious system guides many of our decisions, and that it can be sidelined by too much information. And it has shown that decisions requiring creativity benefit from letting the problem incubate below the level of awareness—something that becomes ever-more difficult when information never stops arriving.

The research so far should give pause to anyone addicted to incoming texts and tweets. More information can lead to objectively poorer choices, and to choices that people quickly regret.

Decision science has only begun to incorporate research on how the brain processes information, but the need for answers is as urgent as the stakes are high. During the BP oil-well blowout last year, Coast Guard Adm. Thad Allen, the incident commander, estimates that he got 300 to 400 *pages* of emails, texts, reports, and other messages every day. It's impossible to know whether less information, more calmly evaluated, would have let officials figure out sooner how to cap the well, but Allen tells NEWSWEEK's Daniel Stone that the torrent of data might have contributed to what he calls the mistake of failing to close off air space above the gulf on day one. (There were eight near mid-air collisions.) A comparable barrage of information assailed administration officials before the overthrow of the Egyptian government, possibly producing at least one misstep: CIA Director Leon Panetta told Congress that Hosni Mubarak was about to announce he was stepping down—right before the Egyptian president delivered a defiant, rambling speech saying he wasn't going anywhere. "You always think afterwards about what you could have done better, but there isn't time in the moment to second-guess," said White House Communications Director Dan Pfeifler. "You have to make your decision and go execute." As scientists probe how the flow of information affects decision making, they've spotted several patterns. Among them:

Total Failure to Decide

Every bit of incoming information presents a choice: whether to pay attention, whether to reply, whether to factor it into an impending decision. But decision science has shown that people faced with a plethora of choices are apt to make no decision at all. The clearest example of this comes from studies of financial decisions. In a 2004 study, Sheena Iyengar of Columbia University and colleagues found that the more information people confronted about a 401(k) plan, the more participation fell: from 75 percent to 70 percent as the number of choices rose from two to 11, and to 61 percent when there were 59 options. People felt overwhelmed and opted out. Those who participated chose lower-return options—worse choices. Similarly, when people are given information about 50 rather than 10 options in an online store, they choose lower-quality options. Although we say we prefer more information, in fact more can be "debilitating," argues Iyengar, whose 2010 book *The Art of Choosing* comes out in paperback in March. "When we make decisions, we compare bundles of information. So a decision is harder if the amount of information you have to juggle is greater." In recent years, businesses have offered more and more choices to cater to individual tastes. For mustard or socks, this may not be a problem, but the proliferation of choices can create paralysis when the stakes are high and the information complex.

Many Diminishing Returns

If we manage to make a decision despite info-deluge, it often comes back to haunt us. The more information we try to assimilate, the more we tend to regret the many forgone options. In a 2006 study, Iyengar and colleagues analyzed job searches by college students. The more sources and kinds of information (about a company, an industry, a city, pay, benefits, corporate culture) they collected, the less satisfied they were with their decision. They knew so much, consciously or unconsciously, they could easily imagine why a job not taken would have been better. In a world of limitless information, regret over the decisions we make becomes more common. We chafe at the fact that identifying the best feels impossible. "Even if you made an objectively better choice, you tend to be less satisfied with it," says Iyengar.

A key reason for information's diminishing or even negative returns is the limited capacity of the brain's working memory. It can hold roughly seven items (which is why seven-digit phone numbers were a great idea). Anything more must be processed into long-term memory. That takes conscious effort, as when you study for an exam. When more than seven units of information land in our brain's inbox, argues psychologist Joanne Cantor, author of the 2009 book *Conquer Cyber Overload* and an emerita professor at the University of Wisconsin, the brain struggles to figure out what to keep and what to disregard. Ignoring the repetitious and the useless requires cognitive resources and vigilance, a harder task when there is so much information.

It isn't only the quantity of information that knocks the brain for a loop; it's the rate. The ceaseless influx trains us to respond instantly, sacrificing accuracy and thoughtfulness to the false god of immediacy. "We're being trained to prefer

<table>
</table>

Decision: Where Should I Get My News?

- **Choices:** Print versus online. Blog versus old-media site. Drudge Report versus Huffington Post RSS feeds versus Twitter.
- **Noise:** Can you trust what you read in newspapers? Can you trust what you read on the Internet? Are liberals more or less trustworthy than conservatives? Do you want to know a lot about one thing or a little about everything?
- **Best Strategy:** Mix it up. Read the top story in *The New York Times*—and then let the bloggers tell you what it missed.

Decision: Should I Run for President?

- **Choices:** A posh gig on cable versus leader of the free world. Millions in greasy lobbying dollars versus a flat rate of $400,000 per year. An ounce of privacy versus endless questions about your place of birth.
- **Noise:** Input from political pros, pundits, your spouse, your spiritual adviser; and Ohio-based plumbers.
- **Best Strategy:** Write a book. If you run out of material before you hit page 200 forget it.

Decision: Which Jeans Should I Buy?

- **Choices:** Low-rise versus high-waisted. Boot-cut versus straight-legged. Regular cut versus painter's pants with a hammer loop.
- **Noise:** Input from fashion blogs, celebrity photos, store employees, and your hips.
- **Best Strategy:** Find a pair that fits. Buy 20 of them.

Decision: Which Coffee Drink Should I Order?

- **Choices:** Dunkin' Donuts versus Starbucks. Fattening frappe versus low-cal Venti versus grande. Fair trade versus cruel exploitation of low-wage workers.
- **Noise:** Input from TV ads, liberal bloggers, Dr. Atkins, and your nagging caffeine headache.
- **Best Strategy:** Find a cup that meets at least two of your requirements. Buy it till the end of time.

an immediate decision even if it's bad to a later decision that's better," says psychologist Clifford Nass of Stanford University. "In business, we're seeing a preference for the quick over the right, in large part because so many decisions have to be made. The notion that the quick decision is better is becoming normative."

'Recency' Trumps Quality

The brain is wired to notice change over stasis. An arriving email that pops to the top of your BlackBerry qualifies as a change; so does a new Facebook post. We are conditioned to give greater weight in our decision-making machinery to what is latest, not what is more important or more interesting. "There is a powerful 'recency' effect in decision making," says behavioral economist George Loewenstein of Carnegie Mellon University, "We pay a lot of attention to the most recent information, discounting what came earlier." Getting 30 texts per hour up to the moment when you make a decision means that most of them make all the impression of a feather on a brick wall, whereas Nos. 29 and 30 assume outsize importance, regardless of their validity. "We're

fooled by immediacy and quantity and think its quality," says Eric Kessler, a management expert at Pace University's Lubin School of Business. "What starts driving decisions is the urgent rather than the important."

Part of the problem is that the brain is really bad at giving only a little weight to a piece of information. When psychologist Eric Stone of Wake Forest University had subjects evaluate the vocabulary skills of a hypothetical person, he gave them salient information (the person's education level) and less predictive information (how often they read a newspaper). People give the less predictive info more weight than it deserves. "Our cognitive systems," says Stone, "just aren't designed to take information into account only a little."

The Neglected Unconscious

Creative decisions are more likely to bubble up from a brain that applies unconscious thought to a problem, rather than going at it in a full-frontal, analytical assault. So while we're likely to think creative thoughts in the shower, it's much harder if we're under a virtual deluge of data. "If you let things come at you all the time, you can't use additional information to make a creative leap or a wise judgment," says Cantor. "You need to pull back from the constant influx and take a break." That allows the brain to subconsciously integrate new information with existing knowledge and thereby make novel connections and see hidden patterns. In contrast, a constant focus on the new makes it harder for information to percolate just below conscious awareness, where it can combine in ways that spark smart decisions.

One of the greatest surprises in decision science is the discovery that some of our best decisions are made through unconscious processes. When subjects in one study evaluated what psychologist Ap Dijksterhuis of the Radboud University of Nijmegen in the Netherlands calls a "rather daunting amount of information" about four hypothetical apartments for rent—size, location, friendliness of the landlord, price, and eight other features—those who decided unconsciously which to rent did better. ("Better" meant they chose the one that had objectively better features.) The scientists made sure the decision was unconscious by having the subjects do a memory and attention task, which tied up their brains enough that they couldn't contemplate, say, square footage.

There are at least two ways an info-glut can impair the unconscious system of decision making. First, when people see that there is a lot of complex information relevant to a decision, "they default to the conscious system," says psychologist Maarten Bos of Radboud. "That causes them to make poorer choices." Second, the unconscious system works best when it ignores some information about a complex decision. But here's the rub: in an info tsunami, our minds struggle to decide if we can ignore this piece . . . or that one . . . but how about that one? "Especially online," says Cantor, "it is so much easier to look for more and more information than sit back and think about how it fits together."

Even experience-based decision making, in which you use a rule of thumb rather than analyze pros and cons, can go off the rails with too much information. "This kind of intuitive decision making relies on distilled expertise," says Kessler. "More information, by overwhelming and distracting the brain, can make it harder to tap into just the core information you need." In one experiment, M.B.A. students choosing a (make-believe) stock portfolio were divided into two groups, one that was inundated with information from analysts and the financial press, and another that saw only stock-price changes. The latter reaped more than twice the returns of the info-deluged group, whose analytical capabilities were hijacked by too much information and wound up buying and selling on every rumor and tip—a surefire way to lose money in the market. The more data they got, the more they struggled to separate wheat from chaff.

Which brings us back to the experimental subjects Angelika Dimoka has put in an fMRI scanner. The prefrontal cortex that waves a white flag under an onslaught of information plays a key role in your gut-level, emotional decision-making system. It hooks up feelings about various choices with the output of the rational brain. If emotions are shut out of the decision-making process, we're likely to overthink a decision, and that has been shown to produce worse outcomes on even the simplest tasks. In one classic experiment, when volunteers focused on the attributes of various strawberry jams they had just rated, it completely scrambled their preferences, and they wound up giving a high rating to a jam they disliked and a low rating to one they had found delicious.

How can you protect yourself from having your decisions warped by excess information? Experts advise dealing with emails and texts in batches, rather than in real time; that should let your unconscious decision-making system kick in. Avoid the trap of thinking that a decision requiring you to assess a lot of complex information is best made methodically and consciously; you will do better, and regret less, if you let your unconscious turn it over by removing yourself from the info influx. Set priorities: if a choice turns on only a few criteria, focus consciously on those. Some people are better than others at ignoring extra information. These "sufficers" are able to say enough: they channel-surf until they find an acceptable show and then stop, whereas "maximizers" never stop surfing, devouring information, and so struggle to make a decision and move on. If you think you're a maximizer, the best prescription for you might be the "off" switch on your smart phone.

Critical Thinking

1. Do the research findings reported in this article have face validity to you?
2. If Internet use does, indeed, rewire the brain, what should parents, teachers, and policy makers do with that knowledge? Should schools change to complement or counteract such effects?

The Digital Disruption
Connectivity and the Diffusion of Power

ERIC SCHMIDT AND JARED COHEN

The advent and power of connection technologies—tools that connect people to vast amounts of information and to one another—will make the twenty-first century all about surprises. Governments will be caught off-guard when large numbers of their citizens, armed with virtually nothing but cell phones, take part in mini-rebellions that challenge their authority. For the media, reporting will increasingly become a collaborative enterprise between traditional news organizations and the quickly growing number of citizen journalists. And technology companies will find themselves outsmarted by their competition and surprised by consumers who have little loyalty and no patience.

Today, more than 50 percent of the world's population has access to some combination of cell phones (five billion users) and the Internet (two billion). These people communicate within and across borders, forming virtual communities that empower citizens at the expense of governments. New intermediaries make it possible to develop and distribute content across old boundaries, lowering barriers to entry. Whereas the traditional press is called the fourth estate, this space might be called the "interconnected estate"—a place where any person with access to the Internet, regardless of living standard or nationality, is given a voice and the power to effect change.

For the world's most powerful states, the rise of the interconnected estate will create new opportunities for growth and development, as well as huge challenges to established ways of governing. Connection technologies will carve out spaces for democracy as well as autocracy and empower individuals for both good and ill. States will vie to control the impact of technologies on their political and economic power.

Some countries, primarily major connected powers such as the United States, EU member states, and the Asian economic powerhouses (led by China and to a lesser extent India) will manage to regulate the interconnected estate within their own borders in ways that strengthen their respective values. But not all states will be able to control or embrace the empowerment of the individual. Connection technologies will add to the strains of less developed societies—forcing them to become more open and accountable while also giving governments new tools to constrain opposition and become more closed and repressive. There will be a constant struggle between those striving to promote what United States. Secretary of State Hillary Clinton has called "the freedom to connect" and those who view that freedom as inimical to their political survival.

Dealing with this dilemma will pose particular challenges for democratic nations that share common principles of openness and freedom. Their ideals will clash with well-founded concerns about national security. In order to avoid yielding the advantage to countries such as China, which seek to extend their values of control and censorship, countries such as the United States and the EU member states will have to hold tightly to freedom and openness.

Democratic governments will most likely be tempted to further their national interests through the same combination of defense, diplomacy, and development on which they relied during the Cold War and the decades after. But these traditional tools will not be enough: although it remains uncertain exactly how the spread of technology will change governance, it is clear that old solutions will not work in this new era. Governments will have to build new alliances that reflect the rise in citizen power and the changing nature of the state.

Those alliances will have to go far beyond government-to-government contacts, to embrace civic society, nonprofit organizations, and the private sector. Democratic states must recognize that their citizens' use of technology may be a more effective vehicle to promote the values of freedom, equality, and human rights globally than government-led initiatives. The hardware and software created by private companies in free markets are proving more useful to citizens abroad than state-sponsored assistance or diplomacy.

Although it is true that governments and the private sector will continue to wield the most power, any attempts to tackle the political and economic challenges posed by connection technologies will fail without the deep involvement of the other rising powers in this space—namely, nongovernmental organizations and activists. The real action in the interconnected estate can be found in cramped offices in Cairo, the living rooms of private homes throughout Latin America, and on the streets of Tehran. From these locations and others, activists and technology geeks are rallying political "flash mobs" that shake repressive governments, building new tools to skirt firewalls and censors, reporting and tweeting the new online journalism, and writing a bill of human rights for the Internet age. Taken one by one, these efforts may be seen as impractical or insignificant, but together they constitute a meaningful change in the democratic process.

The Revolution Will Be Podcast

The idea of technology empowering citizens for good or for ill is not a new phenomenon, nor is there a lack of precedents of governments dealing with how to react to this phenomenon. The arrival of the printing press in the fifteenth century is an interesting case in point. Although Johannes Gutenberg's invention was truly revolutionary, its promise of increased access to information was limited by those who owned the presses and decided what to publish and where it could be distributed. Repressive governments or other institutions, moreover, had the power to use the printing press as a tool for control (by generating propaganda) or oppression (by outlawing anti-government or antichurch writings).

In the twentieth century, with the advent of radio and television, nations—and those wealthy or powerful enough to gain access to the airwaves—could control and even dictate much of what was heard and seen. Radio and television proved to be powerful propaganda tools for states that knew what to do with them. North Korea—where people can only watch state-sponsored channels—is a modern-day version of what was common in Eastern Europe before the fall of the Berlin Wall. Even when unlicensed radio emerged in the first half of the Cold War, and satellite television began to spread during the second half, few people had the hardware, knowledge, or expertise to develop their own programs, let alone to secure a broadcast studio or airtime.

Despite these limits, many people chose to watch and listen to information broadcast through independent sources, which had previously been unavailable to the masses. These listeners and viewers included many who worked in governments—often putting themselves at significant risk of getting caught, losing their livelihood, or worse. A similar phenomenon is occurring today in places such as Iran and Syria, where government officials seeking unvarnished news of the world beyond their borders use so-called proxy servers and circumvention technology to access their own Facebook or e-mail accounts—platforms their governments regularly block.

The Iranian Revolution of 1979 illustrates the shift from broadcast media to another set of communications tools. To be sure, huge social forces were at work in Iran in the 1970s, including unhappiness with the shah's corrupt and repressive regime and pressure from the international community. But many historians believe that one of the keys to the revolution was the ability of Ayatollah Ruhollah Khomeini to spread his message using a simple device: the cassette tape. Using an extensive network, Khomeini distributed tapes of his speeches to more than 9,000 mosques. As *Time* magazine wrote, the "78-year-old holy man camped in a Paris suburb [and] direct[ed] a revolution 2,600 miles away like a company commander assaulting a hill."

The United States. government was wary of the power of the cassette tape in Iran, both because this new technology was too difficult to control and because Washington's eyes were fixed on the Soviet bloc and the cassette tape's possible use as a tool for spreading communist propaganda. In not using this technology, the United States missed out on a powerful opportunity to promote its values and policies and empower lesser-known democratic leaders. By the mid-1970s, cassette manufacturers had broken into emerging markets, and suddenly what had begun as a new entertainment device had become an effective communications tool.

In the decade that followed, technology helped achieve another significant step in reducing the power of intermediaries and in short-circuiting regimes bent on silencing opposition voices. Activists and human rights campaigners in the Soviet Union and Eastern Europe used photocopiers and fax machines to spread their own messages and foment unrest. The technology of today holds even more promise: comparing the uncertain dial tone of the fax machine with the speed of today's handheld devices is like comparing a ship's compass to the power of global positioning systems.

Eclipse of the Intermediaries

Today, people are far more likely to complain about having to sort through too much information than to have none at all. Perhaps the most revolutionary aspect of this change lies in the wealth of platforms that allow individuals to consume, distribute, and create their own content without government control.

This does not mean that intermediaries have suddenly become irrelevant, of course. Companies that provide access to the Internet or software applications are critical for exchanging information, and governments or state-owned companies retain the power to block access. But this power is diminishing, because not even governments can stop, control, or spy on all sources of information all the time. Meanwhile, the involvement of diaspora communities in bringing change to their homelands has vastly increased, creating new sources of financial support and international pressure. And an entire cottage industry has emerged with the goal of finding and creating holes in porous firewalls.

The combination of these new technologies and the desire for greater freedom is already changing politics in some of the world's most unlikely places. In Colombia in 2008, an unemployed engineer named Oscar Morales used Facebook and the free Internet-based telephone service Skype to orchestrate a massive demonstration against the Revolutionary Armed Forces of Colombia. He was able to muster the largest protest against a terrorist group in history and the sort of high-profile blow to militants that no Colombian president has been able to achieve in the past 40 years. In Moldova in 2009, young people, frustrated and angry over a collapsing economy and fraying society, gathered in the streets of Chisinau after a rigged election. They used messages on Twitter to turn a small protest of 15,000 people into a global event. As international and internal pressure continued to rise, the rigged election was overturned, and a new election brought to power the first non-communist government in Moldova in more than 50 years. And in Iran last year, YouTube videos, Twitter updates, and Facebook groups made it possible for activists and citizens to spread information that directly challenged the results of the country's flawed presidential election.

Yet for all the inspiring stories and moments of hope abetted by the use of connection technologies, the potential of such technologies to be manipulated or used in dangerous ways should not be underestimated. The world's most repressive regimes and violent transnational groups—from al Qaeda and the Mexican drug cartels to the Mafia and the Taliban—are effectively using technology to bring on new recruits, terrify local populations, and threaten democratic institutions. The Mexican drug cartels, in order to illustrate the consequences of opposition, spread graphic videos showing decapitations of those who cooperate with law enforcement, and al Qaeda and its affiliates have created viral videos showing the killings of foreigners held hostage in Iraq.

The same encryption technologies used by dissidents and activists to hide their private communications and personal data from the state are used by would-be terrorists and criminals. As relatively inexpensive encryption technology continues to proliferate on the commercial market, there is little doubt that autocrats and hackers will make use of it, too. Finding the balance between protecting dissidents and enabling criminals will be difficult at best.

Afghanistan's telecommunications networks provide a useful case study in how connection technologies can both help and harm a nation. Since United States. and NATO forces first launched military operations there in 2001, cell-phone access in Afghanistan has grown from zero to 30 percent. This growth has had clear positive effects: mobile-based programs enable women to run call centers from their cell phones, provide access to remote medical diagnoses, and give farmers real-time information on commodity prices. And the 97 percent of Afghans who do not have bank accounts can save and access money with their cell phones through mobile money transfers. The salaries for 2,500 Afghan National Police officers in Wardak Province are transmitted through this technology, which allows them to then transfer money to their families using text messaging.

At the same time, the Taliban have become increasingly savvy about using mobile technology to malicious and deadly effect. Taliban militants have used cell phones to coordinate attacks, threaten local populations, and hold local businesses hostage, either by blowing up cell towers or by forcing them to power down between 6 PM and 8 AM, the period when Taliban militants carry out evening operations. In February 2009, Taliban inmates in Kabul's Policharki prison used cell phones to orchestrate a number of coordinated attacks on Afghan government ministries. In Afghanistan—and Iraq, too—it is not uncommon for insurgents to use cell phones to detonate roadside bombs remotely.

Cats and Mice

Realists describe international relations as anarchic and dominated by self-interested states. Although there is little doubt about the dominant role states will and should play in the world, there is a great deal of debate about exactly how dominant they will be going forward. In these pages in 2008, Richard Haass, the president of the Council on Foreign Relations, described a "nonpolar world" that is "dominated not by one or two or even several states but rather by dozens of actors possessing and exercising various kinds of power." In the interconnected estate, a virtual space that is constrained by different national laws but not national boundaries, there can be no equivalent to the Treaty of Westphalia—the 1648 agreement that ended the Thirty Years' War and established the modern system of nation-states. Instead, governments, individuals, nongovernmental organizations, and private companies will balance one another's interests.

Not all governments will manage the turbulence left in the wake of declining state authority in the same way. Much remains uncertain, of course, but it seems clear that free-market and democratic governments will be the best suited to manage and cope with this maelstrom. The greatest danger to the Internet among these countries—perhaps best defined as the members of the Organization for Economic Cooperation and Development—will be the overregulation of the technology sector, which has thus far thrived on entrepreneurial investment and open networks.

Perhaps no country has more carefully considered the implications of allowing its citizens access to connection technologies than China. The regime's goals are clear: to control access to content on the Internet and to use technology to build its political and economic power. Beijing has arrested online activists and used the country's thriving online bulletin boards to spread its propaganda. All of this is part of a strategy to ensure that the technology revolution extends, rather than destroys, the one-party state and its value system. Around the world, the Chinese model of Internet control has been copied by nations such as Vietnam and actively promoted in Asian and African countries where China is investing heavily in natural resources. And Beijing has moved to co-opt international institutions, such as the International Telecommunications Union, in order to gain global credibility and rally allies behind its efforts to control its citizens' communication.

But thanks to the work of activists and nongovernmental organizations operating inside and outside China, Beijing has learned that its attempts to establish total control of the Internet will not always work. The regime has recently been caught off-guard by the use of cell phones, blogs, and uploaded videos to encourage labor protests and report on industrial accidents, environmental problems, and incidents of corruption. The July 2009 demonstrations by ethnic Uighurs in Xinjiang drew international media attention even after Beijing completely shut down all Internet connections in the region; Uighur activists used social networks and so-called microblogs to spread news among targeted audiences abroad, including the Uighur diaspora. These kinds of cat-and-mouse games will no doubt continue, but in the short run there is doubt that Beijing's attempts to control access to information will largely succeed.

The intersection of connection technologies and state power is also playing out in the other BRIC nations: Brazil, India, and Russia. In each of these states, the willingness to welcome new technology in the service of economic growth has generally prevailed over fears about how the Internet can be used by criminals, terrorists, or political troublemakers—but not always. Last spring, for example, Alexei Dymovsky, a police officer in southern Russia, was arrested after he posted a tell-all video on YouTube exposing corruption in Russia's police force.

The acceptance, or lack thereof, of connection technologies can also vary within the governments of democracies. Turkey is a case in point. The country's judiciary has blocked YouTube, but the president has spoken out against the ban. The court ruling was prompted by a series of blogs and videos that depicted the founder of the Turkish state, Kemal Atatürk, in a potentially offensive manner. This internal dispute in Turkey raises the question about whether countries can continue to protect their version of historical events in the age of the interconnected estate.

International observers should also keep their eyes on a small group of hyperconnected states—Finland, Israel, and Sweden, among others—that have relatively strong central governments, stable economies, and vibrant technology and innovation sectors. These nations have already demonstrated their ability to embrace technology and the good sense to invest in broadband and research. Their governments' research and development budgets represent an exceptionally high percentage of GDP. States that invest in research and infrastructure stand to benefit down the road.

Riding the Tsunami

States in the developing world—grouped here as "partially connected" nations—face a different set of opportunities and challenges in incorporating connection technologies. The stakes are especially high for those with weak or failed central governments, underdeveloped economies, populations that are disproportionately young and unemployed, and cultures that lend themselves to opposition and dissent, and also for those contending with outside pressures from large and engaged diasporas living in technologically advanced nations. The sudden influx of connection technologies into these societies will threaten the status quo, leaving fragile governments in potentially unstable positions.

On the bright side, the spread of technology in partially connected nations such as Egypt is breaking down traditional barriers of age, gender, and socioeconomic status. Most of this is due to the rise of cell phones, which have the potential to create the twenty-first-century equivalent of last century's green revolution, a movement that used advanced agricultural technologies and processes to increase food yields worldwide. In Pakistan, for example, there were only 300,000 cellphone users in 2000; in August 2010, that number was closer to 100 million. Such dramatic changes in connectivity are having an impact on the ground. In Kenya, for example, a company called Safaricom has developed a program to transfer money using cell phones, which has lowered the transaction costs for remittances, expanded access to bank accounts for underserved populations, and streamlined the microfinance process.

In some partially connected countries, such as Côte d'Ivoire, Guinea, Kyrgyzstan, and Pakistan, connection technologies are shifting, albeit slowly, the nature of civil society. A growing number of activists work anonymously and part time; websites are replacing physical offices, with followers and members instead of paid staff; and local groups use free, open-source platforms instead of having to rely on foreign donors. At the same time, homegrown companies are filling gaps left by governments, offering language and job-skills training, financial services, health care, and the pricing of commodities. Today's activists are local and yet highly global: they import tools from abroad for their own purposes while exporting their own ideas.

As technology continues to spread, many governments in partially connected societies are seeing more costs than benefits. This is particularly true for those that struggle to maintain their political legitimacy. Anything that questions the status quo, the party in power, or the façade of stability poses a threat. For such governments—including the autocratic, the corrupt, and the unstable—the potential of quick and unexpected mini-rebellions is particularly worrisome. In many cases, the only thing holding the opposition back is the lack of organizational and communications tools, which connection technologies threaten to provide cheaply and widely.

Over the last several years, regimes that carried out ham-handed crackdowns have grown more subtle and sophisticated. The actions of the Iranian government surrounding the country's 2009 elections are a case in point. In the weeks leading up to the vote, Tehran sporadically blocked certain websites, prevented access to text messaging, and slowed down Internet connection speeds. On the day of the election itself, the regime turned off all forms of digital connectivity and kept them down for days and even weeks (although a number of activists were able to use proxy and circumvention technology to get around the stoppage). Members of the country's Revolutionary Guards posed as virtual activists and tried to catch online dissenters in the act. What is perhaps most ominous, Iranian communications officials—employing anonymous engineers and addresses—created websites encouraging people to post pictures of the protests. They then used the sites to identify, track, and, in some cases, detain protesters.

Whether or not partially connected countries follow the Iranian example may depend on the balance between internal political stability and the need for economic growth. Those nations faced with the task of restarting or maintaining stagnant or slowly growing economies are more likely to allow their citizens and businesses to adopt new technologies and to maintain the free flow of information that is vital to foreign investment.

Technology, on the Edge

A second and equally large group of developing countries are the "connecting nations"—places where technological development is still nascent and where both governments and citizens are testing out tools and their potential impact. In these states, connection technologies are not yet sufficiently prevalent to present major opportunities or challenges. Although these states will invariably rise into the ranks of the partially connected, it is too early to determine what this will mean for the relationship among citizens, their governments, and neighboring nations.

Some of these states, such as Cuba, Myanmar (also called Burma), and Yemen, have tried to wall off access to certain technologies entirely. For example, they have confined access to cell phones to the elite; this, however, has led to a communications black market, which is most often used for daily communication but harbors the capacity to foment opposition. Activists in these states and in their diasporas—such as those working along Myanmar's border with Thailand—try daily to break the information blockade. In the short term, the regimes that govern these nations will do their best to maintain monopolies on the tools of communication.

An even larger group of these connecting states can be called "open by default"—that is, states that are, in principle, open to the import and use of connection technologies but whose governments might periodically introduce restrictive controls, whether fueled by a paranoid elite class, bureaucratic corruption, perceived security threats, or other factors. These countries, which are found across Africa, Central America, and Southeast Asia, are potential agricultural exporters and havens for light industry. For the ruling governments in these states, one imagines that the drive to create sustainable, diverse, and more open economies will often take precedence over fears that opponents armed with cell phones will threaten the regime's survival.

Finally, there is a small but globally significant group of nations—the so-called failed states—that are characterized by chaos and an inability to act consistently even on the most important issues. Such states are natural havens for criminal groups and terrorist networks that may have local grievances but harbor regional and global ambitions. Somalia is one notable example of this dynamic. Although much of the activity of the country's rebels and insurgents is directed at targets within Somalia's borders, some offer international terror networks, arms traffickers, and drug lords undisturbed territory for recruiting followers or spreading their ideology. Although connection technologies can serve as creative oudets for citizen innovation in such countries, they also offer the opportunity to export terrorist and criminal behavior.

Tear Down This Wall

Efforts by democratic governments to foster freedom and opportunity will be far stronger if they recognize the vital role technology can play in enabling their citizens to promote these values—and that technology is overwhelmingly provided by the private sector.

Companies whose products or services revolve around information technology—be they producers of cell-phone handsets, manufacturers of routers that are the building blocks of firewalls, or providers of Internet platforms—deal in a commodity that is inherently political. In the interactive world of Web 2.0, the prime mission of some of the technology sector's fastest-growing corporations is to provide cross-border connections. Little wonder that the old-guard officials who dominate repressive regimes see these companies as little more than the arms dealers of the information age. That said, although the United States and other countries can publicly warn Chinese officials to abide by international human rights agreements, companies can actually act—by publicizing how governments around the world censor content or simply cut off their citizens from the world. Cell-phone companies play a particularly important role in this effort, because in many parts of the world the cell phone is one of the few resources local populations can use to stand up to abuses.

The nonprofit sector and individual activists around the globe also face new opportunities. In the interconnected estate, they will continue to shape government and corporate behavior by promoting freedom of expression and by protecting citizens from threatening governments. But at times, they will have to adjust their tactics to reflect the new environment in which they operate. This means, among other things, ensuring that efforts to expose wrongdoing do not strengthen governments apt to make nationalistic appeals; working behind the scenes when that route will produce better, faster results; and using the technology that the private sector creates for their own ends. A website called Herdict, for example, collects data on blocked sites in real time, creating a public log of disruptions to the free flow of online information and enabling an unprecedented level of user-generated transparency.

For both companies and the nonprofit sector, the interconnected estate provides a place where they can join together in new alliances to multiply their impact. One example is the Global Network Initiative, an organization that brings together information technology companies, human rights groups, socially responsible investors, and academics in an effort to promote free expression online and protect privacy. (Google is one of the founding corporate members.) GNI has issued specific guidelines for companies and other groups forced to confront governments that censor content or ask for information about users. Under this arrangement, companies agree to let outside assessors determine their compliance with the guidelines and all members agree to promote common goals.

Coalitions of the Connected

Continuous innovation—and the increasing population of the interconnected estate—will pose new, difficult challenges for people and governments the world over. Even the best-informed and most active users of technology will find themselves caught in a blur of new devices and services. In an era when the power of the individual and the group grows daily, those governments that ride the technological wave will clearly be best positioned to assert their influence and bring others into their orbits. And those that do not will find themselves at odds with their citizens.

Democratic states that have built coalitions of their militaries have the capacity to do the same with their connection technologies. This is not to suggest that connection technologies are going to transform the world alone. But they offer a new way to exercise the duty to protect citizens around the world who are abused by their governments or barred from voicing their opinions.

Faced with these opportunities, democratic governments have an obligation to join together while also respecting the power of the private and nonprofit sectors to bring about change. They must listen to those on the frontlines and recognize that their citizens' use of technology can be an effective vehicle to promote the values of freedom, equality, and human rights globally. In a new age of shared power, no one can make progress alone.

Critical Thinking

1. Under what conditions is it prudent for governments to control connection technologies? What kinds of controls and uses are defensible?

2. Schmidt and Cohen write, "Yet for all the inspiring stories and moments of hope abetted by the use of connection technologies, the potential of such technologies to be manipulated or used in dangerous ways should not be underestimated." What are viable options for mitigating harmful effects?

Eric Schmidt is Chair and CEO of Google. He is a Member of the President's Council of Advisers on Science and Technology and Chair of the New America Foundation. **Jared Cohen** is Director of Google Ideas. He is an Adjunct Fellow at the Council on Foreign Relations and the author of *Children of Jihad* and *One Hundred Days of Silence: America and the Rwanda Genocide*.

From *Foreign Affairs*, November/December 2010, pp. 75–85. Copyright © 2010 by Council on Foreign Relations, Inc. Reprinted by permission of Foreign Affairs. www.ForeignAffairs.com

Journalist Bites Reality!

How broadcast journalism is flawed in such a fundamental way that its utility as a tool for informing viewers is almost nil.

STEVE SALERNO

It is the measure of the media's obsession with its "pedophiles run amok!" story line that so many of us are on a first-name basis with the victims: Polly, Amber, JonBenet, Danielle, Elizabeth, Samantha. And now there is Madeleine. Clearly these crimes were and are horrific, and nothing here is intended to diminish the parents' loss. But something else has been lost in the bargain as journalists tirelessly stoke fear of strangers, segueing from nightly-news segments about cyberstalkers and "the rapist in your neighborhood" to prime-time reality series like *Dateline*'s "To Catch a Predator." That "something else" is reality.

According to the U.S. Department of Justice, in a given year there are about 88,000 documented cases of sexual abuse against juveniles. In the roughly 17,500 cases involving children between ages 6 and 11, strangers are the perpetrators just 5% of the time—and just *3%* of the time when the victim is under age 6. (Further, more than a third of such molesters are themselves juveniles, who may not be true "predators" so much as confused or unruly teens.) Overall, the odds that one of America's 48 million children under age 12 will encounter an adult pedophile at the local park are startlingly remote. The Child Molestation Research & Prevention Institute: "Right now, 90 percent of our efforts go toward protecting our children from strangers, when what we need to do is to focus 90% of our efforts toward protecting children from the abusers who are not strangers." That's a diplomatic way of phrasing the uncomfortable but factually supported truth: that if your child is not molested in your own home—by you, your significant other, or someone else you invited in—chances are your child will never be molested anywhere. Media coverage has precisely inverted both the reality and the risk of child sexual assault. Along the way, it has also inverted the gender of the most tragic victims: Despite the unending parade of young female faces on TV, boys are more likely than girls to be killed in the course of such abuse.

We think we know Big Journalism's faults by its muchballyhooed lapses—its scandals, gaffes, and breakdowns—as well as by a recent spate of insider tell-alls. When Dan Rather goes public with a sensational exposé based on bogus documents; when the *Atlanta Journal-Constitution* wrongly labels Richard Jewell the Olympic Park bomber; when *Dateline* resorts to rigging explosive charges to the gas tanks of "unsafe" trucks that, in *Dateline*'s prior tests, stubbornly refused to explode on their own; when the *New York Times*' Jayson Blair scoops other reporters working the same story by quoting sources who don't exist. . . . We see these incidents as atypical, the exceptions that prove the rule.

Sadly, we're mistaken. To argue that a decided sloppiness has crept into journalism or that the media have been "hijacked by [insert least favorite political agenda]" badly misses the real point; it suggests that all we need to do to fix things is filter out the gratuitous political spin or rig the ship to run a bit tighter. In truth, today's system of news delivery is an enterprise whose procedures, protocols, and underlying assumptions all but guarantee that it cannot succeed at its self-described mission. Broadcast journalism in particular is flawed in such a fundamental way that its utility as a tool for illuminating life, let alone interpreting it, is almost nil.

"You Give Us 22 Minutes, and We'll Give You . . . What, Exactly?"

We watch the news to "see what's going on in the world." But there's a hitch right off the bat. In its classic conception, newsworthiness is built on a foundation of anomaly: *man-bites-dog,* to use the hackneyed journalism school example. The significance of this cannot be overstated. It means that, by definition, journalism in its most basic form deals with what life *is not*.

Today's star journalist, however, goes to great lengths to distance himself from his trade's man-bites-dog heritage. To admit that what he's presenting is largely marginalia (or at best "background music") deflates the journalist's relevance in an environment where members of Major Media have come to regard themselves as latter day shamans and oracles. In a memorable 2002 piece, "The Weight of the Anchor," columnist Frank Rich put it this way, regarding the then-Big 3 of Brokaw, Jennings, and Rather: "Not quite movie stars, not quite officialdom, they are more famous than most movie stars and more powerful than most politicians."

Thus, journalism as currently practiced delivers two contradictory messages: that what it puts before you (a) is newsworthy (under the old man-bites-dog standard), but also (b) captures the *zeitgeist.* ("You give us 22 minutes, we'll give you the world," gloat all news radio stations across the country.) The news media cannot simultaneously deliver both. In practice, they fail at both. By painting life in terms of its oddities, journalism yields not a snapshot of your world, but something closer to a photographic negative.

Even when journalism isn't plainly capsizing reality, it's furnishing information that varies between immaterial and misleading. For all its *cinema-verité* panache, embedded reporting, as exemplified in Iraq and in *Nightline*'s recent series on "the forgotten war" in Afghanistan, shows only what's going on in the immediate vicinity of the embedded journalist. It's not all that useful for yielding an overarching sense of the progress of a war, and might easily be counterproductive: To interpret such field reporting as a valid microcosm is the equivalent of standing in a spot where it's raining and assuming it's raining everywhere.

Journalism's paradoxes and problems come to a head in the concept of *newsmagazination,* pioneered on *60 Minutes* and later the staple tactic of such popular clones as *Dateline, 48 Hours,* and *20/20.* One of the more intellectually dishonest phenomena of recent vintage, newsmagazination presents the viewer with a circumstantial stew whipped up from:

- a handful of compelling sound-bites culled from anecdotal sources,
- public-opinion polls (which tell us nothing except what people *think* is true),
- statistics that have no real evidentiary weight and/or scant relevance to the point they're being used to "prove,"
- logical flaws such as *post hoc ergo propter hoc* (after the fact) reasoning,
- faulty or, at best, unproven "expert" assumptions, or "conventional wisdom" that is never seriously examined,
- a proprietary knowledge of people's inner thoughts or motives (as when a White House correspondent discounts a president's actual statements in order to reveal to us that president's "true agenda"), etc.

Case in point: On Nov. 5, 2004, NBC's *Dateline* built a show around the dangers of gastric bypass surgery. The topic was a natural for *Dateline,* inasmuch as *The Today Show*'s own Al Roker, who did much of the reporting, had undergone the surgery and achieved a stunning weight loss. In setting the scene, anchor Stone Phillips noted that the expected mortality rate for gastric bypass is 1 in 200. (Translation: The *survival* rate is 199 in 200, or 99.5%.) Phillips then handed off to Roker; the affable weatherman spent a few cheery moments on his own success, then found his somber face in segueing to the tragic saga of Mike Butler, who died following surgery. The Butler story consumed the next 30 minutes of the hour long broadcast, punctuated by

the obligatory wistful soliloquy from Butler's young widow. So, in covering a procedure that helps (or at least doesn't kill) roughly 99.5% of patients, *Dateline* elects to tell the story in terms of the 0.5% *with tragic outcomes.* Had NBC sought to equitably represent the upside and downside of gastric bypass, it would've devoted 1/200th of the show—a mere 18 seconds—to Butler. Further, wouldn't it have been journalistically responsible for *Dateline* to devote a good portion of the broadcast to the risks of morbid obesity itself, which far outweigh the risks of surgical bypass?

Do the Math . . . *Please*

One underlying factor here is that journalists either don't understand the difference between random data and genuine statistical proof, or they find that distinction inconvenient for their larger purpose: to make news dramatic and accessible. The media need a story line—a coherent narrative, ideally with an identifiable hero and villain. As Tom Brokaw once put it, perhaps revealing more than he intended, "It's all storytelling, you know. That's what journalism is about." The mainstream news business is so unaccustomed to dealing with issues at any level of complexity and nuance that they're wont to oversimplify their story to the point of caricature.

The best contemporary example is the Red State/Blue State dichotomy, invoked as an easy metaphor to express the philosophical schism that supposedly divides "the two Americas." Watching CNN's Bill Schneider hover over his maps on Election Night 2004, drawing stark lines between colors, one would've thought there were no Republicans in California, or that a Democrat arriving at the Texas border would be turned back at gunpoint. Well, guess what: The dichotomy doesn't exist—certainly not in the way journalists use the term. It's just a handy, sexy media fiction. Although California did wind up in the Kerry column in 2004, some 5.5 million Californians voted for George W. Bush. They represented about 45% of the state's total electorate and a much larger constituency in raw numbers than Bush enjoyed *in any state he won,* including Texas. Speaking of Texas: That unreconstituted Yankee, John Kerry, collected 2.8 million votes there. *Two point eight million.* Yet to hear the media tell it, California is deep, cool Blue, while Texas is a glaring, monolithic Red. Such fabrications aren't just silly. They become institutionalized in the culture, and they color—in this case literally—the way Americans view the nation in which they live.

The mythical Red State/Blue State paradigm is just one of the more telling indications of a general disability the media exhibit in working with data. A cluster of random events does not a "disturbing new trend!" make—but that doesn't stop journalists from finding patterns in happenstance. Take lightning. It kills with an eerie predictability: about 66 Americans every year. Now, lightning could kill those 66 people more or less evenly all spring and summer, or it could, in theory, kill the lot of them on one *really* scary Sunday in May. But the scary Sunday in May wouldn't necessarily mean we're going to have a year in which lightning kills 79,000 people. (No more than if it killed a half-dozen people named Johanssen on that Sunday would it mean that lightning is suddenly targeting Swedes.) Yet you can bet that if *any* half-dozen people are killed by lightning one Sunday, you'll soon see a special report along the lines of, *LIGHTNING: IS IT OUT TO GET US?* We've seen this propensity on display with shark attacks, meningitis, last year's rash of amusement-park fatalities, and any number of other "random event clusters" that occur for no reason anyone can explain.

Journalists overreact to events that fall well within the laws of probability. They treat the fact that something happened as if we never before had any reason to think it *could* happen—as if it were a brand-new risk with previously unforeseen causation. Did America become more vulnerable on 9/11? Or had it been vulnerable all along? Indeed, it could be argued that America today is far *less* vulnerable, precisely because of the added vigilance inspired by 9/11. Is that how the media play it? Similarly, a bridge collapse is no reason for journalists to assume in knee-jerk fashion that bridges overall are any less safe than they've been for decades. Certainly it's no reason to jump to the conclusion that the nation's infrastructure is crumbling, which is how several major news outlets framed the collapse of the Interstate 35W Bridge this past summer. As Freud might put it, sometimes a bridge collapse is just a bridge collapse. Alas, journalism needs its story line.

For a textbook example of the intellectual barrenness of so much of what's presented even as "headline" news, consider the Consumer Confidence Index and media coverage of same. For decades, such indices have been telling America how it feels about its economic prospects. The best known index has been compiled each month since 1967 by the Conference Board, a nonprofit organization dating to 1916. The Board's index is an arbitrary composite of indicators rooted in five equally arbitrary questions mailed to 5000 households. ("Do you see jobs as being easier or harder to get next year?") On Tuesday, October 30, 2007, the Board reported that its latest CCI had dipped to a two-year low. The media jumped on the story, as is ever the case when the CCI dips. (CCI upticks are seldom reported with the same fervor.) Like many of its counterparts nationally, no doubt, a Philadelphia network affiliate sent its consumer-affairs reporter trudging out to find consumers who lacked confidence. She succeeded.

Few reporters bother to mention that, customarily, there has been only a tenuous connection between CCI numbers and actual consumer spending or the overall health of the economy as objectively measured. In fact, just days after the release of the downbeat CCI, the Labor Department reported that the economy had generated 166,000 new jobs in October—twice the forecast. That statistic, which measures reality, got nowhere near the same play as the CCI, which measures perception.

Let's recap. We have a fanciful metric that's just a compilation of opinion, which is layered with further opinion from passersby, and then subjected to in-studio analysis (still more opinion). All of which is presented to viewers as . . . news.

The problem for society is that giving headline prominence to meaningless or marginal events exalts those events to the status of conventional wisdom. "Reporting confers legitimacy and relevance," writes Russell Frank, Professor of Journalism

Ethics at Penn State University. "When a newspaper puts a certain story on page one or a newscast puts it at or near the top of a 22-minute program, it is saying to its audience, in no uncertain terms, that 'this story is important.'" The self-fulfilling nature of all this should be clear: News organizations decide what's important, spin it to their liking, cover it *ad nauseam,* then describe it—without irony—as "the 800-pound gorilla" or "the issue that just won't go away." This is not unlike network commercials promoting sit-coms and dramas that "everyone is talking about" in the hopes of getting people to watch shows that apparently no one is talking about.

Tonight at 11 . . .
the Apocalypse!

Far worse than hyping a story that represents just 0.5% reality, is covering "news" that's *zero* percent reality: There literally is no story. Even so, if the non-story satisfies other requirements, it will be reported anyway. This truism was not lost on the late David Brinkley, who, towards the end of his life, observed, "The one function that TV news performs very well is that when there is no news, we give it to you with the same emphasis as if there were."

On June 9, 2005, as part of its ongoing series of "Security Updates," CNN airs a special report titled "Keeping Milk Safe." Over shots of adorable first-graders sipping from their pint cartons, CNN tells viewers that the farm-to-shelf supply chain is vulnerable at every point, beginning with the cow; with great drama, the report emphasizes the terrifying consequences such tampering could have. Nowhere does the network, mention that in the history of the milk industry, *no incident of supply-chain tampering has ever been confirmed,* due to terrorism or anything else.

Similarly, after the Asian tsunamis struck over Christmas 2004, *Dateline* wasted no time casting about for an alarmist who could bring the tragedy closer to home: the familiar *Could It Happen Here?* motif. The show's producers found Stephen Ward, PhD, of the University of California at Santa Cruz. In January, *Dateline*'s East Coast viewers heard Ward foretell a geological anomaly in their very own ocean that could generate the equivalent of "all the bombs on earth" detonating at once. The event Ward prophesied would unleash on New York City a wave containing "15 or 20 times the energy" of the Asian tsunamis. As a helpful backdrop, *Dateline* treated its viewers to spectacular visuals from *The Day After Tomorrow,* showing Manhattan's heralded landmarks disappearing beneath an onrushing, foamy sea.

But for sheer overwrought absurdity, it's hard to beat what took place in mid-September 1999. For six full days, journalists behaved as if there was one story and one story only: Hurricane Floyd. The TV tempest commenced as the actual tempest still lolled hundreds of miles offshore, with no one certain how much of a threat Floyd posed, or whether it might fizzle before it hit land (as so often happens—Katrina has changed the way we think about hurricanes, but Katrina was a once-in-a-generation event). This was Saturday. By Tuesday the hurricane-in-absentia had engulfed the nightly news. While residents of areas in Floyd's projected path evacuated, the other side of the highway was clotted with news crews on their way *in.* By Wednesday all of the networks had their parka-clad correspondents standing on some coastal beach, each correspondent bent on looking wetter and more windblown than the next. Sprinkled among all this were the requisite interviews with men (and women) on the street—as well as in insurance companies, emergency-services offices, local restaurants, and the like. Bereft of an actual hurricane to show during this feverish build-up, *The Today Show* aired old footage of Hurricane Hugo's plunder of Charleston, in sledgehammer foreshadowing of the disaster to come.

Floyd caused a fair amount of damage when it finally hit on Thursday: 57 deaths and an estimated $6 billion in property loss. But here's where things get curious. By the time Floyd blew in, media interest clearly had ebbed. On television at least, coverage of the aftermath was dispatched in a day or so, with occasional backward glances occupying a few moments of air time in subsequent newscasts. Bottom line, the coverage of Floyd *before* it was a real story dwarfed the coverage given the storm once it *became* a story. Evidently the conjured image of tidal waves crashing on shore was more titillating to news producers than film of real life homeowners swabbing brownish muck out of their basements.

Today's newspeople have substantially improved on one of the timeless axioms of their craft: "If it bleeds, it leads." They prefer the mere prospect of bad news to most other kinds of news that did occur. The result is journalism as Stephen King might do it: the dogged selling of the cataclysm 'round the corner, complete with stage lighting and scenes fictionalized for dramatic purposes. Sure, the camera loves suspense. But . . . is suspense news? Is it really news that someone *thinks* a hurricane *might* kill thousands? It might kill no one, either, which is historically closer to the truth. Honest journalism would wait to see what the storm does, then report it.

Granted, Floyd blew in during a slow week. Following, though, is a sampling of the events that were largely ignored while the assembled media were waiting for Floyd:

- The House of Representatives took a hard stand on soft money, approving limits on campaign spending.
- The Equal Employment Opportunity Commission launched an investigation of corporate America's fondness for cash balance pension plans, an issue that affected millions of workers, and stood to affect millions more.
- The 17-member Joint Security Commission released a chilling report on America's handling of security-clearance applications. This, let us remember, was two years before the terror attacks of 9/11.
- The terrorist bombings in Russia and the gruesome, continuing holocaust in East Timor.

The advance billing given to Floyd bespeaks a gloomy trend in broadcast news' continuing slide toward theater. We witnessed this same phenomenon during the run-up to Desert Storm, Y2K, and the Clinton impeachment, among others.

The Crusades— Postmodern Style

Nowhere are these foibles more noticeable—or more of a threat to journalistic integrity—than when they coalesce into a cause: so-called "advocacy" or "social" journalism. To begin with, there are legitimate questions about whether journalism should even have causes. Does the journalist alone know what's objectively, abstractly good or evil? What deserves supporting or reforming? The moment journalists claim license to cover events sympathetically or cynically, we confront the problem of what to cover sympathetically or cynically, where to draw such lines and—above all—who gets to draw them. There are very few issues that unite the whole of mankind. Regardless, as Tom Rosenstiel of the Project for Excellence in Journalism told *USA Today,* "News outlets have found they can create more . . . identity by creating franchise brands around issues or around a point of view."

Even worse, the data on which journalists premise their crusades are drawn from the same marginalia discussed above. When Francisco Serrano was discovered to be living in the Minnesota high school he once attended, the media covered the 2005 story as if every American high school had a half-dozen homeless people living in it. The actual episode, though exceedingly rare if not one-of-a-kind, became a window to the nation's social failings.

In his thinking and methodology, today's journalist resembles the homicide cop who, having settled on a suspect, begins collecting evidence specifically against that suspect, dismissing information that counters his newfound theory of the crime. Too many journalists think in terms of buttressing a preconceived argument or fleshing out a sense of narrative gained very early in their research. This mindset is formalized in journalism's highest award: the Pulitzer Prize. Traditionally, stories deemed worthy of Pulitzer consideration have revealed the dark (and, often as not, statistically insignificant) underbelly of American life. In 2007 the Pulitzer for "public-service journalism" went to *The Wall Street Journal,* for its "creative and comprehensive probe into backdated stock options for business executives. . . ." The *Journal* reported on "possible" violations then under investigation at 120 companies. There are 2764 listed companies on the New York Stock Exchange; NASDAQ adds another 3200. Not to dismiss the sincerity and diligence of the *Journal*'s work, but what's the final takeaway here? That 120 companies (0.02) "possibly" cheated? Or that—so far as anyone knows—at least 5844 others didn't?

Food for thought: Every time I fly, I'm amazed that these huge, winged machines get off the ground, stay off the ground, and don't return to ground until they're supposed to. Think about the failure rate of commonplace products: Light bulbs burn out. Fan belts snap. Refrigerators stop refrigerating. But planes don't crash. Actuarially speaking, they simply don't. The entire process of commercial flight and the systems that support it is remarkable. Do you fully understand it? I don't. I'm sure lots of people don't. Still, you won't win a Pulitzer for a piece that sheds light on the myriad "little miracles" that conspire to produce aviation's normalcy, stability and success. You'd be laughed out of today's newsrooms for even proposing such a piece (unless you were doing it as the kind of feel-good feature that editors like to give audiences as gifts for the holidays). Have a flight go down, however—*one* flight, *one* time—and have a reporter find some overworked ATC operator or other aberration that may have caused the disaster, and *voila!* You're in Pulitzer territory for writing about something that—statistically—never happens.

Just as journalists who run out of news may create it, journalists who run out of real causes may invent them. It's not hard to do. All you need is a fact or two, which you then "contextualize" with more so-called expert opinion. December 10, 2004 was a banner night for exposing those well-known dens of iniquity that masquerade as Amish settlements. Stories about rape and incest among the Amish appeared on both *Dateline* and *20/20.* The *Dateline* story even made reference to the principal character in the story that aired an hour later on *20/20*—which gives you some idea how common the abuse may be, if seasoned journalists must choreograph their exposés around the same incident. That brings us to Elizabeth Vargas and her question for *20/20*'s expert on Amish affairs: Just how widespread *is* this abuse? Amid stock footage of adorable children strolling down a dusky road in suspenders and bonnets, the expert tells America that it's "not a gross exception."

What kind of reporting is that? Does it indicate that 1% of Amish children are abused? Ten percent? Forty percent? Who knows?

This is what passes for investigative journalism nowadays.

Their World . . . and They're Welcome to It

The world we're "given" has an indisputable impact on how Americans see and live their lives. (How many other events are set in motion by the "truths" people infer from the news?) Here we enter the realm of iatrogenic reporting: provable harms that didn't exist until journalism itself got involved.

In science journalism in particular, the use of anecdotal information can create impressions that would be comical, were it not for the amount of public alarm they generate.

Pop quiz: How many Americans have died of Mad Cow Disease? Before you answer, let's look to Britain, where the scare began in earnest around 1995 after a few herd of cattle were found to be infected. First of all, in the cows themselves, what we call "Mad Cow" is technically *bovine spongiform encephalopathy,* or BSE. When BSE species-jumps to humans, it manifests itself as something called *variant Creutzfeldt Jacob Disease,* or *v*CJD. ("Non-variant" CJD occurs independently of cows and can even be inherited.) A link between BSE and *v*CJD was established in 1996. British reporters went scurrying to find epidemiologists who were alarmed by the discovery, some of whom obligingly put the death toll in the coming years above 500,000.

By late 2006, the end of Mad Cow's first documented decade, the U.K. had confirmed a total of 162 human deaths—nothing to be glib about. But that's a long way from 500,000. And here in the U.S.? The CDC describes two confirmed deaths, both involving people born and raised abroad. A third case involves a man from Saudi Arabia who remains alive at this writing.

Not what you might've expected, eh?

Nevertheless, when a New Jersey woman, Janet Skarbek, became convinced that an outbreak had killed off her neighbors, she found a warm welcome in newsrooms. Her dire pronouncements touched off a mini-hysteria. Even after the CDC eliminated *v*CJD as a factor, the media kept fanning the fires of public concern, typically by quoting Dr. Michael Greger, a part-time chef and full-time alarmist who labels Mad Cow "the plague of the 21st Century." When journalists want a fatalistic sound bite on the disease, they dial Greger's number.

However history may remember Mad Cow as an actual pathology, this much is sure: The media-inflamed scare has been fatal to jobs—most directly in the meat-packing industry, but in related enterprises as well. It has soured consumers on beef. It has caused volatile swings in livestock prices. It has mandated new protocols that add hundreds of thousands of dollars to the average cattle rancher's cost of doing business. It has caused us to cut ourselves off from key beef suppliers, fomenting minor crises in diplomacy and commerce. A 2005 survey reckoned the total cost of Mad Cow to U.S. agricultural interests at between $3.2 billion and $4.7 billion. This, for something that has killed far fewer Americans in 10 years than the 200 who die each month from *choking* on food or food substances.

To hear the media tell it, we're under perpetual siege from some Terrifying New Disease That Threatens to End Life as We Know It. It's too soon to render verdicts on the ultimate impact of avian flu, but that pathogen would have to wipe out many millions in order to justify the hype. Lyme Disease? The Cleveland Clinic has this to say: "Although rarely fatal and seldom a serious illness, Lyme Disease has been widely publicized, frequently overdramatized, and sometimes linked to unproven conditions." Is it coincidence that visits to national parks began tracking downward in 1999, amid media coverage that made it sound as if deer ticks and the rest of Mother Nature's foot-soldiers had declared war on humankind? Maybe. Maybe not.

In science reporting and everywhere else, there's no minimizing the psychic effects of regularly consuming a world-view rooted in peculiarity, much of which is pessimistic. In a 2003 Gallup poll, just 11% of respondents rated crime in their own neighborhoods as "very serious" or "extremely serious," yet 54% of those same respondents deemed crime in America as a whole "very serious" or "extremely serious." The catch-22 should be apparent: If crime were that pervasive, it would have to be occurring in a lot more than 11% of the respondents' "own neighborhoods." Such an enigmatic skew can only be explained in terms of the difference between what people personally experience—what they know firsthand—and the wider impressions they get from the news.

Figuratively speaking, we end up drowning in the tides of a hurricane that never makes shore.

I give you, herewith, a capsule summary of your world, and in far less than 22 minutes:

- The current *employment* rate is 95%.
- Out of 300 million Americans, roughly 299.999954 million were not murdered today.
- Day after day, some 35,000 commercial flights traverse our skies without incident.
- The vast majority of college students who got drunk last weekend did not rape anyone, or kill themselves or anyone else in a DUI or hazing incident. On Monday, they got up and went to class, bleary-eyed but otherwise okay.

It is not being a Pollyanna to state such facts, because they *are* facts. Next time you watch the news, keep in mind that what you're most often seeing is trivia framed as Truth. Or as British humorist/philosopher G.K. Chesteron whimsically put it some decades ago, "Journalism consists in saying 'Lord Jones is dead' to people who never knew Lord Jones was alive."

Critical Thinking

1. If ratings and sales figures indicate that the public is attracted to "intellectually bare" content, should media owners give media consumers what they want? Why or why not?

2. Should feedforward standards and rules differ for news vs entertainment media? Why or why not?

From *Skeptic* by Steve Salerno, volume 14, number 1, 2008, pp. 52–59. Copyright © 2008 by Skeptic Magazine. Reprinted by permission of Millenium Press.

Girls Gone Anti-Feminist

Is '70s feminism an impediment to female happiness and fulfillment?

SUSAN J. DOUGLAS

This was the Spice Girls moment, and debate: Were these frosted cupcakes really a vehicle for feminism? And how much reversion back to the glory days of prefeminism should girls and women accept—even celebrate—given that we now allegedly had it all? Despite their Wonderbras and bare thighs, the Spice Girls advocated "girl power." They demanded, in their colossal, intercontinental hit "Wannabe," that boys treat them with respect or take a hike. Their boldfaced liner notes claimed that "The Future Is Female" and suggested that they and their fans were "Freedom Fighters." They made Margaret Thatcher an honorary Spice Girl. "We're freshening up feminism for the nineties," they told the *Guardian*. "Feminism has become a dirty word. Girl Power is just a '90s way of saying it."

Fast-forward to 2008. Talk about girl power! One woman ran for president and another for vice president. Millions of women and men voted for each of them. The one who ran for vice president had five children, one of them an infant, yet it was verboten to even ask whether she could handle the job while tending to a baby. At the same time we had a female secretary of state, and the woman who had run for president became her high-profile successor. And we have Lady Gaga, power girl of the new millennium. Feminism? Who needs feminism anymore? Aren't we, like, so done here? Okay, so some women moaned about the sexist coverage of Hillary Clinton, but picky, picky, picky.

Indeed, eight years earlier, career antifeminist Christina Hoff Sommers huffed in her book, *The War Against Boys: How Misguided Feminism Is Harming Our Young Men,* that girls were getting way too much attention and, as a result, were going to college in greater numbers and much more likely to succeed while boys were getting sent to detention, dropping out of high school, destined for careers behind fast-food counters, and so beaten down they were about to become the nation's new "second sex." Other books like *The Myth of Male Power and The Decline of Males* followed suit, with annual panics about the new "crisis" for boys. Girl power? Gone way too far.

Fantasies of Power

In 1999, one year before Sommers' book came out, the top five jobs for women did not include attorney, surgeon or CEO. They were, in order, secretaries, retail and personal sales workers (including cashiers), managers and administrators, elementary school teachers and registered nurses. Farther down among the top 20 were bookkeepers, receptionists, cooks and waitresses. In 2007, when presumably some of the privileged, pampered girls whose advantages over boys Sommers had kvetched about had entered the workforce, the top five jobs for women were, still, secretaries in first place, followed by registered nurses, elementary and middle school teachers, cashiers and retail salespersons.

Farther down the line? Maids, child care workers, office clerks and hairdressers. Not a CEO or hedge fund manager in sight. And, in the end, no president or vice president in 2008. But what about all those career-driven girls going to college and leaving the guys in the dust? A year out of college, they earn 80 percent of what men make. And 10 years out? A staggering 69 percent.

Since the early 1990s, much of the media have come to overrepresent women as having made it—completely—in the professions, as having gained sexual equality with men, and having achieved a level of financial success and comfort enjoyed primarily by the Tiffany's-encrusted doyennes of Laguna Beach. At the same time, there has been a resurgence of dreck clogging our cultural arteries—*The Man Show, Maxim, Girls Gone Wild.* But even this fare was presented as empowering, because while the scantily clad or bare-breasted women may have *seemed* to be objectified, they were really on top, because now they had chosen to be sex objects and men were supposedly nothing more than their helpless, ogling, crotch-driven slaves.

What the media have been giving us, then, are little more than fantasies of power. They assure girls and women, repeatedly, that women's liberation is a *fait accompli* and that we are stronger, more successful, more sexually in control, more fearless and more held in awe than we actually are. We can believe that any woman can become a CEO (or president), that women have achieved economic, professional and political parity with men, and we can expunge any suggestion that there might be anyone living on the national median income, which for women in 2008 was $36,000 a year, 23 percent less than their male counterparts.

Yet the images we see on television, in the movies, and in advertising also insist that purchasing power and sexual power are much more gratifying than political or economic power. Buying stuff—the right stuff, a lot of stuff—emerged as the dominant way to empower ourselves. Women in fictional settings can be in the highest positions of authority, but in real life maybe not such a good idea. Instead, the wheedling, seductive message to young women is that being decorative is the highest form of power—when, of course, if it were, Dick Cheney would have gone to work every day in a sequined tutu.

Enter Enlightened Sexism

Not that some of these fantasies haven't been delectable. I mean, Xena single-handedly trashing, on a regular basis, battalions of stubblefaced, leather-clad, murdering-and-raping barbarian hordes? Or *Buffy the Vampire Slayer* letting us pretend, if just for an hour, that only a teenage girl can save the world from fang-toothed evil? What about an underdog law student, dismissed by her fellow classmates as an airheaded bimbo, winning a high-profile murder case because she understood how permanents work, as Elle did in *Legally Blonde?* Or let's say you've had an especially stupid day at work and as you collapse on the sofa desperately clutching a martini (hold the vermouth), you see a man on TV tell his female boss that the way she does things is "just not the way we play ball," and she responds drolly, "Well, if you don't like the way I'm doing things, you're free to take your balls and go straight home"? (Yes, *The Closer.*) Oooo-weeee.

So what's the matter with fantasies of female power? Haven't the media always provided escapist fantasies; isn't that, like, their job? And aren't many in the media, belatedly, simply addressing women's demands for more representations of female achievement and control? Well, yes. But here's the odd, somewhat unintended consequence: These demanded-and-delivered, delicious media-created fantasies have been driven by marketing, and they use that heady mix of flattery and denigration to sell us everything from skin cream to glutestoning shoes.

So it's time to take these fantasies to the interrogation room and shine a little light on them.

One force at work is embedded feminism: the way in which women's achievements, or their desire for achievement, are simply part of today's cultural landscape.

But the media's fantasies of power are also the product of another force that has gained considerable momentum since the early and mid-1990s: enlightened sexism. Enlightened sexism is a response, deliberate or not, to the perceived threat of a new gender regime. It insists that women have made plenty of progress because of feminism—indeed, full equality, has allegedly been achieved. So now it's okay, even amusing, to resurrect sexist stereotypes of girls and women. Enlightened sexism sells the line that it is precisely through women's calculated deployment of their faces, bodies, attire, and sexuality that they gain and enjoy true power—power that is fun, that men will not resent,

and indeed will embrace. True power here has nothing to do with economic independence or professional achievement: it has to do with getting men to lust after you and other women to envy you. Enlightened sexism is especially targeted to girls and young women and emphasizes that now that they "have it all," they should focus the bulk of their time and energy on being hot, pleasing men, competing with other women, and shopping.

Enlightened sexism is a manufacturing process that is constantly produced by the media. Its components—anxiety about female achievement; renewed and amplified objectification of young women's bodies and faces; dual exploitation and punishment of female sexuality; dividing of women against each other by age, race and class; and rampant branding and consumerism—began to swirl around in the early 1990s, consolidating as the dark star it has become in the early 21st century.

The Seed of Feminism's Demise

Some, myself included, have referred to this state of affairs and this kind of media mix as "postfeminist." But I am rejecting this term. It has gotten gummed up by many conflicting definitions. And besides, this term suggests that somehow feminism is at the root of this when it isn't—it's good, old-fashioned, grade-A sexism that reinforces good, old-fashioned, grade-A patriarchy. It's just much better disguised, in seductive Manolo Blahniks and a million-dollar bra.

Enlightened sexism is feminist in its outward appearance (of course you can be or do anything you want) but sexist in its intent (hold on, girls, only up to a certain point, and not in any way that discomfits men). While enlightened sexism seems to support women's equality, it is dedicated to the undoing of feminism. In fact, because this equality might lead to "sameness"— way too scary—girls and women need to be reminded that they are still fundamentally female, and so must be emphatically feminine.

Thus, enlightened sexism takes the gains of the women's movement as a given, and then uses them as permission to resurrect retrograde images of girls and women as sex objects, still defined by their appearance and their biological destiny.

Consequently, in the age of enlightened sexism there has been an explosion in makeover, matchmaking and modeling shows, a renewed emphasis on breasts (and a massive surge in the promotion of breast augmentation), an obsession with babies and motherhood in celebrity journalism (the rise of the creepy "bump patrol"), and a celebration of "opting out" of the workforce.

Feminism thus must remain a dirty word, with feminists (particularly older ones) stereotyped as man-hating, child-loathing, hairy, shrill, humorless and deliberately unattractive lesbians. More to the point, feminism must be emphatically rejected because it supposedly prohibits women from having any fun, listening to Lil' Wayne or Muse, or dancing to Lady Gaga, or wearing leggings. As this logic goes, feminism is so 1970s—grim, dowdy, aggrieved and passé—that it is now an impediment to female happiness and fulfillment. Thus, an amnesia about the women's movement, and the rampant, now illegal, discrimination that produced it, is essential, so we'll forget that politics matters.

Because women are now "equal" and the battle is over and won, we are now free to embrace things we used to see as sexist, including hypergirliness. In fact, this is supposed to be a relief.

Thank God girls and women can turn their backs on stick-in-the-mud, curdled feminism and now we can jiggle our way into that awesome party. Now that women allegedly have the same sexual freedom as men, they actually prefer to be sex objects because it's liberating. According to enlightened sexism, women today have a choice between feminism and antifeminism, and they just naturally and happily choose the latter because, well, antifeminism has become cool, even hip.

The Irony of It All

Enlightened sexism has cranked out media fare geared to girls and young women in which they compete over men, many of them knuckleheads (*The Bachelor, Flavor of Love*); compete with each other (*America's Next Top Model*); obsess about relationships and status (*The Hills*) or about pleasing men sexually (most music videos); and are fixated by conspicuous consumption (*Rich Girls, My Super Sweet 16, Laguna Beach,* and that wonderful little serpent of a show *Gossip Girl*). Yet I can assure you that my female students at the University of Michigan—academically accomplished, smart and ambitious—have flocked to these shows. Why?

This is the final key component to enlightened sexism: irony, the cultivation of the ironic, knowing viewer and the deployment of ironic sexism. Irony offers the following fantasy of power: the people on the screen may be rich, spoiled, or beautiful, but you, oh superior viewer, get to judge and mock them, and thus are above them. With a show like MTV's *My Super Sweet 16,* in which a spoiled brat has her parents buy her everything from a new Mercedes to a Vegas-style show to make sure her Sweet 16 party is, like, the most totally awesome ever, viewers are not merely (or primarily) meant to envy the girl. Animated stars superimposed on the scenes accompanied by a tinkling sound effect signal that we are also meant to see the whole exercise as over-the-top, ridiculous, exaggerated, the girl way too shallow and narcissistic. The show—indeed many 'reality' shows—elbow the viewer in the ribs, saying, "We know that you know that we know that you know that you're too smart to read this straight and not laugh at it."

For media-savvy youth, bombarded their entire lives by almost every marketing ploy in the book, irony means that you can look as if you are absolutely not seduced by the mass media, while then being seduced by the media, wearing a knowing smirk. Viewers are flattered that they are sophisticated, can see through the craven self-absorption, wouldn't be so vacuous and featherbrained as to get so completely caught up in something so trivial. The media offers this irony as a shield.

What so much of this media emphasizes is that women are defined by our bodies. This is nothing new, of course, but it was something millions of women hoped to deep-six back in the 1970s. Indeed, it is precisely because women no longer have to exhibit traditionally "feminine" *personality* traits—like being passive, helpless, docile, overly emotional, dumb and deferential to men—that they must exhibit hyperfeminine *physical* traits—cleavage, short skirts, pouty lips—and the proper logos linking this femininity to social acceptance. The war between embedded feminism and enlightened sexism gives with one hand and takes away with the other. It's a powerful choke leash, letting women venture out, offering us fantasies of power, control and love and then pulling us back in.

This, then, is the mission at hand: to pull back the curtain and to note how these fantasies distract us from our ongoing status—still, despite everything—as second-class citizens.

Trapped in the Media's Funhouse

Many producers insist that mass media are simply mirrors, reflecting reality, whatever that is, back to the public. Whenever you hear this mirror metaphor, I urge you to smash it. Because if the media are mirrors, they are funhouse mirrors. You know, the wavy kind, where your body becomes completely distorted and certain parts—typically your butt and thighs—become huge while other parts, like your knees, nearly disappear. This is the mass media—exaggerating certain kinds of stories, certain kinds of people, certain kinds of values and attitudes, while minimizing others or rendering them invisible.

This is even more true today than it was thirty years ago because specific media outlets targeted to specific audiences traffic in an ever-narrower range of representations. These media also set the agenda for what we are to think about, what kinds of people deserve our admiration, respect and envy, and what kinds don't.

Thus, despite my own love of escaping into worlds in which women solve crimes, can buy whatever they want, perform life-saving surgeries and find love, I am here to argue, forcefully, for the importance of wariness, with a capital W. The media have played an important role in enabling us to have female cabinet members, in raising awareness about and condemning domestic violence, in helping Americans accept very different family formations than the one on *Leave It to Beaver,* and even in imagining a woman president. But let's not forget that in the United States, we have the flimsiest support network for mothers and children of any industrialized country, nearly 2 million women are assaulted each year by a husband or boyfriend, and 18 percent of women have reported being the victim of a completed or attempted rape. White women still make 75 cents to a man's dollar, and it's 62 cents for Black women and only 53 cents for Latinas. The majority of families with children in poverty are headed by single women.

It is only through tracing the origins of these images of female power that we can begin to untangle how they have offered empowerment at the cost of eroding our self-esteem, and keeping millions in their place. Because still, despite everything, what courses through our culture is the belief—and fear—that once women have power, they turn into Miranda Priestly in *The Devil Wears Prada*—evil, tyrannical, hated. And the great irony is that if some media fare is actually ahead of where most women are in society, it may be thwarting the very advances for women that it seeks to achieve.

This essay was adapted from Susan J. Douglas' new book, Enlightened Sexism: The Seductive Message that Feminism's Work is Done *(Times Books, March).*

Critical Thinking

1. What factors, in what proportion, would you estimate are salient in forming a preteen girl's self perception? Where do media fit on your list?

2. How does the article *enlightened sexism?* In your experience, do media consumers get the irony?

SUSAN J. DOUGLAS is a professor of communications at the University of Michigan and an *In These Times* columnist. Her latest book is *Enlightened Sexism: The Seductive Message That Feminism's Work Is Done* (2010).

UNIT 2
Telling Stories

Unit Selections

Learning Outcomes

After reading this Unit, you should be able to

- Summarize factors that have contributed to newspapers' decline.

- Assess the potential of proposals to reinvent and reinvigorate news media.

- Describe the relationship of media and politics in terms of feedforward and feedback agendas.

- Evaluate implications of evolution in how news and information are accessed and disseminated.

- Describe media implications of the attention economy. Relate these to gatekeeping, filtering, editing.

- Propose ethical boundaries for media roles in political revolution.

Student Website
www.mhhe.com/cls

Internet References

Fairness and Accuracy in Reporting
www.fair.org
Organization of News Ombudsmen (ONO)
www.newsombudsmen.org
Television News Archive
www.tvnews.vanderbilt.edu

News (noun plural but singular in construction): 1. a report of recent events; 2. previously unknown information, as in "I've got *news* for you"; 3. something having a specified influence or effect, e.g., "the virus was bad news"; 4. material reported in a newspaper or news periodical or newscast; 5. matter that is newsworthy; 6. newscast (Merriam-Webster, m-w.com)

One of the functions mass media serve is distribution of news. Media transmit stories—about the past, about the day's events, about people, places, and things. Intentionally or not, the stories create heroes and villains, incite emotions, influence political agendas, set our moral compasses.

News, by definition, is timely: It is "news," not "olds." Decisions regarding what stories to report and how to report them are made under tight deadlines. Media expert Wilbur Schramm has noted that "hardly anything about communication is so impressive as the enormous number of choices and discards and interpretations that have to be made between [an] actual news event and the symbols that later appear in the mind of a reporter, an editor, a reader, a listener, or a viewer. Therefore, even if everyone does his job perfectly, it is hard enough to get the report of an event straight and clear and true." Schramm's comments point to the tremendous impact of selectivity in crafting news messages. The process is called *gatekeeping.*

Gatekeeping is necessary. The people who research and put together news stories cannot logistically cover or report every event that happens in the world from one edition or broadcast or posting to the next. The concerns associated with the reality of gatekeeping relate to whether the gatekeepers abuse the privilege of deciding what information or viewpoints mass audiences receive. Simply being selected for media coverage lends an issue, an event, or an individual a certain degree of celebrity— the "masser" the medium, the greater the effect.

Traditional news media are under enormous pressure to remain competitive in a changing media environment. Daily United States newspaper circulation peaked at 62.3 million in 1990. Since then, market share in large markets has dropped as much as 10 percent per year. In 2000 there were 1,480 daily newspapers in the United States; in 2010 the number dropped to 1,302. A 2010 survey of 1,040 adults ages 18 and over indicated 20 percent of respondents ages 18–49 read a newspaper daily, compared with 42 percent of respondents age 50 and older. Television remained the most preferred source of news (52 percent ages 18–49; 69 percent age 50 +), followed by print newspapers (19 percent ages 18–49; 35 percent age 50 +) and online sites (34 percent ages 18–49; 16 percent age 50 +). Among online news sites, CNN has the most monthly unique visitors (65,657,000 in mid-2010 data), followed by Yahoo! News (56,038,000), MSNBC (47,950,000), *the New York Times* (32,360,000), AOL News (29,858,000), and the Huffington Post (24,393,000). The average time spent per person on a *New York Times* site visit in 2009 was 12 minutes and 36 seconds, a drop of 24 minutes from 2008. Time spent at the *Wall Street Journal* site was on average 7 minutes, at USATODAY. com 12 minutes, at Washingtonpost.com 11 minutes.

In 2010, the average American spent 70 minutes each day consuming news. In 2010, 17 percent of Americans said they

© Lars A. Niki

got no news of any kind on the day before they were called for the survey.

In his novel *The Evening News,* Arthur Hailey observed: "People watch the news to find out the answers to three questions, Is the world safe? Are my home and family safe? and, Did anything happen today that was interesting?" Given cursory answers to those questions, viewers are satisfied that they are "keeping up," although the total amount of news delivered in a half-hour newscast would, if set in type, hardly fill the front page of a daily newspaper. Many adults report that they are too busy to follow the news, or are suspicious of the media, or find the news too depressing. In one recent study, 27 percent of television viewers described themselves as "stressed" while watching the evening news (51 percent reported feeling "stressed" watching Martha Stewart). Availability and consumption of *information,* however, is on the rise. Knowledge of sports and celebrities has increased, while knowledge of local and national politics has decreased.

The articles in this section explore the changing landscape of contemporary news and information coverage and consumption, significant changes in the news business that both reflect and shape messages in the media pipeline. "The Reconstruction of American Journalism" reviews turning points in the collapse of newspapers, which depend on diminishing advertising revenue to run their businesses. "Retreating from the World" discusses the status of international news coverage where, "with fellowships, grants and freelance contracts, new entries into the foreign-news business are providing alternatives for journalists intent on reporting from overseas, for editors who need to augment their reports and for readers looking to supplement the now-limited offerings of newspapers and television stations." "Capital Flight" analyzes the implications of reduction in the Washington, DC–based press corps.

"Overload!: Journalism's Battle for Relevance in an Age of Too Much Information" offers an intriguing application of insights from cognitive psychology to analyzing media consumers' response to information overload. "Learning to Love the New Media" looks at news in the digital media world and concludes "there isn't any point in defending the old ways. Consumer-obsessed, sensationalist, and passionate about their work, digital upstarts are undermining the old media—and they may also be pointing the way to a brighter future."

"The Toppling," "Whence the Revolution" and "North Korea's Digital Underground" offer differing perspectives on news and political change. All three are in some fashion gatekeeping case studies, and all three speak to feedforward versus feedback considerations in crafting news stories.

Communicating news and information is a critical function of mass media, and the degree to which media effectively perform and are perceived to effectively perform their gatekeeping and watchdog functions are of critical importance. In his book *Tuned Out: Why Americans Under 40 Don't Follow the News,* David T. Z. Mindich writes,

Robert Putnam's 2000 book, *Bowling Alone,* charted the decay of what the author called 'social capital,' the important resource of public and quasi-public dialogue. For example, Putnam discovered that more people bowl than ever before, but fewer bowl in leagues; hence, the title of his book. But bowling is just the start. The last half century has seen a decline in membership in unions, Elks clubs, and PTAs; fewer people give dinner parties, speak in public, go to church, and attend the theater. . . . Putnam convincingly demonstrated a correlation between the lack of social capital and news consumption. The same people who join groups and write their representatives also read newspapers. The same people who have trust in the system, and their ability to change it, use the news for ammunition. The same people who distrust each other, drop out of society, and become isolated, find news irrelevant to their lives.

It is arguable that a decline in careful and credible coverage of important events and issues among media has contributed to decline in social capital. However, in a market-driven media climate, it is difficult for traditional news media to sustain an economically viable hard-news orientation when a declining number of consumers express interest in that product.

The Reconstruction of American Journalism

Many recent articles have addressed the perilous future of journalism. What is different about this one, aside from the breadth of the authors' research, is that it focuses resolutely on a particular function of the press, what it calls "accountability journalism," and that it lays out a series of usable—though ambitious—ideas that, taken together, would build an ecosystem beneficial to the health of accountability journalism in the commercial, nonprofit, and public news sectors. We hope you see the report as framing the discussion, and that you will join in a conversation about it on our website at cjr.org/reconstruction.—The Editors

LEONARD DOWNIE JR. AND MICHAEL SCHUDSON

American journalism is at a transformational moment, in which the era of dominant newspapers and influential network news divisions is rapidly giving way to one in which the gathering and distribution of news is more widely dispersed. As almost everyone knows, the economic foundation of the nation's newspapers, long supported by advertising, is collapsing, and newspapers themselves, which have been the country's chief source of independent reporting, are shrinking—literally. Fewer journalists are reporting less news in fewer pages, and the hegemony that near-monopoly metropolitan newspapers enjoyed during the last third of the twentieth century, even as their primary audience eroded, is ending. Commercial television news, which was long the chief rival of printed newspapers, has also been losing its audience, its advertising revenue, and its reporting resources.

Newspapers and television news are not going to vanish in the foreseeable future, despite frequent predictions of their imminent extinction. But they will play diminished roles in an emerging and still rapidly changing world of digital journalism, in which the means of news reporting are being re-invented, the character of news is being reconstructed, and reporting is being distributed across a greater number and variety of news organizations, new and old.

The questions that this transformation raises are simple enough: What is going to take the place of what is being lost, and can the new array of news media report on our nation and our communities as well as—or better than—journalism has until now? More importantly—and the issue central to this report—what should be done to shape this new landscape, to help assure that the essential elements of independent, original, and credible news reporting are preserved? We believe that choices made now and in the near future will not only have far-reaching effects but, if the choices are sound, significantly beneficial ones.

Some answers are already emerging. The Internet and those seizing its potential have made it possible—and often quite easy—to gather and distribute news more widely in new ways. This is being done not only by surviving newspapers and commercial television, but by startup online news organizations, nonprofit investigative reporting projects, public broadcasting stations, university-run news services, community news sites with citizen participation, and bloggers. Even government agencies and activist groups are playing a role. Together, they are creating not only a greater variety of independent reporting missions but different definitions of news.

Reporting is becoming more participatory and collaborative. The ranks of news gatherers now include not only newsroom staffers, but freelancers, university faculty members, students, and citizens. Financial support for reporting now comes not only from advertisers and subscribers, but also from foundations, individual philanthropists, academic and government budgets, special interests, and voluntary contributions from readers and viewers. There is increased competition among the different kinds of news gatherers, but there also is more cooperation, a willingness to share resources and reporting with former competitors. That increases the value and impact of the news they produce, and creates new identities for reporting while keeping old, familiar ones alive. "I have seen the future, and it is mutual," says Alan Rusbridger, editor of Britain's widely read *Guardian* newspaper. He sees a collaborative journalism emerging, what he calls a "mutualized newspaper."

The Internet has made all this possible, but it also has undermined the traditional marketplace support for American journalism. The Internet's easily accessible free information and low-cost advertising have loosened the hold of large, near-monopoly news organizations on audiences and advertisers. As this report will explain, credible independent news reporting cannot flourish without news organizations of various kinds, including the print and digital reporting operations of surviving newspapers. But it is unlikely that any but the smallest of these news organizations can be supported primarily by existing online revenue. That is why—at the end of this report—we will explore a variety and mixture of ways to support news reporting, which must include non-market sources like philanthropy and government.

The way news is reported today did not spring from an unbroken tradition. Rather, journalism changed, sometimes dramatically, as the nation changed—its economics (because of the growth of large retailers in major cities), demographics (because of the shifts of population from farms to cities and then to suburbs), and politics (because early on political parties controlled newspapers and later lost power over them). In the early days of the republic, newspapers did little or no local reporting—in fact, those early newspapers were almost all four-page weeklies, each produced by a single proprietor-printer-editor. They published much more foreign than local news, reprinting stories they happened to see in London papers they received in the mail, much as Web news aggregators do today. What local news they did provide consisted mostly of short items or bits of intelligence brought in by their readers, without verification.

Most of what American newspapers did from the time that the First Amendment was ratified, in 1791, until well into the nineteenth century was to provide an outlet for opinion, often stridently partisan. Newspaper printers owed their livelihoods and loyalties to political parties. Not until the 1820s and 1830s did they begin to hire reporters to gather news actively rather than wait for it to come to them. By the late nineteenth century, urban newspapers grew more prosperous, ambitious and powerful, and some began to proclaim their political independence.

In the first half of the twentieth century, even though earnings at newspapers were able to support a more professional culture of reporters and editors, reporting was often limited by deference to authority. By the 1960s, though, more journalists at a number of prosperous metropolitan newspapers were showing increasing skepticism about pronouncements from government and other centers of power. More newspapers began to encourage "accountability reporting" that often comes out of beat coverage and targets those who have power and influence in our lives—not only governmental bodies, but businesses and educational and cultural institutions. Federal regulatory pressure on broadcasters to take the public service requirements of their licenses seriously also encouraged greater investment in news.

A serious commitment to accountability journalism did not spread universally throughout newspapers or broadcast media, but abundant advertising revenue during the profitable last decades of the century gave the historically large staffs of many urban newspapers an opportunity to significantly increase the quantity and quality of their reporting. An extensive *American Journalism Review* study of the content of ten metropolitan newspapers across the country, for the years 1964–65 and 1998–99, found that overall the amount of news these papers published doubled.

The concept of news also was changing. The percentage of news categorized in the study as local, national, and international declined from 35 to 24 percent, while business news doubled from 7 to 15 percent, sports increased from 16 to 21 percent, and features from 23 to 26 percent. Newspapers moved from a preoccupation with government, usually in response to specific events, to a much broader understanding of public life that included not just events, but also patterns and trends, and not just in politics, but also in science, medicine, business, sports, education, religion, culture, and entertainment.

These developments were driven in part by the market. Editors sought to slow the loss of readers turning to broadcast or cable television, or to magazines that appealed to niche audiences. The changes also were driven by the social movements of the 1960s and 1970s. The civil rights movement taught journalists in what had been overwhelmingly white and male newsrooms about minority communities that they hadn't covered well or at all. The women's movement successfully asserted that "the personal is political" and ushered in such topics as sexuality, gender equity, birth control, abortion, childhood, and parenthood. Environmentalists helped to make scientific and medical questions part of everyday news reporting.

Is that kind of journalism imperiled by the transformation of the American news media? To put it another way, is independent news reporting a significant public good whose diminution requires urgent attention? Is it an essential component of public information that, as the Knight Commission on the Information Needs of Communities in a Democracy recently put it, "is as vital to the healthy functioning of communities as clean air, safe streets, good schools, and public health?"

Those questions are asked most often in connection with independent reporting's role in helping to create an informed citizenry in a representative democracy. This is an essential purpose for reporting, along with interpretation, analysis and informed opinion, and advocacy. And news reporting also provides vital information for participation in society and in daily life.

Much of newspaper journalism in other democracies is still partisan, subsidized by or closely allied with political parties. That kind of journalism can also serve democracy. But in the plurality of the American media universe, advocacy journalism is not endangered—it is growing. The expression of publicly disseminated opinion is perhaps Americans' most exercised First Amendment right, as anyone can see and hear every day on the Internet, cable television, or talk radio.

What is under threat is independent *reporting* that provides information, investigation, analysis, and community knowledge, particularly in the coverage of local affairs. Reporting the news means telling citizens what they would not otherwise know. "It's so simple it sounds stupid at first, but when you think about it, it is our fundamental advantage," says Tim McGuire, a former editor of the Minneapolis *Star Tribune*. "We've got to tell people stuff they don't know."

Reporting is not something to be taken for granted. Even late in the nineteenth century, when American news reporting was well established, European journalists looked askance, particularly at the suspicious practice of interviewing. One French critic lamented disdainfully that the "spirit of inquiry and espionage" in America might be seeping into French journalism.

Independent reporting not only reveals what government or private interests appear to be doing but also what lies behind their actions. This is the watchdog function of the press—reporting that holds government officials accountable to the legal and moral standards of public service and keeps business and professional leaders accountable to society's expectations of integrity and fairness.

Reporting the news also undergirds democracy by explaining complicated events, issues, and processes in clear language. Since 1985, explanatory reporting has had its own Pulitzer Prize category, and explanation and analysis is now part of much news and investigative reporting. It requires the ability to explain a complex situation to a broad public. News reporting also draws audiences into their communities. In America, sympathetic exposes of "how the other half lives" go back to the late nineteenth century, but what we may call "community knowledge reporting" or "social empathy reporting" has proliferated in recent decades. Everyone remembers how the emotionally engaging coverage by newspapers and television of the victims of Hurricane Katrina made more vivid and accessible issues of race, social and economic conditions, and the role of government in people's lives. At its best, this kind of reporting shocks readers, as well as enhances curiosity, empathy, and understanding about life in our communities.

In the age of the Internet, everyone from individual citizens to political operatives can gather information, investigate the powerful, and provide analysis. Even if news organizations were to vanish en masse, information, investigation, analysis, and community knowledge would not disappear. But something else would be lost, and we would be reminded that there is a need not just for information, but for news judgment oriented to a public agenda and a general audience. We would be reminded that there is a need not just for news but for newsrooms. Something is gained when reporting, analysis, and investigation are pursued collaboratively by stable organizations that can facilitate regular reporting by experienced journalists, support them with money, logistics, and legal services, and present their work to a large public. Institutional authority or weight often guarantees that the work of newsrooms won't easily be ignored.

Something is gained when reporting, analysis, and investigation are pursued collaboratively by stable organizations.

The challenge is to turn the current moment of transformation into a reconstruction of American journalism, enabling independent reporting to emerge enlivened and enlarged from the decline of long-dominant news media. It may not be essential to save any particular news medium, including printed newspapers. What is paramount is preserving independent, original, credible reporting, whether or not it is popular or profitable, and regardless of the medium in which it appears.

Accountability journalism, particularly local accountability journalism, is especially threatened by the economic troubles that have diminished so many newspapers. So much of the news that people find, whether on television or radio or the Internet, still originates with newspaper reporting. And newspapers are the source of most local news reporting, which is why it is even more endangered than national, international or investigative reporting that might be provided by other sources.

At the same time, digital technology—joined by innovation and entrepreneurial energy—is opening new possibilities for reporting. Journalists can research much more widely, update their work repeatedly, follow it up more thoroughly, verify it more easily, compare it with that of competitors, and have it enriched and fact-checked by readers. "Shoe leather" reporting is often still essential, but there are extraordinary opportunities for reporting today because journalists can find so much information on the Internet. *Los Angeles Times* reporters Bettina Boxall and Julie Cart won the 2009 Pulitzer Prize for explanatory reporting by using both the Internet and in-person reporting to analyze why the number and intensity of wildfires has increased in California. They found good sources among U.S. Forest Service retirees by typing "Forest Service" and "retired" into a Google search and then interviewing the people whose names came up. "The Internet," Boxall said, "has made basic research faster, easier, and richer. But it can't displace interviews, being there, or narrative." At the same time, consumers of news have more fresh reporting at their fingertips and the ability to participate in reportorial journalism more readily than ever before. They and reporters can share information, expertise, and perspectives, in direct contacts and through digital communities. Taking advantage of these opportunities requires finding ways to help new kinds of reporting grow and prosper while existing media adapt to new roles.

These are the issues that this report—based on dozens of interviews, visits to news organizations across the country, and numerous recent studies and conferences on the future of news—will explore, and that will lead to its recommendations.

What is happening to independent news reporting by newspapers? Metropolitan newspaper readership began its long decline during the television era and the movement of urban populations to the suburbs. As significant amounts of national and retail advertising shifted to television, newspapers became more dependent on classified advertising. Then, with the advent of multichannel cable television and the largest wave of non-English-speaking immigration in nearly a century, audiences for news became fragmented. Ownership of newspapers and television stations became increasingly concentrated in publicly traded corporations that were determined to maintain large profit margins and correspondingly high stock prices.

Quarterly earnings increasingly became the preoccupation of some large newspaper chain owners and managers who were far removed from their companies' newsrooms and the communities they covered. To maintain earnings whenever advertising revenues fell, some owners started to reverse some of their previous increases in reporting staffs and the space devoted to news. Afternoon newspapers in remaining multipaper cities were in most cases merged with morning papers or shut down. In many cities, by the turn of the century—even before websites noticeably competed for readers or Craigslist attracted large amounts of classified advertising—newspapers already were doing less news reporting.

The Internet revolution helped to accelerate the decline in print readership, and newspapers responded by offering their content for free on their new websites. In hindsight, this may have been a business mistake, but the motivation at the time was to attract new audiences and advertising for content on the Internet, where most other information was already free. Although the readership of newspaper websites grew rapidly, much of the growth turned out to be illusory—just momentary and occasional visits from people drawn to the sites through links from the rapidly growing number of Web aggregators, search engines, and blogs. The initial surge in traffic helped to create a tantalizing but brief boomlet in advertising on newspaper websites. But the newfound revenue leveled off, and fell far short of making up for the rapid declines in revenue from print advertising that accelerated with the recession.

The economics of newspapers deteriorated rapidly. Profits fell precipitously, despite repeated rounds of deep cost-cutting. Some newspapers began losing money, and the depressed earnings of many others were not enough to service the debt that their owners had run up while continuing to buy new properties. The Tribune chain of newspapers, which stretched from the *Los Angeles Times* and the *Chicago Tribune* to *Newsday, The Baltimore Sun,* and the *Orlando Sentinel,* went into bankruptcy. So did several smaller chains and individually owned newspapers in large cities such as Minneapolis and Philadelphia. In Denver, Seattle, and Tucson—still two-newspaper towns in 2008—longstanding metropolitan dailies stopped printing newspapers. More than one hundred daily papers eliminated print publication on Saturdays or other days each week.

In just a few years' time, many newspapers cut their reporting staffs by half and significantly reduced their news coverage. *The Baltimore Sun*'s newsroom shrank to about 150 journalists from more than 400; the *Los Angeles Times*'s to fewer than 600 journalists from more than 1,100. Overall, according to various studies, the number of newspaper editorial employees, which had grown from about 40,000 in 1971 to more than 60,000 in 1992, had fallen back to around 40,000 in 2009.

In most cities, fewer newspaper journalists were reporting on city halls, schools, social welfare, life in the suburbs, local business, culture, the arts, science, or the environment, and fewer were assigned to investigative reporting. Most large newspapers eliminated foreign correspondents and many of their correspondents in Washington. The number of newspaper reporters covering state capitals full-time fell from 524 in 2003 to 355 at the beginning of 2009. A large share of newspaper reporting of government, economic activity, and quality of life simply disappeared.

A large share of newspaper reporting of government, economic activity, and quality of life simply disappeared.

Will this contraction continue until newspapers and their news reporting no longer exist? Not all newspapers are at risk. Many of those less battered by the economic downturn are situated in smaller cities and towns where there is no newspaper competition, no locally based television station, and no Craigslist. Those papers' reporting staffs, which never grew very large, remain about the same size they have been for years, and they still concentrate on local news. A number of them have sought to limit the loss of paid circulation and advertising in their print papers by charging non-subscribers for access to most of their Web content. They are scattered across the country from Albuquerque, New Mexico, to Lawrence, Kansas, to Newport, Rhode Island. Although they have not attracted many paid Web-only subscribers, their publishers say they have so far protected much of their print circulation and advertising.

Larger newspapers are seriously looking into ways to seek payment for at least some of the news they put online. Their publishers have been discussing various proposals from Internet entrepreneurs, including improved technologies for digital subscriptions, micropayments (on the model of iTunes) to read individual news stories, single-click mechanisms for readers to make voluntary payments, and business-to-business arrangements enabling newspapers to share in the ad revenue from other sites that republish their content. Whether "information wants to be free" on the Internet has become a highly charged, contentious issue, somewhat out of proportion to how much money may be at stake or its potential impact on news reporting.

Only a few large newspapers are already charging for digital news of special interest. Both *The Wall Street Journal* and the *Financial Times* sell subscriptions for access to their websites, and the *Journal* also has decided to charge for its content on mobile devices like BlackBerrys and iPhones. The *Milwaukee Journal Sentinel* sells subscriptions to avid Green Bay Packers football fans for its Packer Insider site, and the *Pittsburgh Post-Gazette* offers paid membership to a niche website of exclusive staff blogs, videos, chats, and social networking.

One entrepreneurial venture, Journalism Online, claims that publishers of hundreds of daily and weekly newspapers have signed letters of intent to explore its strategy for enabling online readers to buy digital news from many publications through a single password-protected website. A Silicon Valley startup named Attributor has developed technology to "fingerprint" each news organization's digital content to determine where it shows up on other websites and what advertising is being sold with it. Attributor offers to negotiate with Internet advertising networks to share that revenue with publishers who join its Fair Syndication Consortium. The Associated Press recently announced a strategy for tracking news produced by AP and its member newspapers through the Internet, and then seeking payment for it.

Entrepreneurs have also proposed ways in which news consumers could allow their reading habits on the Internet to be monitored so that news organizations could sell highly targeted groups of readers to advertisers at high prices. Google offers publishers some ways to use its search engine to seek payment for their digital news. But given the Internet's culture of relatively free access to an infinite amount of information, no one knows whether any of these approaches would lead to new economic models for journalism.

There have been suggestions that philanthropists or foundations could buy and run newspapers as endowed institutions, as though they were museums. But it would take an endowment of billions of dollars to produce enough investment income to run a single sizeable newspaper, much less large numbers of papers in communities across the country.

U.S. Senator Ben Cardin of Maryland has introduced legislation to allow newspapers to become nonprofits for educational purposes under section 501(c)(3) of the tax code, similar to charities and educational and cultural nonprofits. Philanthropic contributions to them would be tax-deductible. But the bill, which has not moved anywhere in Congress, does not address how a newspaper that is losing money, especially one saddled with significant debt or other liabilities, could be converted into a viable nonprofit.

For all this, many newspapers are still profitable, not counting some of their owners' overhanging debt, which may be resolved through ongoing bankruptcy reorganizations and ownership changes. And many newspapers are extensively restructuring themselves to integrate their print and digital operations, creating truly multimedia news organizations in ways that should produce both more cost savings—and more engaging journalism.

A growing number of newspapers also are supplementing their reduced resources for news reporting by collaborating with other newspapers, new kinds of news organizations, and their own readers. In the most extensive collaboration, Ohio's eight largest newspapers—*The Plain Dealer* in Cleveland, *The Akron Beacon Journal, The* (Canton) *Repository, The Columbus Dispatch, The* (Cincinnati) *Enquirer,* the *Dayton Daily News, The* (Toledo) *Blade*, and *The* (Youngstown) *Vindicator*—have formed the Ohio News Organization. They share state, business, sports, arts, and entertainment news reporting, various kinds of features, editorials, photographs, and graphics. The newspapers work independently and competitively on enterprise and investigative reporting, to which their editors say they can each now devote more of their smaller number of reporters.

A growing number of newspapers are collaborating on stories with other newspapers, new kinds of news organizations, and their own readers.

The Star-Ledger in Newark has created a separate community news service that hired three-dozen younger, lower-paid journalists to report from surrounding New Jersey towns. *The Seattle Times* has agreed to share news website links and some reporting with what editor David Boardman calls Seattle's "most respected neighborhood blogs," to which residents contribute news to be edited by professional journalists.

As newspapers sharply reduce their staffs and news reporting to cut costs and survive, they also reduce their value to their readers and communities. At the same time, they are disgorging thousands of trained journalists who are now available to start and staff new kinds of local news organizations, primarily online. This sets the stage for a future for local news reporting in which the remaining economically viable newspapers—with much smaller staffs, revenues, and profits—will try to do many things at once: publish in print and digitally, seek new ways to attract audience and advertisers, invent new products and revenue streams, and find partners to help them produce high-quality news at lower cost. They will do all of this in competition—and in collaboration—with the new, primarily online, news organizations that are able to thrive.

Why can't television and radio make up for the loss of reporting by newspapers? Some local television stations sometimes produce exemplary local and regional reporting, as demonstrated by the winners of the 2009 DuPont Award. A two-year investigation by WTVT, a Fox affiliate in Tampa, of criminal justice in nearby Hardee County led to the release of a truck driver wrongfully imprisoned for vehicular manslaughter. WFAA in Dallas, an ABC affiliate that has won more than a dozen national awards, received a special citation for three notable investigative reports in a single year.

Still, even in their best years, most commercial television stations had far fewer news reporters than local newspapers, and a 1999 study of fifty-nine local news stations in nineteen cities found that 90 percent of all their stories reported on accidents, crimes, and scheduled or staged events. In recent years, with their ratings and ad revenues in rapid decline and their once extravagant profit margins imperiled, many local television stations have made further cuts in already small news staffs. The number of television stations producing local news of their own is steadily shrinking. Some stations, such as KDNL, the ABC affiliate in St. Louis, and WYOU, serving Scranton and Wilkes-Barre in Pennsylvania, have dropped local news altogether. At 205 stations around the country, newscasts are now produced by other stations in the same cities.

In the past, the Federal Communications Commission required station owners to show they were serving the public interest before their broadcasting licenses could be renewed. But the FCC no longer effectively enforces the public-service requirement. Some cable television systems offer all-news local channels produced by the cable company itself or by broadcast station owners. The cable news channels, which recycle a relatively few news programs throughout the day, are usually lower cost, smaller-audience versions of host or collaborating broadcast stations.

On radio, with the exception of all-news stations in some large cities, most commercial stations do little or no local news reporting. A growing number of listeners have turned to public radio stations for national and international news provided by National Public Radio. But only a relatively small number of those public radio stations also offer their listeners a significant amount of local news reporting. And even fewer public television stations provide local news coverage.

Congress created the current system of public radio and television in 1967. Through the quasi-independent Corporation for Public Broadcasting, the federal government funnels about $400 million a year to program producers and to hundreds of independent public radio and television stations that reach every corner of the country. The stations, which are owned by colleges and universities, nonprofit community groups, and state and local governments, supplement relatively small CPB grants with fundraising from individual donors, philanthropic foundations, and corporate contributors. Most of the money is used for each station's overhead costs and fundraising, rather than news reporting.

Three-fourths of the CPB's money goes to public television, which has never done much original news reporting. The Public Broadcasting Service, collectively owned by local public television stations and primarily funded by the CPB, is a conduit for public affairs programs produced by some larger stations and independent producers that consist mostly of documentaries, talk shows, and a single national news discussion program, *The NewsHour with Jim Lehrer,* on weeknights.

Because PBS has no production capacity of its own, it does not do any news reporting. But as a distributor of programming, it is exploring how to improve public television news in what a Pew Foundation-funded PBS consultant described as an often dysfunctional, entrenched culture with "too many silos"—meaning the many individual stations, production organizations, and programming groups—that have not worked well together on news reporting. An internal PBS study reportedly recommends the creation of a destination public news website, with content from throughout public television and radio. David Fanning, the longtime executive producer of *Frontline,* has proposed going further. Fanning wants to create a full-fledged national reporting organization for public television with its own staff and funding. Realizing either his proposal or the vision of the PBS study would require a major realignment of public media relationships and funding. Neither would increase independent local news reporting by public television stations.

While the audience for public radio of about 28 million listeners each week is just over one-third of the 75 million weekly viewers of public television, it has been growing substantially for several decades, driven largely by its national news programs. NPR's *Morning Edition* and *All Things Considered* are the most popular programs on public radio or television. And *Morning Edition*'s audience of nearly 12 million listeners alone has been about a third larger than that for NBC's *Today.* Although NPR also has lost revenue during the recession and laid off staff for the first time in a quarter century, it recently launched an ambitious website with national news updates and stories. It also hired its first editor for investigative reporting, Brian Duffy, who is working on accountability journalism projects with reporters at NPR and local public radio stations. NPR has seventeen foreign bureaus, more than all but a few American newspapers, and six U.S. regional bureaus.

But only a small fraction of the public radio stations that broadcast NPR's national and international news accompany it with a significant amount of local news reporting. Those that do tend to be large city, regional, or state flagship stations. Some of these operations are impressive. Northern California Public Broadcasting, for instance, with stations in San Francisco, San Jose, and Monterey, has a thirty-person news staff reporting on the state's government and economy, education, environment, and health. Its KQED public radio and television stations in San Francisco have announced a collaboration with the Graduate School of Journalism at the University of California, Berkeley to launch in 2010 an independent nonprofit Bay area news organization with $5 million seed money from local businessman Warren Hellman. The new entity's reporters, working with KQED journalists and Berkeley students, will cover local government, education, culture, the environment and neighborhoods for its own website, other digital media, and public radio and television.

Some public radio stations have sought advice from CPB, asking how they could expand and finance local news coverage, using journalists who had worked at local newspapers. A just-completed CPB Public Radio Task Force Report put "supporting significant growth in the scale, quality, and impact of local reporting" near the top of its recommendations for further increasing the audience for public radio.

Under Vivian Schiller, National Public Radio's new CEO, NPR has taken steps to help member stations with local news coverage. NPR is a nonprofit that supplies national and international news and cultural programming—but not local news—to about 800 public radio stations. These stations are owned and managed by 280 local and state nonprofits, colleges, and universities that support NPR with their dues. Schiller says her goal, approved by the board of member station representatives that governs NPR, is "to step in where local newspapers are leaving." In its most ambitious project, NPR has created a digital distribution platform on which it and member stations can share radio and website reporting on subjects of local interest in various parts of the country, such as education or the environment.

Overall, however, local news coverage remains underfunded, understaffed, and a low priority at most public radio and television stations, whose leaders have been unable to make—or uninterested in making—the case for investment in local news to donors and Congress.

What are the new sources of independent news reporting? Different kinds of news organizations are being started by journalists who have left print and broadcast, and also by universities and their students, Internet entrepreneurs, bloggers, and so-called "citizen journalists." Many of these new organizations report on their communities. Others concentrate on investigative reporting. Some specialize in subjects like national politics, state government, or health care. Many are tax-exempt nonprofits, while others are trying to become profitable. Most publish only online, avoiding printing and delivery costs. However, some also collaborate with other news media to reach larger audiences through newspapers, radio, and television, as well as their own websites. Many of the startups are still quite small and financially fragile, but they are multiplying steadily.

The startups are financially fragile. Their staffs and audiences are small, and they are scattered unevenly around the country.

Several new local news organizations, each different from the others, can be found in San Diego. The reporting staff of the daily newspaper there, *The San Diego Union-Tribune,* has been halved by a series of cuts both before and after its sale by the Copley family in May 2009 to a Los Angeles investment firm, Platinum Equity, which had no previous experience in journalism.

Five years ago, frustration with the *Union-Tribune*'s coverage of the city prompted a local businessman, Buzz Woolley, to fund the launch of an online-only local news organization, Voice of San Diego. The dozen reporters who work out of its light-filled newsroom in a new Spanish mission-style building near San Diego Bay focus on local accountability journalism. The site has no recipes or movie reviews or sports. The young journalists, most of whom came from newspapers, do enterprise and investigative reporting about San Diego government, business, housing, education, health, environment, and other "key quality of life issues facing the region," said executive editor Andrew Donohue. "We want to be best at covering a small number of things. We're very disciplined about not trying to do everything."

Voice of San Diego's impact has been disproportionate to its steadily growing but still relatively modest audience of fewer than 100,000 unique visitors a month. Its investigations of fraud in local economic development corporations, police misrepresentation of crime statistics, and the city's troubled pension fund, among other subjects, have led to prosecutions, reforms, and the kind of national journalism awards—from Sigma Delta Chi and Investigative Reporters and Editors—typically given to newspapers. To increase their reach, Voice journalists appear regularly on the local NBC television station, the all-news commercial radio station, and the public radio station, giving those outlets reporting they otherwise would not have.

Voice of San Diego's investigations have led to prosecutions, reforms, and national journalism awards.

The current $1 million annual budget of the Voice of San Diego, which is a nonprofit, comes from donors like Woolley, from foundations, advertising, corporate sponsorships, and contributions from citizen "members," like those who support local public radio and television and cultural institutions. "We don't count on mass traffic, but rather a level of loyalty," said publisher Scott Lewis. "We're seeking loyal people like those who give to the opera, museums or the orchestra because they believe they should be sustained."

They rent newsroom space from one of their supporters, the San Diego Foundation, which, like hundreds of other community foundations around the country, is a collection of local family funds with a professional staff to offer advice to the donors of these funds. Lewis said the foundation recommends contributions to the Voice. At the same time, the national Knight Foundation has been encouraging such foundations to support news and information needs in their communities through a program of matching grants. Knight and the San Diego Foundation recently gave Voice of San Diego matching grants of $100,000 each to increase its coverage of local neighborhoods and communities "underserved" by other news media.

Across town, the San Diego News Network has launched a quite different, for-profit local news website that resembles the *Union-Tribune* newspaper's website much more than it does Voice of San Diego. SDNN aggregates news and information from its own small reporting staff, freelancers, San Diego-area weekly community newspapers, radio, and television stations, and bloggers. It covers most of the subjects the newspaper does, from local events, business, and sports to entertainment, food, and travel, but with less independent reporting. Local entrepreneurs Barbara Bry and her husband Neil Senturia, and former *Union-Tribune* website editor Chris Jennewein, have raised $2 million from local investors and want to create a network of similar sites in as many as forty cities; they hope to attract more advertisers and become profitable. Jennewein said that he expects cities like San Diego, which long had a single dominant newspaper, to spawn many kinds of news entities. "There's going to be fragmentation," he said. "It may be a good thing. We have to think of there being a new news ecosystem."

The most unusual San Diego startup is The Watchdog Institute, an independent nonprofit local investigative reporting project based on the campus of San Diego State University. Lorie Hearn, who was a senior editor at the *Union-Tribune,* persuaded her former newspaper's new owner, Platinum Equity, to contribute money to the startup so that Hearn could hire investigative reporters who had worked for her at the *Union-Tribune.* In return, Hearn will provide the newspaper with investigative stories at a cost lower than if Hearn and the other Watchdog Institute journalists were still on its payroll. She intends to seek more local media partners, along with philanthropic donations, while training San Diego State journalism students to help with the reporting.

There are other examples of local news startups around the country. The nonprofit website St. Louis Beacon, launched by Margaret Freivogel and a dozen of her colleagues who were bought out or laid off by the venerable *St. Louis Post-Dispatch,* does in-depth reporting and analysis in targeted "areas of concentration," including the local economy, politics, race relations, education, health, and the arts. Freivogel's budget of just under $1 million comes primarily from foundations and local donors, advertisers, and corporate sponsors. In Minneapolis, the nonprofit MinnPost website relies on a mix of full-time, part-time, contract, and freelance journalists for the site's news reporting, commentary, and blogs. Editor Joel Kramer's budget of more than $1 million a year includes foundation grants and a significant amount of advertising.

Some of the startups are experimenting with what is being called "pro-am" journalism—professionals and amateurs working together over the Internet. This includes, for example, ProPublica, the nation's largest startup nonprofit news organization with three-dozen investigative reporters and editors. Amanda Michel, its director of distributed reporting, recruited a network of volunteer citizen reporters to monitor progress on a sample of 510 of the six thousand projects approved for federal stimulus money around the country. "We recruited people who know about contracts," Michel said. "We need a definable culture" of people with expertise on targeted subjects, "not just everybody."

Much smaller local and regional websites founded by professional journalists—ranging from the for-profit New West network of websites in Montana and neighboring states to the nonprofit New Haven Independent in Connecticut—regularly supplement reporting by their relatively tiny staffs with contributions from freelancers, bloggers, and readers. The fast-increasing number of blog-like hyperlocal neighborhood news sites across the country depend even more heavily for their news reporting on freelancers and citizen contributors that is edited by professional journalists. In Seattle, among the most Internet-oriented metropolitan areas in the country, pro-am neighborhood news sites are proliferating. "We believe this could become the next-generation news source" in American cities, said Cory Bergman, who started Next Door Media, a group of sites in five connecting Seattle neighborhoods. "The challenge is to create a viable economic model." Bergman and his wife Kate devised a franchise model, in which the editor of each site, a professional journalist, reports news of the neighborhood and curates text, photo, and video contributions from residents. Editors earn a percentage of their site's advertising revenue.

Several affluent suburban New Jersey towns outside New York City also have become test tubes for these kinds of hyperlocal news websites, some of which have been launched by big news organizations experimenting with low-cost local newsgathering. At the state level, other new, nonprofit news organizations are trying to help fill the gap left when cost-cutting newspapers pulled reporters out of state capitals. The Center for Investigative Reporting, a three-decade-old Berkeley-based nonprofit that had long produced award-winning national stories for newspapers and television, has started California Watch with foundation funding to scrutinize that state's government, publishing its reporting in dozens of news media throughout California and on its own website.

The Center for Independent Media, with funding from a variety of donors and foundations, operates a network of non-profit, liberal-leaning political news websites in the capitals of Colorado, Iowa, Michigan, Minnesota, and New Mexico, all battleground states during the 2008 presidential election. David Bennahum, a journalist and business consultant, launched the sites in 2006 with the stated mission of producing "action-able impact journalism" about "key issues." Meanwhile, Texas venture capitalist John Thornton and former *Texas Monthly* editor Evan Smith have raised $3.5 million from Thornton and his wife, other Texas donors, including entrepreneur T. Boone Pickens, and foundations to start the nonprofit Texas Tribune in Austin, where they are hiring fifteen journalists to do independent, multimedia reporting about state government, politics, and policy for its website and other Texas news media.

Not surprisingly, most of these startups are financially fragile. In Chicago, a former *Tribune* reporter, Geoff Dougherty, trained scores of volunteers to help a handful of paid reporters find news in the city's neighborhoods for his nonprofit website, the Chi-Town Daily News. But, in the summer of 2009, after four years of operation with a variety of foundation grants, Dougherty announced he could not raise enough money to keep going as a nonprofit. He said he would instead seek investors for some of kind of commercial local news site.

There are notable startups on the national and international front as well. The for-profit GlobalPost, for example, with money from investors, Web advertising, and fee-paying clients, produces independent foreign reporting with a string of sixty-five professional stringers. On the home front, Politico has a news staff of seventy, and delivers scoops, gossip, and commentary on national politics and government. Revenue comes mostly from advertising online and via its weekly print version, and by corporations and groups seeking to influence legislation and policy.

Meanwhile, as it separates from Time Warner and transitions from an Internet portal to a generator of Web content, AOL also is betting on special-interest, advertising-supported, professionally produced news websites like Politico's. AOL has launched or purchased such Web startups as Politics Daily for politics and government, Fanhouse for sports, Bloging Stocks for business, and TMZ for celebrities and entertainment. It also is experimenting with small local new sites like Patch.com in suburban Connecticut and New Jersey. And like Politico, AOL has been hiring experienced journalists from struggling news media.

The quality of news reporting by most of the national, regional, and local startups is generally comparable to, and sometimes better than, that of newspapers, as can be seen by their collaboration with traditional newspapers on some stories. Small neighborhood news startups generally report on their communities in more detail than newspapers can, even though the quality of reporting and writing may not be comparable.

Collectively, the newcomers are filling some of the gaps left by the downsizing of newspapers' reporting staffs, especially in local accountability and neighborhood reporting. However, the staffs of most of the startups are still small, as are their audiences and budgets, and they are scattered unevenly across the country. Their growth, role, and impact in news reporting are still to be determined by a variety of factors explored later in this report.

What kind of news reporting has been spawned by the blogosphere? The boon and bane of the digital world is its seemingly infinite variety. It offers news, information and, especially, opinion—on countless thousands of websites, blogs, and social networks. Most are vehicles for sharing personal observations, activities, and views in words, photographs, and videos—sometimes more than anyone would want to know. A large number also pass along, link to, or comment on news and other content originally produced by established news organizations. And many of the participants—bloggers, political and special interest activists and groups, governments and private companies, and Internet entrepreneurs—generate various kinds of news reporting themselves.

Lumped together as the "blogosphere," these sites are sometimes seen as either the replacement for—or the enemy of—established news media. In fact, the blogosphere and older media have become increasingly symbiotic. They feed off each other's information and commentary, and they fact-check each other. They share audiences, and they mimic each other through evolving digital journalistic innovation.

A few blogs have grown into influential, for-profit digital news organizations. Upstairs in a loft newsroom in New York's Chelsea neighborhood, Josh Marshall's Talking Points Memo staff is combining traditional news reporting with an openly ideological agenda to create an influential and profitable national news website. TPM has grown from former print reporter Marshall's one-man opinion blog into a full-fledged, advertising-supported digital news institution with a small group of paid reporters and editors in New York and Washington. In 2008, TPM won a George Polk Award for its investigation of the political firings of U.S. attorneys during the Bush administration.

Marshall described TPM as "narrating with reporting and aggregation"—including the involvement of "an audience with high interest and expertise. We have a consistent, iterative relationship with our audience—people telling us where to look," Marshall said. "But all the information, stories, and sources are checked professionally by our journalists."

Marshall also believes in "the discipline of the marketplace," and has not taken foundation money or philanthropic donations. Only advertising and small contributions from readers support TPM's still relatively small $600,000 annual budget. Its first outside investment is coming from a group led by Netscape founder Marc Andreesen to help Marshall expand his reporting staff and advertising sales.

TPM's combination of news reporting, analysis, commentary, and reader participation is the model in varying forms for many blogs on the Internet. Some of the more widely read and trusted independent bloggers specialize in subjects they know and have informed opinions about, such as politics, the economy and business, legal affairs, the news media, education, health care, and family issues. Freelance financial journalist Michelle Leder, for example, turned her interest in the fine print of SEC filings into the closely watched Footnoted blog, which is supported by both her freelance income and expensive subscriptions for investors to an insider version of her blog.

They also are creating new ways to report news. In 2008, Kelly Golnoush Niknejad, a Columbia University journalism school graduate, launched a blog called Tehran Bureau, to which Iranian and other journalists contribute reporting from inside Iran and from the diaspora of Iranian exiles. In 2009, Tehran Bureau joined in a partnership with the public television program *Frontline,* which provides the blog with editorial and financial support and hosts its website. *Frontline* and Tehran Bureau also are collaborating on a documentary.

For most of the millions of its practitioners, blogging is still a hobby for which there is little or no remuneration, even if the blog is picked up or mentioned by news media or aggregation sites. Residents of Baltimore, for example, can currently choose among a variety of blogs about life there. Baltimore Crime posts contributions from readers about what they see happening in the streets. Investigative Voice, started by two journalists from the defunct *Baltimore Examiner* newspaper, and Bmore News, owned by a public relations firm, focus on the city's African-American community. Inside Charm City posts press releases from local businesses and government agencies. Blog Baltimore aggregates reader contributions with stories from local news media. The anonymous Baltimore Slumlord Watch blogger posts photos of abandoned and derelict buildings, identifies the property owners, names the city council members in whose districts the buildings are located, provides links to city and state agencies.

The most ambitious local blog there is Baltimore Brew, launched in 2009 by Fern Shen, a former reporter for *The Baltimore Sun* and *The Washington Post,* who has recruited freelancers, including other former *Sun* journalists, to contribute reporting about the city and its neighborhoods, mostly without pay for the moment. Shen, who runs the blog from her kitchen table with money from an initial angel investor, acknowledged taking advantage of buyouts and layoffs that took about 120 journalists out of the *Sun*'s newsroom in less than a year. "The folks that used to do things for a paycheck are now doing them for cheap or for free," she said. "Somebody has to get these reporters back to work again." She is hoping to take advantage of being named "best local blog" by the *Baltimore City Paper* to raise revenue from prospective advertisers and eventually create a paying business for herself and her contributors.

National online news aggregators have created business models for mass audiences and advertising they hope will make them profitable. They aggregate blogs and some reporting of their own with links to and summaries of news reported by other media, along with plentiful photographs and videos. The small staff at Newser, for example, rewrites stories taken from news media websites. The Drudge Report's Matt Drudge, who has been at it much longer, simply links to other sites' content, along with bits of occasionally reliable media and political gossip. Founders Ariana Huffington of Huffington Post and Tina Brown of The Daily Beast, who are media celebrities themselves, have attracted numerous freelance contributors and volunteer bloggers, including big-name writers, to supplement their relatively small writing and editing staffs. Huffington Post on the left and Drudge on the right also display clear ideological leanings in their selection of stories, links and blogs.

Newspapers complain that some aggregators violate copyrights by using their work without payment or a share of the aggregators' advertising revenue, although the aggregators also link to the original stories on the papers' websites. At issue, besides the trade between paying the papers on the one hand and driving some readers to their sites on the other, is the current state of copyright law, which has not kept up with issues raised by digital publication. It has not been decided, for example, how much of a story can be republished, or in what form, before the prevailing principle of "fair use" is violated.

In a departure from other for-profit aggregators, The Huffington Post has joined with the American News Project, a nonprofit print and video investigative reporting entity, to invest in a The Huffington Post Investigative Fund, a legally separate nonprofit based in Washington with about a dozen investigative journalists and initial funding of $1.75 million, including $500,000 from Huffington Post. The fund's editor, former *Washington Post* investigative editor Larry Roberts, said it will provide reporting on national subjects for use by The Huffington Post and other news media, much the way that ProPublica does. He said that he has a commitment from Huffington that the project would be editorially independent and nonpartisan.

The fast-growing number of digital startups, ambitious blogs, experiments in pro-am journalism, and other hybrid news organizations are not replacing newspapers or broadcast news. But they increasingly depend on each other—the old media for news and investigative reporting they can no longer do themselves and the newcomers for the larger audiences they can reach through newspapers, radio, and television—and for the authority that these legacy media outlets still convey. The many new sources of news reporting have become, in the span of a relatively few years, significant factors in the reconstruction of American journalism.

How are colleges and universities contributing to independent news reporting? A number of universities are publishing the reporting of their student journalists on the states, cities, and neighborhoods where the schools are located. The students work in journalism classes and news services under the supervision of professional journalists now on their faculties. The students' reporting appears on local news websites operated by the universities and in other local news media, some of which pay for the reporting to supplement their own. In southern Florida, for example, *The Miami Herald, The Palm Beach Post,* and *Sun Sentinel* have agreed to use reporting from journalism students at Florida International University.

The University of Missouri is unique in having run its own local daily newspaper, the *Columbia Missourian,* since 1908, when its journalism school opened. This valuable journalism laboratory has professional editors and a reporting staff of journalism students. Other universities, meanwhile, publish local news websites. In New York, Columbia's journalism school operates several sites with reporting by its students in city neighborhoods, and investigative reporting by students in the school's Stabile Center for Investigative Journalism has appeared in several major news outlets.

Students at the Graduate School of Journalism at the University of California at Berkeley also do reporting in several San Francisco area communities for the school's neighborhood news websites, and the graduate school has plans for its 120 students to work with professional journalists, beginning next year, at the local news website it is starting with San Francisco's KQED public radio and television. The Walter Cronkite School of Journalism at Arizona State University in Phoenix operates the Cronkite News Service, which provides student reporting to about thirty client newspapers and television stations around the state. And the Capital News Service of the University of Maryland's Philip Merrill College of Journalism operates news bureaus in Washington and Maryland's capital in Annapolis. Northwestern University students staff a similar Medill School of Journalism news service in Washington.

Universities also are becoming homes for independent nonprofit investigative reporting projects started by former newspaper and television journalists. Some are run by journalists on their faculties, while others, such as The Watchdog Institute at San Diego State University, are independent nonprofits that use university facilities and work with faculty and students. For example, Andy Hall, a former *Wisconsin State Journal* investigative reporter, started the Wisconsin Center for Investigative Journalism as an independent, foundation-supported nonprofit on the campus of the University of Wisconsin in Madison. Its reporting by professional journalists, interns, and students appears in Wisconsin newspapers, public radio and television stations, and their websites.

In Boston, Walter Robinson, a former Pulitzer Prize-winning *Globe* investigative reporter, and students in his investigative reporting seminars at Northeastern have produced eleven front-page pieces for the *Globe* since 2007. And a group of former local television and newspaper journalists on the faculty at Boston University recently launched the New England Center for Investigative Journalism in its College of Communications, staffed by the journalist faculty members and their students, in collaboration with the *Globe,* New England Cable News, and public radio station WBUR.

How can fledgling news reporting organizations keep going? Money is obviously a major challenge for nonprofit news organizations, many of which are struggling to stay afloat. Raising money from foundations and other donors and sponsors consumes a disproportionate amount of their time and energy. Advertising and payments from media partners for some stories account for only a fraction of the support needed by most news reporting nonprofits.

Nearly twenty nonprofit news organizations—ranging from the relatively large and well-established Center for Investigative Reporting and Center for Public Integrity to relatively small startups like Voice of San Diego and MinnPost—met last summer to form an Investigative News Network to collaborate on fundraising, legal matters, back-office functions, website development, and reporting projects. Joe Bergantino, a former Boston television investigative reporter who is director of the New England Center for Investigative Reporting at Boston University, said such collaboration is vital "if we're all going to be back next year."

A number of national foundations—led by Knight and including Carnegie, Ford, Hewlett, MacArthur, Open Society Institute, Pew, and Rockefeller, among others—have made grants to a variety of nonprofit reporting ventures in recent years. A study by the Knight-funded J-Lab at American University in Washington estimated that, altogether, national and local foundations provided $128 million to news nonprofits from 2005 into 2009.

Nearly half of that money, however, has been given by major donors to a handful of relatively large national investigative reporting nonprofits, including ProPublica, the Center for Investigative Reporting at Berkeley, and the Center for Public Integrity in Washington. Some foundations fund only national reporting on subjects of particular interest to their donors or managers—such as health, religion, or government accountability. Grants for local news reporting are much smaller and usually not high priorities for foundations, many of which do not make any grants for journalism.

But the future of news reporting is a priority for the Knight Foundation, whose money comes from a family that once owned twenty-six newspapers. Knight has given tens of millions of dollars to nonprofit reporting projects and university journalism instruction, and is encouraging the hundreds of community foundations around the country to join with it in supporting local journalism, as the San Diego Foundation has done with the Voice of San Diego and the Greater St. Louis Community Foundation with the St. Louis Beacon. Knight conducts an annual seminar with leaders of community foundations to encourage grants to local news nonprofits and has started its matching grants initiative to donate with them. "The bottom line," said Eric Newton, Knight's vice president, "is that local news needs local support." Knight foundation president Alberto Ibarguen has also been talking with national foundations for the past two years to encourage more of them to provide more support for local news reporting.

Some foundations have recognized the importance of news reporting to the advancement of their other objectives, while trying to protect the independence of the reporting. The Kaiser Family Foundation, which has long supported health care policy research, started its own nonprofit news organization in 2009. The California Healthcare Foundation, which also funds research, has given $3.2 million to the Annenberg School of Communication and Journalism at the University of Southern California to support a team of six California newspaper journalists for three years to expand health care reporting in the state. Michael Parks, an Annenberg faculty member and a former *Los Angeles Times* executive editor, directs the team, which has helped newspapers in half a dozen California cities report on local hospitals, the pattern of Medicare reimbursements to doctors, and causes of mortality in the state's central valley. "We went to newspapers and asked what stories they have wanted to do, but were unable to do—no resources, no expertise, whatever," Parks said. "We can help."

What other new sources are there for public information?
The Internet has greatly increased access to large quantities of "public information" and news produced by government and a growing number of data-gathering, data-analyzing, research, academic, and special interest activist organizations. Altogether, these sources of public information appear to be a realization of what Walter Lippmann envisioned nearly ninety years ago when he argued that, in an increasingly complex world, journalism could serve democracy only by relying on agencies beyond journalism for dependable data. He urged journalists to make greater use of what he termed "political observatories"—organizations both in and out of government that used scientific methods and instruments to examine human affairs.

Digital databases, for example, enable journalists and citizens to find information in a fraction of the time it would have taken years ago—if it could have been found at all. Routine documents a reporter once had to obtain in a reading room of a government agency or by filing a Freedom of Information Act request can now be found online and are easy to download.

Access to much of the information is dependent on new online intermediaries. Neither house of Congress, for instance, nor any city council of the twenty-five largest American cities nor most state legislative houses make an individual legislator's roll-call votes available in easily usable form, for example. However, that information is now available online for a fee from three different Congress-watching organizations and for free on the websites OpenCongress.org, GovTrack.us, and Washingtonpost.com. Princeton's Center for Information Technology Policy has created a keyword-searchable online database of federal court records that is much less cumbersome to use than the database maintained by the courts themselves.

Some of this public information comes from government agencies that have been around for a long time, like the Government Accountability Office or the Security and Exchange Commission. Others, like the Federal Election Commission (1975) or the Environmental Protection Agency, which produces the Toxic Release Inventory (1986), or the individual departments' and agencies' inspectors general (most of them established through the Inspectors General Act of 1978) are products of the past several decades. All produce abundant information and analysis about government and what it regulates, information that both resembles and assists news reporting.

Outside government, advocacy groups and nongovernmental organizations have sometimes created what resemble news staffs to report on the subjects of their special interest. It is then up to journalists to separate the groups' activist agendas from their information gathering, which, in many cases, the journalists have grown to trust. Taxpayers for Common Sense, founded in 1995, for example, has painstakingly gathered data on congressional "earmarking" that is the starting point for journalists who report on how members of Congress add money to appropriation bills for projects sought by special interests, constituents, and campaign contributors.

Besides their own version of reporting, governments and interest groups also are opening up increasing numbers of digital databases to journalists and citizens. For instance, ProPublica and the Washington-based Sunlight Foundation have created a downloadable database of two years of federal filings from 300 foreign agents on their lobbying of Congress.

A database is not journalism, but, increasingly, sophisticated journalism depends on reliable, downloadable, and searchable databases. The federal government alone has fourteen statistical agencies and about sixty offices within other agencies that produce statistical data. Such data, said Columbia professor of public affairs Kenneth Prewitt, a former director of the U.S. Census Bureau, "has an assumed precision that the journalistic world is trained to question." It needs to be evaluated carefully and skeptically.

The accessibility of so much more public information changes the work of journalists and the nature of news reporting. It provides reporters new shortcuts to usable, usually reliable information, saving them and their news organizations time and money. It runs the risk of drowning reporters in deep seas of data, but it makes possible richer and more comprehensive and accurate reporting.

What needs to be done to support independent news reporting? We are not recommending a government bailout of newspapers, nor any of the various direct subsidies that governments give newspapers in many European countries, although those subsidies have not had a noticeably chilling effect on newspapers' willingness to print criticism of those governments. Nor are we recommending direct government financing or control of television networks or stations.

Most Americans have a deep distrust of direct government involvement or political influence in independent news reporting, a sentiment we share. But this should not preclude government support for news reporting any more than it has for the arts, the humanities, and sciences, all of which receive some government support.

There has been a minimum of government pressure in those fields, with a few notable exceptions. The National Endowment for the Arts came under fire in the 1990s, for example, for the controversial nature of some of the art it helped sponsor with federal funds. So any use of government money to help support news reporting would require mechanisms, besides the protections of the First Amendment, to insulate the resulting journalism as much as possible from pressure, interference, or censorship.

From its beginning, the U.S. government has enacted laws providing support for the news media, with varying consequences. In the year following enactment of the First Amendment, Congress passed the Post Office Act of 1792 that put the postal system on a permanent foundation and authorized a subsidy for newspapers sent through the mail, as many were at the time. Those early newspapers also could mail copies to one another free of charge, creating the first collaborative news reporting. This subsidy assisted the distribution of news across the growing country for many years. While the First Amendment forbade the federal government from abridging freedom of the press, the founders' commitment to broad circulation of public information produced policies that made a free press possible.

Nearly two centuries later, the Newspaper Preservation Act of 1970, in a specific exception to antitrust laws, allowed newspapers in the same city to form joint operating agreements to share revenue and costs in what proved to be a futile attempt to prevent single-newspaper monopolies in most cities. This intervention did not work as intended, and most joint operating agreements ended with just one of the newspapers surviving.

An antitrust exemption that would allow newspapers to act together to seek payment for the digital distribution of their news would not be any wiser or do much more to support independent reporting. Antitrust laws forbid industries from setting prices in concert, which we do not think is desirable or necessary for newspapers. Individually, newspapers are already contemplating various ways to charge for digital content, and they do not need an antitrust exemption to continue.

We are not advocating or discouraging specific ways for news organizations to seek payment for digital content. We believe the marketplace will determine whether any of the many experiments will ultimately be successful. And we believe that managers of news organizations are best positioned to shape and test responses to them. For example, newspapers should develop detailed information about their digital audience to sell more targeted, and higher-priced, advertising to accompany specific digital content, while protecting individual readers' privacy. They also should experiment with digital commerce that does not conflict with their news reporting, such as facilitating the purchase of books they review. To borrow a phrase from another digital news context, we see a long tail of possible revenue sources—payment for some kinds of unique digital content, online commerce, higher print subscription prices, even new print products—being added to diminished but still significant advertising revenues.

There is unlikely to be any single new economic model for supporting news reporting. Many newspapers can and will find ways to survive in print and online, with new combinations of reduced resources. But they will no longer produce the kinds of revenues or profits that had subsidized large reporting staffs, regardless of what new business models they evolve. The days of a kind of news media paternalism or patronage that produced journalism in the public interest, whether or not it contributed to the bottom line, are largely gone. American society must take some collective responsibility for supporting independent news reporting in this new environment—as society has, at much greater expense, for public needs like education, health care, scientific advancement, and cultural preservation—through varying combinations of philanthropy, subsidy, and government policy.

American society must take some collective responsibility for supporting independent news reporting in this new environment.

Our recommendations are intended to support independent, original, and credible news reporting, especially local and accountability reporting, across all media in communities throughout the United States. Rather than depending primarily on newspapers and their waning reporting resources, each sizeable American community should have a range of diverse sources of news reporting. They should include a variety and mix of commercial and nonprofit news organizations that can both compete and collaborate with one another. They should be adapting traditional journalistic forms to the multimedia, interactive, real-time capabilities of digital communication, sharing the reporting and distribution of news with citizens, bloggers, and aggregators.

To support diverse sources of independent news reporting, we specifically recommend:

1. The Internal Revenue Service or Congress should explicitly authorize any independent news organization substantially devoted to reporting on public affairs to be created as or converted into a nonprofit entity

or a low-profit Limited Liability Corporation serving the public interest, regardless of its mix of financial support, including commercial sponsorship and advertising. The IRS or Congress also should explicitly authorize program-related investments by philanthropic foundations in these hybrid news organizations—and in designated public service news reporting by for-profit news organizations.

Any of the startup news reporting entities are already tax-exempt nonprofits recognized by the IRS under section 501(c)(3) of the tax code. Some magazines with news content, including *Harper's* and *Mother Jones,* as well as public radio and television stations, also have been nonprofits for years. All are able to receive tax-deductible donations, along with foundation grants, advertising revenue, and other income, including revenue from for-profit subsidiaries. Their nonprofit status helps assure contributors and advertisers that they are primarily supporting news reporting rather than the maximization of profits. Tax deductibility is an added incentive for donors, and the nonprofit's tax exemption allows any excess income to be re-invested in resources for reporting.

However, neither the IRS nor Congress has made clear what kinds of news organizations qualify as nonprofits under section 501(c)(3), which specifies such charitable activities as the advancement of education, religion, science, civil rights, and amateur sports. News reporting is not one of the "exempt purposes" listed by the IRS, which has granted 501(c)(3) nonprofit recognition to startup news organizations individually by letter rather than categorically. News organizations cannot be certain whether they would qualify—or whether they would be able to keep their 501(c)(3) status, depending, for example, on how much advertising or other commercial income they earn or the extent to which they express political opinions.

The IRS has not made clear whether a certain amount of a nonprofit news organization's advertising revenue might be considered "unrelated business income" subject to tax or even might be regarded as an impediment to continued nonprofit status. And, while its regulations stipulate that a 501(c)(3) nonprofit "may not attempt to influence legislation as a substantial part of its activities and it may not participate in any campaign activity for or against political candidates," it is not clear whether that restricts political editorial opinion apart from the endorsement of candidates.

Congress should add news organizations substantially devoted to public affairs reporting to the list of specifically eligible nonprofits under section 501(c)(3), regardless of the amount of their advertising income. Or the IRS itself should rule that such news organizations are categorically eligible under the criteria already established by Congress. The IRS also should explicitly allow news nonprofits to express editorial opinions about legislation and politics without endorsing candidates or lobbying. The Obama administration, in which the president and some officials have expressed their openness to ways to help preserve public interest news reporting, should weigh in on these policy decisions.

A possible alternative for news organizations is a Low-profit Limited Liability Corporation, known as an L3C, a hybrid legal entity with both for-profit and nonprofit investments to carry out socially useful purposes. Both private investors and foundations could invest in an L3C, with private investors able to realize a limited profit. A small but growing number of states, beginning with Vermont in 2008, have passed laws enabling the creation of L3Cs to make it more economically feasible to set up businesses for charitable or education purposes that might have difficulty attracting sufficient capital as either commercial firms or nonprofits. Illinois, Michigan, Wyoming, and North Dakota also have recently enacted L3C laws.

Each of the state laws was written to enable foundations to make "program-related investments" in the new hybrid organizations. The IRS created the concept of program-related investments in the 1960s to enable foundations to make socially useful grants to for-profit ventures. But foundations have been hesitant to make such grants because they are not certain which ones the IRS would allow. Congress or the IRS should provide a process by which a qualifying journalistic organization seeking a program-related investment from a foundation could be assured that it would qualify.

Nonprofit news organizations should, as some already have, individually and collectively through collaboration, develop professional fundraising capabilities like those of advertising departments for commercial news organizations. They also should develop other sources of revenue, including advertising, partnerships, and innovative marketing of their reporting to other news media and news consumers.

2. Philanthropists, and national foundations, and community foundations should substantially increase their support for news organizations that have demonstrated a substantial commitment to public affairs and accountability reporting.

Philanthropically supported institutions are central to American society. Philanthropy has been essential for educational, research, cultural, and religious institutions, health and social services, parks and the preservation of nature, and much more. With the exception of public radio and television, philanthropy has played a very small role in supporting news reporting, because most of it had been subsidized by advertising.

Led by the Knight Foundation and individual donors like Buzz Woolley and Herbert and Marion Sandler, foundations and philanthropists have begun to respond to the breakdown of that economic model by funding the launch of nonprofit news startups and individual reporting projects, as discussed earlier. But foundations are not yet providing much money to sustain those startups or to underwrite all of their journalism rather than only their reporting on subjects of special interest to each foundation or donor.

Foundations should consider news reporting of public affairs to be a continuous public good rather than a series of specific projects under their control or a way of generating interest and action around causes and issues of special interest to them. They should ensure that there is an impermeable wall between each foundation's interests and the news reporting it supports, and they should make their support of accountability journalism a much higher priority than it has been for all but a few like the Knight Foundation.

These steps would represent major shifts in the missions of most national foundations. Their model of grant-making has relied on documenting specific "outcomes," explained Eric Newton of the Knight Foundation, and it is not easy to measure the impact of news reporting. "News is not like electricity," Newton said. "When there's a news blackout, you don't know what you're not getting." But what communities are now missing in news reporting is becoming increasingly apparent as newspaper and television station newsrooms empty out.

It is time for other national foundations to join with Knight in a concerted effort to preserve public affairs news reporting, and because of the importance of local news, the nation's more than 700 community foundations should take the lead in supporting news reporting in their own cities and towns. Community foundations, which manage collections of donor-advised local philanthropic funds, have large assets and make large gifts. Donations from the twenty-five largest community foundations alone in 2007 totaled $2.4 billion. If community foundations were to allocate just 1 percent of their giving to local news reporting, it would roughly equal all the money that all foundations have spent annually to support news reporting in recent years.

Some community foundations have taken the first steps in this direction. Several donor-advised funds of the Greater St. Louis Community Foundation are among donors to the St. Louis Beacon. The San Diego Foundation has been a key supporter of the Voice of San Diego. The Minneapolis Foundation received a Knight grant to encourage its donors to help MinnPost pay for reporting on local subjects like education and poverty, in which the foundation has a longstanding interest and record of grant-giving.

Community foundations also should consider funding public affairs and accountability reporting not only by nonprofits but also by local commercial newspapers that no longer have the resources to fund all of it themselves. For example, James Hamilton, director of Duke University's DeWitt Wallace Center for Media and Democracy has proposed that local foundations finance specific accountability reporting projects, individual reporters, or the coverage of some subjects at the Raleigh *News & Observer*. That would not be such a big step beyond the journalism produced by nonprofits like ProPublica or the Center for Investigative Reporting that many commercial news media are already publishing and broadcasting.

3. Public radio and television should be substantially reoriented to provide significant local news reporting in every community served by public stations and their websites. This requires urgent action by and reform of the Corporation for Public Broadcasting, increased congressional funding and support for public media news reporting, and changes in mission and leadership for many public stations across the country.

The failure of much of the public broadcasting system to provide significant local news reporting reflects longstanding neglect of this responsibility by the majority of public radio and televisions stations, the Corporation for Public Broadcasting, and Congress. The approximately $400 million that Congress currently appropriates for the CPB each year is far less per capita than public broadcasting support in countries with comparable economies—roughly $1.35 per capita for the United States, compared to about $25 in Canada, Australia, and Germany, nearly $60 in Japan, $80 in Britain, and more than $100 in Denmark and Finland. The lion's share of the financial support for public radio and television in the United States comes from listener and viewer donations, corporate sponsorships, foundation grants, and philanthropic gifts.

It is not just a question of money, but how it is spent. Most of the money that the CPB and private donors and sponsors provide public broadcasting is spent on broadcast facilities, independent television production companies, and programming to attract audiences during fund-raising drives. In many metropolitan areas, the money supports more stations and signals than are necessary to reach everyone in the community.

At the same time, outside of a relatively few regional public radio station groups, very little money is spent on local news coverage by individual public radio and television stations. The CPB itself, in its new Public Radio Audience Task Force Report, acknowledged that "claiming a significantly larger role in American journalism requires a much more robust newsgathering capacity—more 'feet on the street' with notebooks, recorders, cameras, and more editors and producers to shape their work" for broadcast and digital distribution by public radio stations. "The distance between current reality and the role we imagine—and that others urge upon public radio—is large," the report concluded. And that distance is immense for the vast majority of public television stations that do no local news reporting at all.

The CPB should declare that local news reporting is a top priority for public broadcasting and change its allocation of resources accordingly. Local news reporting is an essential part of the public education function that American public radio and television have been charged with fulfilling since their inception.

The CPB should require a minimum amount of local news reporting by every public radio and television station receiving CPB money, and require stations to report publicly to the CPB on their progress in reaching specified goals. The CPB should increase and speed up its direct funding for experiments in more robust and creative local news coverage by public stations both on the air and on their websites. The CPB should also aggressively encourage and reward collaborations by public stations with other local nonprofit and university news organizations.

National leaders of public radio and television who have been meeting privately to discuss news reporting should bring their deliberations into the open, reduce wasteful rivalries among local public stations, regional and national public media, and production entities, and launch concerted initiatives to increase local news coverage. The CPB should encourage changes in the leadership of public stations that are not capable of reorienting their missions.

Congress should back these reforms. In its next reauthorization of the CPB and appropriation of its budget, Congress should change its name to the Corporation for Public Media, support its efforts to move public radio and television into the digital age, specify public media's local news reporting mission, and significantly increase its appropriation. Congress should also reform the governance of the reformed corporation by broadening the membership of its board with appointments by such nonpolitical sources as the Librarian of Congress or national media organizations. Ideological issues that have surfaced over publicly supported arts, cultural activities, or national news coverage should not affect decisions about significantly improving local news reporting by public media.

4. Universities, both public and private, should become ongoing sources of local, state, specialized subject, and accountability news reporting as part of their educational missions. They should operate their own news organizations, host platforms for other nonprofit news and investigative reporting organizations, provide faculty positions for active individual journalists, and be laboratories for digital innovation in the gathering and sharing of news and information.

In addition to educating and training journalists, colleges and universities should be centers of professional news reporting, as they are for the practice and advancement of medicine and law, scientific and social research, business development, engineering, education, and agriculture. As discussed earlier, a number of campuses have already started or become partners in local news services, websites and investigative reporting projects, in which professional journalists, faculty members and students collaborate on news reporting. It is time for those and other colleges and universities to take the next step and create full-fledged news organizations.

Journalists on their faculties should engage in news reporting and editing, as well as teach these skills and perform research, just as members of other professional school faculties do. The most proficient student journalists should advance after graduation to paid residencies and internships, joining fully experienced journalists on year-round staffs of university-based, independently edited local news services, websites, and investigative reporting projects.

As in many professional fields, integrating such practical work into an academic setting can be challenging. Although much basic news reporting is routine, enterprise and accountability journalism, which by definition bring new information to light, can grow into society-changing work not so dissimilar from academic research that makes original contributions to knowledge in history and the social sciences. The capacity of the best journalists to combine original investigation with writing and other communications skills can enhance the teaching and research missions of universities.

Funding for university news organizations should come from earmarked donations and endowments, collaborations with other local news organizations, advertising, and other sources. Facilities, overhead, and fund-raising assistance should be provided by the colleges and universities, as is the case for other university-based models of professional practice. Reporting on specialized subjects in which university researchers can offer

relevant expertise in such fields as the arts, business, politics, science, and health could be assisted by faculty and students in those disciplines, funded in part by research grants, so long as independent news judgment is not compromised.

University news organizations should increase their collaboration with other local news nonprofits, including local public radio and television stations, many of which are owned by colleges and universities themselves and housed on their campuses. They also should collaborate with local commercial news media, providing them with news coverage and reporting interns, as some journalism schools and their news services do now. They should provide assistance for hyperlocal community news sites and blogs.

Universities should incubate innovations in news reporting and dissemination for the digital era. They could earn money for this from news media clients, as the Walter Cronkite School at Arizona State University does for research and development work for Gannett. Universities are among the nation's largest nonprofit institutions, and they should play significant roles in the reconstruction of American journalism.

5. A national Fund for Local News should be created with money the Federal Communications Commission now collects from or could impose on telecom users, television and radio broadcast licensees, or Internet service providers and which would be administered in open competition through state Local News Fund Councils.

The federal government already provides assistance to the arts, humanities, and sciences through independent agencies that include the National Endowment for the Arts, the National Endowment for the Humanities, the National Science Foundation, and the National Institutes of Health. The arts and humanities endowments each have budgets under $200 million. The National Science Foundation, with a budget of $6 billion, gives out about 10,000 grants a year. The National Institutes of Health has a budget of $28 billion and gives 50,000 grants. In these and other ways, the federal government gives significant support to individuals and organizations whose work creates new knowledge that contributes to the public good.

The Federal Communications Commission uses money from a surcharge on telephone bills—currently more than $7 billion a year—to underwrite telecom service for rural areas and the multimedia wiring of schools and libraries, among other things. In this way, the FCC supports the public circulation of information in places the market has failed to serve. Local news reporting, whose market model has faltered, is in need of similar support.

The FCC should direct some of the money from the telephone bill surcharge—or from fees paid by radio and television licensees, or proceeds from auctions of telecommunications spectrum, or new fees imposed on Internet service providers— to finance a Fund for Local News that would make grants for advances in local news reporting and innovative ways to support it. Commercial broadcasters who no longer cover local news or do not otherwise satisfy unenforced public-service requirements could also pay into such a fund instead.

In the stimulus bill passed in early 2009, Congress required the FCC to produce by February 17, 2010, a strategic plan for universal broadband access that specifies its national purposes. One of those purposes should be the gathering and dissemination of local news in every community, and the plan should include roles for the FCC and the federal government in achieving it.

The Fund for Local News would make grants through state Local News Fund Councils to news organizations—nonprofit and commercial, new media and old—that propose worthy initiatives in local news reporting. They would fund categories and methods of reporting and ways to support them, rather than individual stories or reporting projects, for durations of several years or more, with periodic progress reviews.

Local News Fund Councils would operate in ways similar to the way state Humanities Councils have since the 1970s, when they emerged as affiliates of the National Endowment for the Humanities. Organized as 501(c)(3) nonprofits, they have volunteer boards of academics, other figures in the humanities, and, in some places, gubernatorial appointees, all serving limited terms. Local News Fund Council boards should be comprised of journalists, educators, and community leaders representing a wide range of viewpoints and backgrounds.

Grants should be awarded in a transparent, public competition. The criteria for grants should be journalistic quality, local relevance, innovation in news reporting, and the capacity of the news organization, small or large, to carry out the reporting. A Fund for Local News national board of review should monitor the state councils and the quality of news their grants produced, all of which should be available on a public Fund for Local News website.

We understand the complexity of establishing a workable grant selection system and the need for strict safeguards to shield news organizations from pressure or coercion from state councils or anyone in government. As stated earlier, we recognize that political pressure has played a role at times in the history of the arts and humanities endowments and in public broadcasting. But these organizations have weathered those storms, and funding for the sciences and social sciences has generally been free of political pressure. With appropriate safeguards, a Fund for Local News would play a significant role in the reconstruction of American journalism.

6. More should be done—by journalists, nonprofit organizations and governments—to increase the accessibility and usefulness of public information collected by federal, state, and local governments, to facilitate the gathering and dissemination of public information by citizens, and to expand public recognition of the many sources of relevant reporting.

With the Internet, the compilation of—and access to—public information, such as government databases, is far easier than ever before. Yet much of this information is not easily available, and the already useable information is not being fully exploited by journalists. Optimal exploitation of these information sources is central to the mission of journalism, as it is to the practice of democratic governance. Governments, nongovernmental organizations, and news organizations should accelerate their efforts to make public information more accessible and to use it for news reporting.

With the Obama administration taking the lead, governments should fulfill "open government" promises by rapidly making more information available without Freedom of Information Act requests. News organizations should work with government agencies to use more of this information in their reporting. The federal government has some 24,000 websites, a massive bounty of information that should be made more accessible by opening closed archives, digitizing what is not yet available online, and improving its organization and display so everyone can use it easily.

News organizations should also move more quickly and creatively to involve their audiences and other citizens in the gathering and analysis of news and information, as Josh Marshall has done with readers of his TPM blogs, Minnesota Public Radio has done with its Public Insight Network of radio listeners, and ProPublica's Amanda Michel is doing with her citizen reporters. Local news organizations should collaborate with community news startups that utilize citizen reporting, as *The Seattle Times* has committed to do with neighborhood blogs. University scholars should archive and analyze these experiments and produce guidelines for "best practices."

Involving thousands of citizens in the collection and distribution of public information began long before computers and the Internet. For over a century, the Audubon Society has relied on thousands of local volunteers for a national bird count that might be termed pro-am scientific research. This is similar to the reporting that volunteers all over the world do for Human Rights Watch, or the information-gathering that health workers do for the Centers for Disease Control and Prevention. The original gathering and reporting of information also includes expert investigations like those of the inspectors general in federal agencies. All of this work amounts to "adjunct journalism"—public information gathering, analysis, and reporting that is adjunct to the news reporting journalists do and available for them to use. It should be fully integrated into what journalists, scholars, and the public recognize as reporting in the public interest.

Where Do We Go from Here?

What is bound to be a chaotic reconstruction of American journalism is full of both perils and opportunities for news reporting, especially in local communities. The perils are obvious. The restructuring of newspapers, which remain central to the future of local news reporting, is an uphill battle. Emerging local news organizations are still small and fragile, requiring considerable assistance—as we have recommended—to survive to compete and collaborate with newspapers. And much of public media must drastically change its culture to become a significant source of local news reporting.

Yet we believe we have seen abundant opportunity in the future of journalism. At many of the news organizations we visited, new and old, we have seen the beginnings of a genuine reconstruction of what journalism can and should be. We have seen struggling newspapers embrace digital change and start to collaborate with other papers, nonprofit news organizations, universities, bloggers, and their own readers. We have seen energetic local reporting startups, where enthusiasm about new forms of journalism is contagious, exemplified by Voice of San Diego's Scott Lewis when he says, "I am living a dream." We have seen pioneering public radio news operations that could be emulated by the rest of public media. We have seen forward-leaning journalism schools where faculty and student journalists report news themselves and invent new ways to do it. We have seen bloggers become influential journalists, and Internet innovators develop ways to harvest public information, such as the linguistics doctoral student who created the GovTrack .us Congressional voting database. We have seen the first foundations and philanthropists step forward to invest in the future of news, and we have seen citizens help to report the news and support new nonprofit news ventures. We have seen into a future of more diverse news organizations and more diverse support for their reporting.

We have seen into a future of more diverse news organizations and more diverse support for their reporting. It is all within reach.

All of this is within reach. Now, we want to see more leaders emerge in journalism, government, philanthropy, higher education, and the rest of society to seize this moment of challenging changes and new beginnings to ensure the future of independent news reporting.

Critical Thinking

1. What is *accountability journalism?* Do you agree that it is "as vital to the functioning of communities as clean air, safe streets, good schools, and public health"?

2. Summarize the writers' six recommendations for supporting diverse sources of independent news reporting. All of them assume sources of non-commercial financial support, most of them governmental. What are pros and cons of each?

LEONARD DOWNIE JR. is vice president at large and former executive editor of *The Washington Post* and Weil Family Professor of Journalism at Arizona State University's Walter Cronkite School of Journalism and Mass Communication. MICHAEL SCHUDSON is a professor of communication at Columbia University's Graduate School of Journalism. Additional research was provided by Christopher W. Anderson, an assistant professor of communications at the College of Staten Island.

This version of The Reconstruction of American Journalism is drawn from a longer report commissioned by Columbia's Graduate School of Journalism and its dean, Nicholas Lemann. The full version is available in pdf format at columbiajournalismreport.org. The school thanks the Charles H. Revson Foundation for its support of this project, as well as the Surdna Foundation and Barbara G. Fleishman.

Retreating from the World

In the face of heightened globalization and with the United States engaged in two wars, many mainstream news organizations have turned their backs on foreign news. Newspapers and television networks alike provide much less of it. Many outlets have shuttered overseas bureaus. But a handful of promising startups offer some hope for the future.

JODI ENDA

During more than two decades at the Chicago Tribune, Colin McMahon reported from bureaus in Mexico City, Moscow, Baghdad and Buenos Aires. He served as foreign editor, directing a cadre of correspondents as they covered the invasion of Iraq, the war in Afghanistan, the Palestinian uprising. He was dispatched to Jerusalem for six months. It was a heady life of globe-trotting that not only allowed him to be a witness to history, but to bring stories from the far corners of the globe home to readers in America's third-largest city readers who live in Chicago's distinctively ethnic neighborhoods, who often have intensely close ties to far-flung places and who might not get such a rich diet of news—breaking or enterprise—were it not for Colin McMahon.

Now McMahon goes by the title of "national content editor." Once again he oversees the Tribune's foreign news operation. This time, however, McMahon does not direct a staff of foreign correspondents.

The paper has none.

The Chicago Tribune, like many other newspapers, eliminated its storied foreign bureaus during the last decade's repeated rounds of belt tightening. Instead of overseeing reporters in the field and helping to shape articles that will form a unique international report, McMahon runs a desk that receives foreign and national stories from the Tribune's largest sister paper, the Los Angeles Times. His staff then picks some of those stories, edits them, trims them if need be and places them alongside wire service reports to create nation/world "modules" for the Chicago Tribune and six other Tribune Co. papers.

"We take the content and we edit it here and add info-boxes, graphics and other material," McMahon explains. "So we are the central editing and design house for seven Tribune Company newspapers. We send it fully designed. They drop it in."

Each day, McMahon feeds three to five foreign stories in prefab modules to the Tribune, the Baltimore Sun, the Orlando Sentinel and Fort Lauderdale's Sun-Sentinel—all of which used to have foreign bureaus—as well as the Hartford Courant, the Morning Call in Allentown, Pennsylvania, and the Daily Press in Newport News, Virginia. Rarely do any of those stories land on a front page. That would complicate the module. If he has big news, McMahon creates a refer, a potentially sizable box that summarizes the story on page one and directs interested readers to the appropriate page inside.

Modules. Content editor. Central editing and design house. Intentionally or not, Tribune Co. has hit upon the perfect words to describe a modern, industrialized, assembly line approach to foreign (and sometimes national) news. And while the chain's particular method of providing identical pages for a variety of papers might not be the national norm, its pared-down vision of foreign reporting is.

Eighteen newspapers and two chains have shuttered every one of their overseas bureaus in the dozen years since AJR first surveyed foreign coverage for the Project on the State of the American Newspaper (see "Goodbye, World," November 1998). All but two of them eliminated their last bureau sometime after 2003, the year the United States invaded Iraq and the last time AJR conducted the survey. Many other papers and chains reduced their coterie of foreign correspondents, meticulously choosing which bureaus to close. What's more, an untold number of regional and local papers have dramatically decreased the amount of foreign news they publish. Television networks, meanwhile, slashed the time they devote to foreign news and narrowed their focus largely to war zones.

Remarkably, NPR is the only mainstream media organization that serves up a heartier foreign report, with more bureaus and correspondents than in the past, to a chiefly American-based audience, according to the survey. While Bloomberg News also has opened more foreign bureaus, a majority of the terminals where their stories appear are overseas. The "big four" national newspapers—the Wall Street Journal, New York Times, Washington Post and Los Angeles Times—all continue to have vibrant foreign reports, though each has closed some foreign bureaus in recent years.

As the mainstream media steadily retrench, a mix of start-ups has stepped in to help fill the news vacuum. With fellowships, grants and freelance contracts, new entries into the foreign-news business are providing alternatives for journalists intent on reporting from overseas, for editors who need to augment their reports and for readers looking to supplement the now-limited offerings of newspapers and television stations.

There is no pretending they can completely make up for the formerly dynamic coverage in many national and regional outlets.

In closing all their outposts abroad, a number of newspapers—most notably the Boston Globe, Newsday, the Philadelphia Inquirer and some Tribune Co. papers—put an end to long, much heralded traditions of delivering foreign news in their own way to their own readers, of covering patches of the globe that their audiences had a particular, sometimes singular, interest in. They covered breaking news and big stories, to be sure. But, perhaps more often, correspondents from these papers were ahead of the news or off it completely, telling stories about interesting people, places and customs that you just couldn't read anywhere else.

They had passports. They wandered. And they took their readers with them.

Many editors say that kind of reporting was a luxury. Now, with some noteworthy exceptions, it is a relic, gone the way of paper tape and the pica pole. Unlike those artifacts of days past, foreign bureaus were not replaced by new technology. They were not replaced at all.

Colin McMahon and his counterparts across the country have learned to make do. Rarely do they contend they are doing more with less, the can-do mantra of the early years of budget cuts. They merely do the best they can.

McMahon is one of the lucky ones. He has his pick of stories produced by L.A. Times foreign correspondents and relies less on wire services than his counterparts at many midsize papers. He might not have his own staff of reporters, but most readers are unlikely to know the difference. It could be worse.

"I'm happy with a lot of the things that we do," McMahon says. "I'm happy with this approach. It's easy for the reader and it makes a lot of sense for the new reality."

"I'm not happy with the new reality, though. I think this is the best solution, but I wish it were 2004 again, when I was a foreign correspondent. I don't think there's anybody at this newspaper, including the editor, who wouldn't want 13 foreign correspondents."

Jon Sawyer was less accepting of the "new reality."
Sawyer had long been the Washington bureau chief for the St. Louis Post-Dispatch, but he made his name reporting and writing major projects from distant shores. By his count, he traveled to five dozen countries, many more than once and for weeks at a time, during three decades as a newspaper reporter.

"There were a number of big, regional papers that were determined to have their own voice and report on global issues," Sawyer recalls now. "That was changing, and changing quite rapidly, in the early 2000s."

The swift decline and, in some cases, wholesale disappearance of original foreign reporting at some of the nation's premier papers created a yawning journalistic void. Increasingly, big-city newspapers relied solely on wire services to provide foreign news. Space tightened again and again. Local, local, local became louder, louder, louder. No longer did papers have the space to run fascinating yarns about how people lived in remote, little-known villages thousands of miles away. They barely had the staff necessary to cover their own backyards. Neither did they have the resources to develop foreign stories that were not only interesting but also important—stories that might explain a culture or a country in ways that either foretold or underscored key global developments in places like Pakistan, China or Congo.

So when the Pulitzer family sold the Post-Dispatch and 13 other newspapers to Lee Enterprises in 2005 (see "Lee *Who?*" June/July 2005), Sawyer—fresh from reporting in the Middle East—decided to chart a new course. He asked Emily Rauh Pulitzer, the wealthy widow of newspaper magnate Joseph Pulitzer Jr., for seed money to allow him to build a program that would support the kind of international stories the Post-Dispatch and other papers seldom would produce.

The idea, Sawyer says, was to help finance reporters—young Jon Sawyers, if you will—who would go overseas for weeks at a time and produce in-depth projects for regional newspapers and broadcast outlets. His hope, Sawyer says, was that once reporters produced one or two such stories with help from outside, they would be able to make the case that their employers should pay for future projects themselves. In that way, the money would have a ripple effect.

Enter the nonprofit Pulitzer Center on Crisis Reporting (see "Funding for Foreign Forays," February/March 2008).

Sawyer is one of a handful of journalists trying to step into the foreign news breach with inventive and varied upstarts. John Schidlovsky is another. He founded the nonprofit International Reporting Project to finance foreign reporting in 1998—when he began to witness what then was a gradual decline in international coverage—but has expanded and shifted the center's course to meet the changing needs of journalists. A newer addition to the mix is Philip Balboni, who in January 2009 launched GlobalPost, a for-profit Internet venture that pays freelance reporters based overseas for regular submissions to its round-the-clock news report. (See "Foreign Affairs," April/May 2008.)

None of these endeavors replicates the old model of hiring reporters, paying them a living wage, providing them benefits sending them and their families overseas with generous expense accounts and housing allowances and interpreters and "fixers," and dedicating prime real estate in the paper or on nightly newscasts to their reports. Whether those days are over or simply on hiatus at most media outlets is anyone's guess. The new models—for-profit and non—require journalists to be more resourceful and nimble to make a (frequently modest) living, patching together freelance gigs and travel grants that allow them to report from overseas.

The organizations founded by Sawyer, Schidlovsky and Balboni have become the beneficiaries of the great migration of reporters from daily newspapers. Each of their organizations has been inundated with entreaties from foreign correspondents who have left the news organizations that they feel abandoned them or, perhaps more to the point, their readers. "These are really talented people who have many years of working for major newspapers behind them," says Schidlovsky. "They could still be working for the Los Angeles Times, the Chicago Tribune, the Philadelphia Inquirer, if those papers didn't downsize."

Even some reporters who remain at papers that have a foreign presence, including the New York Times and Washington Post, occasionally seek outside funding for specific projects that their papers wouldn't otherwise undertake, say Schidlovsky and Sawyer. Both of their organizations, which underwrite individual projects, have partnered with reporters from large papers to produce stories with foreign datelines. The Washington, D.C.-based International Reporting Project has worked with journalists from "almost every organization in the country," says Schidlovsky, himself a former foreign correspondent for the Baltimore Sun.

Both the IRP and the Pulitzer Center prefer to finance journalists working on stories that are unlikely to be reported elsewhere, often in developing and under-covered parts of the world. The need is great. Schidlovsky says he receives 300 applications for about 40 grants a year. Since he founded it a dozen years ago, he says, the program has sent 174 reporters overseas to a total of 92 countries, for five weeks at a time, and given them another four weeks to work on their projects in Washington. It has sent 156 senior editors to foreign countries for two weeks of intensive learning.

When he started the IRP, Schidlovsky intended to provide lengthy training—and kind of a mini-master's degree—to reporters who were employed by newspapers and hoped to become traditional foreign correspondents. But as one paper after another closed foreign bureaus, he realized he needed not only to teach reporters how to work overseas, but to get them there—fast. Few applicants to his program could afford to spend an entire semester learning about international reporting. They had to just do it.

Phil Balboni has a wholly different approach. He doesn't send journalists overseas; instead, he pays reporters who have traveled abroad on their own dimes to write for him. The founder and past president of New England Cable News (see Broadcast Views, October 2002), Balboni was dissatisfied with foreign news coverage long before the latest cutbacks. As many as four decades ago and throughout what most people regard as the zenith of international news, he judged the range and variety of stories as "modest, at best, and insufficient." In 2006 and 2007, he wrote a business plan for an Internet-based foreign news service that he hoped would make a profit and meet what by then had become a gaping need. Ultimately, Balboni raised $10 million from wealthy investors, including Ben Taylor, former publisher of the Boston Globe.

Nearly two years ago, Balboni and Executive Editor Charles Sennott—a former foreign correspondent for the Globe—launched GlobalPost. In October of this year, the site had 1,278,000 unique visitors, Balboni says.

GlobalPost produces a wide-ranging daily foreign report of relatively short stories written each month by 100 to 120 reporters who have planted themselves around the globe and support themselves with freelance gigs. None of the writers will get rich working for the Boston-based enterprise, which pays them $250 for stories of 600 to 800 words. The 50 or 60 reporters who are on contract to write at least one story a week also receive shares of stock in the privately owned company. Larger projects and video reports command higher prices, Balboni says. Despite the low pay, he says, there are more journalists who want to write for the website than it can accommodate.

"We can present a fantastic smorgasbord of reporting that is interesting and important but that is not on the agenda of AP," says Philip Balboni, founder of the online foreign news startup GlobalPost.

"Most of the people writing for us are seasoned journalists," Balboni says, reaffirming Schidlovsky's experience. "They are committed to being in a place for a substantial period of time."

Unlike the nonprofit outfits, GlobalPost earns most of its money through advertising. It also syndicates its content to newspapers, websites, radio stations and television networks in the United States and abroad, Balboni says. A third source of revenue is membership, which costs $2.95 a month or $29.95 a year. Though most parts of globalpost.com can be accessed at no cost, the nearly 600 readers who have signed up to be members are privy to additional content. They also get to vote, once a week, on a story they'd like to read. The top vote-getter then is ordered up from a GlobalPost reporter.

Balboni views his as an all-purpose site, with news and features that touch on most of the big stories going on in the world. He boasts that he has readers not only in the United States, but in almost every country in the world.

Says Balboni, "We can present a fantastic smorgasbord of reporting that is interesting and important but that is not on the agenda of AP."

Jon Sawyer is not enamored of the smorgasbord approach. Smorgasbords, after all, are speedy, inexpensive and, well, their fare generally cools quickly.

Shrinking Foreign Coverage

To get a sense of the amount of foreign news in United States newspapers, AJR selected two papers from each of the four Census-designated regions of the country: the Northeast, Midwest, South and West. We then randomly selected seven dates between January and June, making sure to include each day of the week. Using microfilm and hard copies, we looked through the entire edition of each newspaper and counted the number of foreign stones. Foreign stories included hard news, features, editorials, columns and, generally, travel stories. We included stories with domestic bylines if they focused on foreign events or issues.

The papers we chose were the Philadelphia Inquirer, Providence Journal, St. Louis Post-Dispatch, Cincinnati Enquirer, Tampa Tribune, Dallas Morning News, Fresno Bee and Portland's Oregonian.

The findings? A drastic decline in the amount of foreign news. Over the past quarter-century, foreign news in the dailies examined by AJR fell by 53 percent, with the largest drop coming in the St. Louis Post-Dispatch. That paper printed three-fourths fewer foreign stories in 2010 than in 1985. The Dallas Morning News had the smallest drop in foreign stories among the eight, printing one-fifth fewer.

The percentage of staff-produced foreign stories in the eight papers also fell sharply, from 15 percent in 1985 to 4 percent in 2010.

When newspapers printed foreign news in 1985, they were more likely to go longer, with stories more than 400 words out-numbering shorter pieces by nearly two to one. And although this year's foreign stories were still more likely to be longer, the ratio narrowed.

Foreign news never played a starring role on the front page of these dailies. In 1985, 9 percent of foreign stories appeared on page 1, compared with only 6 percent in 2010.

Research for this chart was conducted by Priya Kumar.

1985	Total Stories	Editorials and Op/Eds	Less than 400 Words	More than 400 Words	Staff-written	Other Sources	Page 1	Notes
Philadelphia Inquirer	101	12	30	71	26	75	15	
Providence Journal	75	16	26	49	13	63	7	*One story listed staff and wire services
St. Louis Post-Dispatch	92	20	47	45	15	76	8	*One story had no byline, so unsure of source
Cincinnati Enquirer	57	12	27	30	7	51	5	*One story listed staff and wire services
Dallas Morning News	75	11	34	41	18	57	6	
Tampa Tribune	96	18	27	69	4	93	8	*One story listed staff and wire services
The Oregonian	115	11	27	88	11	104	8	
Fresno Bee	78	13	36	42	8	70	6	
TOTAL	689	113	254	435	102	589	63	
2010								
Philadelphia Inquirer	62	4	16	46	2	60	6	
Providence Journal	38	8	16	22	2	36	0	
St. Louis Post-Dispatch	24	5	6	18	3	21	4	
Cincinnati Enquirer	33	3	18	15	0	33	0	
Dallas Morning News	59	0	31	28	4	55	6	
Tampa Tribune	33	2	25	8	1	32	1	
The Oregonian	41	2	10	31	2	39	1	
Fresno Bee	31	1	13	18	0	31	1	
TOTAL	321	25	135	186	14	307	19	

Tall and graying, Sawyer sits with his back to a window six floors above Massachusetts Avenue in Washington's chic Dupont Circle neighborhood. He is surrounded by mementos of his years on the road, photos and knickknacks from the glory days of late 20th century American journalism. Yet he is not living in the past, pining for what he (and many others) refer to as "the golden era." His computer screen is evidence of his adroit transition to the 21st century.

Sawyer adjusts his mouse and clicks to proudly display project after project financed by the Pulitzer Center on Crisis Reporting, which in nearly five years has amassed an annual budget upward of $1.7 million. The center produces 50 to 60 projects a year, far fewer than GlobalPost. That's OK with Sawyer. His are stories that dig deeply into the kind of issues generally ignored by the mainstream media: a child bride's struggles in Sudan, birth control in rural India, Maoist insurgents in Nepal, disappearing wetlands in China. "We're not interested in covering things that are going to get covered" by other outlets, Sawyer says.

It's an impressive display. Yet the center didn't work out the way Sawyer planned. "Unfortunately, the pace of retreat from media outlets was astounding," he says. "When I started the Pulitzer Center, the Post-Dispatch, the Inquirer, the big regional papers were what I thought would be my big platform. For the most part I was wrong. They no longer have foreign editors. There's no budget for freelancers. There's no space in the papers."

Like Schidlovsky at the IRP, Sawyer had to alter his approach. Rather than partner with regional papers, he works more often with more nationally focused outlets, including the Washington Post, The Atlantic, PBS' "NewsHour." He offers travel grants directly to journalists and works with them to place their stories. The grants typically run from $3,000 to $10,000 but are sometimes substantially larger. More than three-quarters of the reporters he finances are freelancers, Sawyer says.

That "new reality"—most of the journalists he backs don't have regular paychecks—has prompted Sawyer to find ways to give them small stipends and to help them market their work. The reporters come up with ideas and submit brief proposals that contain budget estimates, placement plans and descriptions about the long-term value of each project. That last point is critical: Sawyer wants stories that have a shelf life.

The Pulitzer Center also expects reporters to blog from the field while working on their projects. The blogs keep the website fresh and also give the center's staff ammunition to place upcoming projects in traditional media outlets. That, after all, is the goal. Sawyer wants projects that will be published and reproduced far beyond the center's website. So he and his full-time staff of nine (plus four interns) peddle the stories, primarily to newspapers and television outlets, which typically pay the reporters small amounts for their work.

The center expands its reach with an educational component, something Sawyer describes as part marketing, part journalism, part consciousness raising in the sense that it enhances students' awareness of and interest in critical global issues. The Global Gateway program sends journalists to classrooms across the country to discuss their Pulitzer Center projects with middle school, high school and university students. In some cases, the journalists mentor students who are working on video projects of their own. In others, they help teachers draw links between global and local issues. The goal is to build a larger audience for international news, now and for the future, and to provide the reporters with additional income in the form of honoraria.

The Pulitzer Center, born five years ago out of one man's desire to salvage the kind of international reporting that his newspaper used to pursue, has financed the projects of 180 journalists and worked to place them in outlets all over the country. It is but one response to the "new reality," one way to try to bridge the foreign news gap.

"Things are lost," Sawyer says, "and things are gained."

A common refrain among editors whose papers have cut foreign reporting is that not only is it outrageously expensive, it can—thanks largely to the Internet—be found elsewhere. In other words, not all that much is lost.

"There are still a lot of places where you can read that kind of coverage," says Arnie Robbins, editor of the St. Louis Post-Dispatch, whose paper seldom sends reporters overseas anymore—just as Sawyer foresaw. "You can read it all online. So even though there are fewer voices out there, it's more accessible."

But in the next breath, Robbins points to one of the flaws in that line of thinking: "Many editors would say—*I* would say—we're concerned about the lack of voices in foreign coverage. When you have fewer voices, you're concerned not about the accuracy, but the context."

It's true that anyone eager to read anything about nearly anyplace in the world can do so online. If your local paper doesn't carry enough foreign news to satisfy you, you can read the New York Times, either in the flesh or on the Web. Or the Washington Post, or the Los Angeles Times or the Wall Street Journal or one of several specialized publications, such as Foreign Policy. You can peruse globalpost.com or pulitzer-center.org or internationalreportingproject.org. You can go to the websites of countless international policy foundations and nonprofits, international institutes and university programs and read what their experts are up to. And you can read oh-so-many foreign newspapers, conveniently translated into English by high-tech wizardry. Foreign news really does abound.

If you look for it.

But how many people do that?

W. Joseph Campbell, a former foreign correspondent who teaches international journalism and media at American University, says many people don't go the extra length to seek out foreign news if it's not in front of them, either on the front page of their newspaper or on the nightly TV newscast. They take the easy route; they go "news-less."

"If you really are enthralled by, fascinated by, a particular topic internationally, it's easier than ever to find good, solid reporting," Campbell says. However, he continues, "You're more likely to find a serendipitous story, one you weren't looking for but find compelling, in a newspaper than online."

In other words, people who are especially engaged by another country or steeped in an international issue can and will find lots of stuff about it if they look online. The casual newspaper reader or television viewer, on the other hand, the person who doesn't Google Phnom Penh or Nairobi or nuclear nonproliferation, is less likely to trip across a story that catches his or her eye, less likely than before to accidentally discover something new and interesting about a place. Less likely to come upon that old-fashioned yarn.

And there are consequences.

The Internet, says Leslie H. Gelb, president emeritus and board senior fellow of the Council on Foreign Relations, is "no substitute" for solid, in-country reporting by experienced, unbiased journalists. Foreign reporting, he says, is essential to an informed electorate as well as to the development of foreign policy.

"You can say, 'What the devil difference does it make?' The difference that it makes is that the United States is still the most important country in the world," says Gelb, formerly a reporter and editor for the New York Times and a senior official for the State and Defense departments. "Even China will say that America is the leader on any international issue. The interested public in America absolutely has to have reliable information about what's going on in all those countries. Otherwise, our leaders do dumb things, and the American people never know about it. It's just that important.

"Just look at getting into Iraq or into Afghanistan," he says. "There were very few people who knew these countries who could tell us what it would be like once the boots were on the ground there, what we would be running into. We developed that capacity after the fact. . . .You need reporters on the ground who know those places who can do the reporting. It's very unlikely to come from papers in those countries. That's not their tradition, particularly in Asia."

Stephen Hess, senior fellow emeritus at the Brookings Institution, is of the same mind. It is a "great tragedy," he says, when news outlets close their foreign bureaus. Even the organizations that still send reporters overseas often concentrate almost exclusively on war coverage. "Take away places where Americans are fighting, and it's even more pathetic a picture," Hess says.

Indeed, an AJR report in the summer of 2002 revealed that, after the terrorist attacks of the previous year, newspapers beefed up their foreign coverage, sent more reporters abroad and devoted more space to international stories than at any time since the Cold War.

"The two stories dominating the foreign report, Afghanistan and the Middle East, are certainly filled with bombs and disaster. Those two stories are eating most of the space allotted for foreign news, even if that space has increased somewhat since the attacks on the World Trade Center and the Pentagon," Stephen Seplow wrote more than eight years ago (see "Closer to Home," July/August 2002). "Those caveats aside, there does seem to be a new acceptance of the notion that what happens abroad affects local readers as residents of the world's most important country. It deserves good play. And more space should be devoted to it.

"How long will this last?" Seplow asked. "The general consensus: The appetite for foreign news will remain hearty for some time; it will slowly dissipate, but it is not likely to become anemic again in the foreseeable future."

In hindsight, those post-9/11 years appear to have been a blip.

Just six years after that story appeared in AJR, the Project for Excellence in Journalism reported in July 2008 that international news was "rapidly losing ground at rates greater than any other topic area." According to the PEJ report, "The Changing Newsroom," 64 percent of newsroom executives said that in the previous three years, their papers had reduced the amount of space apportioned to foreign news. And 46 percent said they set aside fewer resources to cover foreign stories. Just 10 percent considered foreign coverage "very essential," the report said.

During the Cold War, newspapers and television stations saw a distinct need to cover foreign news, particularly from the Soviet Union and Europe, Hess says. When the Iron Curtain ceased to exist about two decades ago, "that was a good excuse for cutting back," he says.

Airtime on the three major networks illustrates the shift. In 1989, the year the Berlin Wall fell, ABC, CBS and NBC devoted a combined 4,828 minutes to international news, according to a tally by the Tyndall Report, which monitors network broadcasts. By 2000, after more than a decade of steady decline, the three networks aired only 2,127 minutes of international news during newscasts that totaled between 14,500 and 16,000 minutes, the Tyndall Report says.

Foreign coverage by the networks increased with the terrorist attacks in 2001, and reached a peak in 2006, with 3,059 minutes of international news. Last year, despite the United States' involvement in two wars, the networks allotted only 2,070 minutes to foreign news—less than they had during the relative calm of 2000.

During the first 10 months of 2010, coverage has increased somewhat, to 2,247 minutes. Andrew Tyndall, publisher of the report that bears his name, attributes the uptick this year to two events: the Haitian earthquake and the rescue of Chilean miners.

Not only are the networks devoting less time to foreign news, the reports they do air emanate less often from their bureaus and more frequently from reporters who parachute in to cover specific stories. This doesn't bother Tyndall, who attributes the shift to improved technology and travel, which make it easier for reporters both to move around the globe and to transmit stories than in decades past.

"If you're going to cover Haiti, does it matter if you're sending someone from the Mexico City bureau or from Miami?" Tyndall asks. "You send them down to Chile, does it

Shuttered Bureaus

The following newspapers and newspaper companies have eliminated their foreign bureaus since AJR began a series of surveys of international coverage in 1998.

- Baltimore Sun
- Boston Globe
- Boston Herald
- Chicago Tribune
- Copley Newspapers
- Cox Newspapers
- Ft. Lauderdale's Sun-Sentinel
- Fort Worth Star-Telegram
- Miami Herald
- Newark's Star-Ledger
- New Orleans' Times-Picayune
- New York Post
- Newsday
- Orange County Register
- Orlando Sentinel
- Philadelphia Inquirer
- St. Petersburg Times
- San Francisco Chronicle
- San Jose Mercury News
- Washington Times

really matter what airport they left from to get there? Even in the heyday of foreign news coverage, there were vast areas of the world where they didn't have a bureau."

For the past few years, NBC has dedicated more time to international news than its competitors. In 2009, for instance, NBC's newscasts included 722 minutes of international news, compared with 664 and 686 for ABC and CBS, respectively Tyndall reports. Still, that's a far cry from the 1,490 minutes of international news that NBC aired in 1989.

Alexandra Wallace, an NBC News senior vice president, says things started to change about four years ago, for two reasons: The ad market softened and technology allowed reporters "to do more with less."

"I hate to use such a business-y term, but we right-sized our organization," Wallace says.

She acknowledges that the right-sizing has come at a time when Americans' involvement in foreign countries has increased, not only because the nation is caught up in two wars, but because of the global economy and the Internet. "I think the population is engaged in the rest of the world in a way that it probably wasn't before," she says. "This generation is absolutely global. Their Facebook friends are in Dubai."

But how much does NBC report on Dubai? If you search several NBC websites, you might come up with a clip on the world's tallest building, which opened there in early 2010. You'd be hard-pressed to learn much else about the emirate.

No matter how much editors and producers say they value foreign news, statistics show that they don't value it enough to bestow the kind of time or space to it that they did in the past. The Tyndall Report illustrates the decline among television networks. An AJR analysis of eight regional newspapers shows a similar drop in that medium. Consider: On seven days in 1985, the Cincinnati Enquirer, Dallas Morning News, Fresno Bee Philadelphia Inquirer, Providence Journal, St. Louis Post-Dispatch, Tampa Tribune and Portland's Oregonian collectively published 689 foreign stories, editorials and op-eds (see box "Shrinking Foreign Coverage"). On seven days this year, the same papers printed just 321 such pieces. In 1985, 102 of the stories—almost 15 percent—were staff-written; this year, only 14—or 4.3 percent—of them were.

"Some of it is hard to measure," says American University's Campbell, "but it's a real loss."

There are three approaches to foreign reporting: Don't do it (use the wires), do it sporadically (parachute in) or do it all the time (maintain bureaus).

Roy Gutman is an avid all-the-timer.

Gutman was based in Bonn, Germany, as Newsdays European bureau chief in 1992 when, during a trip to the former Yugoslavia, he first heard the term "ethnic cleansing." He spent months in the region ferreting out a story that would horrify the world: Bosnian Serbs had set up a network of concentration camps, where they imprisoned, beat, starved and murdered Muslims. With the endorsement of top state officials, whole villages were deported and women systematically raped. Gutman's work in 1992 and 1993 prompted the closure of some of the worst camps, and the United Nations High Commissioner for Refugees credited him with saving 5,000 to 6,000 lives.

"If Newsday had not let me follow my nose in the Balkans, I'm sure that the ethnic cleansing, genocide, would have been reported, but who knows when, how, to what degree and to what extent it would have been a clear-cut story instead of 'on the one hand, on the other hand,'" Gutman says now.

Working in a bureau and getting to know a country or a region of the world enable reporters to pick up on things that outsiders—even seasoned journalists (and former foreign correspondents) who parachute in for days or weeks—would be much less likely to learn, he says. When you cover city hall or the police department or county courts, you go there day in and day out, get to know the terrain, learn the issues, develop sources, become a presence. Covering a piece of the world is like covering any other beat—writ large. You have to do basic, shoe-leather reporting. You have to get to know the place, the people, the pulse.

Unfortunately, Gutman says, very few newspapers spend the time or money to get to know the world anymore. They have downsized so much that if they have foreign bureaus at all, they tend to be in war zones, places where the story is obvious and, to a great extent, dictated by government actions. Fewer reporters from fewer news outlets have time to get off the beaten path, to do what Gutman did when he followed his nose—uncovered human atrocities.

"It's so sad," he says. "American journalism, it seems to me, when applied to the world, has done exceptionally good work, and it's vital for the American public and for the democracy. And to be pulling back as we are having to is more than hurting, it's really tragic."

Newsday, which Tribune Co. sold to Cablevision in 2008, no longer has foreign correspondents. Top editors did not return repeated phone calls for this story, and a spokesman said no editor was available for comment. The paper won four Pulitzer Prizes for international reporting between 1985 and 2005. One, in 1993, went to Gutman.

Gutman now serves as foreign editor for McClatchy, working from its Washington bureau. In the four years since he accepted that job, his budget has been halved. "We've had to shrink almost every year," he says.

Gone are McClatchy bureaus in Jerusalem, Berlin, Nairobi, Moscow, Tokyo and Rio de Janeiro. "Baghdad went from being a very expensive and major operation to a pared-down operation" in which McClatchy this year shared a correspondent with the Christian Science Monitor, Gutman says. (The partnership ends January 1.) There was some good news: McClatchy opened bureaus in Kabul and Mexico City and has maintained those in Beijing and Cairo. The chain uses stringers to cover Jerusalem and Islamabad.

"I'm excited for what we still have," says McClatchy Foreign Editor Roy Gutman, whose roster of foreign bureaus has shrunk. "I'm depressed for what we've lost."

"I'm excited for what we still have. I'm depressed for what we've lost," Gutman says. "Literally, you don't want to lose anything. You need to be everywhere. We're not covering Europe or Russia right now, which is egregious. It's not as important a story to America right now as Mexico or Afghanistan, but big things happen there."

"What we've done is reduce ourselves, in a sense, to a series of war bureaus as kind of an irreducible minimum, plus Beijing," he says. "If you have to do a triage, those are places you cannot leave. But there's all the rest of the news that we're not covering the way that we'd like to."

Although he admires some of the stories produced by organizations like the Pulitzer Center and the International Reporting Project, Gutman doesn't think they adequately fill the void. To really sense what's going on in a region, to catch the nuance and notice trends, you have to be in-country, he avers.

"Some of the projects coming out of there are absolutely first class," Gutman says. "But they are projects. You wouldn't be able to spot the shift in Pakistan policy in the tribal areas based on a three-month project. And that's the test. What are the turning points?. . . You have to follow your nose."

As Gutman sees it, there are two major impediments to foreign coverage: money and interest. Maintaining a bureau costs hundreds of thousands of dollars a year in correspondents' salaries, rent and supplies, money for local staff and $4,000 or $5,000 a month in travel expenses, he says. Even if you can afford the upfront expenditure, you face a significant problem on the back end, as newspaper editors shun foreign news in favor of local stories.

"Foreign is not everybody's top priority," Gutman says. "I like to be competitive on the daily coverage. In a number of our papers, something we regard as a first-class foreign story could be a brief. But other papers devote significant space to stories we feel are important."

Fortunately for Gutman and his correspondents, the people who run McClatchy still value what they do, even if some individual editors at the chain's 30 daily newspapers don't. And, in an ironic twist, Gutman says, his reporters' stories often receive better play in non-McClatchy papers that subscribe to the McClatchy-Tribune News Service. "We do offer an alternative to the [New York] Times' coverage, which tends to be long and exhaustive, and AP's, which is shorter, tighter and tends to be re-led [with new tops] and often fact-laden. We try to be well-written," he says.

In days gone by, a number of newspapers and chains provided alternatives to the wires and the New York Times, Washington Post, Wall Street Journal and Los Angeles Times. Now, you can count them on one hand. "We've lost those extra voices," Gutman says. "So we're losing the fabric of coverage."

For a long time, the Baltimore Sun was revered for its national and foreign reporting. Nothing was off limits to its journalists, recalls Robert Ruby, the paper's last foreign editor. "It regarded its readers as adults and as people who were interested in the world. And the world extended beyond Baltimore, it extended beyond Maryland, it extended beyond the United States. There was this very untypical belief that the Sun could tell the story for its readers better than anyone else could on a given day. And if the story was in Moscow, so be it. If the story was in Annapolis, so be it. That was the DNA of the paper. The economic model for much of the 20th century could support that idea."

Ruby left the paper in 2006 and now directs communications for the Revenue Watch Institute, a New York-based nonprofit that "promotes the responsible management of oil, gas and mineral resources." (Initially, the organization was financed by the Open Society Institute.) Ruby says things started changing at the Sun when Tribune Co. bought its parent company, Times Mirror, in 2000.

"There's a smaller newshole. What goes into the newshole in almost every case is shorter than it used to be," he says. "If one really thinks that all news can be homogenized, then the argument that it doesn't matter who writes it would be correct. I don't happen to believe that. If you accept the argument that you only need one person covering a story, then having different voices doesn't matter. But I don't buy that either. . . . I think we would all agree that there are many different stories to write about, say, the White House on any given day. There are many ways of writing about what Congress does. Certainly, it's reasonable to believe that we're losing something, readers are losing something, intelligence is losing something, if we only have one or two or three voices coming from Moscow or Jerusalem or Lima."

When it shuttered its last foreign bureau, in Jerusalem, in 2006, the Philadelphia Inquirer closed the door on an era in which its reporters felt that, at home or abroad, nothing was impossible. If they had a good idea, they pursued it. And it paid off in a paper rich with stories—important, interesting and, very often, prize-winning—that you just couldn't find anywhere else. (Disclosure: I worked at the Inquirer during that era.)

Vernon Loeb was an Inquirer foreign correspondent based in the Philippines from 1989 to 1992, when the paper had six foreign bureaus. Now the deputy managing editor for news, he oversees a newsroom staff that plummeted in size from 680 during the fat and happy years—"back in the day," Loeb says—to 280 today. Its recent trajectory is one for the ages: corporate-mandated cutbacks, higher profit margins, new owners, bankruptcy, buyouts, layoffs, empty desks, more new owners, much uncertainty. The paper is now in the hands of creditors of the local group that acquired the Inquirer from McClatchy in 2006.

To hear Loeb tell it, the Inquirer still has grand aspirations, but it lacks the resources to accomplish them all. So it scales back, strives to be the best at less, concentrates on local news and covers the world in spurts.

"For foreign news, we mainly use the wires, and we send our own reporters out pretty robustly when there are stories that really speak powerfully to Philadelphia in some fashion or that are of such magnitude that it almost cries out to send somebody," he says.

Haiti cried out. In the aftermath of the earthquake in January, the Inquirer sent two reporters to the Caribbean country. Feature writer Melissa Dribben traveled with Philadelphia-area medical professionals who volunteered to aid victims. She ended up producing a series of stories about a Haitian-American nurse practitioner who left his home in Florida to join the relief effort. Former Jerusalem correspondent Michael Matza flew to Haiti with doctors from a Camden, New Jersey, hospital and also wrote about a woman whose arm was amputated by a surgeon from the University of Pennsylvania. Both reporters returned to the island later in the year and, all told, spent four weeks there, Loeb says.

The Inquirer also sent a reporter to Afghanistan for a month to embed with troops alongside a local doctor. And it sent Dribben to Hungary after a sightseeing boat capsized in the Delaware River, drowning two students from the small Hungarian town of Mosonmagyaróvár.

"We still have foreign ambitions, and we still do foreign reporting, but it's much more episodic," Loeb says. "Our readers now get more news from the New York Times and the Washington Post and Los Angeles Times. Do the readers notice that? I don't even know.

"When we had our own bureaus and could tailor our own coverage, it probably made a difference. Foreign reporting was more a part of the fabric of the paper," he says, choosing the same term as Gutman.

"By the same token, look, we're living in the real world here." The real world of bankruptcy, of struggling to survive.

The "new reality."

Local. Local. Local.

"Our bread and butter is local and regional coverage," Loeb says. "It's not foreign and national coverage. I don't think that's probably going to change anytime soon, as much as I'd love to open six foreign bureaus again. Most of the top editors here have been national or foreign correspondents. We know how to cover the world and the nation. We're going to do it when we can give our readers something special."

Though it no longer has foreign bureaus—and slashed its national staff from seven bureaus to a lone Washington reporter who concentrates on projects—the Inquirer still saves space on the front page each day for some foreign and national news, Loeb says. In that way, it is different from many regional papers. "Most of our readers get all their news from us," he says, tacitly rejecting the notion that newspapers don't need to provide foreign news because it is available elsewhere. "We are the indispensable news source for a lot of people, and they count on us for foreign and national news."

Not so the Detroit News. In March 2009, the News, which is owned by MediaNews Group, and its partner in a joint operating agreement, the Gannett-owned Detroit Free Press, reduced home delivery to three days a week to save money. A scaled-back version of the papers is available at newsstands on other days. "The amount of newshole available for foreign news has been curtailed," says News Managing Editor Don Nauss.

The News relies on the Associated Press for most of its foreign news and on Bloomberg for business news from overseas. "We aren't aware of any significant complaints," Nauss says. "I don't think people in general look to us for that coverage."

The News last had a foreign correspondent—in Germany—in 2003. Detroit is an automobile town, and the correspondent, Daniel Howes, focused on the auto industry and the merger between Chrysler and Daimler. When Howes returned to Detroit, the bureau remained empty and then closed. Editors considered opening a bureau in Japan or, alternately, in Southern California, where a number of Asian automakers base their United States sales offices. They did neither.

"That all kind of fell by the wayside as our business changed," Nauss says. Daimler sold Chrysler to an equity firm and the newspaper's resources tightened. "Some of our ambitions had to be pared back. . . .

"There's no question that newspapers in the past 20 to 25 years have reduced their troops on the ground abroad, and I'm sure that has some impact on our isolationist views of the world. But we have to face the reality of what we can do monetarily."

The News will send reporters overseas on occasion. In 2010, such parachuting was limited to Haiti, to cover Michigan's response to the earthquake.

At the Post-Dispatch, in another industrial Midwestern city, Arnie Robbins made precisely the same decision and dispatched a reporter and a photographer to document St. Louisans' relief work in Haiti.

Although he laments his paper's diminished foreign coverage, Robbins says the tradeoff is worth it. Money and space, both less abundant than they once were, now are given to hard-hitting local stories, the kind that require digging, the kind that make a difference.

"It's about priorities. Our priority is primarily local," Robbins says. "It's increasingly public service, investigative reporting, high-impact enterprise, which takes time. If I had to choose between that and overseas travel, I'd take local high-impact investigative enterprise."

Some papers, primarily those that view themselves as national or international in scope, still spend a lot of money on foreign coverage. The Wall Street Journal has 35 foreign bureaus; the New York Times, 24. The Washington Post maintains 17 bureaus and the Los Angeles Times, 13. Though each paper's international coverage remains strong, each one has closed some bureaus during the past seven or eight years.

Then there's NPR, one of the very few mainstream news outlets that has completely bucked the trend to trim. In the past decade, its foreign bureaus have mushroomed from six to 17, and it has part-time correspondents in two more, says Senior Foreign Editor Loren Jenkins. The calculation was simple, Jenkins says: "It was perceived that this was an area that needed coverage, and we were the people to do it."

It didn't hurt that while most other media outlets were experiencing enormous revenue losses, NPR received an infusion of money. There were two principal reasons. Its audience, which grew consistently through the 1990s, shot up after September 11, 2001, when many public radio stations around the country switched their focus from music to news, says Ellen Weiss, NPR's senior vice president for news. That shift translated into increased payments from member stations that air NPR programs and more listener donations to the nonprofit, which relies heavily on the largesse of its audience. To top it off, when she died in late 2003, Joan Kroc, widow of McDonald's founder Ray A. Kroc, left NPR more than $200 million—an amount that the Washington Post reported was more than twice as large as the organization's operating budget at the time.

The combination allowed NPR to add three foreign bureaus between 2003 and 2006 alone, during the same period when regional newspapers were shuttering their overseas offices and bringing their correspondents home.

Now, a full 30 percent of what NPR broadcasts in reports from its correspondents and on-air interviews is international in scope, Jenkins says. He and Weiss emphasize that, while it covers Iraq, Afghanistan and Pakistan, NPR also sends reporters to parts of the globe that many news outlets ignore, places where the United States is not involved in wars.

Weiss is particularly proud of NPR's presence in sub-Saharan Africa—in Dakar, Nairobi and Johannesburg. "While there is a lot of conflict there," she says, "the purpose is to explain to people that Africa is far more important and intricate than conflict and genocide."

Fewer than 10 blocks west of NPR's headquarters in downtown Washington stands the bland, brick box of a building that houses the city's dominant newspaper. Jenkins worked for the Washington Post in 1983, when he won a Pulitzer Prize for international reporting for his coverage of Israel's invasion of Beirut and its aftermath. He and Douglas Jehl, the Post's foreign editor, share a keenness for foreign reporting.

But Jehl and his colleagues at the Post have had to make the difficult decisions that Jenkins and Weiss have not. The paper has closed some foreign bureaus and opened others, for a net loss of three since 2003.

Like so many papers from coast to coast, the Post has gone through a series of painful cutbacks and compressions. A number of its best-known and most seasoned reporters have taken advantage of repeated buyout offers—the capital's think tanks, foundations, nonprofits and PR shops are littered with former Posties—and its staff is stretched thin. Nonetheless, Jehl asserts that the paper is committed to foreign coverage, in part because it is so closely linked to official Washington.

"It's expensive, but it's vital to a paper that is for and about Washington, and I think we have a staff that is large enough to provide insightful, penetrating, value-added coverage to the parts of the world that matter most going forward," he says. "We certainly are smaller than the [New York] Times and the [Wall Street] Journal. We're certainly a lot smaller in terms of foreign coverage than Bloomberg, Reuters, the BBC. It does mean we need to pick our shots. But I think we can and are doing a terrific job covering the world through the prism of what matters most to Washington, to American foreign policy and, in some ways, [to] the way the world's evolving."

Top Post editors opted to maintain the bulk of their foreign bureaus even as they decided in late 2009 to close the paper's remaining national bureaus in New York, Los Angeles and Chicago. It previously had shut down bureaus in Miami, Austin and Denver. Then-Post media writer Howard Kurtz, who this fall departed for The Daily Beast, called the move "a significant retrenchment."

"The money-saving move, coming on the heels of four rounds of early-retirement buyouts and the closing or merging of several sections, is the clearest sign yet of the newspaper's shrinking horizons in an era of diminished resources," Kurtz wrote in November of last year. He quoted Executive Editor Marcus Brauchli as saying that the paper could "effectively cover the rest of the country from Washington."

Jehl says the same claim could not be made about covering the world. It might save money, but at great cost.

"We do feel, in terms of foreign coverage, that you cannot replace the kinds of insight and sourcing and understanding gained by living in a foreign country and immersing yourself in that culture. The task of becoming a sophisticated observer and translator of foreign countries is difficult," says

Backpack Journalism Overseas

To broadcast live from Baghdad in 1991, reporters needed more than two dozen cases of equipment that took five people to operate, says former CNN senior Pentagon correspondent Jamie McIntyre. When McIntyre filed his last live report for the network from the Iraqi capital in February 2008, he did so through a Webcam in a MacBook Pro via a satellite Internet transmitter.

"When you're a TV reporter and you're doing everything yourself, it does change the way you tell a story," says McIntyre, now an adjunct professor at the Philip Merrill College of Journalism at the University of Maryland. McIntyre covered the trial of Salim Hamdan, Osama bin Laden's driver and bodyguard, at Guantánamo Bay in summer 2008 without a crew. "I was doing a lot of the logistics myself, which meant I wasn't spending as much time in the courtroom."

Broadcast organizations increasingly rely on smaller one- or two-person operations in most of their foreign bureaus, a strategy that makes sense when money is tight and technology reduces the need for large crews. Most integrate multimedia tools into their reporting, but some journalists want to see the industry do more to capitalize on the unique storytelling opportunities that video journalism offers.

"When we think about opening new bureaus, I think smaller rather than larger," says Alexandra Wallace, a senior vice president of NBC News. "As long as you can keep quality and quantity up, the reality is it takes fewer people to do what it took many people to do, and that's really, truly based on technology."

An individual digital correspondent costs far less than a full-fledged bureau, but Wallace emphasizes that newsworthiness trumps budgetary concerns when it comes to foreign coverage. "We feel like we have the right amount of people overseas," she says. The network has 14 foreign bureaus and an editorial presence in another four countries.

The shift toward mobile journalists, or digital correspondents, is also part of ABC News' approach. Three years ago, the network sent seven digital correspondents to form solo bureaus around the world (see "Armies of One," December 2007/January 2008). At first they primarily produced content for the Web and radio, but many eventually got more on-air exposure, says Kate O'Brian, ABC's senior vice president for news. ABC has an editorial presence in 19 cities around the world.

Both network executives say that most of the foreign stories that make it onto the TV newscast are hard news; features typically run only digitally.

"Particularly with our overseas digital reporters, you'll find that when they file for our ABC News iPad app, they'll file a different sort of story, because they don't have the time constraints television has," O'Brian says.

Ian Williams, NBC's Bangkok-based correspondent, acknowledges that it's difficult to balance Covering the meat-and-potatoes stories with ferreting out new angles and perspectives. But the Internet gives more mileage to a reporter's notebook, he says. Curious viewers who want more context for a story they see on television can turn to the Web for blog posts, photographs and extended interviews.

Williams and both network executives say decisions on how many people to send and which tools they use depend on what the story is about. Correspondents use whatever the right platform is at the right moment, Wallace says, though she adds that ultimately NBC is a television company.

The use of Web tools as secondary components to a mainstream media product irks Jane Stevens, one of the early advocates of back-pack reporting. Stevens, who calls herself a "Webcentric" journalist, embraced the video journalism movement beginning in 1996 and now directs media strategies for the World Company, which owns Kansas' Lawrence Journal-World.

Network news ratings are down because people in today's news ecosystem want more context than they can get in a two-minute story, Stevens says. She praises BBC's use of special reports pages (bbc.co.uk/news/special_reports/), archived by year and organized into geographic and subject categories. The pages, which compile stories, graphics, maps and photos related to a specific topic, give readers a comprehensive look at BBC's coverage of a particular issue and offer background information when related news breaks.

Transitioning into a truly multimedia environment is difficult when mainstream media organizations remain married to their original platforms, and Stevens has little faith that they will adapt. She tracks niche Web-based operations and cites GlobalPost . . . as the most successful digital-native outlet for foreign news.

"Organizations that just go after the immediate lose a lot of ability to tell the whole story," Stevens says. "The idea that you could have one person covering Europe is really reaching into the absurd."

Competition has always been the industry's lifeblood, but today's 24-hour news cycle places a premium on getting information out rather than telling a compelling story. And that means media organizations aren't taking advantage of emerging styles of storytelling, says Tom Kennedy, former managing editor for multimedia at washingtonpost.com.

"There's this ingrained reflex of 'let's keep moving to the next thing,'" Kennedy says. "And while I understand that influence and respect the need to do that, I think that leaves open an entirely different form of coverage."

Traditional broadcast pieces are often reporter driven. But technological advances and ever-shrinking equipment mean a backpack journalist can produce a piece that connects with the viewer on a more intimate level. Using documentary-style techniques, video journalism can capture a subject telling his or her own story through words or actions with little reporter involvement. Emotion and empathy can convey cultural and historical nuances more viscerally than a reporter's commentary.

"It's been so mystifying to me why organizations have been slow to do even modest experimentation" with this type of storytelling, says Kennedy, who now heads the consulting and training company Tom Kennedy Multimedia. "A very well-funded person or company needs to create a short documentary cable channel that goes beyond what Current TV is doing that plants the flag for feature stories."

Although news organizations may differ in how they integrate new technology into their repertoire, most agree that multimedia has been a boon to foreign coverage.

"I think the new ways that we work and the new technologies that we use are really quite liberating, and I'm really quite optimistic about foreign news," NBC's Williams says. "It's enhancing us rather than undermining us."

—Priya Kumar

Priya Kumar (2priyak@gmail.com) is a Washington, D.C.-based writer.

Jehl, formerly a correspondent in the New York Times' Cairo bureau. "You've got language, you've got culture, you've got logistics, you have the enormous gulf between what your readers know and the realities on the ground and the task of interpreting and making sense of that."

Certainly, Jehl acknowledges, there have been sacrifices.

"We recognize that with a staff of our size, we couldn't cover all parts of the world equally, particularly when the paper's mission is to cover Washington," he says. "We decided to leave unfilled our bureaus in Rio and Johannesburg in order to throw more resources at Afghanistan and Pakistan, to reopen a bureau in the Arab world outside of Baghdad and to make sure we were covering China as vigorously as we can."

Just as some regional papers choose to cover international stories that have particular resonance with their readers, the Post concentrates much of its foreign coverage on issues and countries pertinent to its audience. But there is a big difference. The Post's stock in trade is not coverage of local stories, but of national ones. So its international report tends to have foreign policy implications.

"We're providing readers everywhere with a report that's framed around what matters most to a capital and to a government that remains the most powerful and influential in the world," Jehl says. "It's not like we're providing localized

coverage. I think we're providing coverage that reflects developments that are most important out there."

He also dismisses heavy reliance on the wires or other organizations, such as GlobalPost, reasoning that his reporters put foreign developments in context for their readers in a way that the rest do not.

And so, Jehl says, the Post will continue to spend millions of dollars a year on foreign bureaus. That said, the paper has saved money by directing most foreign correspondents to close freestanding offices and work out of their homes, and by hiring some reporters on a contract basis, which allows the Post to pay them less and to withhold benefits.

Los Angeles Times Foreign Editor Bruce Wallace says international reporting "is an integral part of the Los Angeles Times. It's part of the corporate mission to do this kind of reporting."

"What we want to do is to maintain our news coverage, maintain the ability of correspondents to travel widely and to report intensively, and so we try to save money in other places," Jehl explains.

The Post's cuts have been nothing compared with those undertaken by the Los Angeles Times, which closed 43 percent of its foreign bureaus when it went from 23 in 2003 to 13 today. The downsizing is even more striking when you consider that the L.A. Times is providing foreign coverage for all the Tribune Co. papers, several of which also closed bureaus in the recent past.

In fact, just seven years ago, other Tribune Co. newspapers— the Baltimore Sun, Chicago Tribune, Orlando Sentinel, Fort Lauderdale's Sun-Sentinel and Newsday (which the chain has since sold)—had 25 foreign bureaus among them. None of those papers has any bureaus today.

Although the rest of the chain obliterated its bureaus, the L.A. Times' foreign editor, Bruce Wallace, says the paper "has made a commitment" to foreign reporting. "Foreign news is an integral part of the Los Angeles Times. It's part of the corporate mission to do this kind of reporting. We get our stories on the front page almost daily. Our A section opens with world news. The other thing we're doing is our

Farewell to Foggy Bottom

The number of newspapers and newspaper chains covering the State Department has shrunk dramatically since 2003, the last time AJR conducted its foreign reporting survey. Today just six newspaper reporters spend at least half of their time covering foreign affairs and the State Department, compared with 13 seven years ago.

BOSTON GLOBE
Farah Stockman

CHRISTIAN SCIENCE MONITOR
Howard LaFranchi

LOS ANGELES TIMES
Paul Richter

MCCLATCHY
Warren P. Strobel

NEW YORK TIMES
Mark Landler

WASHINGTON POST
John Pomfret

Who Covers What

The number of foreign correspondents employed by United States newspapers has decreased markedly since the last AJR census, taken in 2003. A count largely conducted in July shows that 10 newspapers and one chain employ 234 correspondents (including one vacancy) to serve as eyes and ears to global events. In 2003, AJR found 307 full-time correspondents and pending assignments. The current list includes a combination of staffers and contract writers, who were not included in 2003. They were counted this time to reflect changes in the industry. If only full-time correspondents were listed, the current total would be far lower. Stringers are not included in the tally.

The chart lists domestically based reporters who spend a portion of their time covering foreign news, but they are not included in the total. The same is true for reporters who are based in the United States and cover border issues.

Twenty papers and companies have cut their foreign bureaus entirely since AJR conducted its first census of foreign correspondents in 1998. Only six papers and chains dedicate reporters in Washington, D.C., to cover the foreign affairs beat, down from 13 in 2003.

The current list includes the Associated Press and Bloomberg News, which were not included in previous AJR surveys.

As for television networks, where airtime for foreign news has declined dramatically over the years, the numbers do not precisely reflect the reality of staffing levels. Some networks this year were more open in their responses than others, so a direct comparison to previous surveys is impossible. NBC distinguished between full-fledged bureaus and editorial presence, listing 14 bureaus and an editorial presence in four other countries. "Editorial presence" means that the organization has at least one representative, who may be a staffer, on contract or a freelancer. In the 2003 count, the networks listed 42 bureaus with full-time correspondents. This year, ABC and CNN declined to distinguish between bureaus and editorial presence, simply listing the cities where they have some representation. CBS declined to provide any information.

One bright spot is the growing international presence of NPR, which has 17 foreign bureaus. NPR had six foreign bureaus a decade ago.

Research for this chart was conducted by Priya Kumar.

correspondents increasingly write for other parts of the paper" on such subjects as the arts, entertainment, business and global health. "It infuses all of the paper and the website with more of a global feel, a global reach. It's stitched into the fabric of the paper," he says, invoking the same language as Gutman and Loeb.

"What the company decided to do," Wallace says, "is make the commitment to stay in the game. But they also decided they couldn't replicate it throughout the company. That's not a bad decision. . . . I think the most important thing to realize is that world news is not icing on the cake. It's not something to get rid of when you're thinking of ways to save money."

Wallace says his staff might be smaller, but it's still "robust" and large enough to produce a daily report along with enterprise reporting. "You do need a staff of a certain size. Otherwise you become a boutique operation. Which has been done," he says. "But those operations didn't survive."

"Those operations" would include the ones run by the L.A. Times' sister papers, most notably the Chicago Tribune and Baltimore Sun, which in 2003 staffed 10 and five foreign bureaus, respectively. Editors at the Sun declined interview requests. But at the chain's flagship Chicago Tribune, Colin McMahon, the editor who compiles the foreign news for most Tribune Co. papers, says he is satisfied both with Wallace's foreign report and with his own paper's decision to plow money

formerly spent on foreign bureaus into local investigative and watchdog reporting.

"Before, we were a pseudo national paper in the Midwest," McMahon says. "We're not that anymore. Now we're a day-to-day watchdog paper. It's a stronger identity than we had before. . . .

"What you don't get is that story about a Chicagoan in Siberia. I think that that brings something to the report, but it's not a make-or-break thing. Most readers want to know about the Chicago City Hall and how it affects their lives.

"That's a great bit of chocolate that we miss."

McMahon provided plenty of that "chocolate" when he was in the field, with beautifully crafted stories that gave Chicagoans a true taste of wherever he happened to be in the world. He wrote vividly about a Jewish Autonomous Region in Russia that was bereft of Jews; about the impact of Iraq's guerrilla war on one Baghdad neighborhood; about the alarming, violent deaths of Mexican peasants who dared to oppose one state's governor. He went to Pisco, Peru, to explore the strained relations between Peru and Chile and used the grape brandy that shares the port city's name as a symbol of the discord.

Some of the stories were weighty, some less so. Each shed light on faraway lands and people and cultures, on corners of the world that wouldn't otherwise be in the media spotlight.

And, for the most part, no longer are.

The Overseas Press Corps

[Numbers reflect current bureau total, with 2003 total in parentheses]

Albuquerque Journal 0 (0)

- Border issues: *Rene Romo*

Arizona Republic 1 (1)

- Mexico City: *Chris Hawley (half-paid by USA Today)* *Only counted once in overall total of correspondents*
- Border issues: *Dennis Wagner*

Christian Science Monitor 7 (7)

- Baghdad: *Jane Arraf (Cost of bureau shared with McClatchy)*
- Beijing: *Peter Ford*
- Istanbul: *Scott Peterson*
- Johannesburg: *Scott Baldauf*
- Mexico City: *Sara Miller Llana*
- New Delhi: *Ben Arnoldy*
- Paris: *Bob Marquand*

Dallas Morning News 1 (4)

- Mexico City: *Alfredo Corchado*

El Paso Times

No foreign correspondents, but extensive coverage of Mexico.

Houston Chronicle 1 (3)

- Mexico City: *Dudley Althaus*
- Border issues/drug war: *Dane Schiller*

Los Angeles Times 13 (24)

- Baghdad: *Ned Parker*
- Beijing: *Barbara Demick, Megan Stack, David Pierson*
- Beirut: *Borzou Daragahi*
- Cairo: *Jeffrey Fleishman*
- Islamabad: *Alex Rodriguez*
- Jerusalem: *Edmund Sanders*
- Johannesburg: *Robyn Dixon*
- Kabul: *Laura King*
- London: *Henry Chu*
- Mexico City: *Ken Ellingwood, Tracy Wilkinson*
- Moscow: *Vacant*
- New Delhi: *Mark Magnier*
- Seoul: *John Glionna*

McClatchy 4 (Knight Ridder 8)

- Beijing: *Tom Lasseter*
- Cairo: *Hannah Allam (spent half year in Baghdad in a bureau shared with Christian Science Monitor)*
- Kabul: *Dion Nissenbaum*
- Mexico City: *Tim Johnson*

Miami Herald

No foreign correspondents, but Jim Wyss, who is based in Miami, covers the northern tier of South America. The Herald listed 3 foreign bureaus in 2003.

New York Times 24 (27)

- Baghdad: *Steve Myers, Anthony Shadid, Timothy Williams, Nada Bakri*
- Beijing: *Mike Wines, Ed Wong, Andrew Jacobs, Sharon LaFraniere, Ian Johnson*
- Beirut: *Robert Worth*
- Berlin: *Michael Slackman*
- Cairo: *David Kirkpatrick*
- Caracas: *Simon Romero*
- Dakar: *Adam Nossiter*
- Hong Kong: *Keith Bradsher*
- Islamabad: *Jane Perlez, Sabrina Tavernise*
- Jakarta: *Nori Onishi*
- Jerusalem: *Ethan Bronner, Stephen Farrell, Isabel Kershner*
- Johannesburg: *Barry Bearak, Celia Dugger*
- Kabul: *Alissa Rubin, Carlotta Gall, Dexter Filkins, Rod Nordland, Rich Oppel*
- London: *John Burns, Landon Thomas, Sarah Lyall*
- Mexico City: *Randal Archibold, Damien Cave, Elisabeth Malkin*
- Moscow: *Cliff Levy, Ellen Barry*
- Mumbai: *Vikas Bajaj*
- Nairobi: *Jeffrey Gettleman*
- New Delhi: *James Yardley, Lydia Polgreen, Hari Kumar*
- Paris: Steven *Erlanger, Alan Cowell (Based in International Herald Tribune office), Marlise Simons, John Tagliabue*
- Rome: *Rachel Donadio*
- São Paulo: *Alexei Barrionuevo*
- Shanghai: *David Barboza*
- Tokyo: *Martin Fackler, Hiroko Tabuchi (IHT)*

San Antonio Express-News 0 (1)

- Border issues: *Lynn Brezosky*

San Diego Union-Tribune 1 (1)

- Tijuana: *Sandra Dibble*
- Border issues: *Morgan Lee*

San Jose Mercury News

No foreign correspondents, but John Boudreau covers the Pacific Rim.

USA Today 5 (4)

- Beijing: *Calum MacLeod, Sunny Yang*
- Hong Kong: *Kathy Chu*
- London: *Traci Watson*
- Kabul: *William M. Welch*
- Mexico City: *Chris Hawley (Shared with Arizona Republic) *Only counted once in overall total of correspondents*

Wall Street Journal 35 (36)

Franchise staff based abroad totals 129. Franchise staff comprises the news departments of the United States, Asia and Europe editions of the Wall Street Journal and WSJ.com.

- Baghdad
- Bangkok
- Beijing

- Beirut
- Berlin
- Brussels
- Buenos Aires
- Dubai
- Frankfurt
- Hong Kong
- Istanbul
- Jakarta
- Jerusalem
- Johannesburg
- Kabul
- Kuala Lumpur
- Lagos
- London
- Manila
- Mexico City
- Moscow
- Mumbai
- New Delhi
- Paris
- Prague
- Rio de Janiero
- Rome
- São Paulo
- Seoul
- Shanghai
- Singapore
- Taipei
- Tokyo
- Toronto
- Zurich

Washington Post 17 (20)

- Baghdad: *Ernesto Londono, Liz Sly*
- Beijing: *(Andrew Higgins in accreditation process)*
- Berlin: *Michael Birnbaum (Opening Jan. 1)*
- Bogotá: *Juan Forero*
- Cairo: *Leila Fadel (Opening Jan. 1)*
- Islamabad: *Karin Brulliard*
- Jerusalem: *Janine Zacharia*
- Kabul: *Joshua Partlow*
- London: *Anthony Faiola*
- Mexico City: *William Booth*
- Moscow: *Kathy Lally, Will Englund*
- Nairobi: *Sudarsan Raghavan*
- New Delhi: *Emily Wax, Rama Lakshmi*
- Paris: *Ed Cody*
- Shanghai: *Keith Richburg*
- Tehran: *Thomas Erdbrink*
- Tokyo: *Chico Harlan*

Associated Press

Global staff of 3,700 employees working in 304 locations in 116 countries; 2,400 are newsgatherers. Six international regional editing hubs:
- Bangkok: Asia-Pacific desk
- Cairo: Middle East desk
- Johannesburg: sub-Saharan Africa desk
- London: Europe-Africa desk
- Mexico City: Latin America desk
- New York: North America desk

Bloomberg News

Global staff of more than 2,300 in 146 bureaus (101 are foreign) in 72 countries. Content syndicated to more than 450 media outlets in 66 countries with a combined circulation of 78 million people. A breakdown of the number of correspondents based abroad was not available.

Americas

- Bogotá
- Brasília
- Buenos Aires
- Calgary
- Caracas
- Lima
- Mexico City
- Monterrey
- Montreal
- Ottawa
- Quito
- Rio de Janeiro
- Santiago
- São Paulo
- Toronto
- Vancouver

Europe/Mideast/Africa

- Abu Dhabi
- Abuja
- Accra
- Almaty
- Amman
- Amsterdam
- Ankara
- Athens
- Belfast
- Belgrade
- Berlin
- Bratislava
- Brussels
- Bucharest
- Budapest
- Cairo
- Cape Town
- Copenhagen
- Doha
- Dubai
- Dublin
- Dusseldorf
- Edinburgh
- Frankfurt
- Geneva
- Helsinki
- Istanbul
- Jerusalem
- Johannesburg
- Kiev
- Kuwait
- Lagos
- Lisbon
- Ljubljana

- London
- Luxembourg
- Madrid
- Manama
- Milan
- Moscow
- Munich
- Nairobi
- Nicosia
- Oslo
- Paris
- Prague
- Riga
- Riyadh
- Rome
- Sofia
- St. Petersburg
- Stockholm
- Tallinn
- Tel Aviv
- Toulouse
- Vienna
- Vilnius
- Warsaw
- Zagreb
- Zurich

ASIA/ASIA PACIFIC
- Auckland
- Bangalore
- Bangkok
- Beijing
- Canberra
- Colombo
- Hanoi
- Hong Kong
- Islamabad
- Jakarta
- Karachi
- Kuala Lumpur
- Manila
- Melbourne
- Mumbai
- New Delhi
- Osaka
- Perth
- Seoul
- Shanghai
- Singapore
- Sydney
- Taipei
- Tokyo
- Wellington

Television and Radio

NBC 14
- Baghdad
- Bangkok
- Beijing
- Beirut
- Cairo
- Germany
- Havana
- Islamabad
- Jordan*
- Kabul
- London
- Moscow
- Saudi Arabia*
- South Korea*
- Syria*
- Tel Aviv
- Tehran
- Tokyo

*Editorial presence, not full-fledged bureau.

ABC
- Baghdad
- Beijing
- Buenos Aires
- Dubai
- Havana
- Hong Kong
- Islamabad

- Jerusalem
- Johannesburg
- Kabul
- London
- Mexico City
- Moscow
- Nairobi
- New Delhi
- Paris
- Rome
- Seoul
- Tokyo

Would not distinguish between full-time bureaus and editorial presence.

CBS

The Los Angeles Times reported that as of January 2010, cutbacks would leave bureaus in London and Tokyo and small offices in half a dozen other cities. A CBS News spokesperson said the network has a broader foreign presence, but wouldn't provide details.

CNN
- Abu Dhabi
- Amman
- Baghdad
- Bangkok
- Beijing

- Beirut
- Berlin
- Bogota
- Buenos Aires
- Cairo
- Chennai
- Dubai
- Havana
- Hong Kong
- Islamabad
- Istanbul
- Jakarta
- Jerusalem
- Johannesburg
- Kabul
- Lagos
- London
- Madrid
- Mexico City
- Moscow
- Mumbai
- Nairobi
- New Delhi
- Paris
- Rome
- Santiago
- Seoul
- Tokyo

Would not distinguish between full-time bureaus and editorial presence.

FOX 6 (6)

- Baghdad
- Islamabad
- Jerusalem
- Kabul
- London
- Rome

NPR 17

- Baghdad
- Beijing
- Berlin
- Bogotá*
- Cairo
- Dakar
- Istanbul
- Jakarta
- Jerusalem
- Johannesburg*
- Kabul
- London
- Mexico City
- Moscow
- Nairobi
- New Delhi
- Islamabad
- Rome
- Shanghai

Part-time correspondents not counted in the total.

Critical Thinking

1. Is "local, local, local became louder, louder, louder" a reflection of feedforward or feedback? Is there a decreasing interest among the American public in international news? If so, is that a result of decreasing mainstream media coverage? Or has a decreasing interest in international news resulted in less of a market for selling it?

2. Analyze the pros and cons of two models for filling the international reporting void: (1) competitive grant funding such as that provided by the International Reporting Project and Pulitzer Center grants and (2) freelance contracting, such as Phil Balboni's GlobalPost.

JODI ENDA (jaenda@gmail.com) writes about politics and government from Washington, D.C. She previously covered the White House, presidential campaigns and Congress for Knight Ridder and was a national correspondent for the Philadelphia Inquirer. Enda wrote about declining coverage of federal agencies and departments in AJR's Summer issue.

From *American Journalism Review*, Winter 2010, pp. 14–31. Copyright © 2010 by the Philip Merrill College of Journalism at the University of Maryland, College Park, MD 20742-7111. Reprinted with permission.

Capital Flight

Watchdog reporting is at an alarming low at many federal agencies and departments whose actions have a huge impact on the lives of American citizens.

JODI ENDA

After an explosion killed 29 coal miners in West Virginia in early April, the Washington Post and the New York Times quickly produced lengthy exposés detailing a plethora of safety breaches that preceded the nation's worst coal mining disaster in a quarter century. The Times reported that mining companies thwarted tough federal regulations enacted after a spate of deaths four years earlier simply by appealing citations. The Post wrote that federal regulators had cited the Upper Big Branch mine for a whopping 1,342 safety violations in the past five years, 50 times in the previous month alone.

These are the kind of powerful stories that can goad public officials to make changes—sometimes life-saving changes—by shedding light on dangerous conditions. They also are the kind of stories that more and more often come too late, or not at all.

Just ask the families of the 29 miners.

As daily newspapers continue to shed Washington bureaus and severely slash their staffs, fewer reporters than ever are serving as watchdogs of the federal government. Rare is the reporter who is assigned to cover one of the many federal departments, agencies or bureaus that are not part of the daily news cycle. Even if they are large, even if they are central to how Americans live their lives, most parts of the federal government—the very offices that write the rules and execute the decisions of Congress and the president—remain uncovered or undercovered by the mainstream media. Consider that not one newspaper has a reporter who works in the newsroom of the Department of Agriculture, which, with a staff of 104,000, is one of the government's largest employers. Trade publications and bloggers pick up a bit of the slack but have neither the audience nor the impact of more traditional media outlets.

Throughout much of this nation's history, it has been newspapers that set the standard for reporting that is hard-hitting, meaningful, thought-provoking, exhaustive, consequential. In the last half century, in particular, newspapers sought to be more impartial and professional, and less partisan, as they disclosed misdeeds involving Democrats and Republicans alike. Think Pentagon Papers, Watergate, Iran-contra, Jack Abramoff, campaign finance.

Networks and cable television news outlets certainly have reporters in Washington, but they concentrate on politics and the story of the day out of the White House, the Capitol and the most visible departments, such as Defense, State, Justice and Homeland Security. National Public Radio has beefed up its Washington coverage the past several years, and its reporters—many of them former newspaper writers—do have time for enterprise. Yet when it comes to departments, it sticks to the same handful as television.

Now that so many newspapers have forsaken the capital, it should not be surprising that the quality of reporting on the federal government has slipped. The watchdogs have abandoned their posts. How that plays out in the long run—for journalism, for democracy—has yet to be determined. Perhaps one day, websites, or a future medium, will pick up where newspapers left off. In the short term, though, the dearth of in-depth government reporting is palpable.

Newspaper reporters who remain in the capital tend to focus on the big issues of the moment (health care, Wall Street), their congressional delegations and politics. Scoops are measured in nanoseconds and posted online the moment they are secured (and sometimes prior to that). Good, old-fashioned shoe-leather reporting? You can find it here and there, kind of like the typewriter.

"Dealing with agencies can be very time-consuming," says Bill Lambrecht, the lone reporter remaining in the once-exalted Washington bureau of the St. Louis Post-Dispatch, a Lee Enterprises-owned newspaper. "The kind of source work that you need to do—calling people at night, filing FOIAs [Freedom of Information Act requests]—to bird-dog the agencies that invariably try to put up obstructions to giving you what you should get takes a lot of time."

Perhaps that's why only one Washington-based newspaper reporter covers the Mine Safety and Health Administration, which oversees mines in every state in the country, on anything close to a regular basis.

"The Courier-Journal [in Louisville] historically has had a great interest and desire to cover the coal mining industry and safety issues related to coal mining. That commitment hasn't diminished at all in recent years," says James Carroll, the Gannett newspaper's Washington reporter. "Being a one-man bureau, however, you have to pick your shots. Disasters obviously get a lot of media that don't normally cover this. And we do that ourselves. If there's an accident, we spend a lot of time on it. But in between, we try to keep an eye on anything significant that MSHA does. We know it will have a great impact on Kentucky."

Carroll, who has won numerous awards for regional reporting from Washington, says he keeps tabs on MSHA "when they're proposing safety initiatives and when they're not putting out safety initiatives.... With MSHA, we try to revisit issues that nobody else is covering." For years, he's been tracking government activity on "float dust," coal dust that floats in the air and can lead to black lung disease and cause fires in underground mines. In the 1990s, the Courier-Journal reported that mining companies were falsifying records on coal dust, prompting the federal government to crack down.

"Over the years since then we've tried to revisit this story from time to time, absent any immediate event," Carroll says. "With the changing administrations, now it looks like there is going to be some new energy coming up with regulations on coal dust."

It is those types of stories, the "in-between" ones that track government's progress or lack of it, that so many Washington reporters either choose to or are forced to skip. Many have little interest in what they consider to be "unsexy" process stories that take a lot of time to report, require research and source-building, and don't necessarily pan out or land on the front page. But for reporters like Lambrecht and Carroll, who made their names by patiently following turn-of-the-screw stories, the issue is one of time.

It is those types of stories, the "in-between" ones that track government's progress or lack of it, that so many Washington reporters either choose to or are forced to skip.

"It goes without saying that when bureaus are operating with fewer people and fewer resources, they have to be more selective about what they go after," says Lambrecht, whose own bureau gradually decreased from seven full-time reporters and one part-time reporter in the late 1980s to five, then three and, since the end of 2008, just him. Since then, he has had to scale back on the type of hard-hitting stories he previously wrote about the Environmental Protection Agency, the Agriculture Department and the Food and Drug Administration, to name a few. His plight is shared by countless Washington reporters, survivors of layoffs, buyouts and closures. "Part of the bureau reduction around town also meant focusing much more, and sometimes exclusively, on congressional delegations

and issues that have a direct impact on a region or locality," Carroll says.

Like Lambrecht, Carroll has to sandwich reporting on regulatory agencies—in addition to MSHA, he follows specific issues at the Federal Aviation Administration, the National Transportation Safety Board, the FDA and the Pentagon—in between stories about politics and Kentucky's congressional delegation, which includes Senate Minority Leader Mitch McConnell, the Republican who has led his party's efforts to block President Obama's agenda.

"It's a real challenge because you have day-to-day things that are breaking all the time. And you have additional responsibilities, like blogs," Carroll says. "You have to treat your enterprise stories like daily stories. . . . Otherwise, you'll never get to them."

To be sure, the decline in coverage of federal departments, bureaus and agencies started long before newspapers began shuttering their Washington bureaus.

Nine years ago, AJR documented how newspapers and wire services had shifted from covering government "buildings"—shorthand for a blanket approach to reporting on departments and agencies—to covering issue-oriented beats. Reporters abandoned their desks in what once had been bustling pressrooms in stately federal buildings all across the capital and worked from modern news bureaus in staid rooms that often resembled insurance offices. At the time, bureau chiefs explained in what might be described as lockstep language that the change was a way to bring alive coverage of dry policy issues, to engage readers who had tuned out incremental Washington stories.

"There's been a real castor-oil quality of coverage," Kathleen Carroll, then Knight Ridder's Washington bureau chief and now executive editor of the Associated Press, said in 2001. "If you look back at the way Washington stories were written in the past, you see that it's just boring as hell."

Bureau chiefs trumpeted their move to issue-related coverage, saying that by leaving the daily drudgery to the wires, they had more time and more resources to devote to investigative and enterprise reporting.

But toward what end? Did journalists use their newfound freedom from daily coverage to keep closer tabs on what really was happening behind the imposing façades of federal buildings? Did they do a better job of telling readers what was going on before and after, rather than during, press conferences? Did they forgo the dull, incremental stuff to better serve the American people, to make sure their elected and appointed officials were using taxpayers' money wisely and honestly, using sound judgment, serving the public good? Were they better watchdogs?

The evidence suggests the answer is no. Certainly, there have been some standout stories in the past decade—Knight Ridder stood virtually alone in questioning the Bush administration's march to war in Iraq; Copley News Service sent a corrupt member of Congress to prison. But it is no secret that the story of Washington newspaper bureaus in the 2000s is one of cutbacks and closures, and less coverage.

"When I joined the Dallas Morning News' D.C. bureau in early 2003, we had 11 people. We now have three. Back then, we did indeed have a full-time Pentagon writer, a Supreme Court writer and a writer who covered the Justice Department, homeland security and immigration. All three took buyouts several years ago," says Todd Gillman, Washington bureau chief for the Belo-owned newspaper. "Now, with three reporters, we no longer structure any coverage around agencies. We are more scattershot. Or flexible. However you prefer."

A near-revolutionary shift in the Washington press corps was well documented in a 2009 report by the Pew Research Center's Project for Excellence in Journalism. The report concluded that newspapers with Washington bureaus declined by more than half from the mid-1980s to 2008 (when additional reductions took place). Conversely, there was tremendous growth in special interest or niche media, including newsletters, and nearly a tenfold increase in the number of foreign reporters in the capital.

The widespread constriction of newspaper bureaus, coming as it did after the move toward issue-based reporting, has served to further limit coverage of the "real" Washington, the workaday, off-camera Washington charged with getting things done.

"To me, what's happening—and it goes back over a period of time—is that there are some parts of Washington that I would argue are overcovered, like the White House. There's a tremendous amount of pack journalism going on over there; everybody has to do a stand-up in front," says Clark Hoyt, who is completing a three-year stint as the New York Times' public editor in mid-June and was formerly Washington editor for now-defunct Knight Ridder. (The chain was acquired by McClatchy in 2006.) "The numbers of reporters in Washington have not necessarily gone down. It's just the composition of the press corps and what they cover has changed dramatically."

Parts of the capital are woefully ignored, says Hoyt, who makes clear he does not speak for the Times. A case in point, he says, is the Agriculture Department. In years past, the Des Moines Register "had a powerhouse Washington bureau" whose reporters landed the paper four Pulitzer Prizes for national reporting between 1968 and 1985 and were finalists for two others. "These were stories that grew out of intense coverage of the Agriculture Department," Hoyt says. "I don't know how many people are in the pressroom of the Agriculture Department on a daily basis, but I'll bet you that most of them work for special-interest publications."

"To me, that story has been replicated all over town in different places where newspapers once identified local affinities that were important to the economy, that were important to local readers because they really touched their lives in some ways. I think a lot of that coverage has dried up."

Chris Mather, communications director at the Agriculture Department, concurs. The USDA is covered by smaller local papers in communities that are beneficiaries of its largesse, especially as a result of the federal stimulus, but much less frequently by the Washington press corps, she says. The department's pressroom, or what's left of it, is dominated by wire services—Thomson Reuters, Bloomberg News, the Associated Press and Dow Jones—National Journal and Agri-Pulse, which has a website and weekly e-newsletter on farming and rural issues. The Register's sole remaining Washington reporter was, remarkably, not on her radar. (Philip Brasher, whose blog says he covers agriculture, energy and climate issues for the Gannett-owned Register, did not return repeated phone calls from AJR.)

At a time when critical or salacious stories are in vogue, many communications officials are content to be ignored. Mather, though, is keen for her department to receive attention. "The difficulty we have at USDA is that there are very few people out there who understand the breadth of our portfolio," Mather says. "Reporters think that we are here just to advocate for farmers and ranchers. We definitely do that, but we do a lot more than that."

For instance, she says, the department made 113,000 home loans last year through its Rural Development Agency. It also financed fire stations, schools and infrastructure in rural areas, as well as broadband support for telemedicine. Now, she says, Agriculture Secretary Tom Vilsack is focusing on ways to rebuild and revitalize rural America with greater access to broadband Internet connections, development of biofuels, programs to mitigate climate change and ways for consumers to connect with local food producers. Publicity for the programs is sparse, particularly out of Washington.

"Rural America continues to suffer," Mather says. "The poverty level is higher, the education level lower. It's suffering because people are leaving those communities. They don't have water treatment systems that work; the schools aren't what they used to be."

It could be a great story: Where are these people going? What kind of jobs can they get? Are they putting pressure on the social service system? Who's doing the work they left behind? What's the impact on the cities and suburbs that receive them? What about the schools? Does this migration affect the nation's food supply?

It's a story Mather would love to see. "When we start talking about our new approach," she says, "you see this light bulb go off in reporters' heads after about 20 minutes."

Agriculture—like mining—might be a hard sell to readers of large, urban papers whose closest connection with rural America often is a neighborhood farmers market. But it is up to reporters to connect the dots, to explain the impact of rural poverty on the food that makes its way to grocers in Manhattan or Los Angeles, for example, or of mining issues on electricity and climate change nationwide.

"We're making the largest broadband investment in rural America in history," Mather says. "It will bolster the national economy if these businesses are able to thrive and people stay in these communities. It's unfortunate people are not interested in the story."

The happiest press secretary in Washington might well be Scott Wolfson of the Consumer Product Safety Commission. Having endured a period of bad press in the final years of the Bush administration, the CPSC now is on the offensive, fighting unsafe products and reveling in coverage. Wolfson credits the new chairman, Inez Tenenbaum, whom he characterizes as something of a publicity machine. Tenenbaum has made herself available for countless interviews, and she traveled the country and even the world to demonstrate that the Obama administration takes consumer safety seriously, he says.

"We do not want there to be a downtime in the media's coverage of CPSC. We are trying to be transparent and proactive, to let the media know how we are trying to solve the problems of the past for two key reasons: to give parents greater confidence in the safety of products in the marketplace and to give them confidence that their children or themselves won't be hurt by products in their homes."

The press office also is putting out videos on YouTube, writing blogs and tweeting. And the press is responding, Wolfson says. But that's hardly the case for many other departments, bureaus and agencies. Indeed, a clear majority get little, if any, coverage. Even large departments often go begging for coverage out of Washington.

The Department of Housing and Urban Development has been the subject of more stories than usual in the past year because of the foreclosure crisis, says Jerry Brown, deputy assistant secretary for the Office of Public Affairs. But normally, he says, no newspaper or wire service reporters are assigned to cover HUD full time, and the number of newspaper reporters who check in with the department from time to time has dropped as papers have eliminated real estate sections and housing beats. Still, HUD gets publicity from trade publications and housing magazines as well as blogs, Brown says. And, as with the Agriculture Department, local papers cover it when HUD grants money to community projects.

But is anyone serving as a watchdog? During the Bush administration, National Journal's Edward Pound broke a story that federal prosecutors were investigating whether then-HUD Secretary Alphonso R. Jackson had steered contracts to friends. This May, Jackson's lawyers announced that the Justice Department had decided not to file charges. Even so, Jackson was plagued by so many allegations of misconduct regarding contracts and favoritism that he resigned in 2008.

Pound, a well-known Washington investigative reporter and veteran of U.S. News & World Report, the New York Times, the Wall Street Journal and USA Today, no longer works as a journalist. He left National Journal last year to be director of communications for the federal Recovery Accountability and Transparency Board. He laments the lack of coverage of nuts-and-bolts Washington, saying it never was great, and now it's worse.

"A lot of these agencies never were covered the way they should have been covered because they weren't sexy stories. It's not some sex scandal on the Hill or some intelligence screwup," Pound says. "HUD is a very good example of how reporters aren't really covering these agencies very well. I'm loath to stick it to the reporters. I know what the pressures are on people to just churn it out, churn it out. The economics of the business are so much a factor now."

A lot of these agencies never were covered the way they should have been covered because they weren't sexy stories. It's not some sex scandal on the Hill or some intelligence screwup.

What's more, he says, "So much of what's out here in Washington is glitz reporting."

It's a sure bet that more Americans recognize the names Tareq and Michaele Salahi than could identify Shaun Donovan. The former are the Virginia socialites whose claim to fame is crashing President Obama's first state dinner in November. So notable are they that the president included a quip about them in his address to the White House Correspondents' Association dinner in May. The latter is the secretary of HUD, who oversees 9,000 employees and a $43.5 billion 2010 budget, plus stimulus money.

Likewise, how many Americans can name the chairman of the Federal Trade Commission? It is Jon Leibowitz. According to the commission's website, the FTC "deals with issues that touch the economic life of every American." Certainly, the commission receives attention on big stories about consumer rip-offs and unfair trade practices. But much of the publicity comes from blogs and websites, making it unavailable to those without Internet access. Like so many other places in town, this one has seen a diminution of its traditional corps of newspaper reporters. Consequently, to get the word out, its press office has learned to be "creative," says Cecelia J. Prewett, the public affairs director.

"It definitely makes for an on-your-toes press person," Prewett says. "Evidently, it used to be much simpler. You'd know who your contact was, you'd call and—boom!—they'd be interested. Now there's much targeting to be done." Prewett, who started at the FTC in late November, says she frequently has to help reporters—even those from the largest, most-respected newspapers—sell stories to their editors. "You have to do a lot more embargoing of information so that you can help them convince their editor, because the resources are so tight. You have to help them pitch it to their editor. You're not having to convince one person, you have to convince two."

The FTC has adjusted to the shift away from newspapers with Washington bureaus and toward websites without bureaus by changing tactics, from the way it conducts press conferences to the way it issues press releases, says Claudia Bourne Farrell, a senior press officer who has been with the commission for 16 years.

"Five years ago, if we were having a press conference, we'd send out a release and expect 8 to 10 cameras and a roomful of reporters. That no longer happens. Because we don't fill up the room, we do Webcasts of our news releases and two-way audio conferences so reporters can call up and listen and ask questions," she explains. "Five years ago, material produced by the Division of Consumer and Business Education was largely written—paper publications and/or Web-based publications. They were words. In the last several years, that division has taken to producing videos."

"It underscores what I said about having to work smarter," Farrell continues. Still, there's a downside. "I think our Division of Consumer and Business Education is very creative and gifted at developing consumer education. But about 45 percent of the country is on the other side of the digital divide."

Ralph Nader does not mince words. As far as the consumer advocate and frequent presidential candidate is concerned, the failure of the Washington press corps to cover departments, agencies and bureaus—the guts of the federal government—has cost American lives.

"The danger is *danger*," he says. "Health and safety agencies are letting people die that they can save . . . It's a very, very sad state of affairs."

Example No. 1 in his mind is the National Highway Traffic Safety Administration's treatment of Toyota Motor Corp., maker of the popular Toyota and Lexus vehicles. "NHTSA has had six investigations on Toyota in the last two to three years. They haven't subpoenaed one document yet from Toyota. That's a story," Nader said earlier this spring.

In November, a Los Angeles Times investigation by Ralph Vartabedian and Ken Bensinger reported that, since 2001, more than 1,000 Toyota and Lexus owners had complained that their vehicles accelerated suddenly, against the drivers' wishes. Many instances ended in crashes, and 19 people died. They wrote that those complaints led NHTSA to open eight investigations, and that Toyota responded to two of them by recalling 85,000 vehicles. NHTSA closed the other six investigations because it did not find a defect.

But the Times disclosed that the investigations "systematically excluded or dismissed the majority of complaints by owners that their Toyota and Lexus vehicles had suddenly accelerated, which sharply narrowed the scope of the probes." A second story by the same reporters later in November called Toyota to task for blaming the cases of sudden acceleration solely on floor mats. The L.A. Times' own investigation pointed to electronic throttles, the reporters wrote. Subsequently, the National Academy of Sciences undertook a 15-month investigation to determine whether electronic vehicle controls can cause sudden acceleration.

Similar to the mining stories by the New York Times and the Washington Post, these were strong and damning. Also similar to those stories, they came after disaster struck. In late September, Toyota issued what, at the time, was its largest U.S. recall—of 3.8 million vehicles. The recall was prompted by a fiery crash near San Diego in August, when a California Highway Patrol officer and three members of his family were killed after their Lexus ES 350 suddenly took off, sped out of control, flew off an embankment, rolled several times and burst into flames.

In April, NHTSA slapped Toyota with a $16.4 million fine—the maximum it is allowed to levy—for failing to disclose for months that faulty pedals in 2.3 million vehicles could cause them to accelerate suddenly. NHTSA has been criticized for acting too slowly as thousands of consumers complained—and dozens died—and congressional Democrats began work this spring on legislation to grant NHTSA greater authority.

Vartabedian and Bensinger were Pulitzer Prize finalists, and their reporting shed needed light on a deadly issue, light that likely helped prod the Obama administration and Congress to take another look at NHTSA as well as at Toyota. Not a bad feat from 3,000 miles away—the reporters are based not in Washington, but in California. Some argue that makes no difference, that with access to records on the Internet, reporters can cover Washington from anywhere.

Washington-based reporters from just four news organizations—the AP, the Detroit News, the Detroit Free Press and Automotive News—regularly check in with NHTSA, says a public affairs specialist there, who was one of just a handful of spokespersons who refused to speak for attribution for this article. Reporters from Bloomberg and USA Today call fairly often, as does the Los Angeles Times (from L.A.) and Jalopnik, a car blog, the spokesperson says. Routine NHTSA press conferences (not those about Toyota) attract just two or three print reporters.

One of those reporters is Justin Hyde, a business writer who represents half of the Detroit Free Press' Washington bureau. Hyde's beat is automotive news, a high-profile job for a Motor City daily. And Hyde says he is given a lot of time by the Gannett-owned paper to do his job well. Last year, he co-wrote an eight-part series on the bankruptcies of General Motors and Chrysler.

The Toyota story, he says, was hard to get because the Japanese company withheld much of the pertinent information about sudden acceleration. However, Hyde says that NHTSA officials were "fairly responsive" and that data about complaints are available online.

So why didn't the Washington press corps write about the Toyota investigations earlier? Nader blames the migration away from "building" coverage.

"These agencies are not being covered on a regular basis," he says. "They're being covered thematically. So if EPA puts out something on carbon dioxide regulation, they'll cover that. But if OSHA [the Occupational Safety and Health Administration] doesn't put out anything for four years, they don't cover that. It's the end of the beat reporter. There's nobody I can consistently call on NHTSA or FDA and know that they're there every day."

When reporters aren't on top of an agency or department, they often miss inaction. Advocates argue that was the real story of the first decade of this century. The Bush administration systematically rolled back regulatory enforcement, but little was written about it. As Nader puts it: "You don't want to be investigated or covered? Don't do anything."

The Center for Auto Safety, a consumer organization founded by Nader in 1970, lists an overwhelming amount of information about recalls, defects and complaints on its website, autosafety.org. Clarence Ditlow, the group's executive director, says that during the second term of George W. Bush's presidency, NHTSA "virtually stopped issuing any fines. And there was no journalistic coverage of that."

It's only now, with the Obama administration confronting record-setting Toyota recalls, that fines are coming back into fashion, he says. But that doesn't mean journalists should be less vigilant.

"You simply need to have journalists who are willing to pull teeth," Ditlow says. "Could Toyota have been discovered earlier? I think so . . . If there'd been coverage of Toyota and NHTSA reaching deals to exclude certain types of complaints, I think that would have precluded what they did." For instance, Ditlow says that NHTSA excluded from its investigations complaints in which Toyota drivers said the brakes failed to stop runaway vehicles or the sudden acceleration lasted a long time. "If you look at the San Diego event where four people were killed, the brakes couldn't stop the vehicle and it was a long-duration event," he says. "The very premise on which they curtailed the investigation was false.

"A death is a death!"
And a death is a story.

In fact, Nader says about the only things he can count on reporters to cover are disasters—plane crashes, mine explosions, auto deaths. He called it a "tombstone mentality." But after the initial flood of coverage, the follow-up is noticeably minuscule.

The words "regulatory agencies" are eye-glazing for many, if not most, Washington journalists. Give 'em a juicy story about politics—the sleaze of a John Edwards, the slide of a Charlie Crist, the slurs and slams that fly between the powers on Pennsylvania Avenue and K Street—over a substantive (read: boring) policy (read: homework) story any day of the week. Without a doubt, many a Washington journalist would rather pore over transcripts of Sunday morning talk shows for a mini-scoop that anyone else on the planet could find online than wade through government records that might yield an exclusive yet hard-to-find exposé of the Pulitzer variety.

Perhaps that's why an article in the New York Times Sunday magazine recently posited that Politico's Mike Allen, author of a popular e-mail tip sheet called "Playbook" that dishes scooplets and news summaries along with birthday wishes for insiders, might be the most powerful journalist in Washington. Some bloggers and columnists have disputed the title, but not the fact that Allen is one of the capital's best known scribes. To be sure, Allen is a hard-working, knowledgeable journalist. He has reported for the Washington Post, the New York Times and Time magazine. He has covered the White House and presidential campaigns. Like many Washington writers of the 21st century, he has enhanced his fame by appearing regularly on TV. But Allen's selling point is his ability to be a human vacuum cleaner. He is on top of everything, but he's not an expert at any one thing. And while Allen is fortunate to work for one of the few news outlets that actually has increased its Washington presence the past few years, he also is symbolic of the direction this town's reporting has taken of late.

Short is in.
Blogs are in.
And.
Tweets.
R.
In.

Coverage of the inner workings of the bureaucracy, the behind-the-scenes actions that affect everyday Americans? Not so much.

"It's changed dramatically, and all for the worse," George Condon, former Washington bureau chief for Copley News Service, says of Washington journalism. Condon was forced to close down the bureau in November 2008, two years after its reporters won a Pulitzer for the chain and Copley's flagship paper, the San Diego Union-Tribune, for revealing that Rep. Randy "Duke" Cunningham, a California Republican, had taken millions in bribes. Condon, who now covers the White House for CongressDaily, ticked off a few of the Washington bureaus that have closed in recent years: Newhouse, Cox, Media General. There are more that have shut down, of course, including numerous one- or two-person bureaus. And many that have merged (most notably Tribune Co. bureaus, including the Los Angeles Times') and shrunk.

Each bureau had expertise based on the industries in the areas where their newspapers were located, Condon notes. For Copley, with its Southern California base, that meant immigration and border policies and the military; for Media General, which has several outlets in Florida, that meant NASA. Reporters assigned to those beats developed deep and reliable sources in agencies and departments, expertise that their newspapers no longer have.

"You're not getting the voice filled by AP," Condon says. "Just calling a press secretary or the person whose name is on a press release is not the same thing as knowing who the decision maker is before the decision is made."

Few reporters who have been laid off or bought out (Condon represents the latter) end up at other newspapers, given that they generally aren't hiring, especially in Washington bureaus. CongressDaily, part of National Journal Group, is published twice a day, on paper and online, when Congress is in session. Condon points out that none of the 11 reporters who worked for Copley's Washington bureau landed at a newspaper.

Where are all these old-fashioned newspaper reporters going? Some have left the field, putting their skills to use at think tanks, nonprofits, research organizations, foundations and public relations firms. Some have gone to brand-name websites, such as Politico, The Daily Beast, AOL News and Politics Daily. For the most part, those reporters cover politics or breaking news and have little opportunity to develop the sources and do the kind of digging required to uncover the stories people don't know about, but should.

After two decades at the Los Angeles Times, one of them in the Washington bureau, Josh Meyer, quit early this year to become director of education and outreach for Northwestern University's Medill National Security Journalism Initiative in Washington. Meyer says he took the job for the entrepreneurial opportunities it provides, but he acknowledges that he became frustrated when real estate developer Sam Zell bought Tribune Co. and combined and slashed staff in all of its papers'

Washington bureaus. His national security and terrorism beat was broadened to include the Justice Department, making it difficult to cover any of them as well as he would have liked, Meyer says.

"People don't want specialists anymore," he says. "It takes a long time to understand how things work and to get people to talk to you and crack intelligence agencies and the FBI and even the White House. If you don't have that, you're relegated to writing off the news."

Now, through Northwestern's Washington journalism program, Meyer will be conducting investigative projects on national security issues with groups of 10 graduate students assigned to him for three months at a time.

"We're also trying to figure out," he says, "who's going to pick up the slack from the carnage of the major media outlets."

Mary Jacoby, for one.

A former reporter for the Wall Street Journal and several other publications, Jacoby now is a media entrepreneur. In 2009, she founded Main Justice (mainjustice .com), a website that covers "insider news" about the Justice Department. It is just one of the upstart specialty or niche publications attempting to fill the void left by newspaper bureaus—and providing jobs to the capital's many unemployed or underemployed journalists.

"I saw that no one was really covering Justice," Jacoby explains. "The big papers never covered it in depth," and when cutbacks came, coverage "really fell off a cliff." Jacoby says there's "hardly anyone" in the Justice Department's pressroom and "dust on the desks." Further, she says, "very few people show up for the daily press gaggle."

Jacoby, who used her own money and raised some venture capital to start the site, teamed up with Kenny Day, now her publisher, when Legal Times laid him off and closed its Washington operation. They have hired five reporters and employ others on a contract basis. Jacoby says she wants to "revolutionize" how the department and its employees are covered by delving into certain legal topics, such as white-collar crime, and writing about lawyers "as personalities."

She likens her website to the Politico of the Justice set.

Other specialty sites have popped up to cover topics newspapers have pulled back on, including Scotusblog.com, which focuses on the Supreme Court. That newspapers have reduced their coverage of the High Court—the pinnacle of an entire branch of government—would have been unthinkable in an earlier time. But that withdrawal has left an opening for the site, which boasts that it hired the "dean" of the Supreme Court press corps, Lyle Denniston, a 52-year veteran of the beat (and onetime AJR columnist). Denniston, who previously wrote about the court for the Baltimore Sun and other papers, says he is reveling in his newfound editorial freedom and virtually unlimited space. The downside of the new outlet, he says, is that the audience is relatively small. "Now my audience is in the tens of thousands, not the hundreds of thousands," he says. The upside is that it is sophisticated, composed mainly of professionals and academics, so "we can write at a level of technicality and scope greater than any daily newspaper could use."

Perhaps the best-known of the specialty websites is Kaiser Health News, which is funded primarily by the Kaiser Family Foundation and launched on June 1, 2009, the same day Congress opened its debate on health care legislation, says Laurie McGinley, executive editor for news.

"We're a niche operation. We're writing for people who are interested in health care," says McGinley, formerly the Wall Street Journal's deputy Washington bureau chief for global economics. "The great thing is, given what happened in Congress, there's a lot more general interest than there was before."

KHN, as it is known, lists 16 reporters and editors and one Web producer on the site. Its stories read much as they would if written for a mainstream newspaper—and other news outlets are encouraged to reproduce them for free. The ultimate goal, McGinley says, is to reach a wider audience, not just Washington insiders.

Although plenty of reporters covered the health care debate during the past year, many wonder to what extent they will follow up as the administration drafts the rules and regulations that will determine exactly how the new law is applied. After all, congressional reporters who covered the politics and the substance of the legislation before it passed now must move on to other hot-button issues facing Congress, such as financial regulation, immigration and the Supreme Court nomination of Elena Kagan, not to mention what could be game-changing midterm elections in November.

"That's where we can make a big contribution," McGinley says. "Now that the traditional media are moving on to other things," KHN can "fill in the blanks."

A number of other newspaper refugees have gone to Environment & Energy Publishing, known as E&E, which hired 45 reporters and editors for four daily online publications on environment and energy policy. "Most of the people we've hired over the last three years have been laid off from regional papers," says Editor in Chief Kevin Braun, who put that number at 18. (See "Endangered Species," December 2008/January 2009.)

But Braun, who co-founded E&E in 1998, is careful to say that his sites are not intended to replace traditional media. His 2,000 subscribers pay in the neighborhood of $5,000 a year, he says, adding that total readership is about 40,000. E&E's target audience is not Mr. and Ms. Public, but insiders: Congress members and staffers, lobbyists and officials at federal agencies, major law firms, multinational corporations, energy companies and utilities, financial institutions, environmental organizations, foreign governments, universities and state governments.

"Our bread-and-butter issues are not of interest to the general public," Braun says. On the occasions that it does have general-interest stories, E&E makes them available through a partnership with the New York Times.

The fact is that niche or specialty publications tend to be geared toward specialty audiences, not the broad readership that newspapers have long targeted. Even if there are more reporters than ever before in the capital, the question arises as to whether they are covering federal departments, agencies and bureaus in a way that is useful to most Americans.

Who has replaced the newspaper reporters who once filled the pressroom desks at places like the departments of Agriculture, Justice, and Housing and Urban Development?

The answer seems to be no one and everyone.

Beyond the professional journalists seeking refuge at websites are the now-ubiquitous citizen journalists and others, such as bloggers at nonprofits and advocacy groups, who also are working to "fill in the blanks." These are dedicated individuals, some of whom have a point of view, some of whom do not, with varying degrees of training and commitment to the values that journalists hold dear. Many journalists scorn them; others rationalize that, given the demise of traditional outlets, there's no alternative. This can be described as an "if not them, who?" approach to the world of untrained scribes.

To those inside and outside government who want their issues covered accurately and without bias, the "who" makes a big difference.

"The level of expertise has largely disappeared," says Caroline Smith DeWaal, food safety director at the Center for Science in the Public Interest, a consumer advocacy organization. She says most major news outlets, in the past, had reporters who focused primarily on food safety. Now, few do. "One possible effect of this is that when the administration makes a major announcement, you don't have the quality of questions or the quality of analysis that you used to have. The media act strictly as reporters of information. They can't dissect the policy at the level they used to."

Even at places like the Pentagon, which, thanks to two wars, has not shed its corps of print reporters, press secretaries field regular queries from online reporters, bloggers and other "nontraditional media," including advocates, says Marine Col. Dave Lapan, director of press operations there.

"One of the biggest changes I have encountered in my career in public affairs is the exponential increase in news-gathering organizations and individuals and the volume of requests for information," Lapan said in an e-mail interview. "I don't think the effect on defense policy of these changes is yet known."

As a result of the mushrooming number of news outlets, there is a split between experienced beat journalists who understand the practices, policies, and unique culture and language of the Defense Department and the drop-ins, who do not. "One of our challenges," Lapan says, "is in providing information to the myriad sources who don't cover the beat and don't have the depth of knowledge and understanding."

Eliot Brenner, director of public affairs for the Nuclear Regulatory Commission, has watched the transformation of Washington coverage. He outlines a progression in which newspaper reporters have gone from producing in-depth stories to following a wire-service approach of filing and updating and, now, to writing in the fast, nonstop method of the digital world.

"We're seeing a transition where reporters are consumed with feeding the electronic ether," he says.

Every reporter knows what that means: less depth, less triple- or even double-checking, a greater chance for errors. Brenner says he has no problems with newspaper coverage of the NRC—the Washington Post, Wall Street Journal and New York Times still cover it regularly—but that he must stay on top of non-newspaper websites and quickly correct any mistakes. Further, he says, because these niche sites tend to concentrate on narrow issues, they don't offer the benefits of mainstream outlets—that is, a general readership.

"Now, we're paying more attention to blogs, but you have to take them with a grain of salt," he says. "Their readership tends to be smaller and made up of true believers."

Gary Bass, executive director of OMB Watch, a nonprofit research and advocacy organization that closely monitors the White House Office of Management and Budget, says non-journalism websites can be useful if they provide links to the underlying materials they are writing about. Otherwise, he says, it's hard to know which sites are reliable. As an example, he says that last year, there were "thousands upon thousands of citizen inspector generals" who wrote about how federal stimulus money was being used.

"As the news media has cut back, I think we've seen this growth in citizen journalism," Bass says. "The strength is that a lot of these accountability issues are covered. The weakness is that you don't have editors—not only for the writing quality, but also for accuracy."

A common refrain among regulatory agency staffers and advocates alike is that things haven't been the same since Cindy Skrzycki left the Washington Post. In 1993, Skrzycki began writing a weekly column called "The Regulators," and she later wrote a book called *The Regulators: The Anonymous Power Brokers Who Shape Your Life.* The title explains exactly how she views coverage of departments, bureaus and agencies: not as the regurgitation of mind-numbing bureaucratic gobbledygook, but as the discovery, interpretation and exploration of the truly important stuff of Washington, the otherwise hidden decisions that touch real people in beyond-the-Beltway America.

Skrzycki is addicted to regulation in the same way a baseball writer might be addicted to the game. She practically breathes it. "I just thought it was the most fascinating part of government and the most unsupervised part of government. These people are not elected. They really affect our lives," she says. She might have been the only reporter at the Post who regularly covered numerous agencies and bureaus, but she was ever vigilant. When she left the Post in 2005, Skrzycki continued her column at Bloomberg News until last year.

She eagerly rattles off some of the regulatory issues she covered over the years: auto safety, distracted driving among truck drivers, federal preemption of regulatory matters, tires, immigration and employment, liquor regulations, lobbying, food safety (chicken, eggs, meat), ergonomics, the environment, communications, nuclear power, alcohol labeling, import laws regarding socks—socks!—Internet gambling, ozone, mercury, airplane drinking water, lead, Medicare, Medicaid, small and big business, and spyware.

"I don't think there's anyone in Washington now who has a 20-year overview of how these things have played out over the years and how they repeat themselves and how the problems don't get fixed," says Skrzycki, who now teaches nonfiction writing at the University of Pittsburgh and is a business correspondent for GlobalPost, a website that launched last year to fill another emerging gap—international reporting. "Covering regulation is a long, tedious process. It doesn't happen by press conference. If you don't have people dedicated to doing that, it's likely not to get done. . . . I was spread pretty thin, but I did know all the major legislation that was moving, everything that was going on at the agencies. I had great sources."

It is through the slow, methodical, old-school skill of source development that government reporters often get their best stories. That can take time, and it's harder to do when deadlines are measured in hours or minutes and not days. But it is these sources, people in little-known offices of agencies and bureaus, who are bothered by what they see, who might pick up the phone and tip off a trusted reporter. Skrzycki says she was the beneficiary of many such calls over the years, the kind of call she would have hoped someone in NHTSA would have made concerning Toyota.

"If you have fewer and fewer reporters out there who are recognizable, who people can call, tip, it's likely things are going to go on for longer than they might," Skrzycki says. "It's always good to have reporters watching, checking in."

If you have fewer and fewer reporters out there who are recognizable, who people can call, tip, it's likely things are going to go on for longer than they might.

Some of her sources (who also are her fans) echo that sentiment. "Cindy used to track regulatory issues. Unless there is a silo-based issue [one that fits neatly into a beat], there isn't someone you can go to at the Washington Post, New York Times, Wall Street Journal and say, 'Look what OMB is doing,' " says OMB Watch's Bass.

Apparently, no one called a reporter to say, "Look what the Minerals Management Service is doing." Prior to the explosion of the Deepwater Horizon drilling platform in the Gulf of Mexico in April, little had been written about the MMS in recent years, save for a sex scandal from 2002 to 2006. After the rig exploded, killing 11 workers and dumping millions of gallons of oil into the Gulf of Mexico, journalists and Congress members alike started paying attention to the Interior Department agency, which granted permission to BP and other oil companies to drill in the gulf. Among the revelations that came out in the weeks after the explosion was that the agency, which both promotes and regulates offshore drilling, failed to get permits intended to protect endangered species.

Interior Secretary Ken Salazar announced that he would reduce the conflict of interest within MMS by abolishing the agency and dividing its functions among three new entities. Skrzycki's book addresses the built-in tensions in a number of federal agencies.

"You have agencies that have these dual missions both to promote the industry and to police them," she says. "These things often come into conflict. And the recent blowup with BP and the Minerals Management agency is an example of that."

Even though President Obama announced before the spill that he was going to expand offshore drilling, it appears that no one was looking into the agency that would regulate it. "You have all these inherent conflicts," Skrzycki said. "It means that the enforcement part of the regulatory system is not pure. And, sometimes, you get results like this. This is something that the press certainly never looks into or even probably knows about until you have a big incident like this."

MMS spokesman Nicholas Pardi says there are a number of reporters who contact the agency regularly, though none covers it full time. Most of the reporters cover issues such as energy (especially oil and gas) or the environment, and report on other agencies as well, he says. Still, Pardi insists the agency is frequently in the news because it provides oil and gas production numbers and information about offshore rig safety during hurricanes. He declines to speculate about whether the press should have been writing about the inherent conflict between MMS's dual functions.

"Our movements are pretty closely monitored, because we're responsible for regulating such a large industry," Pardi says. Since the Gulf of Mexico explosion, he adds, "people have been doing a lot of research about the agency. And we welcome that. We want to be transparent."

Skrzycki cut her journalistic teeth covering the steel industry for the American Metal Market, a trade publication that she credits with teaching her the importance of the people who write the regulations. Take the health care law: "There will be hundreds of rules coming out of HHS [the Department of Health and Human Services] and the Centers for Medicare and Medicaid Services. That's a huge story. The implementation of that law will be in regulations. And they're going to be so important, and there's going to be so much lobbying."

It's a valid point. While most reporters cover lobbyists as they work to persuade members of Congress and their staffs, few pay attention to (or even see) the lobbyists who roam the halls of other government buildings, meeting with administrators who write rules and regulations. It's not surprising, since few reporters roam those halls themselves. For sure, it is more difficult to wander around government buildings, poking your head in offices, than it used to be. In the post-9/11 era, it's impossible to walk into many buildings without an appointment. Nevertheless, with some effort, it can be done.

Neil Kerwin, president of American University and, like Skrzycki, a regulatory aficionado, says it must be done. Casting a spotlight on the writing and enforcement of regulations "changes priorities," says Kerwin, who founded AU's Center for the Study of Rulemaking and wrote a book titled *Rulemaking: How Government Agencies Write Law and Make Policy*. Public pressure on agencies, he says, "will cause them to try to fix the faults of the system. That's where I would encourage journalists to spend more time. . . .

"I believe the most important law in America is being written by administrative agencies," Kerwin says. And, more than ever before, the administrators writing the rules are receiving information from advocacy groups and lobbyists, he says. It's not their fault, Kerwin asserts, because the government doesn't have the money to provide independent research on every issue that needs a rule. But that makes it even more important for journalists to watch over the regulatory process.

"The person who needs to be educated is the average American," Kerwin says. "You sit here and you watch the health care bill going through what it went through. As an afterthought, we won't know the impact until HHS writes the rules. How are they going to write them? Who's going to write them? How much guidance will they get from the Congress?. . . . Does the government have resources? I rarely see that covered. . . .

"Cindy," he says of Skrzycki, "was a lonely voice out there."

The Post did not replace Skrzycki. But it did run her column for a while after she went to Bloomberg. And National Editor Kevin Merida insists that, despite repeated rounds of buyouts that have reduced the Post's editorial staff, the paper's devotion to federal coverage remains strong.

"I think buyouts have an effect on a newsroom. But it hasn't reduced our commitment to covering the federal government, because that's the heart of what we do," Merida says. "That's central for us. That's kind of where we live. Politics and government is the heart of our core franchise coverage."

Like so many of its counterparts, the Post shifted years ago from covering "buildings" to covering issues. That means a number of reporters follow topics that require them to touch base with more than one department or agency. It may or may not mean that they follow the agency closely. "We don't have people attached to buildings per se, for instance, the Agriculture Department or HUD," Merida says. "But through issues, we intersect with the federal government."

Lyndsey Layton writes for the Post about food safety and consumer issues, and Kimberly Kindy writes about government accountability, an assignment that has led to post-disaster investigations of both Toyota and mining. Further, Merida says, the Post is strengthening its coverage of the federal government, regulatory agencies in particular, through blogs. Cecilia Kang is writing about the Federal Communications Commission on her technology blog, and Zach Goldfarb covers the SEC on a new blog called Market Cop.

The blog posts tend to be faster and shorter than newspaper stories, and some compete with niche publications. "There are a lot of specialized audiences that want selected news given to them any time they want it wherever they are," Merida says, adding that blogs provide the Post a way to develop more mobile "apps" for agency coverage. "We'll find ways to serve those specialized audiences."

As Washington bureaus grapple with contracting staffs and increasing pressures to produce for multiple media platforms, there is one that has had the luxury—in terms of staff and money—to set its own course. And the course Bloomberg News has chosen is to beef up coverage of departments and agencies, says Washington Executive Editor Al Hunt. The bureau went so far as to create a regulatory team of 10 reporters and three editors. Some reporters still cover issue-oriented beats, but all in all, Hunt says, "we think it's better to cover buildings."

Hunt says the need to cover agencies has increased because the Obama administration is much more given to regulation than administrations past, both because the financial crisis shone a spotlight on some of government's shortcomings and because the deficit has limited Washington's options to solve problems in more expensive ways.

"We think it's very important in most agencies," he says. "The FTC, the SEC and the FDIC [Federal Deposit Insurance Corporation] particularly now are in a period of tremendous regulatory attention. If you don't focus on those agencies, you're going to miss a lot of that. Fifteen or 20 years ago, the FDIC was a pretty sleepy agency. No one would accuse it of being a sleepy agency today. . . .

"I've been in Washington for 40 years, and I have never seen a time where there is so much attention paid to the regulatory issue" by the federal government.

Bloomberg is able to place one, two and occasionally three reporters on departments and agencies because of its remarkable size. Unlike so many Washington bureaus, this one has grown—substantially—in recent years. The bureau now numbers 140, about double what it was a decade ago and 30 percent larger than it was five years ago, Hunt says. It has a seasoned staff peopled with many illustrious former newspaper reporters, including Hunt, a veteran of the Wall Street Journal and a familiar television commentator. Along with its staff, the bureau's reach has grown significantly. Once a financial media outlet primarily for wealthy CEOs, investors, bankers and the like, Bloomberg now distributes a much broader daily report through its famed (and pricey) terminals, but also on its website; in Bloomberg Businessweek magazine, which it bought late last year; through its global television operation; and to hundreds of newspapers that subscribe to the Washington Post's newswire.

Hunt is reluctant to criticize bureaus that don't cover agencies. "I think a lot of people don't do it that way because they've cut back," he says. "If instead of 10 reporters, you only have five reporters, it's tough to cover institutions."

The New York Times makes no bones about the manner in which it covers the capital. "We don't cover buildings, which would be a remarkably bureaucratic and reader-unfriendly way of organizing ourselves," Richard Stevenson, deputy Washington bureau chief, said in an e-mail interview. "We cover subject matter, and encourage our reporters to follow the story when it cuts across the boundaries of departments or agencies, or between Washington and the rest of the world."

Perhaps if the Times or another paper had written about the conflicted relationship between MMS and the oil industry it regulates before the latest disaster, no one would have paid attention and nothing would have changed. It likely would have been viewed as a dullish insider story about a flawed government bureaucracy, something to bury inside the A section. After the explosion, it was a front-page story that definitely grabbed attention.

Too late.

Talk to anyone about coverage of the Mine Safety and Health Administration and you'll undoubtedly hear about Ellen Smith. Smith is managing editor of Mine Safety & Health News, a biweekly newsletter published from Pittsford, New York. She has been covering mining since 1987 and has won 29 journalism awards. It's easy to see why. She's a walking encyclopedia of mining information, about flammability and inspection requirements, about underground conveyor belts and rescue chambers. And she has the ability to explain the intricacies to a general, non-mining audience. But she doesn't. Smith's newsletter, which costs $525 to $625 a year, is distributed to insiders.

Smith understands why Washington newspaper reporters don't cover MSHA— "It's not sexy . . ."—so whenever disasters occur, she finds herself translating mining-ese to non-mining reporters. She teaches them how to search MSHA's database and what the information they find there means. She did that in April in West Virginia, just as she did following three mining disasters in five months in 2006.

Eventually, Smith knows, most of the reporters will go back to their newspapers and ignore mining until the next disaster. Except, primarily, for Smith (who has two part-time reporters under contract in Washington), plus James Carroll of Louisville's Courier-Journal and Ken Ward Jr. of the Charleston Gazette in West Virginia. Each of these journalists covers the mining industry differently, and each goes out of his or her way to praise the other two. Carroll, the only one in Washington, asserts that he has the advantage of being able to show his face at MSHA's office and at hearings on Capitol Hill.

"Within the limits of the time you have as a one-person bureau, it does really help when you're at a committee hearing to spend time chatting with the staff," he says. "It's helpful to have that face-to-face contact. They know who you are. It shows your level of interest in the subject matter. It's one of those intangible things that helps you do your job as a reporter.

"Newspapers would say they don't need to have people in Washington," he continues. "By the same token, you could say you don't need to have somebody in City Hall, in the police headquarters, you could just dial it in. They—editors—would argue about that. Well, I'd say the same thing for Washington . . . I think it's a mistake for newspapers not to see Washington as just as vital to local coverage as any other beat."

Ward, who covers not only mining but all things environmental, says his paper hasn't had a reporter in Washington for more than two decades. In the 19 years he has been with the independently owned Gazette, Ward has been to MSHA's national office exactly once, when he came to the capital because he won a journalism fellowship and wanted to attend the luncheon. He doesn't view his location as a disadvantage.

"If I were in Washington, I might have different and higher-level sources in the agency that I went to lunch with or had drinks with or something, but a sense of perspective outside the Beltway is not necessarily a bad thing," he says.

In fact, Ward does something to unearth stories that a lot of Washington reporters *used* to do: He reads the Federal Register.

"The job of these agencies is to implement a law that Congress passed. They do that by writing regulations and by enforcement. You can find out what they're doing without being in Washington. You can read the regulations. You can file FOIA requests. You can do that from afar."

Like Carroll, Ward tries to cover MSHA and other agencies "in between" disasters. "We started doing stories in 2001 about how the Bush administration was tearing down the safety net for miners," he says. "They were halting work on new regulations. They were reversing existing regulations. They were trying to be more friendly to coal.

"We were doing stories about that in 2001–2005. Then in 2006, six miners died in the Sago mine [in West Virginia], and all of a sudden reporters discovered that, oh, the Bush administration was dismantling MSHA."

But the Gazette, with its circulation of less than 50,000, doesn't have the influence that large newspapers have. And the large papers don't provide the kind of sustained day in day out coverage of agencies that might bring change.

Not one large, national paper covers MSHA consistently, according to spokeswoman Amy Louviere. She says that in addition to the three regulars, she occasionally hears from reporters who work for papers in Salt Lake City, Pittsburgh and Lexington, Kentucky. In the 15 years that Louviere has been with MSHA, the press operation has shrunk from four people to just her.

Phil Smith, director of communications for the United Mine Workers, says that since the April mine explosion in West Virginia, he has tried to persuade more reporters to stick with the story. "I think it would make a difference," he says. "When the mine operators know that there's going to be media scrutiny of what they're doing and MSHA knows there's going to be scrutiny in how they are enforcing the law, I think it's obvious they would do things differently.

"I have talked to several hundred reporters from print media, from radio, from television and bloggers. I encouraged all them: 'You guys can't do what you always do when the story's not so sexy and the funerals are over.'

"But something else always comes up."

This year it's the oil spill in the gulf.

Attention spans are short. News bureaus, those that remain, are thin. The federal bureaucracy is massive, and no newspaper could possibly cover all of it. However, when Washington teemed with newspaper bureaus fully stocked with reporters, there was always a chance that one or two would pay attention to this department or that agency. It's still possible.

But it happens less and less.

"I like to think a lot of us got into this profession because we did want to make government accountable and help people understand how government works," Carroll says. "That should be one of our top priorities—to be watchdogs. But in this environment, it's more of a challenge. If you're the only guy answering the phone, doing the blog, doing the Web update and writing for tomorrow's paper? Then you want to go talk to sources? You just do the very best you can."

"I like to think a lot of us got into this profession because we did want to make government accountable and help people understand how government works. That should be one of our top priorities—to be watchdogs."

"Tomorrow's paper" may well prove to be anachronistic. The question for Washington is whether "yesterday's" reporting—the time-consuming, source-building, questioning, triple-checking and following up that hold officials' feet to the fire; the painstaking digging that tells readers or viewers or clickers or scrollers things that no one else is telling them—will become a relic as well.

Critical Thinking

1. Summarize Jodi Enda's concerns is terms of *feedforward* and *feedback* agendas of reporting. Which loss is the greater concern?

2. Why have many of the Washington bureaus shut down? Is diminishing depth of coverage driven more by lack of resources or lack of audience interest? Would greater audience interest lead to increased reporting resources? Would increased reporting resources lead to greater audience interest?

JODI ENDA (jaenda@gmail.com) writes about politics and government from Washington. Previously, she covered the White House, presidential campaigns and Congress for Knight Ridder and was a national correspondent for the Philadelphia Inquirer. AJR Assistant Editor Lori Miller (lammiller@comcast.net) contributed to this story.

Overload!

Journalism's Battle for Relevance in an Age of Too Much Information

BREE NORDENSON

In 2007, as part of the third round of strategic planning for its digital transformation, The Associated Press decided to do something a little different. It hired a research company called Context to conduct an in-depth study of young-adult news consumption around the world. Jim Kennedy, the AP's director of strategic planning, initially agreed to the project because he thought it would make for a "fun and entertaining" presentation at the annual meeting. It turned out to be more than that; the AP believed that the results held fundamental implications for the role of the news media in the digital age. Chief among the findings was that many young consumers craved more in-depth news but were unable or unwilling to get it. "The abundance of news and ubiquity of choice do not necessarily translate into a better news environment for consumers," concluded the researchers in their final report. "Participants in this study showed signs of news fatigue; that is, they appeared debilitated by information overload and unsatisfying news experiences. . . . Ultimately news fatigue brought many of the participants to a learned helplessness response. The more overwhelmed or unsatisfied they were, the less effort they were willing to put in."

The idea that news consumers, even young ones, are overloaded should hardly come as a surprise. The information age is defined by output: we produce far more information than we can possibly manage, let alone absorb. Before the digital era, information was limited by our means to contain it. Publishing was restricted by paper and delivery costs; broadcasting was circumscribed by available frequencies and airtime. The Internet, on the other hand, has unlimited capacity at near-zero cost. There are more than 70 million blogs and 150 million websites today—a number that is expanding at a rate of approximately ten thousand an *hour.* Two hundred and ten billion e-mails are sent each day. Say goodbye to the gigabyte and hello to the exabyte, five of which are worth 37,000 Libraries of Congress. In 2006 alone, the world produced 161 exabytes of digital data, the equivalent of three million times the information contained in all the books ever written. By 2010, it is estimated that this number will increase to 988. Pick your metaphor: we're drowning, buried, snowed under.

The information age's effect on news production and consumption has been profound. For all its benefits—increased transparency, accessibility, and democratization—the Internet has upended the business model of advertising-supported journalism.

This, in turn, has led news outlets to a ferocious focus on profitability. Over the past decade, they have cut staff, closed bureaus, and shrunk the newshole. Yet despite these reductions, the average citizen is unlikely to complain of a lack of news. Anyone with access to the Internet has thousands of free news sources at his fingertips. In a matter of seconds, we can browse *The New York Times* and *The Guardian, Newsweek* and *The Economist,* CNN and the BBC.

News is part of the atmosphere now, as pervasive—and in some ways as invasive—as advertising. It finds us in airport lounges and taxicabs, on our smart phones and PDAS, through e-mail providers and Internet search engines. Much of the time, it arrives unpackaged: headlines, updates, and articles are snatched from their original sources—often as soon as they're published—and excerpted or aggregated on blogs, portals, social-networking sites, RSS readers, and customizable homepages like My MSN, My Yahoo, myAOL, and iGoogle. These days, news comes at us in a flood of unrelated snippets. As Clay Shirky, author of *Here Comes Everybody: The Power of Organizing without Organizations,* explains, "The economic logic of the age is unbundling." But information without context is meaningless. It is incapable of informing and can make consumers feel lost. As the AP noted in its research report, "The irony in news fatigue is that these consumers felt helpless to change their news consumption at a time when they have more control and choice than ever before. When the news wore them down, participants in the study showed a tendency to passively receive versus actively seek news."

There has always been a large swath of the population that is not interested in news, of course, just as there has always been a portion that actively seeks it out. What's interesting about the current environment is that despite an enormous increase in available news and information, the American public is no better informed now than it has been during less information-rich times. "The basic pattern from the forties to today is that the amount of information that people have and their knowledge about politics is no worse or no better than it's been over that sixty-year period," explains Michael X. Delli Carpini, dean of the Annenberg School for Communication at the University of Pennsylvania. For example, a 2007 survey conducted by the Pew Research Center for the People & the Press found that 69 percent of Americans could correctly name the vice president, only a slight decrease from the 74 percent who could in 1989.

This phenomenon can be partially explained by our tendency to become passive in the face of too much information. It can also be attributed to the fact that the sheer number of specialized publications, the preponderance of television channels, the wide array of entertainment options, and the personalization and customization encouraged by digital technologies have made it far easier to avoid public-affairs content. "As choice goes up, people who are motivated to be politically informed take advantage of these choices, but people who are not move away from politics," explains Delli Carpini. "In the 1960s, if you wanted to watch television you were going to watch news. And today you can avoid news. So choice can be a mixed blessing."

Markus Prior writes in his book, *Post-Broadcast Democracy: How Media Choice Increases Inequality in Political Involvement and Polarizes Elections,* "Political information in the current media environment comes mostly to those who want it." In other words, in our supersaturated media environment, serendipitous exposure to political-affairs content is far less common than it used to be. Passive news consumers are less informed and less likely to become informed than ever before.

The tragedy of the news media in the information age is that in their struggle to find a financial foothold, they have neglected to look hard enough at the larger implications of the new information landscape—and more generally, of modern life. How do people process information? How has media saturation affected news consumption? What must the news media do in order to fulfill their critical role of informing the public, as well as survive? If they were to address these questions head on, many news outlets would discover that their actions thus far—to increase the volume and frequency of production, sometimes frantically and mindlessly—have only made things more difficult for the consumer.

> **To win the war for our attention, news organizations must make themselves indispensable by producing journalism that helps make sense of the flood of information that inundates us all.**

While it is naïve to assume that news organizations will reduce their output—advertising dollars are involved, after all—they would be wise to be more mindful of the content they produce. The greatest hope for a healthy news media rests as much on their ability to filter and interpret information as it does on their ability to gather and disseminate it. If they make snippets and sound bites the priority, they will fail. Attention—our most precious resource—is in increasingly short supply. To win the war for our attention, news organizations must make themselves indispensable by producing journalism that helps make sense of the flood of information that inundates us all.

The Limits of Human Attention

Ours is a culture of multitasking, of cramming as many activities as possible into as short a period of time as possible. We drive and talk on our cell phones, check e-mail during meetings and presentations, eat dinner while watching TV. In part, says Maggie Jackson, author of *Distracted: The Erosion of Attention and the Coming Dark Age,* such multitasking "is part of a wider value system that venerates speed, frenetic activity, hyper-mobility, etcetera, as the paths to success. That's why we're willing to drive like drunks or work in frenzied ways, although it literally might kill us."

Many young people multitask to the extreme, particularly when it comes to media consumption. I've witnessed my twenty-two-year-old brother watch television while talking on the phone, IMing with several friends, composing an e-mail, and updating his Facebook page. A widely cited 2006 study by the Henry J. Kaiser Family Foundation found that 81 percent of young people engage in some form of media multitasking during a given week. But as cognitive psychologists have long known, human attention is quite limited. Despite our best efforts, when we try to do more than one thing at once, we are less efficient and more prone to error. This is because multitasking is actually a process of dividing attention, of toggling back and forth between tasks.

Acquiring new information requires particularly focused attention, which includes the ability to ignore distractions. In order to absorb the information contained in a CNN newscast, for example, we must not only direct our attention to the person talking, but also filter out the running headlines, news updates, and financial ticker on the lower part of the screen. Torkel Klingberg, a professor of cognitive neuroscience at Karolinska Institute in Sweden and author of *The Overflowing Brain,* puts it simply: "If we do not focus our attention on something, we will not remember it." In other words, attention is a critical component of learning.

Michael Posner, a researcher who has dedicated his career to studying attention and a professor emeritus of psychology at the University of Oregon, explains attention as a system of three networks—alerting, orienting, and executive. Alerting refers to the state of wakefulness necessary to attend to information, while orienting is the process by which we respond to stimuli, such as movement, sound, or noise. Executive attention is the highest-order network, the one that we have conscious control over. If we are trying to study for a test or read a novel, we use it to direct and maintain our focus, as well as to suppress our reaction to competing stimuli like the din of a nearby conversation or television.

The information-saturated environment that we live in is, unsurprisingly, extremely demanding of our attention. Modern life—both at work and at home—has become so information-rich that Edward Hallowell, a Boston-area psychiatrist, believes many of us suffer from what he calls an attention-deficit trait, a culturally induced form of attention-deficit disorder. As he pointed out in a 2005 interview with CNET News, "We've been able to overload manual labor. But never before have we so routinely been able to overload brain labor." According to Hallowell and other psychiatrists, all these competing inputs prevent us from assimilating information. "What your brain is best equipped to do is to think, to analyze, to dissect, and create," he explains. "And if you're simply responding to bits of stimulation, you won't ever go deep." Journalist John Lorinc noted as much in an elegant article on distraction in the April 2007 issue of *The Walrus:*

> It often seems as though the sheer glut of data itself has supplanted the kind of focused, reflective attention that might make this information useful in the first place. The dysfunction of our information environment is an outgrowth of its extraordinary fecundity. Digital communications technology

has demonstrated a striking capacity to subdivide our attention into smaller and smaller increments; increasingly, it seems as if the day's work has become a matter of interrupting the interruptions.

In a recent report, *Information Overload: We Have Met the Enemy and He Is Us,* the research firm Basex concluded that interruptions take up nearly 30 percent of a knowledge worker's day and end up costing American businesses $650 billion annually. Other studies show that interruptions cause significant impairments in performance on IQ tests.

In many ways, the modern age—and the Internet, in particular—is a veritable minefield of distractions. This poses a central challenge to news organizations whose mandate is to inform the public. Research by Pablo Boczkowski, who teaches communication studies at Northwestern University, has revealed that when we consume news online we do so for significantly less time than in print and that we do it while we're working. Further complicating matters is the disruptive nature of online advertising. Intrusive Web advertisements—washingtonpost.com recently featured one in which a Boeing helicopter flies right across the text of a news story—exploit our orienting network, which evolved to respond quickly to novel stimuli. Could we train ourselves to suppress our tendency to be distracted by such advertising? "You can get somewhat better, but it's hard to resist because it'll produce orienting," Posner explains. "The way you resist it is you bring your attention back as quickly as you can." Yet even if we were somehow able to eliminate ads, the sheer number of articles, headlines, and video and audio feeds on news websites makes focused attention difficult. Having to decide where to direct our attention and then maintain it makes reading and retaining news online a formidable task.

The Attention Economy

One of the most useful frameworks for understanding journalism's challenges and behavior in the information age is the notion of the attention economy. Economics is the study of the allocation of resources and the basic principles of supply and demand, after all, and about a decade ago a handful of economists and scholars came up with the concept of the attention economy as a way of wrestling with the problem of having too much information—an oversupply, if you will—and not enough time or people to absorb it all.

The dynamics of the attention economy have created a complicated and hypercompetitive arena for news production and consumption. News media must not only compete with one another, as well as with an ever-increasing assortment of information and entertainment options, but also with the very thing that supports their endeavors—advertising. In fact, the advertising industry has been struggling with the dynamics of the attention economy for a couple of decades now. As the advertising landscape becomes more saturated, advertisers must work harder to get their messages to the consumer. But as Mark Crispin Miller, professor of media ecology at New York University, notes in the *Frontline* documentary *The Persuaders:*

> Every effort to break through the clutter is just more clutter. Ultimately, if you don't have clean, plain borders and backdrops for your ads, if you don't have that blank space, that commons, that virgin territory, you have a very hard time

making yourself heard. The most obvious metaphor is a room full of people, all screaming to be heard. What this really means, finally, is that advertising is asphyxiating itself.

The news media also run the risk of self-asphyxiation in an information landscape crowded with headlines, updates, and news feeds. In order to garner audience attention and maintain financial viability, media outlets are increasingly concerned with the "stickiness" of their content. According to Douglas Rushkoff, host of *The Persuaders* and author of the forthcoming book *Life Incorporated,* the question for these organizations has become, "How do we stick the eyeballs onto our content and ultimately deliver the eyeballs to our sponsors?" As he dryly points out, "That's a very different mandate than how do we make information—real information—available to people. The information economy, then, is a competitive space. So as more people who are information providers think of themselves as competing for eyeballs rather than competing for a good story, then journalism's backwards." The rise of sound bites, headlines, snippets, infotainment, and celebrity gossip are all outgrowths of this attempt to grab audience attention—and advertising money. Visit a cable-news website most any day for an example along the lines of POLICE: WOMAN IN COW SUIT CHASED KIDS (CNN); or MAN BEATS TEEN GIRL WAITING IN MCDONALD'S LINE (FOX News). As Northwestern's Boczkowski points out, "Unlike when most of the media were organized in monopolistic or oligopolistic markets, now they are far more competitive; the cost of ignoring customer preferences is much higher."

Meanwhile, the massive increase in information production and the negligible cost of distributing and storing information online have caused it to lose value. Eli Noam, director of the Columbia Institute for Tele-Information, explains that this price deflation is only partly offset by an increase in demand in the digital age, since the time we have to consume information is finite. "On the whole—on the per-minute, per-line, per-word basis—information has continuously declined in price," says Noam. "The deflation makes it very difficult for many companies to stay in business for a long time."

Thus, we come to the heart of journalism's challenge in an attention economy: in order to preserve their vital public-service function—not to mention survive—news organizations need to reevaluate their role in the information landscape and reinvent themselves to better serve their consumers. They need to raise the value of the information they present, rather than diminish it. As it stands now, they often do the opposite.

More-Faster-Better

"Living and working in the midst of information resources like the Internet and the World Wide Web can resemble watching a firefighter attempt to extinguish a fire with napalm," write Paul Duguid and John Seely Brown, information scientists, in *The Social Life of Information.* "If your Web page is hard to understand, link to another. If a 'help' system gets overburdened, add a 'help on using help.' If your answer isn't here, then click on through another 1,000 pages. Problems with information? Add more."

Like many businesses in the information age, news outlets have been steadily increasing the volume and speed of their output. As the proliferation of information sources on the Web continues at a breakneck pace, news media compete for attention by adding content and features—blogs, live chat sessions with journalists, video and audio streams, and slideshows. Much of this is of excellent quality. But taken together, these features present a quandary: Do we persevere or retreat in the face of too much information? And as the AP study showed, even young news consumers get fatigued.

In psychology, passivity resulting from a lack of control is referred to as "learned helplessness." Though logic would suggest that an increase in available news would give consumers more control, this is not actually the case. As Barry Schwartz, the Dorwin Cartwright Professor of Social Theory and Social Action at Swarthmore College, argues in his book *The Paradox of Choice: Why More is Less,* too many choices can be burdensome. "Instead of feeling in control, we feel unable to cope," he writes. "Freedom of choice eventually becomes a tyranny of choice."

Too many choices can be burdensome: 'Instead of feeling in control, we feel unable to cope. Freedom of choice becomes a tyranny of choice.'

A recent study by Northwestern University's Media Management Center supports this phenomenon. It found that despite their interest in the 2008 election, young adults avoid political news online "because they feel too much information is coming at them all at once and too many different things are competing for their attention." The study participants said they wanted news organizations to display *less* content in order to highlight the essential information. "Young people want the site design to signal to them what's really important . . . instead of being confronted by a bewildering array of choices," write the researchers in their final report, *From "Too Much" to "Just Right": Engaging Millennials in Election News on the Web.*

The instinct that more is better is deeply ingrained in the modern psyche. David Levy, a professor at The Information School of the University of Washington, uses the phrase "more-better-faster" to describe the acceleration of society that began with the Industrial Revolution. According to Levy, we tend to define productivity in terms of speed and volume rather than quality of thought and ideas. "We are all now expected to complete more tasks in a smaller amount of time," writes Levy in a 2007 journal article. "And while the new technologies do make it remarkably efficient and easy to search for information and to collect masses of potentially relevant sources on a huge variety of topics, they can't, in and of themselves, clear the space and time needed to absorb and to reflect on what has been collected." In the case of news production, Swarthmore's Schwartz agrees. "The rhythm of the news cycle has changed so dramatically that what's really been excluded," he says, "is the time that it takes to think."

Implications for Democracy

Our access to digital information, as well as our ability to instantly publish, share, and improve upon it at negligible cost, hold extraordinary promise for realizing the democratic ideals of journalism. Yet as we've seen, many news consumers are unable or unwilling to navigate what Michael Delli Carpini refers to as the "chaotic and gateless information environment that we live in today."

When people had fewer information and entertainment options, journalistic outlets were able to produce public-affairs content without having to worry excessively about audience share. As the Internet and the 24/7 news cycle splinter readership and attention

spans, this is no longer the case. "Real journalism is a kind of physician-patient relationship where you don't pander to readers," says Bob Garfield, a columnist for *Advertising Age* and co-host of NPR's *On the Media.* "You give them some of what they want and some of what you as the doctor-journalist think they ought to have." Unfortunately, many news outlets feel they can no longer afford to strike the right balance.

As information proliferates, meanwhile, people inevitably become more specialized both in their careers and their interests. This nichification—the basis for *Wired* editor Chris Anderson's breakthrough concept of the Long Tail—means that shared public knowledge is receding, as is the likelihood that we come in contact with beliefs that contradict our own. Personalized home pages, newsfeeds, and e-mail alerts, as well as special-interest publications lead us to create what sociologist Todd Gitlin disparagingly referred to as "my news, my world." Serendipitous news—accidentally encountered information—is far less frequent in a world of TiVo and online customization tools.

Viewed in this light, the role of the journalist is more important than ever. "As society becomes splintered," writes journalist and author David Shenk in *Data Smog,* "it is journalists who provide the vital social glue to keep us at least partly intact as a common unit." Journalists work to deliver the big picture at a time when the overload of information makes it hard to piece it together ourselves. "The journalist's job isn't to pay attention simply to one particular field," explains Paul Duguid. "The job is to say, 'Well, what are all the different fields that bear on this particular story?' They give us the breadth that none of us can have because we're all specialists in our own particular area." In other words, the best journalism does not merely report and deliver information, it places it in its full and proper context.

Journalism's New Role

The primacy placed on speed and volume in the information age has led to an uneven news landscape. "There is an over-allocation of resources on breaking and developing news production and constant updates," observes Boczkowski. "I think many news organizations are overdoing it." While headlines and updates are undoubtedly important, their accumulation is problematic. "Increasingly, as the abundance of information overwhelms us all, we need not simply more information, but people to assimilate, understand, and make sense of it," write Duguid and Seely Brown.

The question, then, is how?

As David Shenk presciently noted more than a decade ago, "In a world with vastly more information than we can process, journalists are the most important processors we have." The researchers who conducted the study for the AP concluded that the news fatigue they observed among young adults resulted from "an overload of basic staples in the news diet—the facts and updates that tend to dominate the digital news environment." In other words, the news they were encountering was underprocessed.

"In a world with vastly more information than we can process, journalists are the most important processors we have."

—David Shenk

In order to address the problem, the AP has made a number of changes in the way it approaches news production. For starters, it instituted a procedure it calls 1-2-3 filing, which attempts to reduce news clutter and repetition (the days of endless write-throughs are over) while also acknowledging the unpackaged and real-time nature of news in the digital world. With 1-2-3 filing, reporters produce news content in three discrete parts, which they file separately: a headline, a short present-tense story, and, when appropriate, a longer in-depth account. By breaking down the news in this way, the AP hopes to eliminate the redundancy and confusion caused by filing a full-length article for every new story development. In 1-2-3 filing, each component replaces the previous component: the headline is replaced by the present-tense story, which is then replaced by the in-depth account.

The AP has also launched a series of initiatives aimed at providing consumers with deeper, more analytical content. It has created a Top Stories Desk at its New York headquarters to identify and "consider the big-picture significance" of the most important stories of the day. It has also begun developing interactive Web graphics to help explain complicated and ongoing stories like Hurricane Katrina and the Minnesota bridge collapse. And for 2008, the AP launched "Measure of a Nation," a multimedia series dedicated to examining the election "through the prism of American culture, rather than simply the candidates and the horse race." "Measure of a Nation" packages take a historical approach to covering such notions as myth, elitism, and celebrity in American presidential politics. In one article published in late August, for example, journalist Ted Anthony explains the powerful political influence of the Kennedy family over the past fifty years, drawing parallels between the campaigns of JFK and RFK and that of Barack Obama. As the AP writes in its report, these changes in approach represent "a concerted effort to think about the news from an end-user's perspective, re-emphasizing a dimension to news gathering and editing that can get lost in the relentless rush of the daily news cycle."

Much like educational institutions, the best news organizations help people convert information into the knowledge they need to understand the world. As Richard Lanham explains in *The Economics of Attention,* "Universities have never been simply data-mining and storage operations. They have always taken as their central activity the conversion of data into useful knowledge and into wisdom. They do this by creating attention structures that we call curricula, courses of study." Institutions of journalism do it by crafting thoughtful and illuminating stories. "Journalists who limit their role to news flashes are absolving themselves of any overarching obligation to the audience," writes Shenk in *The End of Patience.* "Mere telling focuses on the mechanics of transmitting information of the moment, while education assumes a responsibility for making sure that knowledge sticks." The most valuable journalism is the kind that *explains.* "The first and foremost role that a journalist plays is to provide the information in a context that we wouldn't be able to get as amateurs," says Delli Carpini. "And I think that's where journalism should be focusing."

As it turns out, explanatory journalism may have a promising future in the market for news. On May 9, in partnership with NPR News, *This American Life* dedicated its hour-long program to explaining the housing crisis. "The Giant Pool of Money" quickly became the most popular episode in the show's thirteen-year history. *CJR* praised the piece (in "Boiler Room," the essay by Dean Starkman in our September/October issue) as "the most comprehensive and insightful look at the system that produced the credit crisis." And on his blog, *PressThink,* Jay Rosen, a journalism professor at New York University, wrote that the program was "probably the best work of explanatory journalism I have ever heard." Rosen went on to note that by helping people understand an issue, explanatory journalism actually creates a market for news. It gives people a reason to tune in. "There are some stories—and the mortgage crisis is a great example—where until I grasp the *whole,* I am unable to make sense of *any* part," he writes. "Not only am I not a customer for news reports prior to that moment, but the very frequency of the updates alienates me from the providers of those updates because the news stream is adding daily to my feeling of being ill-informed, overwhelmed, out of the loop."

> **"There are some stories—and the mortgage crisis is a great example—where until I grasp the *whole,* I am unable to make sense of *any* part."**
>
> —Jay Rosen

Rather than simply contributing to the noise of the unending torrent of headlines, sound bites, and snippets, NPR and *This American Life* took the time to step back, report the issue in depth, and then explain it in a way that illuminated one of the biggest and most complicated stories of the year. As a result of the program's success, *NPR News* formed a multimedia team in late August to explain the global economy through a blog and podcast, both of which are called "Planet Money." And on October 3, *This American Life* and NPR aired a valuable follow-up episode, "Another Frightening Show About the Economy," which examined the deepening credit crisis, including how it might have been prevented and Washington's attempts at a bailout.

Along with supplying depth and context, another function of the modern news organization is to act as an information filter. No news outlet better embodies this aim than *The Week,* a magazine dedicated to determining the top news stories of the week and then synthesizing them. As the traditional newsweeklies are struggling to remain relevant and financially viable, *The Week* has experienced steady circulation growth over the past several years. "The purpose of *The Week* is not to tell people the news but to make sense of the news for people," explains editor William Falk. "Ironically, in this intensive information age, it's in some ways harder than ever to know what's important and what's not. And so I often say to people, 'With *The Week,* you're hiring this group of really smart, well-versed people that read for you fifty hours a week and then sit down and basically give you a report on what they learned that week.'"

Rather than merely excerpting and reprinting content, this slim magazine takes facts, text, and opinions from a variety of sources—approximately a hundred per issue—to create its own articles, columns, reviews, and obituaries. As Falk explains, there's a certain "alchemy" that occurs when you synthesize multiple accounts of a news story. And *The Week*'s success suggests that consumers are willing to pay for this. "We're a service magazine as much as we are a journalism magazine," says Falk. "People work ten, eleven hours a day. They're very busy. There are tremendous demands on their time. There are other things competing for your leisure time—you can go online, you can watch television or a DVD. So what we do is deliver to you, in a one-hour package or less, is a smart distillation of what happened last week that you need to pay attention to."

One ally in journalism's struggle to deal with information overload, meanwhile, may be the digital machinery that brought it about in the first place. While digital archiving and data tagging cannot replace human interpretation and editorial judgment, they have an important role to play in helping us navigate the informational sea. As any news consumer knows, searching for or following a story can be frustrating on the Internet, where information is both pervasive and transient. In its study, the AP observed that young consumers struggled to find relevant in-depth news. So the wire service stepped up an effort begun in 2005 to tag all its articles, images, and videos according to a classification system of major news topics and important people, places, and things. These tags allow consumers, as well as news organizations and aggregators, to more effectively find and link to AP content. A number of other organizations, including *The New York Times* (check out the Times Topics tab on nytimes.com), *The Washington Post,* and CNN have similar projects under way, promising an opportunity to rapidly—and often automatically—provide consumers with a high level of detail, context, and graphical means of explanation.

The website for BBC News may be the best example of how journalistic organizations can deliver context in the digital environment. A news story about the Russia-Georgia crisis, for example, is displayed alongside a list of links to a map of the region, a country profile, an explanation of the crisis, a summary of Russian foreign policy, and related news articles and video footage. All online BBC News stories are presented in this manner, giving consumers multiple ways to learn about and understand an issue. While no American site is this comprehensive, a handful of major news outlets, from CNN to NPR to the *National Journal,* have used this approach in creating special election 2008 Web pages. By linking stories to one another and to background information and analysis, news organizations help news consumers find their way through a flood of information that without such mediation could be overwhelming and nearly meaningless.

Why Journalism Won't Disappear

While it's true that the Web allows the average individual to create and disseminate information without the help of a publishing house or a news organization, this does not mean journalism institutions are no longer relevant. "Oddly enough, information is one of the things that in the end needs brands almost more than anything else," explains Paul Duguid. "It needs a recommendation, a seal of approval, something that says this is reliable or true or whatever. And so journalists, but also the institutions of journalism as one aspect of this, become very important."

Moreover, the flood of news created by the production bias of the Internet could, in the end, point to a new role for journalistic institutions. "We're expecting people who are not librarians, who are not knowledge engineers to do the work of knowledge engineers and librarians," says Jonathan Spira, CEO and chief analyst for the business research firm Basex and an expert in information overload.

In other words, most of us lack the skills—not to mention the time, attention, and motivation—to make sense of an unrelenting torrent of information. This is where journalists and news organizations come in. The fact that there is more information than there are people or time to consume it—the classic economy-of-attention problem—represents a financial opportunity for news organizations. "I think that the consumers, being subjects to this flood, need help, and they know it," says Eli Noam. "And so therefore they want to have publications that will be selecting along the lines of quality and credibility in order to make their lives easier. For that, people will be willing to pay." A challenge could become an opportunity.

In fact, journalism that makes sense of the news may even increase news consumption. As Jay Rosen points out on his blog, explanatory journalism creates a "scaffold of understanding in the users that future reports can attach to, thus driving demand for the updates that today are more easily delivered." In a similar fashion—by providing links to background information and analysis alongside every news story—the BBC gives consumers frameworks for understanding that generate an appetite for more information.

The future of news depends on the willingness of journalistic organizations to adjust to the new ecology and new economy of information in the digital age. "I think in some ways, we need a better metaphor," says Delli Carpini. "The gatekeeping metaphor worked pretty well in the twentieth century, but maybe what news organizations should be now is not gatekeepers so much as guides. You don't want gatekeepers that can say you can get this and you can't get that. You want people who can guide you through all this stuff."

> **"Maybe what news organizations should be now is not gatekeepers so much as guides. You want people who can guide you through all this stuff."**
>
> —Delli Carpini

Ironically, if out of desperation for advertising dollars, news organizations continue to chase eyeballs with snippets and sound bites, they will ultimately lose the war for consumer attention. Readers and viewers will go elsewhere, and so will advertisers. But if news organizations decide to rethink their role and give consumers the context and coherence they want and need in an age of overload, they may just achieve the financial stability they've been scrambling for, even as they recapture their public-service mission before it slips away.

Critical Thinking

1. To what degree do you want news media to filter and interpret information you receive?
2. Describe the media implications of *the attention economy.*

BREE NORDENSON is a freelance writer.

Learning to Love the New Media
Shallow, Divisive, Unreliable

Everyone from President Obama to Ted Koppel is bemoaning a decline in journalistic substance, serious-ness, and sense of proportion. But the author, a longtime advocate of these values, takes a journey through the digital-media world and concludes there isn't any point in defending the old ways. Consumer-obsessed, sensationalist, and passionate about their work, digital upstarts are undermining the old media—and they may also be pointing the way to a brighter future.

JAMES FALLOWS

Just after last fall's midterm elections, Ted Koppel, for 25 years the face of *Nightline* on ABC, wrote in *The Washington Post* about journalism's modern decline. "Much of the American public used to gather before the electronic hearth every evening," Koppel wrote, referring to an era that ran through roughly the 1980s, while Walter Cronkite, Chet Huntley, David Brinkley, Frank Reynolds and Howard K. Smith offered relatively unbiased accounts of information that their respective news organizations believed the public needed to know . . . It was an imperfect, untidy little Eden of journalism where reporters were motivated to gather facts about important issues. We didn't know that we could become profit centers. No one had bitten into that apple yet.

The column was called "The Case Against News We Can Choose," and it said that the shift toward a more market-minded, profit-driven journalism was both irreversible and destructive. "The need for clear, objective reporting in a world of rising religious fundamentalism, economic interdependence and global ecological problems is probably greater than it has ever been," Koppel said. But we were less likely than before to get the fair, steady view we need, because "we are no longer a national audience receiving news from a handful of trusted gatekeepers; we're now a million or more clusters of consumers, harvesting information from like-minded providers."

Anyone who has read, watched, or listened to the news has an idea of what Koppel is worried about. The election cycle just behind us was dominated by very bitter views and accusations, on issues likely to matter very little in the long run. Candidates denounced "the deficit" without seriously proposing to do anything about it. "The question of how the US should tackle its mounting national debt has been relegated to a bunch of Punch and Judy bumper stickers that bear as little relation to its fiscal reality as astrology does to astronomy," a *Financial Times* analyst wrote on the day before the election. "The same applies to infrastructure, education, immigration—pretty much anything

that touches on America's future competitiveness." The same as well for the ongoing wars in Iraq and Afghanistan; nuclear threats from North Korea or Iran; world trends in food and energy. Elections are how we face big issues, except when we can't.

Just before the midterm elections, Barack Obama answered questions from students at George Washington University and made a point like Koppel's. After a young man asked Obama what had surprised him about the actual work of being president, Obama said wryly, "Where do I start?" Then he started with the dysfunction of the modern press.

> I've been surprised by how the news cycle here in Washington is focused on what happens *this minute*. Sometimes it's difficult to keep everybody focused on the long term. The things that are really going to matter in terms of America's success 20 years from now, when we look back, are not the things that are being talked about on television on any given day.

Embedded in complaints like these is a series of related concerns: that the media are doing a worse job than they used to, that their failures make it harder for the country as a whole and for individuals trying to understand the world to do business and make sensible decisions—and that all these trends are only going to get worse.

I am an easy target for this sort of message. Fifteen years ago, I published a book, *Breaking the News,* which argued that a relentless focus on scandal, spectacle, and the "game" of politics was driving citizens away from public affairs, making it harder for even the least cynical politicians to do an effective job, and at the same time steadily eroding our public ability to assess what is happening and decide how to respond. And this was in an era that in retrospect seems innocent. The big, fatherly anchor figures—Brokaw, Jennings, Rather—were still on the evening news shows. Newspapers were mildly concerned about falling circulation rather than in an all-out panic about imminent collapse. Fox News Channel had yet to begin operations, and Craigslist had just started up. To serve the public and to remain in operation, I argued, the news industry had to re-embrace its special role as a business that was not just about business. Journalists should commit themselves to the challenge of making what matters interesting, and resist the slide into the infotainment age. How quaint it all looks now!

But, as I was reminded when I recently talked to people in the news business, historians, political scientists, and others about the current predicament of the news, every previous era looks innocent. Those talks changed my mind about what the press should do next. I haven't changed my mind about the dysfunction of American public life; as I argued a year ago in these pages ("How America Can Rise Again," January/February 2010), most things look promising for America—except our ability to face and solve big problems through our political system. But I no longer think it's worth arguing whether journalism is getting "worse." The fond retrospective view offered by Koppel and others is highly selective, as Koppel himself admits in his article. I now think it's worth facing the inevitability of the shift to infotainment and seeing how we can make the best of it. To show why, let's visit Gawker.

Nick Denton, the founder, owner, and CEO of the dozen or so websites that make up Gawker Media, revels in his role as the unembarrassable and highly publicized bad boy of today's New York media scene. Twice in less than four years, *New York* magazine has run lengthy features about him and his latest offense against good taste. During last fall's midterm election campaign, Gawker paid a 25-year-old man from Philadelphia, whom it left unnamed, for 15 photos from a one-night stand (unconsummated) he had had three years earlier with Christine O'Donnell, who was running for the United States. Senate in Delaware and was best known for her "I'm Not a Witch" ad campaign. Gawker posted the pictures with the headline "I Had a One-Night Stand With Christine O'Donnell." Everything about Gawker's choices in that case violated normal journalistic ethics, from paying a source to spotlighting material with a lot of titillation value and only the faintest possible claim to being "relevant" in public-interest terms. But Denton told me that his only regret was bothering to justify the decision. A follow-up post, signed by "The Staff of Gawker.com," said that O'Donnell's pro-abstinence, anti-masturbation campaign made her fair game:

> She lies about who she is; she tells that lie in service of an attempt to impose her private sexual values on her fellow citizens; and she's running for Senate. We thought information documenting that lie—that O'Donnell does *not* live a chaste life as she defines the word, and in fact hops into bed, naked and drunk, with men that she's just met—was of interest to our readers.

"I don't believe we should have done that defense," Denton told me when I spoke with him at Gawker HQ on Elizabeth Street in Lower Manhattan early this year. "It's helpful when someone is a hypocrite, but we should have just said that our interest is voyeuristic. 'We did this story because we thought you would like it. We thought it was funny, so we thought you'd think it was funny, too.' And there was a tidal wave of traffic and attention."

In his mid-40s, tall and louche, Denton was unshaven and wearing jeans and an untucked shirt when I visited him in an open-plan office filled with people half his age (I in corduroys and blue blazer over a V-neck sweater and Jos. A. Bank shirt, personification of Mr. Square). I had known and liked him in an earlier incarnation, when we were both based in San Francisco and he had started an early news aggregator called Moreover Technologies. And I am interested in him as a pure type. He combines a familiar figure, the Fleet Street rogue (he grew up in London and went to Oxford) willing to tart up and shake up stuffy American newsrooms, with something entirely new: the most refined tools ever created for knowing exactly what an audience wants to see and read, as opposed to someone's opinion of what it should want or "needs" to know. Denton's shtick is to be outrageously impolitic. ("What annoys me about the United States. media? Generally the pompous liberals. I suppose they're useful, but they're such losers, with their endless hand-wringing. They don't know how to fight.") His enterprises, and his rationale for them, present a distillation of the model toward which the news business is trending.

Giving people what they want as opposed to what they should want is a conflict as old as journalism, certainly as it has been practiced in this country. My capsule history of journalism is that for more than a century after the Civil War, American readers and viewers were in various ways buffered from getting exactly what they *wanted* from newspapers and, later, radio and TV news shows. News, like education, aspired to be as interesting as possible but to have an uplifting civic intent.

Regulations, from the "fairness doctrine" to a requirement for "public service" programming, affected radio and TV coverage. And technological and geographic constraints had already played a crucial role in the evolution of newspapers, many of which could operate as regional monopolies or duopolies. You couldn't get the New York papers if you lived in Dallas, so the *Morning News* and *Times Herald* had the whole of Dallas as their audience. Like their counterparts in Atlanta, Los Angeles, or Minneapolis, the families who owned these newspapers valued them not just as (good) businesses but also for their cultural and political roles. When there were only three nationwide broadcast networks, they could have a statesmanlike agreement on covering worthy events, like presidential press conferences, and treating their nightly news shows as prestige loss-leaders aimed at telling a broad Middle American audience what it needed to know. "I grew up when broadcast news was a duopoly," the long-time anchor Tom Brokaw told me, referring to the relative dominance of CBS and his own NBC over ABC news until at least the early 1980s. "I figured I would be one of the people with the hands on the lever in deciding what mattered. It worked for me!"

That's all gone, as Brokaw and everyone else knows. One by one, the buffers between what people want and what the media can afford to deliver have been stripped away. Broadcast TV was deregulated, and cable and satellite TV arose in a wholly post-regulation era. As newspapers fell during the rise of the Internet, and fell faster because of the 2008 recession, the regional papers fell hardest. The survivors, from *The New York Times* to the *National Enquirer,* will be what British newspapers have long been: nationwide in distribution, and differentiated by politics and class. The destruction of the "bundled" business model for newspapers, which allowed ads in the Auto section to underwrite a bureau in Baghdad; the rise of increasingly targeted and niche-ified information sources and advertising vehicles; and the consequent pressure on almost any mass offering except for sports—all of these are steps toward a perfected market for information of all sorts, including news. With each passing month, people can get more of what they want and less of what someone else thinks they should have.

Every news organization recognizes this shift. For instance, a strategy document leaked from AOL just before its acquisition of the Huffington Post said that its route toward survival was to drive the average cost per unit of content down to $84 (from the current $99) and use "search engine optimization" and other techniques to attract an average of 7,000 page views per item, up from the current 1,500. *The Atlantic* is now profitable in part because traffic on our website is so strong. Everyone involved in the site understands the tricks and trade-offs that can increase clicks and raise the chances of a breakout "viral" Web success. Kittens, slide shows, videos, Sarah Palin—these are a few. For us and for other publications, they are complications. For Gawker, they're all that is.

The first thing you see on entering Gawker's loft-size open work area is a huge screen that looks like a nicer, higher-def version of what you might see in a brokerage house. The top part of the screen shows live views of the home pages of the main Gawker properties—Gizmodo, Jezebel, Lifehacker, Deadspin, Gawker itself, and others (excluding Gawker's sex-oriented site, Fleshbot, which accounts for about 5 percent of the company's total traffic). Together, according to Denton, the sites bring in some 32 million unique visitors worldwide a month, about the same as *The New York Times* and twice as many as *The Washington Post*. Meters display the second-by-second traffic to each site. As users log on to a site, and leave, the needles on the meters go up and down to register its popularity. The bottom part of the screen lists specific stories from each of the Gawker Media sites and across the company as a whole, ranked by how many people are viewing them at each moment—and those numbers are listed. As you watch, the stories switch places on the screen, each with a green arrow if it's trending up or a red arrow if it's heading down. When I arrived, "Your Horoscope May Have Changed" still led the chart for all sites but was heading down, while "The Horrible Life of a Disney Employee" was in second place and on the way up. "Loose Rat in New York City Subway Car Crawls on Man's Face," with a 26-second amateur video of exactly that, was the lead item on Gawker.tv, and "The Greatest Scam in Tech," from Gizmodo, was the most popular technology item. (It was about a "free" mobile-phone service called PeepApp.) "The Hilarious Agony of Watching a Computer Illiterate" was in second place among tech items. Two weeks after my visit, as I write this story, "How Good Is Charlie Sheen for a Porn Star's Career?" is No. 1.

I saw more screens as I walked into the central work space, where more than 50 young writers sat side by side at their computers, as if in a coffee shop, at three big tables that ran the length of the room. "How much do the writers think about the rankings?," I asked Denton after saying hello. "Let's ask them!" he said, and we went to the back corner of the room where Gawker.com's writers worked.

"I usually just check the board when I walk by," Brian Moylan said. "You have an idea of what's going to be big and what's not." He and his colleagues agreed that a story's popularity could be predicted—but only to a certain degree. "You can't get a big one every day," he added. His strategy: "I just try to figure out, if I were to go to a party, what would everyone want to talk about? And that is what I'd want to write about."

Across the table from him, Maureen O'Connor emphasized that every item was a crapshoot. "I feel like the biggest breakaway hits are always surprising," she said. The day's surprise hit was hers, about the rearranged dates for zodiac signs. "That was a smallish thing that nobody had picked up from the *Minneapolis Star Tribune*," she said. "I threw it up at the end of the day because I wanted to put up one more post." It took off instantly. (The "reporting" that staff writers do is almost all online.) In February, O'Connor had a predictably huge hit with her article, including a shirtless picture, that led to the resignation of the "Craigslist Congressman," Christopher Lee. "Serendipity is an important part of the operation," Denton added. "The job of journalism is to provide surprise."

That afternoon, Denton and his associates talked me through the other refinements they had learned in what people want—not what they say they want, nor what they "should" want, but what they choose when they have a chance. Some might seem obvious—video everywhere, a website with what Denton called a "rounded personality," meaning one that gives visitors the option of being outraged, amused, diverted, even inspired, as their moods dictate. Others were more surprising.

In the first *New York* profile, in 2007, Denton had said that an active "commenter" community was an important way to build an audience for a site. Now, he told me, he has concluded that courting commenters is a dead end. A site has to keep attracting new users—the omnipresent screens were recording the "new uniques" each story brought to the Gawker world—and an in-group of commenters might scare new visitors off. "People say it's all about 'engagement' and 'interaction,' but that's wrong," he said. "New visitors are a better indicator and predictor of future growth." A little more than one-third of Gawker's traffic is new visitors; writers get bonuses based on how many new viewers they attract.

As for the science of website headlines: "I'm against verbs," Denton told me, even though that day's greatest-hits list included several exceptions ("Rat Crawls . . ."). "It's almost as if you've got to get the whole story into the headline," Brian Moylan said, "but leave out enough that people will want to click." "You can kill a story by using a too-clever headline," Maureen O'Connor said. "The public is not very forgiving of wit in headlines," Denton added. "Or irony. You can get away with one opinionated word, if the rest is literal and clear." O'Connor said she had a further rule: "It can't be more than two lines on the home page. Your eyes can't take it in. You want the dumbest headline possible!" That said, one of the most popular headlines of the previous year had been anything but obvious. It was "Эй, вы можете прочитать запрещенную статью *GQ* про Пуина здесь," or, "Hey, You Can Read the Banned *GQ* Story About Putin Here," for an item on a story about Vladimir Putin not included in *GQ* magazine's Russian edition. John Cook, the Gawker writer who showed it to me, was emphasizing that headline writing was still as much guess-work as science.

Denton said that other journalists would compliment him on snarky items, but those didn't bring in enough new read-ers. Neither did print-industry gossip, which had been Gawk-er's original staple. "We put scoop ahead of satire," by which he meant things like the O'Donnell story, photos they had just acquired that day of Mark Zuckerberg's new house in Califor-nia, and "Favregate."

"If I were running *The New York Times*," Denton said, "the first thing I would do is put numbers next to every story," as Gawker does on its home page—not just include a most-e-mailed list but fully embrace the concept of giving readers more of what they want. If he felt compelled to do "good" for the world, Denton said, he would set up "offshore Gawkers" serving capitals where speech is limited, like Riyadh, Beijing, Tehran. "Zero political content—you don't want to be seen as a 'democ-racy advocate' at all," he said. "Just good, juicy, scurrilous gossip stories about nepotism and corruption and mistresses and Swiss bank accounts. Pictures of their houses! You would want to be seen as having wicked fun. And if you did that for 20 years . . ."

Of course, Denton was omitting good-for-you, public-service-style stories for outrageous effect. In my first "inter-view" with him for this story, conducted over the course of nearly an hour through an instant-message exchange, he said that a market-minded approach like his would solve the business problem of journalism—but only for "a certain kind of journal-ism." It worked perfectly, he said, for topics like those his sites covered: gossip, technology, sex talk, and so on. And then, as an aside: "But not the worthy topics. Nobody wants to eat the bor-ing vegetables. Nor does anyone want to pay [via advertising] to encourage people to eat their vegetables." He continued:

NICK: But, anyway, look at me. I used to cover political reform in post-communist Eastern Europe, which had been my subject at Oxford.

And now I tell writers that the numbers (i.e. the audience) won't support any worthiness. We can't even write stories about moguls like Rupert Murdoch or Barry Diller unless it involves photographs of them cavorting with young flesh.

(I used to enjoy [doing] those stories in the old days, before web metrics.)

But naturally even he admits that the "worthy topics" have their necessary place, and when pressed, he had a surprisingly earnest list of ways to make sure they were covered, from local volunteer efforts to donations by philanthropists.

"I know this is scary for the high-end American journalist," he said when I was about to leave, with as little condescension as he could manage. "If you come from the U.K., it doesn't seem alien."

Scary or not, is this in fact worse than journalism as we have previously known it? It is tempting to conclude that the cacophony we hear now must represent a descent from previous standards. "I am sad at what feels like a decline in our public culture," I was told by Jill Lepore, a professor of American history at Harvard and the author of the recent *The Whites of Their Eyes*, which compares today's Tea Party activ-ists with the original Revolutionary War activists. "It feels like a personally abusive and textually violent time." But she went on to say that it is hard to demonstrate that today's media and result-ing public discussion are, in their totality, worse than before.

For instance: Ted Koppel, a direct descendant of the golden-age greats, illustrates the complexities of even journalism's "best" periods. To Jimmy Carter and senior members of his administration, Koppel's famous *Nightline* program on ABC was a dramatic example of the way media sensationalism could distort, or at least affect, public life. On November 4,1979, exactly one year before Carter would stand for reelection, Ira-nian radicals seized 66 American hostages at the United States. Embassy in Tehran. Within a few days, ABC had launched a nightly 11:30 P.M. special report on the crisis, which soon was called "America Held Hostage: Day 15." Then it was "America Held Hostage: Day 100," and the night before Americans went to the polls, "America Held Hostage: Day 365," with Koppel anchoring the news each night.

There are many reasons Carter lost that election to Ronald Reagan; a prime interest rate of 20 percent during the spring symbolized economic problems that might have been suf-ficient to do him in. But "America Held Hostage" surely played a part. It was an early illustration of the way in which a choice about news coverage—namely, to offer a daily count-down of America's humiliation—converted a problem into an emergency. Koppel told me that years after the hostages were released, he met Jimmy Carter at a ceremony in Washington. "President Carter said there were two people who were better off because of the hostage situation," Koppel told me. "The ayatollah. And me." And all of this notwithstanding Koppel's role as one of the most serious and sophisticated broadcast journalists of his day.

The point is not to debunk the greats but to say that the noble parts of golden-age journalism were not its only parts. The most famous play about American journalism, Ben Hecht and Charles MacArthur's *The Front Page*, is set in a courthouse press room in the 1920s, when reporters swaggered rather than cowered. But its ethics are straight from what many think of as the Gawker playbook: reporters bribe sources, editors hype whatever lurid story will draw a crowd, no one gets too haughty about the "responsibility" of the press. Richard Hofstader's seminal works about unreason and misinformation in Ameri-can public affairs, *The Paranoid Style in American Politics* and *Anti-Intellectualism in American Life*, appeared in the early 1960s and were hardly respectful of the journalism of that time.

"From the standpoint of policy explanation, as opposed to battlefield coverage, the press did a lousy job on the two biggest foreign-policy stories of my adult life—Vietnam and Iraq—and it's doing a poor job now on Afghanistan," I was told by William Whitworth, for 20 years the editor of this magazine. As a young *New Yorker* writer in 1970, Whitworth did a celebrated 20,000-word interview with Eugene Rostow, a Johnson-administration veteran and prominent supporter of the Vietnam War, consisting of repeated requests for him to explain why, exactly, it would matter if the United States "lost" Vietnam. I had asked Whitworth whether he thought that throughout his career the media had gotten better or worse in their ability to examine, as he had done in his Rostow article, the "why" of major policy decisions, beyond the operational "how." He said it was hard to argue that newspapers and TV were overall doing a worse job than during the Korean and Vietnam wars. "What mixes the picture, obviously," he said, "is the advent of the Internet. It provides us with an unprecedented amount of poor and even fake information, but it also give us access to a wider array of good news sources and to very useful public-policy discussions you wouldn't find in newspapers or on television."

"It's not so much that American public life is more idiotic," Jill Lepore said, referring to both press coverage and the public discussion it spawns. "It's that so much more of American life is public. I think that goes a long way to explaining what seems to be a 'decline.' Everything is documented, and little of it is edited. Editing is one of the great inventions of civilization."

She added that since the 1940s, political scientists had tried to measure how well American citizens understood the basic facts and concepts of the nation and world they live in. "It actually is a constant," she said. "There is a somewhat intractable low level of basic political knowledge." When I asked Samuel Popkin, a political scientist at UC San Diego, whether changes in the media had made public discussion less rational than before, he sent back a long list of irrationalities of yesteryear. One I remembered from my youth: the taken-for-granted certainty among some far-right and far-left groups in the 1960s (including in my very conservative hometown) that Lyndon Johnson had ordered the killing of John Kennedy. One I had forgotten: Representative John Anderson of Illinois, who received nearly 6 million votes as an Independent presidential candidate against Ronald Reagan and Jimmy Carter in 1980, three times introduced legislation to amend the Constitution so as to recognize the "law and authority" of Jesus Christ over the United States.

While it's interesting and even useful to know whether today's journalism marks a descent from past standards, what matters more is how it suits today's needs. This depends on how media of the Gawker age, which deliver what the customers want rather than what they "should" have, handle the task of explaining the world. Of course, there will for a long time be a range of publications, all of them subject to the new market pressures but each having its own conception of its culture and the "brand," the reputation and audience it can deliver to advertisers. But existing American media operations must become slightly if steadily more like the Gawkers of the business— we're doing it right here, at the magazine Ralph Waldo Emerson and company founded before the Civil War—and new operations will grow up knowing no other environment. Is this a change to fight?

he News Business has never been stable. Like everything else in American society, it has kept changing, often in dramatic and unforeseen ways. For instance, *Time* and *Newsweek* now seem like legacies practically from the age of the Founders, but they were the result of sudden, market-driven experimentation by young Henry Luce and his imitators in the late 1920s through the Depression years. (The market opportunity identified by Luce and his partner, Briton Haddon, as entrepreneurs fresh out of Yale: people who lived far from the big East Coast cities wanted to know more about national and world affairs than they could learn from their local papers.) National Public Radio seems just as venerable, but when Lyndon Johnson was in the White House, it did not exist. Indeed, the relative stability of big media in the golden-age decades after World War II left a misleading impression of how tumultuous the news business had been through most of America's past. The mid-1940s to the late 1970s was a time when newspapers were fat, national magazines were widely read, and TV news reports were sober and "responsible." Like the idealized sitcoms of the same era—*Father Knows Best, The Donna Reed Show, Happy Days*—they presented as normal and traditional what was in fact an exceptional moment in American existence.

We have created a technology that has wonderful potential, but increases our ability to lie to ourselves and forget it is a lie.

As technological, commercial, and cultural changes have repeatedly transformed journalism, they have always caused problems that didn't exist before, as well as creating opportunities that often took years to be fully recognized. When I was coming into journalism, straight from graduate school, in the 1970s, one of the central complaints from media veterans was precisely that the "college boys" were taking over the business. In the generation before mine, reporters had thought of themselves as kindred to policemen and factory workers; the college grads in the business stood out, from Walter Lippmann (Harvard 1910) on down. A large-scale class shift was under way by the time of Watergate, nicely illustrated by the team of Bob Woodward (Yale '65) and Carl Bernstein (no college degree). The change was bad, in shifting journalists' social sights upward, so they identified more with the doctors and executives who were their college classmates, and less with the non-college, blue-collar Americans whose prospects were diminishing through those years. And it was good, in equipping newspapers and TV channels with writers and analysts who had studied science or economics, knew the history of Russia or the Middle East, had learned a language they could use in the field.

Similarly, the rise of TV changed all of journalism, even for those who worked in print or on the radio. It had effects that were bad, like the disproportionate emphasis on spectacles like car chases or tornadoes. And mixed, like the new importance of physical attractiveness in opening or closing career possibilities for newsmen and (especially) newswomen. And it had effects that were revolutionarily positive. For the first time in human history, people could see events taking place beyond their immediate line of sight. They could therefore envision and, perhaps, understand the world with a richness never possible before. How different would the psychic effect of the first moon landing have been if people had only read about it the next day? Or of the battlefield conditions and relentless casualties of the Vietnam War?

Unless they are different from anything the news business has yet undergone, the technological and market changes now disrupting journalism will have effects that are both good and bad. The reason to point this out is not so we will shrug and say, "Whatever!" It is to identify the likely problems so that we can try to buffer them—and remember that we will be slow to recognize the most beneficial possible effects.

If we accept that the media will probably become more and more market-minded, and that an imposed conscience in the form of legal requirements or traditional publishing norms will probably have less and less effect, what are the results we most fear? I think there are four:

- that this will become an age of lies, idiocy, and a complete Babel of "truthiness," in which no trusted arbiter can establish reality or facts;
- that the media will fail to cover too much of what really matters, as they are drawn toward the sparkle of entertainment and away from the depressing realities of the statehouse, the African capital, the urban school system, the corporate office when corners are being cut;
- that the forces already pulverizing American society into component granules will grow all the stronger, as people withdraw into their own separate information spheres;
- and that our very ability to think, concentrate, and decide will deteriorate, as a media system optimized for attracting quick hits turns into a continual-distraction machine for society as a whole, making every individual and collective problem harder to assess and respond to.

Our protection against these trends is partly defensive, or conservative. Economic history is working against "legacy" news organizations like the BBC, *The New York Times,* NPR, and most magazines you could name. But historical forces don't play out on a set schedule, and can be delayed for a very long time. Economic history is also working against museums, small private colleges, and the farm-dappled French countryside, but none of them has to disappear next week. Even as it necessarily evolves, our news system will be better the longer it includes institutions whose culture and ambitions reach back to the pre-Gawker era, and it would be harder and costlier to try to re-create them after they have failed than to keep them on life support until their owners find a way to fit their values and standards into the imperatives of the new systems.

But the new culture also creates positive opportunities—as, it's worth saying again, every previous disruption has. An odd symbol of the new possibilities is Roger Ailes, the guiding force behind Fox News since its start.

To people who are worried about journalism's future, Ailes would seem a perverse symbol of anything positive. The "news" system he has created is correctly understood to be a political rather than a journalistic operation, and to be free of inner conflict about "getting it right" or "going too far." (Here's the thought-experiment test: What assertion from Glenn Beck on his broadcasts would finally lead Ailes or his producers to say, "Glenn, are you *sure?*" "Real" news operations don't always get the right answer to that question, but asking it is how they can think of themselves as journalists rather than propagandists.) But to me, Ailes is an instructive example because of what he shows about the way discourse will be conducted in the coming journalistic era. Ailes flatly denied my request for an interview on this story, which surprised me. I have interviewed him before, with no harm to either side.

As it happens, what I wanted to ask him about was covered by Tom Junod, of *Esquire,* in a recent profile. The core of Ailes's success, Junod says, has been not simply that Fox was more entertaining to watch than pallid CNN. It has been, in the words of Richard Wald, the former president of NBC News: "You can't beat Roger fighting on territory he's left behind." That is, Fox is doing something different from the other networks. If you say that Glenn Beck got a fact wrong, or if you point out how many of Fox's female on-air broadcasters are babes in very short skirts, Ailes's answer will be "So?" He's doing something new—as Henry Luce did with the power of photographs at *Life* in the 1930s, as Ted Koppel did when satellite connections made *Nightline* the first regular TV show to have live interviews with prominent guests from around the world.

No one knows exactly what forms the next Ailes, Luce, or Koppel will invent. But here, again, are some of the risks of whatever those forms are, along with some possibilities of heading them off in advance:

- **Lies and truthiness.** The regular journalistic reflex is to correct error by applying fact and logic. In moot-court competition, this pays off. In much of the rest of life, it does not. On being told "You're wrong," some people will say "Thanks for the correction!" Most will say "Go to hell."

"There is actually a lot of energy released by opposing 'settled facts,'" I was told by Jay Rosen, of the journalism school at NYU. "The more 'settled' it is, the more furious the energy. When someone points out an error in what Sarah Palin has said, that becomes another example of the liberal media, and it becomes another tool for organizing."

"Liberals love to talk about the erosion of logic and the scientific method," Nick Denton said. One example he discussed: Al Gore's book about irrationality in public life, called *The Assault on Reason,* with passages like this: "The German philosopher Jürgen Habermas describes what has happened as the 'refeudalization of the public sphere.'"

"But what if the answer to a false narrative isn't fact?," Denton says. "Or Habermas? Maybe the answer to a flawed narrative is a different narrative. You change the story." Which is what, he said, Jon Stewart and Stephen Colbert have done.

They don't "fact-check" Fox News, or try to rebut it directly, or fight on its own terms. They change the story not by distorting reality—their strength is their reliance on fact—or creating a fictitious narrative, but by presenting the facts in a way that makes them register in a way they hadn't before.

Jaron Lanier, author of *Digital Maoism,* was blunt when I asked him about Fox's ability to assert a "truth" and have it echo through digital media. "We have created a technology that has wonderful potential, but that enormously increases our ability to lie to ourselves and forget it is a lie," he told me. "We are going to need to develop new conventions and formalities to cut through the lies." Stewart and Colbert have developed one such set of new conventions; others will emerge.

- **Undercovered stories.** This will be a problem, as it has always been. "In a lot of different ways, the new journalism will be better than the old," Steven Waldman, a co-founder of Beliefnet who is now doing a report on the information needs of communities for the Federal Communications Commission, told me. "But there are a few important areas where that is not the case. Especially local, labor-intensive, full-time 'accountability' journalism"—what used to be called "covering City Hall."

Or, as the writer Steven Berlin Johnson, among others, has contended, local coverage could in some ways become much better, as systems arise to match "hyper-local" news—the burglary down the street, the test scores at the neighborhood school—with the audience directly affected by it. "I think in the long run, we're going to look back at many facets of old media and realize that we were living in a desert disguised as a rain forest," Johnson said in 2009 in a speech at the South by Southwest (SXSW) festival in Austin. "There is going to be more content, not less; more information, more analysis, more precision, a wider range of niches covered." Rather than worry about a general collapse of the press, perhaps we should watch carefully for specific failures of local, statehouse, or investigative coverage, and start experimenting now with ways to correct them—through nonprofit coverage or other means that new technologies make possible.

- **Disconnection.** American life is becoming more polarized, and this is a phenomenon bigger than whatever is happening in the media. But the separate spheres of political discussion—Hannity for some people, Maddow for others—may be less of an emergency than is often assumed. "Government is not life," Jeff Jarvis, a Time Inc. veteran and the founder of *Entertainment Weekly,* who now teaches journalism at the City University of New York, told me. "The fact that people want to ignore it is okay." In this view, the political class, fascinated by the process of campaigning and strategizing, dominates the media, imposes its obsession on the public at large, and worries when citizens don't share its passion.

"The people who are mainly interested in politics are crazy in a way," Denton told me. "Maybe I'd rather reach people whose first passion is video games, or fashion, or are retirees or young professional women. Their interest in politics is the normal interest in politics, not as the main source of rage and resentment in their lives or to the exclusion of everything else." The targeting of such communities, ever easier with social media, is not an answer to America's polarization. But it does suggest the possibility of new, complex connections that offset a stark right/left divide.

- **Distractedness.** "If young people are awake, they are connected," Eric Schmidt, the CEO of Google, told me early this year. "When they're walking, when they're in a car, if they wake up at night, when they're in class. This is probably doing something to their brains, but we don't know what." He said that a friend who flies regularly between California and Israel deliberately changes planes in New York, even though there is a nonstop between L.A. and Tel Aviv, so he can use WiFi on the United States. leg of the trip.

At an individual level, I think the "distracted Americans" scare will pass. Either people who manage to unplug, focus, and fully direct their attention will have an advantage over those constantly checking Facebook and their smart phone, in which case they'll earn more money, get into better colleges, start more successful companies, and win more Nobel Prizes. Or they won't, in which case distraction will be a trait of modern life but not necessarily a defect. At the level of national politics, America is badly distracted, but that problem long predates Facebook and requires more than a media solution.

In this turbulent media environment, let's remember something we saw early this year. Television networks have been closing bureaus all around the world. Only a handful of United States. news organizations even pretend to operate a global network of correspondents. Americans are famous for their ineptness in foreign languages. Ten years of military engagement in the Middle East has done little to increase United States. sophistication about Islam or the Middle East.

Yet with all these reasons why the media should have failed, in fact they succeeded. A major event in world history was covered more quickly, with more nuance, involving a greater range of voices and critical perspectives, than would have been conceivable even a few years ago. Within hours of the first protests in Egypt, American and world audiences read dispatches from professional correspondents—on websites, rather than waiting until the next day, as they had to during the fall of the Berlin Wall. They saw TV news footage—including Al Jazeera's, which was carried by few United States. broadcasters but was available on computers or mobile apps. Then the Twitter feeds from and about Egypt, the amateur YouTube videos from the streets, the commentary of contending analysts—all of it available as the story took place. We take this for granted, yet there has been nothing like it before. Even a year ago it would have been hard to imagine how thoroughly, and with what combination of media, voices, and judgments, an event in an Arab capital could have been witnessed around the world.

It is hard now to imagine the possibilities of the new media landscape, or the further problems it will create. "All these possibilities are fantasy until someone actually builds them," Jeff

Jarvis said. "We don't know what we are building. But from a position of optimism and respect for the public, we have to invent tools and see what they become." This message is unsurprising, coming from Jarvis; for years he has scolded the old media for being too slow to adapt to the new.

It was more striking, then, to hear something similar from Tom Brokaw, who was born in 1940 and was 15 years old when his family first got a TV. "We're creating a whole new universe," he told me. "All those planets that are out there, colliding with each other, we don't know which ones will support life and which will burn up."

At no stage in the evolution of our press could anyone be sure which approaches would support life, and which would flicker out. Through my own career I have seen enough publications and programs start—and succeed, and fail—to know how hard it is to foresee their course in advance. Therefore I am biased in favor of almost any new project, since it might prove to be the next *New York Review of Books, Rolling Stone,* NPR, or *Wired* that helps us understand our world. Perhaps we have finally exhausted the viable possibilities for a journalism that offers a useful and accurate perspective. If so, then America's problems of public life can only grow worse, since we will lack the means to understand and discuss them.

But perhaps this apparently late stage is actually an early stage, in the collective drive and willingness to devise new means of explaining the world and in the individual ability to investigate, weigh, and interpret the ever richer supply of information available to us. Recall the uprisings in Iran and Egypt. Recall the response to the tsunami in Indonesia and the earthquake in Haiti. My understanding of technological and political history makes me think it is still early. Also, there is no point in thinking anything else.

Critical Thinking

1. Fallows writes, "One by one, the buffers between what people want and what the media can afford to deliver to them have been stripped away." What do people want? What should news and information media deliver?

2. Fallows lists four outcomes he fears most as the result of media becoming more market-minded. If these things occur, how do you envision their affecting higher education in 20 years?

JAMES FALLOWS is an Atlantic national correspondent; his blog is at jamesfallows.theatlantic.com.

The Toppling

How the media inflated a minor moment in a long war.

Peter Maass

On April 9, 2003, Lieutenant Colonel Bryan McCoy, commander of the 3rd Battalion 4th Marines, awoke at a military base captured from the Iraqis a few miles from the center of Baghdad, which was still held by the enemy. It had been twenty days since the invasion of Iraq began, and McCoy had some personal chores to take care of—washing his socks, for one. Afterward, he walked over to a group of marines under his command who were defacing a mural of Saddam Hussein. As I watched, he picked up a sledgehammer and struck a few blows himself. The men cheered. Then he began preparing for the serious business of the day: leading the battalion into the heart of the city. He expected a house-to-house brawl that would last several days.

The battalion's tanks were followed by Humvees with the barrels of M-16s pointing from every window. But Only a few potshots were fired at the marines, and small groups of Iraqis and their children were on the streets waving. On the radio, McCoy's men told of being served tea. "We're not getting resistance, we're getting cakes," McCoy remarked.

As the battalion neared the center of the city, Colonel Steven Hummer, the regimental commander, ordered it to the Palestine Hotel. The hotel was in Firdos Square, but neither the hotel nor the square was labelled on McCoy's map. All he had was a grid coördinate for an area that was a square kilometre.

The hotel was filled with international journalists, and by three in the afternoon some who had remained in Baghdad during the invasion were probing the city, freed of government minders who had controlled their movements until then. A few of them ran into McCoy as he was examining his map. McCoy turned to Remy Ourdan, a reporter for *Le Monde*. "Where is this damn Palestine Hotel?" he asked. Ourdan indicated the road to take.

Not far away, Captain Bryan Lewis, the leader of McCoy's tank company, spotted a car with "TV" scrawled on its side and shouted from his turret, "Is this the way to the Palestine?" A Danish photographer named Jan Grarup pointed down the avenue—they were heading the right way. Lewis motioned for Grarup to come along, in case further directions were needed. Grarup hopped onto the turret and led the tanks to Firdos Square.

After the marines arrived, a small group of Iraqis gathered around a statue of Saddam Hussein in the middle of the square and tried to bring it down with a sledgehammer and rope. More photographers and TV crews appeared. An American flag was draped over the statue's head. Eventually, a Marine vehicle equipped with a crane toppled the statue. The spectacle was broadcast live around the world.

Some have argued that the events at Firdos were staged, to demonstrate that America had triumphed, the war was over, and the Iraqis were happy. After all, the marines had seized the only place in Baghdad where a large number of foreign reporters could be found—at least two hundred were at the Palestine. And United States. officials were suspiciously quick to appropriate the imagery from Firdos. A few minutes after the toppling, Secretary of Defense Donald Rumsfeld told reporters, "The scenes of free Iraqis celebrating in the streets, riding American tanks, tearing down the statues of Saddam Hussein in the center of Baghdad are breathtaking. Watching them, one cannot help but think of the fall of the Berlin Wall and the collapse of the Iron Curtain."

Propaganda has been a staple of warfare for ages, but the notion of creating events on the battlefield, as opposed to repackaging real ones after the fact, is a modern development. It expresses a media theory developed by, among others, Walter Lippmann, who after the First World War identified the components of wartime mythmaking as "the casual fact, the creative imagination, the will to believe, and out of these three elements, a counterfeit of reality." As he put it, "Men respond as powerfully to fictions as they do to realities [and] in many cases they help to create the very fictions to which they respond." In the nineteen-sixties, Daniel J. Boorstin identified a new category of media spectacle that he called "pseudo-events," which were created to be reported on. But Boorstin was theorizing primarily about political conventions and press conferences, not about events on a battlefield.

The 2004 documentary film "Control Room" featured Al Jazeera journalists who argued that the toppling of Saddam's statue was merely "a show . . . a very clever idea," and that Iraqis had been brought to the square like actors delivered to the stage. Skeptics have also questioned whether the crowd was as large or as representative of popular sentiment as United States. officials suggested. Might it have been just a small group of Iraqis whose numbers and enthusiasm were exaggerated by the cameras? Did the media, which had, with few exceptions, accepted the Bush Administration's prewar claims about weapons of mass destruction, err again by portraying a pseudo-event as real? And were lives lost as a result of this error?

I had followed McCoy's battalion to Baghdad for the *Times Magazine*. I was what the military called a "unilateral" journalist, driving unescorted into Iraq on the first day of the invasion in an S.U.V. rented from Hertz in Kuwait. A few days into the war, I happened to meet McCoy at a staging area in the Iraqi desert north of Nasiriya, and he agreed to let me and a number of other unilaterals follow his battalion to Baghdad. On April 9th, I drove into Firdos with his battalion, and was at his side during some of the afternoon.

My understanding of events at the time was limited. I had no idea why the battalion went to Firdos rather than to other targets. I didn't know who had decided to raise the American flag and who had decided to take down the statue, or why. And I had little awareness of the media dynamics that turned the episode into a festive symbol of what appeared to be the war's finale. In reality, the war was just getting under way. Many thousands of people would be killed or injured before the Bush Administration acknowledged that it faced not just "pockets of dead-enders" in Iraq, as Rumsfeld insisted, but what grew to be a full-fledged insurgency. The toppling of Saddam's statue turned out to be emblematic of primarily one thing: the fact that American troops had taken the center of Baghdad. That was significant, but everything else the toppling was said to represent during repeated replays on television—victory for America, the end of the war, joy throughout Iraq—was a disservice to the truth. Yet the skeptics were wrong in some ways, too, because the event was not planned in advance by the military. How did it happen?

Three days earlier, Marine Regimental Combat Team 7, under the command of Colonel Hummer, arrived at the Diyala Canal, which loops around eastern Baghdad. The center of the city was less than eight miles away, but the regiment did not have orders to seize it. The plan was to stay along the Diyala and send small units on quick raids into the city.

The task of planning the raids was given to two majors on the regiment's staff, John Schaar and Andrew Milburn. Until Diyala, they had not even examined a map of the city, but they quickly concluded that the raids were a bad idea. "We did a little study and thought this was really stupid," Schaar told me not long ago. Raiding units risked becoming trapped in the city, creating an Iraqi version of "Black Hawk Down." Schaar and Milburn also concluded that Iraqi forces could not withstand a direct assault by the regiment; for nearly three weeks, the regiment had blasted through every Iraqi unit in its path.

They then divided central Baghdad into twenty-seven zones, with each battalion responsible for occupying four or five zones (several low-priority zones were unassigned). Schaar and Milburn had received from divisional headquarters a list of about thirty sensitive sites—a hodgepodge that comprised embassies, banks, detention centers, potential nuclear facilities, and hotels,

including the Palestine. The most important targets were in four central zones across the Tigris River from the Republican Palace, which the Army had already seized. Schaar recently sent me a photograph of the twenty-seven-zone invasion map. The map has six thumbtacks marking key targets. One of them, in the central zones, was the Palestine Hotel.

According to Schaar, there was never any doubt about which battalion would be assigned the central zones. "Three-four"—McCoy's battalion—"got tagged to that because they were the sharp guys," he told me.

Bryan McCoy, who has a stocky build and a blunt Oklahoma manner, became known as the regiment's toughest battalion leader. During the drive to Baghdad, McCoy mentioned Sherman's famous dictum that war is cruelty. "My idea of a fair fight," he said, "is clubbing baby harp seals." When McCoy returned from Iraq, he disdained the well-equipped fitness center at the regiment's training base, in California, and built a prisonlike gym that had no air-conditioning or fancy exercise machines, the better, he believed, to accustom his men to the rigors of battle; they weightlifted with sandbags.

The Marine Corps is the smallest branch of the United States. military and the most precarious, because one of the key missions it fulfills—amphibious landings—does not require a separate branch. The Army knows how to conduct amphibious landings, and has done more of them in the past century than the Marines. Moreover, the future of warfare is not likely to revolve around landings on the shores of Tripoli. As McCoy remarked to me one day, "Our existence is always threatened."

This circumstance makes the Corps particularly aware that it must be successful in the halls of Congress as well as on the fields of battle. For that reason, perhaps, marines tend to be friendlier toward the media than other branches of the military; they recognize the value of good stories and images. It is not surprising that the most famous war photograph in American history—the flag-raising at Iwo Jima—depicts marines.

McCoy, who has written a monograph on military leadership, "The Passion of Command," understood the importance of the media. That was one reason he had agreed to let me and ten other unilateral journalists follow his battalion, which already had four embedded journalists. The reporters worked for, among others, the *Times, Time, Newsweek,* the Associated Press, and several photography agencies. McCoy occasionally joined us for coffee in the morning, giving us briefings about the battles along the way to Baghdad, and he made it clear to his men that we were to be welcomed. When he threw a grenade at an Iraqi position one day, a photographer was at his side, and the photograph was widely disseminated.

McCoy heard about the Palestine Hotel from the journalists in his battalion. One of the photographers, Gary Knight, of *Newsweek,* had mentioned it to him on several occasions, because a colleague was having a hard time there; Knight's editors wanted McCoy to know that journalists at the hotel were in peril. "As we got closer to Baghdad, it got ramped up," Knight recalled last year. "It was, like, 'Can you try and persuade the marines to get to the Palestine Hotel?'"

The photographer Laurent Van der Stockt, working with me for the *Times Magazine,* also mentioned the Palestine to McCoy, often while sharing his stash of Cuban cigars with him. Van der Stockt would tell the Colonel what he was hearing from Remy Ourdan, with whom he spoke almost every day on his satellite phone. Ourdan had stayed at the Palestine throughout the invasion, hiding his phone behind a ceiling panel and using it surreptitiously at night or in the early morning, when he would crouch on his balcony and talk in whispers to his editors in Paris.

On the morning of April 9th, as McCoy was washing his socks, Van der Stockt wandered over while talking to Ourdan on the sat phone. Ourdan told Van der Stockt that Iraqi forces had abandoned the center of Baghdad. For the first time, there were no security forces at the Palestine or in the area around it.

"Colonel, my friend at the Palestine Hotel is saying there is nobody in front of us—the city is empty," Van der Stockt said.

McCoy nodded but said the battalion wouldn't get to the center so fast. The Army had met fierce resistance in the western part of the city. The next few hundred yards were of far greater importance to him than a hotel several miles away. Besides, marines do not take orders from French journalists

Van der Stockt told Ourdan that they wouldn't be seeing each other that day.

"But tell the Colonel that Baghdad has fallen!" Ourdan said. "There is no more resistance. The city is open!"

The battalion moved out, and, to McCoy's surprise, faced little opposition. Simon Robinson, a reporter for *Time,* was in the back of McCoy's vehicle when the regiment's commander, Colonel Hummer, ordered the battalion to the Palestine. Robinson vividly recalls the order, because it prompted him to lean forward to remind McCoy that reporters were there. When he did, he saw a satisfied expression spread over McCoy's face.

"He was fully cognizant that he was about to move into an area where there were a lot of journalists and there were going to be opportunities," Robinson told me.

In 1999, Marine General Charles Krulak wrote an influential article in which he coined the term "strategic corporal." Krulak argued that, in an interconnected world, the actions of even a lowly corporal can have global consequences. "All future conflicts will be acted out before an international audience," Krulak wrote. "In many cases, the individual Marine will be the most conspicuous symbol of American foreign policy and will potentially influence not only the immediate tactical situation, but the operational and strategic levels as well."

At Firdos Square, it was a thirty-five-year-old gunnery sergeant, Leon Lambert, who bore out Krulak's thesis. Lambert's background was typical of that of many youths who enlist in the military. His father was a car mechanic with five children. Leon had to get a dishwashing job when he was twelve. One of his brothers joined the Army, another the Air Force. Lambert went for the Marines. By 2003, after almost sixteen years of service, he commanded an M-88 Hercules, a tow truck for tanks that is equipped with a crane.

At 4:30 P.M., as the M-88 rumbled into Firdos not far behind the lead tank, Lambert noticed the statue of Saddam. Installed a year earlier to celebrate the leader's sixty-fifth birthday, it was the sort of totem that American troops had been destroying

across Iraq. On the first day of the invasion, I had watched in the Iraqi border town of Safwan as a Humvee dragged down a billboard of Saddam. Erasing the symbols of regime power is what conquering armies have done for millennia.

Lambert radioed his commander, Captain Lewis, whose tank was carrying the Danish photographer.

"Hey, get a look at that statue," Lambert said. "Why don't we take it down?"

"No way," Lewis responded. He didn't want his men distracted.

There was no hostile fire, or even hostility, other than some shouts from American and West European "human shields," who had remained in Baghdad to symbolically stand in the way of the invaders. The Iraqi forces had fled. Lewis's tanks blocked the streets leading to Firdos while armored personnel carriers disgorged the infantry, which fanned out. Within minutes of the marines' arrival, Firdos had been secured.

When McCoy's Humvee stopped in front of the Palestine, he was surrounded by reporters. In addition to the journalists at the hotel, others who had followed United States. troops to Baghdad began pulling up in their dusty S.U.V.s. One of the reporters, *Newsweek's* Melinda Liu, introduced McCoy to the hotel's manager, who nervously greeted his new boss and led him into the hotel. Striding inside, McCoy held his M-16 at the ready.

Outside, a handful of Iraqis had slipped into the square. Lambert got on the radio and told Lewis that the locals wanted to pull down the statue.

"If a sledgehammer and rope fell off the 88, would you mind?" Lambert asked.

"I wouldn't mind," Lewis replied. "But don't use the 88."

Higher authorities were unaware of these developments. McCoy, Hummer, Rumsfeld, President Bush—they hadn't a clue about the chain of events that Lambert had triggered with a wink, a nod, and a sledgehammer.

One after another, Iraqis swung Lambert's sledgehammer against the statue's base. In a much photographed moment, a former weight lifter got into the action, but only a few inches of plaster fell away. The rope, thrown around the statue's neck, was not sufficient to topple it, either.

"We watched them with the rope, and I knew that was never going to happen," Lambert told me recently. "They were never going to get it down."

At the Palestine, McCoy briefly talked with reporters in the manager's office. Then he walked outside to Firdos Square and saw Lambert's rope flopped around the statue's neck as various Iraqis futilely wielded the sledgehammer. Cameras were everywhere. "A military operation was developing into a circus atmosphere," McCoy recalled when I interviewed him last spring at his home in Tampa, where he serves at Central Command.

Other commanders had already concluded that toppling the dictator's likeness might help get the point across and had tried it elsewhere. A few days into the war, British tanks mounted a raid into the heart of Basra, in the south of the country, where they destroyed a statue of Saddam. The Brits hoped the locals, seeing a strike against a symbol of regime power, would rise up against Saddam. As the British military spokesman, Colonel Chris Vernon, told reporters, "The purpose of that is psychological." The statue was destroyed, but the event wasn't filmed and drew little attention. Similarly, on April 7th, after Army soldiers seized the Republican Palace in Baghdad, their commander, Colonel David Perkins, asked his men to find a statue that could be destroyed. Once one was found—Saddam on horseback—a nearby tank was ordered to wait until an embedded team from Fox News got there. On cue, the tank fired a shell at the statue, blowing it up, but the event had little drama and did not get a lot of TV coverage. No Iraqis were present, and just a few Americans, and the surrounding landscape was featureless.

The situation at the Palestine was different. "I realized this was a big deal," McCoy told me. "You've got all the press out there and everybody is liquored up on the moment. You have this Paris, 1944, feel. I remember thinking, The media is watching the Iraqis trying to topple this icon of Saddam Hussein. Let's give them a hand."

McCoy also considered the "buzz-kill," as he phrased it, of not helping. "Put your virtual-reality goggles on," he continued. "What would that moment have been if we hadn't? It would have been some B reel of Iraqis banging away at this thing and eventually losing interest and going home. There was a momentum, there was a feeling, this atmosphere of liberation. Like a kid trying to whack a piñata and he's not going to get it with a blindfold on, so let's move the piñata so he can knock it. That was the attitude—keep the momentum going."

Captain Lewis, the tank commander, walked over to McCoy and asked whether the marines should finish the job for the Iraqis. McCoy asked if the Iraqis had requested help; Lewis told him they had. A marine asked whether the battalion was authorized to tear down statues; McCoy responded that it would not be a problem.

He got on the radio with Colonel Hummer, who had set up a regimental command post behind the partially destroyed Information Ministry, to update him on the events. Hummer did not have aerial reconnaissance from Firdos, or even a TV. While the rest of the world was watching the scene in the square, the colonel who authorized its climax was blind to the event.

Hummer, in a phone interview recently, explained what happened: "I get this call from Bryan and he says, 'Hey, we've got these Iraqis over here with a bunch of ropes trying to pull down this very large statue of Saddam Hussein.' And he said, 'They're asking us to pull it down.' So I said, 'O.K., go ahead.' And I didn't think much of it after that."

Before signing off, Hummer instructed McCoy to make sure no one got killed by falling debris.

McCoy then issued a brief order to Lewis: "Do it." He also told Lewis not to get anyone killed in the process.

The M-88, with its crane, was the perfect tool. Lambert, who had started everything by handing out the sledgehammer and the rope, was told to finish the job.

Before dawn on September 11, 2001, a twenty-one-year-old second lieutenant named Tun McLaughlin arrived at the Pentagon, where he was a general's assistant. After taking care of some paperwork, he went down to the gym, changed into running clothes, and jogged across Memorial Bridge, along the Jefferson Memorial, until he heard a deep, soft thud. He rushed back to the Pentagon. As people streamed out of the building, McLaughlin made his way into it. The corridors were deserted and were filling with smoke; he could barely see his hand.

A few days later, as a personal token of appreciation for his service in the military, a congressional staffer who worked for Senator Charles Schumer and was a friend of the McLaughlin family presented McLaughlin with a flag bought at the Senate stationery store. Two years later, when McLaughlin was packing to leave for Iraq under McCoy's command, he put the flag in his duffel.

During the invasion, McLaughlin tried to raise the flag several times. On the first attempt, he was preparing to hoist it on top of a building but realized that there was too much shooting going on. Another time, Lambert's M-88 rolled over the flagpole that McLaughlin was about to use. McLaughlin's efforts became an inside joke in his tank company. When McCoy ordered the toppling in Firdos Square, Captain Lewis told McLaughlin to fetch his flag for the mother of all flag pictures. Soon it was handed up to Corporal Edward Chin, who had climbed atop the M-88's crane and was hooking a chain around the statue's head.

"I remember thinking, What am I going to do?" Chin told me. "I didn't want to just wave the flag." At that moment, the wind blew the flag and it stuck to the statue's head. "That worked for me. I later realized the flag was upside down. That is actually a symbol of distress."

McCoy, too busy to keep an eye on the statue, wasn't looking when the flag went up. People watching TV from their sofas in America saw it before he did. When he finally looked up, his first thought was Oh, shit! An American flag would seem like a symbol of occupation. He instantly ordered it taken down.

Around this time, McCoy's superior, Colonel Hummer, got an urgent order from his commander, Major General James Mattis, who had apparently received an urgent order that Hummer assumes originated at the Pentagon.

Get the flag down. Now.

With the breeze keeping the flag in place, Chin had returned to his rigging work. As he was finishing up, he took the flag down of his own volition. It had been on display for just a minute and a half. There had not been time for the orders to reach him.

One of the battalion's lieutenants, Casey Kuhlman, had also realized that the American flag would not be a welcome symbol for Iraqis and other Arabs. Kuhlman had acquired an Iraqi flag during the invasion. "I grabbed it and started going up to the statue," he recalled. "And I didn't get but ten or twenty metres when an older Iraqi man grabbed it from me and it sort of got passed through the crowd and then went up. I thought, My souvenir is gone. But this is a little bit better than a souvenir."

His flag helped create one of the Firdos myths.

Staff Sergeant Brian Plesich, the leader of an Army psychological-operations team, arrived at Firdos after the sledgehammer-and-rope phase had begun. He saw the American flag go up and had the same reaction as Kuhlman: get an Iraqi flag up. Plesich, whom I interviewed last year, told his interpreter to find an Iraqi flag. The interpreter waded into the crowd, and soon an Iraqi flag was raised.

Plesich assumed that the Iraqi flag had got there because of his initiative, and in 2004 the Army published a report crediting him. The report was picked up by the news media ("ARMY STAGE-MANAGED FALL OF HUSSEIN STATUE," the headline in the Los Angeles *Times* read) and circulated widely on the Web, fuelling the conspiracy notion that a psyops team masterminded not only the Iraqi flag but the entire toppling. Yet it was Kuhlman who was responsible for the flag. Plesich's impact at Firdos was limited to using the loudspeakers on his Humvee to tell the crowd, once the statue had been rigged to fall, that until everyone moved back to a safe distance the main event would not take place.

By the time it was over and the sun was setting at Firdos Square, Sergeant Lambert and his M-88 crew had become so famous that even Katie Couric wanted an interview. Lambert had to hide from the spectacle he had unleashed.

"God's honest truth," Lambert told me. "We went inside the 88, we locked the hatches, and the only time we would come out was when we were directed to."

The Palestine was built in the early nineteen-eighties for tourists, who were then visiting Iraq in large numbers, and it was run by the Méridien hotel chain. After Iraq invaded Kuwait, in 1990, and was slapped with international sanctions, the Méridien got rid of its outlaw franchise. The Palestine, with more than three hundred rooms and seventeen floors, stayed open under state control but was outclassed by the Al Rasheed Hotel, which stood on the other side of the Tigris and was surrounded by government ministries and Presidential palaces. For years, the Al Rasheed was favored by foreign journalists who wanted to be close to the action, but they moved out just before the invasion, to get away from the bombs that would presumably destroy the government district. When the Shock and Awe campaign began, a couple of hundred reporters watched from their balconies at the Palestine.

Like everyone else, Pentagon officials viewed TV reports from Baghdad which often noted that the Palestine was the point of broadcast. It was at the hotel that the Information Minister Mohammed Saeed al-Sahhaf, known as Baghdad Bob, held many of his extravagant press conferences.

During the aerial bombardment of Baghdad, the Palestine was not hit, and, once ground troops had moved into the city, most commanders in Baghdad were made aware of the Palestine's do-not-bomb status. But the commanders failed to convey the information to the soldiers in every unit, and this caused the casualties that contributed to the dispatch of McCoy's battalion to Firdos Square.

On April 8th, the day before McCoy's battalion arrived at Firdos, an Army tank that was on the Al Jumhuriya Bridge, over the Tigris, fired a shell at the Palestine, killing two journalists and injuring three others. The tank's crew mistakenly thought that a camera aimed at them from a balcony was a spotting device for Iraqi forces. Journalists at the Palestine were outraged; some thought it was a deliberate attack on the media. Subsequent investigations by the military and reporters found that although key officers on the ground, including brigade and battalion commanders, knew that the Palestine should not be fired on, they did not know the hotel's precise location, because, as McCoy was to learn, it wasn't marked on their maps. The tank's crew did not know that journalists were in the building.

The killings increased media pressure on the Pentagon to insure the hotel's safety, calls and e-mails to Pentagon officials reached a furious pitch, and at a Pentagon press conference a few hours after the attack the Palestine was a major topic. The media demanded that the Pentagon see to it that no further harm came to the journalists at the Palestine.

Some journalists considered the hotel to be a death trap. When the photographer Seamus Conlan came across American troops in the hours before McCoy's battalion showed up, he asked for a rescue mission. "I was sure that today was going to be the day that we got killed by Saddam's enraged and retreating militiamen," Conlan later wrote. "A Marine officer assured me that every journalist in Baghdad was telling him the same thing."

The media have been criticized for accepting the Bush Administration's claims, in the run-up to the invasion, that Iraq had weapons of mass destruction. The W.M.D. myth, and the media's embrace of it, encouraged public support for war. The media also failed at Firdos Square, but in this case it was the media, rather than the government, that created the victory myth.

Because the world's media were based at the Palestine, television networks had the equipment to go live the moment the marines arrived there. It was certainly a legitimate and dramatic story—proof that Baghdad was falling under American control. But problems with the coverage at Firdos soon emerged, including the duration, which was non-stop, the tone, which was celebratory, and the uncritical obsession with the toppling.

One of the first TV reporters to broadcast from Firdos was David Chater, a correspondent for Sky News, the British satellite channel whose feed from Baghdad was carried by Fox News. (Both channels are owned by News Corp.) Before the marines arrived, Chater had believed, as many journalists did, that his life was at risk from American shells, Iraqi thugs, and looting mobs.

"That's an amazing sight, isn't it?" Chater said as the tanks rolled in. "A great relief, a great sight for all the journalists here. . . . The Americans waving to us now—fantastic, fantastic to see they're here at last." Moments later, outside the Palestine, Chater smiled broadly and told one marine, "Bloody good to see you." Noticing an American flag in another marine's hands, Chater cheerily said, "Get that flag going!"

Another correspondent, John Burns, of the *Times,* had similar feelings. Representing the most prominent American publication, Burns had a particularly hard time with the security thugs who had menaced many journalists at the Palestine. His gratitude toward the marines was explidt. "They were my liberators, too," he later wrote. "They seemed like ministering angels to me."

The happy relief felt by some journalists on the ground was compounded by editors and anchors back home. Primed for triumph, they were ready to latch onto a symbol of what they believed would be a joyous finale to the war. It was an unfortunate fusion: a preconception of what would happen, of what victory would look like, connected at Firdos Square with an aesthetically perfect representation of that preconception.

Wilson Surratt was the senior executive producer in charge of CNN's control room in Atlanta that morning. The room, dominated by almost fifty screens that showed incoming feeds from CNN crews and affiliated networks, was filled with not just the usual complement of producers but also with executives who wanted to be at the nerve center of the network during one of the biggest stories of their lives. Surratt had been told by the newsroom that marines were expected to arrive at Firdos any moment, so he kept his eyes on two monitors that showed the still empty square.

"The climax, at the time, was going to be the troops coming into Firdos Square," Surratt told me. "We didn't really anticipate that Hussein was going to be captured. There wasn't going to be a surrender. So what we were looking for was some sort of culminating event."

On that day, Baghdad was violent and chaotic. The city was already being looted by swarms of people using trucks, taxis, horses, and wheelbarrows to cart away whatever they could from government buildings and banks, museums, and even hospitals. There continued to be armed opposition to the American advance. One of CNN's embedded correspondents, Martin Savidge, was reporting from a Marine unit that was taking fire in the city. Savidge was ready to go on the air, under fire, at the exact moment that Surratt noticed the tanks entering Firdos Square. Surratt vividly recalls that moment, because he shouted out in the control room, "There they are!"

He immediately switched the network's coverage to Firdos, and it stayed there almost non-stop until the statue came down, more than two hours later. I asked Surratt whether, by focussing on Firdos rather than on Savidge and the chaos of Baghdad, he had made the right call.

"What were we supposed to do?" Surratt replied. "Not show what was going on in the square? We did the responsible thing. We were careful to say it was not the end. At some point, you've got to trust the viewer to understand what they're seeing."

The powerful pictures from Firdos were combined with powerful words. On CNN, the anchor Bill Hemmer said, "You think about seminal moments in a nation's history . . . indelible moments like the fall of the Berlin Wall, and that's what we're seeing right now." Wolf Blitzer described the toppling as "the image that sums up the day and, in many ways, the war itself." On Fox, the anchor Brit Hume said, "This transcends anything I've ever seen. . . . This speaks volumes, and with power that no words can really match." One of his colleagues said, "The important story of the day is this historic shot you are looking at, a noose around the neck of Saddam, put there by the people of Baghdad."

A visual echo chamber developed: rather than encouraging reporters to find the news, editors urged them to report what was on TV. CNN, which did not have a reporter at the Palestine, because its team had been expelled when the invasion began, was desperate to get one of its embedded correspondents there. Walter Rodgers, whose Army unit was on the other side of the Tigris, was ordered by his editors to disembed and drive across town to the Palestine. Rodgers reminded his editors that combat continued and that his vehicle, moving on its own, would likely be hit by American or Iraqi forces. This said much about the coverage that day: Rodgers could not provide reports of the war's end because the war had not ended. But he understood the imperatives that kept CNN's attention pinned on Firdos Square. "Pictures are the mother's milk of television, and it was a hell of a picture," he said recently.

Live television loves suspense, especially if it is paired with great visuals. The networks almost never broke away from Firdos Square. The event lived on in replays, too. A 2005 study of CNN's and Fox's coverage, conducted by a research team from George Washington University and titled "As Goes the Statue, So Goes the War," found that between 11 A.M. and 8 P.M. that day Fox replayed the toppling every 4.4 minutes, and CNN every 7.5 minutes. The networks also showed the toppling in house ads; it became a branding device. They continually used the word "historic" to describe the statue's demise.

Anne Garrels, NPR's reporter in Baghdad at the time, has said that her editors requested, after her first dispatch about marines rolling into Firdos, that she emphasize the celebratory angle, because the television coverage was more upbeat. In an oral history that was published by the *Columbia Journalism Review,* Garrels recalled telling her editors that they were getting the story wrong: "There are so few people trying to pull down the statue that they can't do it themselves. . . . Many people were just sort of standing, hoping for the best, but they weren't joyous."

Gary Knight, the photographer who followed McCoy's battalion to Baghdad, had a similar problem, as he talked with one of his editors on his satellite phone. The editor, watching the event on TV, asked why Knight wasn't taking pictures. Knight replied that few Iraqis were involved and the ones who were seemed to be doing so for the benefit of the legions of photographers; it was a show. The editor told him to get off the phone and start taking pictures.

Robert Collier, a San Francisco *Chronicle* reporter, filed a dispatch that noted a small number of Iraqis at Firdos, many of whom were not enthusiastic. When he woke up the next day, he found that his editors had recast the story. The published version said that "a jubilant crowd roared its approval" as onlookers shouted, "We are free! Thank you, President Bush!" According to Collier, the original version was considerably more tempered. "That was the one case in my time in Iraq when I can clearly say there was editorial interference in my work," he said recently. "They threw in a lot of triumphalism. I was told by my editor that I had screwed up and had not seen the importance of the historical event. They took out quite a few of my qualifiers."

British journalists felt the same pressure. Lindsey Hilsum, the Baghdad reporter for Britain's Channel 4 News, was instructed by her editors to increase her coverage of Firdos even though she believed the event was trivial. She told the authors of a study titled "Shoot First and Ask Questions Later" that the toppling was a small part of a nine-minute story that she transmitted to London on April 9th; in her view, it was "a small, symbolic event for American television." As she put it, "In London, where they had been watching, they said, 'No, you have to make that section much larger.'"

Robert Capa once said, "If your pictures aren't good enough, you're not close enough," and generations of journalists have followed his maxim. But the opposite can also be true: the farther away you are, the better you can see. At Firdos Square, the farther from the statue you were, the more you could understand.

Very few Iraqis were there. If you were at the square, or if you watch the footage, you can see, on the rare occasions long shots were used, that the square was mostly empty. You can also see, from photographs as well as video, that much of the crowd was made up of journalists and marines. Because of the lo-fi quality of the video and the shifting composition of the crowd, it's hard to give a precise number, but perhaps a quarter to a half consisted of journalists or marines. The crowd's size—journalists, marines, and Iraqis—does not seem to have exceeded several hundred at its largest, and was much smaller for most of the two hours. The Iraqis who were photogenically enthusiastic—sledgehammering the statue, jumping on it after the toppling—were just an excitable subset of all Iraqis there. "I saw a lot of people watching with their arms crossed, not at all celebrating," Collier noted.

Closeups filled the screen with the frenzied core of the small crowd and created an illusion of wall-to-wall enthusiasm throughout Baghdad. It was an illusion that reflected only the media's yearning for exciting visuals, and brings to mind a famous study carried out more than half a century ago, when General Douglas MacArthur, who had just been relieved of his command by President Truman, visited Chicago for a parade and a speech that were expected to attract enormous public support. The study, conducted by the sociologists Kurt and Gladys Lang, found that the Chicago events, as experienced by people who attended them, were largely passionless. But for television viewers the events were dramatic and inspiring, owing to the cropped framing of what they saw.

The Lang study illuminates another distortion that occurred in Baghdad: the extent to which listless crowds lit up when cameras were turned on. In Chicago, the Lang researchers saw crowds shift to the places that cameras pointed toward; people were taking their cues from the lenses. "The cheering, waving, and shouting was often but a response to the aiming of the camera," the study noted.

Just after 5 P.M. local time, Fox News showed about a dozen Iraqis walking into the empty square; these were the first civilians on the site. They were followed and surrounded by an increasing number of journalists; within a minute of the Iraqis arriving at the statue's base, journalists appear to nearly outnumber them. In the first act of iconoclasm, two plaques on the statue's base were torn off by the Iraqis and hoisted in front of the photographers and the cameramen, in much the same way that a prizefighter raises a championship belt above his head as pictures are snapped.

Would the Iraqis have done the same thing if the cameras hadn't been there? At key moments throughout the toppling, the level of Iraqi enthusiasm appeared to ebb and flow according to the number and interest of photographers who had gathered. For instance, when Lambert's sledgehammer made its first appearance, photographers clustered around as one Iraqi after another took a few shots at the base. Not long afterward, many photographers and cameramen drifted off, they had got their pictures. The sledgehammering of the statue soon ceased, too.

An hour after the first Iraqis entered the square, the toppling was at a standstill, because the rope and the sledgehammer were useless. Neither Iraqis nor journalists cared any longer. Many of the Iraqis had moved into the street and gathered around the Humvee that carried Staff Sergeant Plesich and his psychological-operations team, because loudspeakers on Plesich's Humvee were broadcasting in Arabic. These were the first words in Arabic that the Iraqis had heard from their occupiers, and the Iraqis were indeed cheering.

But the area around the base of the statue was virtually empty: Though TV anchors talked excitedly about the statue, Iraqis at the square were no longer paying attention to it. Then Lambert's M-88, having received a green light from Colonel McCoy, lumbered into view, entering from the left of the television screen. On Fox, journalists can be seen hurrying toward the M-88 and the deserted statue. Iraqis do the same, like bees returning to a hive. By the time the M-88 reached the statue's base, the crowd of Iraqis, journalists, and marines had reassembled for the next act. As the Lang study noted of the MacArthur celebrations, "The event televised was no longer the same event as it would have been if television had not been there."

The journalists themselves, meanwhile, were barely photographed at all. The dramatic shots posted on websites that day and featured in newspapers the next morning contained almost no hint of the army of journalists at the square and their likely influence on events. One of the most photographed moments occurred when the statue fell and several dozen Iraqis rushed forward to bash the toppled head; there were nearly as many journalists in the melee, and perhaps more, but the framing of photographs all but eliminated them from view.

"It's one thing if you don't want a photographer in the picture and there's one photographer in a crowd of a thousand," Gary Knight, who now directs the Program for Narrative and Documentary Studies, at Tufts University, told me. "But when you've got three hundred journalists sitting on vehicles, sitting on tanks, it's really important contextually to include that information. Most of the imagery that was published didn't have that context, and so it was misleading."

At the square, I found the reality, whatever it was, hard to grasp. Some Iraqis were cheering, I later learned, not for America but for a slain cleric, Mohammed Sadiq al-Sadr, whose son Moqtada would soon lead a Shia revolt against American occupation. I met an apparently delighted

Iraqi who spoke English, and he told me that his name was Samir and that he felt "free at last." About an hour later, after the statue came down, Samir was cornered by a group of men who accused him of being a spy for Saddam and were shouting, "Kill him!" A marine had to intervene to save his life.

The subsequent years of civil war, which have killed and injured hundreds of thousands of people, have revealed the events at Firdos to be an illusional intermission between invasion and insurgency. For instance, one of the stars of the spectacle—the weight lifter who sledgehammered the statue—was Khadim al-Jubouri, a motorcycle mechanic who had worked for Saddam's son Uday but had fallen out of favor and spent time in prison. When he heard that American troops had arrived, al-Jubouri went to Firdos Square. As anniversaries of the event come around, he gets interviewed by journalists. In 2007, he told the Washington *Post* that, since the toppling, seven relatives and friends had been killed, kidnapped, or forced to flee their homes. Al-Jubouri was happy when the sledgehammer was in his hands, but since then his life had deteriorated. "I really regret bringing down the statue," he told the *Guardian*. "Every day is worse than the previous day."

Among the handful of studies of Firdos Square, the most incisive was George Washington University's, led by Sean Aday, an associate professor of media and public affairs. It concluded that the coverage had "profound implications for both international policy and the domestic political landscape in America." According to the study, the saturation coverage of Firdos Square fuelled the perception that the war had been won, and diverted attention from Iraq at precisely the moment that more attention was needed, not less. "Whereas battle stories imply a war is going on, statues falling—especially when placed in the context of truly climactic images from recent history—imply the war is over," the study noted.

The study examined CNN, Fox, ABC, CBS, and NBC from March 20th to April 20th, cataloguing the footage used each day, what the footage showed, and what was said by anchors and reporters. The study focussed particular attention on Fox and CNN, because they broadcast non-stop news. It found that, in the week after the statue was toppled, war stories from Iraq decreased by seventy per cent on Fox, sixty-six per cent on ABC, fifty-eight per cent on NBC, thirty-nine per cent on CBS, and twenty-six per cent on CNN, even though, in that same week, thirteen United States. soldiers were killed and looting was rampant.

The George Washington University study and other examinations of Firdos—like "Ugly War, Pretty Package," a book by the Boston University associate professor Deborah Jaramillo—suggest that the bullishness of the post-Firdos era stemmed, at least in part, from the myth created at the square. Without the erroneous finality of the statue falling, this argument goes, the notion of "Mission Accomplished" would have been more difficult to assert; the Bush Administration would have had a harder time dismissing an insurgency that, for a fatal interlude, it all but ignored. Conventional wisdom blames the failure in Iraq on the Coalition Provisional Authority, which has been heavily criticized for its inept management of the occupation.

But if the C.P.A. inherited a war rather than a victory, the story of what went wrong after Firdos needs to be revised.

In a way, statue topplings are the banana peels of history that we often slip on. In 1991, when pro-democracy forces led by Boris Yeltsin stood up to a coup by Soviet hard-liners in Moscow, a crowd outside K.G.B. headquarters forced the removal of a statue of Felix Dzerzhinsky, who had led the K.G.B.'s notorious predecessor, the Cheka. The statue was lifted off its pedestal by a crane; its demise seemed to symbolize the end of Soviet-era oppression. Yet within a decade a K.G.B. functionary, Vladimir Putin, became Russia's President, and former K.G.B. officials now hold key political and economic positions.

Throughout the nineteen-nineties, Svetlana Boym, a Soviet-born professor of comparative literature at Harvard, visited the Moscow park where Dzerzhinsky's statue was left on its side, neglected and stained with urine. But over the years, as the power of the security state revived, the statue became the object of fond attention; eventually, Dzerzhinsky was raised to his feet and placed on a pedestal in the park. By studying a statue at not just a dramatic moment but during the course of its existence—construction, toppling, preservation—one can sometimes trace a nation's political evolution, but it takes patience. In "The Future of Nostalgia," Boym's book on history and memory, she described Soviet-era monuments serving as "messengers of power . . . onto which anxieties and anger were projected." The Princeton architectural historian Lucia Allais, who has examined the destruction of monuments during the Second World War, mentioned to me one of the most famous topplings ever—of the statue of King Louis XV in Paris, in 1792, during the French Revolution. The action was portrayed by its authors as a liberation from the power of the monarchy, but they put in its spot a symbol of a new sort of power: the guillotine. These monumental destructions "are usually acts of monumental replacement, which hide continuities of power . . . behind the image of rupture," Allais wrote to me in an e-mail.

Not long ago, Tim McLaughlin, the officer whose flag was placed on the statue at Firdos, unpacked a wooden trunk that stored his military gear after he left the Marines to attend law school. We were at his childhood home, in Laconia, New Hampshire. McLaughlin is tall and large, but his head seems small for his frame, like a child's on a grown-up's body. He majored in Russian at Holy Cross, and his favorite story, by Chekhov, is about a widowed carriage driver who can find no one to share his sorrows with; at the end of a cold night, the driver pours out his heartache to his loyal horse.

In the trunk, McLaughlin found a copy of the United States. Constitution that was on his Pentagon desk on September 11, 2001; it was stained with ash from the fire. He pulled out a sealed envelope that had a Marine Corps insignia on the front. Inside was a letter to his parents, to be opened in the event of his death during the invasion. It was a reminder of the dread that gripped the McLaughlin household in those days.

McLaughlin had kept a list of notable events during the invasion. One day's entry said, "Killed lots of people." Another day: "Drove through house." Yet another: "Lunch w/ villagers."

He opened a diary from which silty grains of sand sprinkled out. On one page, exhausted from fighting and lack of sleep, he had written "disoriented" or "disorienting" four times.

The flag that McLaughlin carried to Iraq lay on the bed, folded in the military manner, crisp and tight. It was returned to him after it was taken down from the Stame at Firdos Square: his parents had fetched it from a safe-deposit box at the local bank for my benefit.

"It's just a flag," McLaughlin said, unfolding it. "A whole lot of fuss has been made over it, but it's not the most important thing to me."

The diaries explain why:

Company volley into buildings. Killed 4 soldiers trying to run away. . . .

My position is good to cut off back door exit. Kill dismounts in grove (3–7?) then 1 swimming across canal. 2 just about in canal. . . .

Covered canal w/.50 cal—killed 2 more.

McLaughlin also wrote of shooting at a fast-moving car that he considered suspicious. After his bullets killed the driver, McLaughlin realized that an innocent man had perished. A few days later, wishing to avoid the same mistake, McLaughlin didn't fire when he spotted a group of suspicious Iraqis just ahead of the battalion. Moments later, the Iraqis got off the first shots in an ambush that killed a marine.

The war icons that McLaughlin cares about are not made of metal. They are made of flesh and blood.

Critical Thinking

1. Analyze the events reported in this article from an ethical perspective. Did anyone cross the line between right and wrong?

2. Wilson Surratt, a senior executive producer at CNN, is quoted as saying, "What were we supposed to do? Not show what was going on in the square? We did the responsible thing. We were careful to say it was not the end. At some point, you've got to trust the viewer to understand what they're seeing." Does this perspective toward gatekeeping work for you?

Whence the Revolution

For the past half-decade, Egyptian workers, journalists, and bloggers have increasingly, and bravely, been standing up to their government.

STEPHEN FRANKLIN

After the policemen had sodomized the bus driver with a broomstick, and after one of the officers had sent a cell-phone video of the attack to other bus drivers in downtown Cairo to make clear that the cops could do as they pleased, and after someone had given the video to Wael Abbas, who posted it on his blog, something unusual happened—at least, something unusual for Egypt.

The video went viral on the Internet. Two officers were charged, convicted, and ultimately given three-year prison terms.

It was an extraordinary moment, this sudden burst of justice back in 2006. Few have dared to point their fingers at police wrongdoing in Egypt. And it's even rarer that the culprits have been punished.

The tumult that has rocked Egypt this winter was clearly sparked by the Tunisian revolution. But the Egyptian uprising didn't begin on Jan. 25. It was rooted in the waves of workers' strikes and protests; the explosion of the Internet as a rallying megaphone for dissent about government abuse, corruption, and a vampire economy where a few flourish while many struggle; and a growing willingness by reporters, writers, and human-rights groups to tell the truth in the face of great risks.

The roots could be seen by anyone who has paid attention to the upheavals that have marked Egyptian society these last few years. But they were dismissed up until now as inconsequential and insufficient.

After all, hadn't the regime brutally slapped down bloggers and anyone who dared to stick out his or her neck? Hadn't it crushed and humiliated political opponents? Hadn't it cowed its college graduates into accepting high unemployment rates and menial low-wage work or into leaving the country in order to land a decent job?

Nobody counted on these disparate groups—including Muslims and Christians—coming together in the streets. Nobody calculated the emotional impact on the Egyptian people when it became clear that the republic of fears and lies was no longer almighty.

And nobody counted on unsung heroes like Wael Abbas. Over the past three years, when officials denied attacks by groups of men on young women in downtown Cairo, Abbas provided videos that showed the opposite. He put up videos depicting police brutally attacking demonstrators.

Nothing in his background suggested that Abbas would become an inspiration for a generation of bloggers. (Cairo's "official" newspaper, *Al Ahram,* called him "Egypt's most well-known blogger.") A recent college graduate from a working-class family when I first met him in 2007, Abbas knew his way around the Internet. He had friends who did as well. But what set him apart was his need to tell the truth that wasn't being told and his unwillingness to give up. Others quit when things got rough. Abbas didn't. He seemed emboldened by the impact he was having. The arrival of the Internet and the explosion of Egyptian bloggers, he said, created the "genie" that the government couldn't put back in the bottle.

Abbas paid a price for his truth telling. Enemies have tied him up in lawsuits. He has searched for steady work, plainly hindered by his reputation as a dissident. Several years ago, I urged him to consider work elsewhere, but he insisted he couldn't leave Egypt. He steadily kept up his blog. When the uprising began this January, he showed some of the first pictures of injured protesters in Alexandria. After his brief detention by police in February, he told ABC News that he had gone into hiding and that many of his friends had been seized by police.

Over the past couple of years, Abbas was far from the only one posting police misconduct online. Last June, Khalid Said, a young businessman, died at an Alexandria café. The police claimed that he had suffocated from a plastic bag of marijuana. Two autopsies backed up the police's claims, authorities declared.

Eyewitness accounts, spread via the Internet and eventually to the Egyptian newspapers, told a very different story. They described how the 24-year-old had been dragged out of the café and beaten by police. They said he had been targeted by police allegedly because he had posted a video online that showed officers sharing the results of a drug bust. Yet the most compelling items posted online of what happened at the café were photos depicting someone who had been so badly beaten that his face was grotesquely contorted.

Thousands joined the Facebook page protesting Said's death. Demonstrations broke out in Alexandria and elsewhere. The government quickly charged the two police officers named by witnesses not with murder but with unlawful arrest and excessive use of force.

While most of the wrongs recounted on the Internet over the past couple of years have not been righted, they have been part of the process of building the movement that's taken to Cairo's streets this winter.

When workers staged protests in 2008 in al Mahala al Kubra, a grim textile-manufacturing town, a Facebook page rallied more than 100,000 supporters across the country. That spurred the formation of a group known as the April 6 Youth Movement, a loose collection of tech-savvy youths, intellectuals, workers, and many from the vast ranks of the unemployed. Their online success encouraged them to join in a call for a national strike in 2009. Hardly anyone showed up, however. The organizers blamed the fizzled turnout on a government crackdown and tight police presence.

The growing protests of Egyptian workers has been a particular focus of journalist and photographer Hossam el Hamalawy, a blogger who's been deep into the action in Cairo's streets this winter. When labor protests accelerated several years ago, his blog was often the place where journalists, who would normally ignore such events, could go to see what was happening. Hamalawy and I met years ago when I was working with an Egyptian human-rights group on a guide for bloggers on how to cover the news—and how to avoid problems with the government as well. (Fearful about his obsession with his work, I've typically ended our talks by reminding him that one cannot live on coffee and cigarettes alone.)

Hamalawy's photos have shown the faces of Egyptian workers as they've overcome their fears to confront their employers—and, at times, their government. Over the past six years, more than 2 million workers have joined in more than 3,300 occupations, demonstrations, or other forms of protest—a development without precedent in Hosni Mubarak's Egypt. In nearly all cases, they were protesting on their own because their unions are shells for the government. On occasion, they have won their battles, with the government conceding just enough to deflate the confrontations.

The workers have protested lethal workplace conditions. They've protested a minimum wage for beginning workers that was stuck at $7 a month for more than 20 years. They protested the government's broken promises of economic reforms. Their biggest victory came last autumn when the government, after fighting lawsuits from labor and human-rights groups, grudgingly boosted the wage base to about $70 a month, still far below what workers say they need.

That may seem like a heaping increase. But state officials last November told *Al Ahram* that a family of four needs to earn more than $120 a month to escape poverty. And for hundreds of thousands of workers in the underground economy, there are no pay rules, no benefits, no workplace protections. They get whatever the boss gives them. That is why about at least 40 percent of the nation lives on $2 a day and why one out of five Egyptians does not earn enough to meet his or her basic food needs, according to a 2008 United Nations Development Program report. Many workers have slipped further into despair as privatization efforts have trimmed already low benefits and wages, taken away their slim hopes of job security, and fed into a strong sense of outrage.

Last summer, the workers' fury reached a crescendo as disgruntled employees from one factory after another gathered in front of the Egyptian parliament on one of Cairo's busiest streets. Such an in-your-face display of angry workers in front of the government was unprecedented. The demonstrators slept on the sidewalks for days on end, often dressing in rags to show their plight.

One broiling day last year, I hung out with workers from one factory, who pounded drums and banged rocks on police barricades to draw attention from the motorists passing by. "We are not going to fight or make trouble," vowed Khaled el Shishawy, a short, muscular man in his 40s who had worked at a factory that had shut down, and was the protesters' acknowledged leader. To calm an earlier protest by the same workers, the government had promised months earlier to help them get severance payments. But nothing happened, so the workers were back on the streets.

The next day, police and government thugs swept all of the demonstrators away from the parliament building, saying that the workers had armed themselves and were violent—claims discounted by Egyptian journalists who had been on the scene. When I met with el Shishawy and leaders of other worker protests several days later, they were not discouraged at all. They swore they would carry on. The problem was their whole effort was so new they were not sure how to organize themselves. They wanted to tell the world about their struggle, but they had no idea how to do so.

Informing the world about what's happening in Egypt hasn't been easy or safe even for those with the right skills. Novelist Alaa al Aswany tried for years to tell the story of the government's corruption and abuse and its blindness toward the massive numbers of poor. State censors blocked the publication of nearly all of his books, and he was planning to leave Egypt. One book, however, got through, and a publisher took a chance on it. The novel, *The Yacoubian Building,* set sales records in Egypt about a decade ago and became a widely popular movie.

The story is a melange of Egyptians' woes. It tells of people so poor they live in shacks on rooftops, of a ruling party that thrives on kickbacks, and of police torture that drives the young into the arms of Muslim extremists.

Because he could not rely on his income as a writer, al Aswany kept up his job as a dentist. Even after the book's success, he kept his practice, in a decrepit office building not far from where I lived in Cairo's Garden City. When I visited him several years ago, he was headed for one of the nighttime salons he held weekly for young writers. But the salons had run into problems. The government was pressuring restaurants to deny him space to hold his meetings. Al Aswany constantly had to search for new places.

For years, al Aswany had written a column for *Al Destour,* a small, struggling leftist paper. Last year, he began writing for *El Shourok,* a new, independent newspaper that is closer to the political center. He stopped writing last fall, however, according to the Committee to Protect Journalists, after the newspaper's bosses warned him and another columnist about "external pressures" to tone down their content.

His column vanished at about the same time that Ibrahim Eissa, a long-term journalism gadfly who has faced dozens of court cases under the government's press laws, was fired as editor of *Al Destour.* The new owners of the newspaper said it had nothing to do with his views. But Eissa insisted that he had been fired after he refused to kill an article written by Mohamed ElBaradei, the former head of the International Atomic Energy Agency, who was building up his status as a leader of a growing political opposition.

During the past year, though, incidents of censorship and the repression of news and opinions have themselves become more of a topic for public discussion. Salama Ahmed Salama, a columnist for *Al Ahram,* weighed in with his view of Eissa's firing.

"An invisible hand is in control of the media," he wrote. "The invisible hand determines the degree to which freedom of expression and publication is permitted. This invisible hand uses the owners of the media, forcing them to shut down mouths that talk and break pens that have gone far."

What's notable here is that *Al Ahram* is not only the nation's largest daily newspaper but the government's mouthpiece. In the deadening tradition of Arab government-run newspapers, it is rare not to see the face of the ruler—Hosni Mubarak—on the front page greeting some dignitary. News that makes the government look bad either doesn't exist or appears as a small item way back among the advertisements.

Salama's is a brave and unusual voice. To be sure, amid competition from TV and new papers, *Al Ahram* has struggled to reshape itself and loosen its authoritarian demeanor. But its role as the government's voice from on high to the masses still pervades many of its workers' thinking. I was reminded of this during a training session I put on last year for *Al Ahram* staffers.

The goal was to create issue-oriented stories that draw in readers by first telling about particular persons or describing a particular scene. This is long a tradition in the West but not in government-run Arab newspapers that like to tell its readers what to think.

The reality portrayed by government-run Arab newspapers is being challenged by voices on the Internet.

Much to my pleasure, the writers and editors embraced the concept. For their homework assignments, many also came up with compelling stories about poor people struggling to survive in Cairo, and the group seemed pleased with the results. But at the end of our meetings, a young editor, who had seemed enthused by the work, complained that the concept didn't fit his newspaper.

"This is not the way we Egyptians think. We don't emphasize the individual or put the individual first," he said.

That's no longer entirely true, however—not since *Al Masry Al Youm* (*Egypt Today*) appeared in 2004, followed by one or two other independent newspapers. *Al Masry Al Youm* doesn't belong to the government or to a party or a religious group as do most Egyptian newspapers. It has emphasized features and investigative reporting. And it has turned loose young reporters, who have pushed back barriers never challenged before. During this winter's uprising, it reported accusations that thugs captured during looting had cards identifying them as police.

Indeed, soon after the Jan. 25 uprising began, the paper's editor, Magdi el Gallad wrote:

"The 25 January 'Day of Anger' was a turning point for mass politics under Mubarak as thousands of demonstrators broke a fear barrier that for decades had kept Egyptians off the streets out of concerns for their safety. Those days are coming to a close."

Critical Thinking

1. From a government perspective, what are the pros and cons of media censorship?
2. How do you decide when the people inciting revolution are the good guys and when they are the bad guys?

North Korea's Digital Underground

To smuggle facts into or out of North Korea is to risk imprisonment and even execution. Yet today, aided by a half-dozen stealthy media organizations outside the country, citizen-journalists are using technologies new and old to break the regime's iron grip on information. Will the truth set a nation free?

Robert S. Boynton

The democratic people's Republic of Korea is the very archetype of a "closed society." It ranks dead last—196th out of 196 countries—in Freedom House's *Freedom of the Press* index. Unlike the citizens of, say, Tunisia or Egypt, to name two countries whose populations recently tapped the power of social media to help upend the existing political order, few North Koreans have access to Twitter, Facebook, or YouTube. In fact, except for a tiny elite, the DPRK's 25 million inhabitants are not connected to the Internet. Televisions are set to receive only government stations. International radio signals are routinely jammed, and electricity is unreliable. Freestanding radios are illegal. But every North Korean household and business is outfitted with a government-controlled radio hardwired to a central station. The speaker comes with a volume control, but no off switch. In a new media age awash in universally shared information—an age of planet-wide instant messaging and texted manifestos—the Democratic People's Republic of Korea remains a stubborn holdout, a regime almost totally in control of its national narrative.

Given this isolation, it's even more remarkable that since 2004, a half-dozen independent media organizations have been launched in Northeast Asia to communicate with North Koreans—to bring news out of the country as well as to get potentially destabilizing information in. These media insurgents have a two-pronged strategy, integrating Cold War methods (Voice of America–like shortwave broadcasts in; samizdat-like info out) and 21st-century hardware: SD chips, thumb drives, CDs, e-books, miniature recording devices, and cell phones. And as with all intelligence-gathering projects, their most valuable assets are human: a network of reporters in North Korea and China who dispatch a stream of reports, whether about the palace intrigue surrounding the choice of Kim Jong Il's successor, or the price of flour in Wŏnsan.

Run on shoestring budgets by North Korean defectors and South Korean and Japanese activists, these groups walk a line between journalism and advocacy. The two Koreas are still at war, and neither side is above employing censorship, disinformation, and outright propaganda. South Korea, for example, blocks access to North Korean websites and broadcasts. Its National Security Law promises lengthy prison sentences for any activity or material that the government judges to be pro–North Korean. Last November, for example, its top court upheld a jail sentence for a woman convicted of possessing instrumental music with composition *titles* that praised the North. It would be naive to assume that these independent news organizations aren't influenced by these pressures. But regardless of where they fit on the South Korean ideological spectrum or whether they fully support the hard line toward North Korea of South Korea's current president, Lee Myung Bak, these new media organizations are helping to create something remarkable: a corps of North Korean citizen-journalists practicing real journalism inside the country.

Their work is illegal and extremely dangerous, and it is producing results. In December 2009, for example, one reporter for the Daily NK, a website based in Seoul, embarrassed Pyongyang by intercepting a copy of Kim Jong Il's annual message, a critical document that sets the ideological tone for the year, *before* it appeared in North Korea's official newspaper, *Rodong Sinmun.* This past December, Open Radio North Korea, a broadcast-news organization, broke the story that a train headed for Pyongyang with gifts from China for Kim Jong Un, the heir apparent, was reportedly sabotaged and derailed, in one of several sporadic and mostly unreported acts of resistance that would have been unthinkable a few years ago.

The sudden availability of so much timely information about what Donald Gregg, the former CIA chief and United States. ambassador in Seoul, once called the world's "longest-running intelligence failure" has shaken up the world of Pyongyang watchers. Until recently, experts could say more or less whatever they wanted about North Korea, because nobody could prove them wrong. Conventional wisdom, planted intelligence, and hoary rumors have long been the coin of the realm.

We've seen how serious the consequences of this uninformed punditry can be. Assured by North Korea experts in 2002 that the regime was "on the brink" of collapse, president George W. Bush saw no point in negotiating with Kim Jong Il, whom he loathed and wasn't inclined to deal with in the first place. Not only did the regime not collapse, but in October 2006 it detonated its first nuclear weapon.

115

The impact of these new groups on journalism has been transformative. Hardly a story about North Korea appears in *The New York Times, The Wall Street Journal,* or *The Washington Post* that hasn't either originated in, or been confirmed by, outlets like the Daily NK or Open Radio North Korea. "The international media gets most of its information on North Korea from them," says Kim Young Sam, an editor of South Korea's oldest monthly magazine, the *Chosun Monthly,* whose sister publication, the newspaper *Chosun Ilbo,* regularly cites their stories. "Nobody else has the resources, contacts, and expertise." Even agents from South Korea's National Intelligence Service (formerly the KCIA) sometimes contact the Daily NK and other such outlets to request information.

Not everyone is a fan. This spring, the North Korean government expressed its displeasure: "We have been entrusted with issuing a strict warning in the name of the Republic to those organizations which will be the first targets for severe punishment." The announcement referred to the news organizations by name, and Pyongyang watchers noted that the phrase *We have been entrusted* indicates the message comes directly from Kim Jong Il. These were no idle threats. Last spring, two North Korean spies posing as defectors were sent to assassinate Hwang Jang Yop, the highest-level North Korean official ever to defect to South Korea. (Hwang died, peacefully, of a heart attack in October.) And in January 2010, a North Korean factory worker was publicly executed by firing squad for phoning news about the price of rice to someone in South Korea.

H oused on the second floor of a dingy commercial building that anyone can find, on a small, winding street just blocks from Seoul's Gyeongbokgung Palace, the Daily NK looks more like a call center than a bustling international news organization. Editors sit in 17 gray cubicles encircling the room. Phones ring and are answered with a grunt, hung up, and then redialed—the paper's routine for communicating with its reporters.

One of the Daily NK's founders, Park In Ho, spends much of his time recruiting and training reporters on the North Korean border with China. Published in Korean, Chinese, English, and Japanese, the site receives 150,000 visits a month. Like most of the other independent news organizations, it receives funds from the National Endowment for Democracy, as well as other NGOs and private donors. The Daily NK, like its peers, pays its North Korean correspondents small monthly retainers (more for scoops), and additional funds that they can use to bribe their way out of difficult situations.

Park tells me about recruiting one of his reporters. "I met him in China through an NGO. He was a graduate of Kim Il Sung University, so was destined to become a member of the elite. The first thing he asked me was to help him get some dynamite, so that he could blow up Kim Jong Il. He thought that everything in North Korea would change if he killed him." They spent three months together, talking and reading books about the history of Northeast Asia. "I wanted him to understand the situation in the region, and persuade him not only that

terrorism was wrong, but that it wouldn't change anything." The man is now a trader inside North Korea, and because his work requires constant travel, he has become one of the Daily NK's most valuable correspondents.

There have been a number of close calls. In 2008, a security officer caught one of the Daily NK's reporters as he was crossing the river into China. The reporter had been surreptitiously recording conversations with party officials, and was carrying three memory cards filled with audio files. North Korea had recently launched several test missiles; the reporter and his contacts were discussing the international reaction.

As he had rehearsed with Park, the reporter told the officer that he was only a cog in a larger operation. He was delivering the cards to a relative in China, who then would sell the information to journalists and give him a cut. You can bribe your way around virtually anything in North Korea, it seems, unless it involves either South Korea or religious materials. If the officer discovered that the reporter was working for the Daily NK, he would be sent to a labor camp, or even executed. The reporter suggested that the officer call his relative in China to confirm his story.

Park works according to a strict protocol. He carries several cell phones, each assigned to a different reporter, and they agree to communicate only at certain times on certain days. Any unscheduled call is cause for suspicion. So when his phone rang, Park answered in his best Chinese-Korean accent. The officer assumed he was speaking to the reporter's relative and demanded $5,000 to release him. After several calls back and forth, the bribe was paid and the reporter freed (though without the memory cards). However, the officer sensed that he was onto a good thing, and tried to enlist Park as a business partner. "He called me every day for a month, like a stalker. He wanted to deal North Korean drugs. He'd send them to me, I'd sell them, and we'd divide the profit," Park says.

Another of Park's sources of high-level intelligence is the widow of a party official who she believes was unjustly purged. She is bitter and gives the information she learns from her children—many of whom have government jobs—to Park during trips she takes to China. She lives near the Yellow Sea and sometimes gets a ride across with local fishermen. During one journey, the fishing boat was boarded by a North Korean naval patrol. The only place for her to hide was among the layers of fish and ice stored in the bowels of the ship. She escaped undetected, but with a bad case of frostbite. Park paid for a two-month stay in a Chinese hospital, where she recovered. "Don't worry about me," she assured him. "I'm too old to remarry, so my looks don't matter."

I n the late 1990s, a daring strategy emerged for using video to supplement information collected through interviews in North Korea. To learn about this, I travel to Osaka, Japan, to meet Ishimaru Jiro, 48, a diminutive, serious man with a neatly trimmed goatee, who works for Asia Press International, a consortium of freelance journalists famous for its coverage of war zones in Afghanistan, Iraq, and elsewhere in the Middle East. During the past 12 years, its reporters in North Korea have shot some of the most dramatic footage ever to emerge from the country.

Ishimaru began making trips to the China–North Korea border in the '90s, interviewing refugees, shooting video, and writing. Twice, he crossed into North Korea legally, and another time he used a forged Chinese passport. One day in 1998, Ahn Chul, one of the young men who moved back and forth over the border, made an extraordinary proposal: "Why are you putting yourself in such danger by shooting video here?" he asked. "Give me a camera, and I'll shoot video inside North Korea."

Ishimaru gave him some rudimentary training in video photography and a camera hidden in a shopping bag. They set a date to meet three months later. The footage Ahn brought out was shocking: filthy, barefoot children scavenging for food, picking kernels of corn from cow manure. Glassy-eyed, the children told the interviewer that their parents had died and they were homeless and alone. The footage was beamed around the world.

The footage that Ahn Chul brought out of North Korea was shocking: filthy, barefoot children scavenging for food, picking kernels of corn from cow manure.

The experiment was so successful that Ishimaru started training other aspiring reporters, using crowded Chinese markets to teach them how to film secretly. Now Ishimaru meets in China with his North Korea–based reporters every few months to pick up and help edit their tapes.

How did a country so closed become porous enough to support such news-gathering by watchers in the South? The answer goes back to the collapse of Communism in the late 1980s, which deprived North Korea of the Eastern Bloc subsidies it had long relied on to sustain its people. In the mid-1990s, a series of floods obliterated several harvests and ushered in a famine that ultimately killed an estimated 1 million North Koreans, or nearly 5 percent of the population. The government food-distribution system collapsed, and people who had relied on it for 50 years didn't know what to do. Many starved. Others, despite great peril, crossed into China in search of food. The number of defectors who traveled through China to South Korea—previously never more than a few each year—increased tenfold between 1998 and 2002.

Once these North Korean defectors made it across the Yalu or Tumen River, they were startled to discover that even the poorest Chinese had higher living standards than they did. Food was abundant. If anything, the Chinese were growing wealthier.

The famine encouraged the spread of open-air markets throughout North Korea. They had begun appearing after Kim Il Sung's death in 1994. People lucky enough to farm small plots of land sold their extra produce. Riots broke out when the police tried to shut the markets down, so the government decided to look the other way. As the markets spread, they soon became places where one could buy not only rice,

but also bootlegged South Korean soap operas and used electronics.

The spread of such trading gave Ishimaru another idea. Could market forces be used not just to get information out but to smuggle footage in? He and his colleagues started with a video about the Kim Il Sung era. Its ideological content was subtle: by praising the decades when life was good and food was plentiful, it was implicitly criticizing the current Kim Jong Il era, in which neither is the case. The video was edited in Japan and sent to China, where a few hundred copies were burned. Traders on the border were eager to get free merchandise, and within days the discs were being bought and sold in markets throughout the country.

Across the border, as the Chinese got richer, they were trading in their Walkmans and cheap computers for iPods and computers with larger hard drives and DVD burners. And what do a billion Chinese do with their old stuff? Sell it to their poor neighbors. (A 2009 survey found that 58 percent of North Koreans had regular access to a cassette recorder with radio, and 21 percent watched videos on video-compact-disc players.) The confluence of these developments created a remarkable journalistic opening: just as defectors in unprecedented numbers were bringing more information out of North Korea, the spread of markets and secondhand technology was creating a conduit for getting more information in. As the North Korea experts Stephan Haggard and Marcus Noland report in a recent study based on their surveys of refugees, "Not only is foreign media becoming more widely available, inhibitions on its consumption are declining as well."

The North Korean Government has always been of two minds when it comes to technology. Despite its guiding philosophy of "self-reliance" (*juche*), it has relied on neighbors to enable it to enter the information age. Its official YouTube videos, Twitter feed, and Facebook accounts are registered in China. Until the late 1990s, all international phone calls were routed through Beijing or Moscow. And what few connections to the Internet the country *does* have come via a cross-border link to China's Unicom.

No more than a few thousand North Korean researchers and high officials have access to the Internet. Most North Korean citizens must settle instead for the Kwangmyong ("Bright Star") intranet portal, which provides access to censored news and official documents and has a rudimentary e-mail service. Launched in 2000, Kwangmyong is based on a Japanese version of Microsoft Windows. It can be accessed at universities and in government offices, as well as in the hundred or so cyber cafés where young people in the country's largest cities go to play games and watch videos.

Owning computers is legal, although they must be registered with the local authorities. Most computers, which generally run on pirated Microsoft software, come from China. The country's only computer-manufacturing company, Morning Panda, produces barely 10,000 a year. If computers are rare, printers are even more so. They are closely monitored because of their potential for spreading anti-regime documents. Similarly, citizens are forbidden to own fax machines, which can be found only in national post offices and in business offices. Sending a fax requires the approval of a high-level employer. Cell phones, both legal and illegal, have become a fact of life only during the past five years.

Radio is the chief technology through which the regime communicates with its citizens and is, for a variety of reasons that include patterns of historical use, the technology of choice for the exile-media outlets. A few target specific audiences. North Korea Reform Radio, founded in 2007, directs its free-market message at government bureaucrats (it recently aired a 44-episode series on China's economic liberalization); North Korea Intellectual Solidarity, or NKIS, a hybrid think tank and news organization, concentrates on the intelligentsia ("The bottom of the population are too ignorant and brainwashed, and the elites are too hardline," says its founder, Kim Heung Kwang).

Much of the programming has a distinct social-media character. Free North Korea Radio's *Voices of the People* features man-on-the-street interviews with North Koreans, their voices digitally distorted before being broadcast back into their country. NK Reform Radio interviews defectors now living in South Korea. Some are unable to fit into South Korean society, and their ambivalence about their new home comes through in their comments—itself evidence of their newfound freedom of speech.

No more than a few thousand North Korean researches and high officials have access to the Internet.

The subject that most interests North Koreans is the country's ruling dynasty: founder Kim Il Sung, his son Kim Jong Il, and his presumed heir, Kim Jong Un. Most of their subjects know little more than the idealized history of the Kims churned out by the state's propaganda mill. They are shocked to learn that Kim Jong Il was born in Russia, and not on the mythic Mount Paektu; Koreans are quite socially conservative and are aghast that he has fathered several children with women other than his wives.

Editors have wasted no time creating a suite of Kim-centric programs. Open Radio North Korea broadcasts an original serial drama called *2012*, whose title refers to the much-anticipated 100th anniversary of Kim Il Sung's birth. It starts with the premise that Kim Jong Il has been incapacitated by a second stroke, and imagines what North Korea might be like in the near future. Radio Free Chosun has dramatized several memoirs about the ruling family, including one by Kim Jong Il's chef. And even NK Reform Radio is getting in on the action with an original drama called *What Did Kim Jong Il Eat During the Famine?*

The bet is that a mix of entertainment and news is more compelling than broadcasts that focus on famine or human-rights abuses (things most North Koreans are well aware of).

The evidence suggests that such programs work. In their surveys of North Korean refugees, Haggard and Noland found a clear correlation between the "consumption of foreign media" and "more negative assessments of the regime and its intentions." Kim Seong Min, the founder of Free North Korea Radio, credits his own political awakening to shortwave-radio programs. As a North Korean propaganda officer, he sometimes listened to the illegal radios he confiscated. One night he heard a South Korean program that contradicted a number of the myths surrounding the Kim family. After a little research, he discovered that the broadcasts were true. *Was* everything *he'd been taught a lie,* he wondered? It wasn't long before he defected.

Without a doubt, North Korea Intellectual Solidarity is the organization that has thought most about the role of technology. Its reporters are equipped with South Korean, rather than Chinese, cell phones, because NKIS technicians believe their encoded protocol is more difficult for North Korean intelligence to track. Not content to buy voice and video recorders off the shelf, NKIS uses customized devices, whose battery life and recording times are reputedly superior. My request to see one is (pleasantly) denied.

The group's technical emphasis comes from its founder, Kim Heung Kwang. Kim was a professor of computer science at Hamhung University of Technology, a branch of the North Korean military. He looks a decade older than his 51 years, and has the haggard mien of someone who has fallen afoul of the authorities. In North Korea, he was training students for careers as engineers or soldiers. The best were recruited by the army's elite hacker units, which reportedly disrupted South Korean and United States. government websites in 2009. Two of his former students defected recently, and now work with him at NKIS.

Kim's facility with technology got him into trouble in the North. "I had several e-books, which I got from China. The national security force arrested me for possessing them," he tells me. The books were pretty innocuous fare, mostly motivational titles like Dale Carnegie's *How to Win Friends and Influence People.* "These weren't anti-regime books, so why was this a crime?" he asks bitterly. "I saw that there wasn't any hope for the North Korean system. I started to dream of going somewhere where I had the freedom to read what I wanted." Kim defected in 2003 and arrived in South Korea a year later.

One of the first things Kim's team created was an e-book called *Window to the Global Village.* A 204-page primer about South Korea and the rest of the world, it is loaded with embedded video, music, photos, and voice files. The three-gigabyte thumb drive had extra space, so he added a math program for children, a fortune-telling program for adults, games, and a bunch of computer tools.

Kim reaches into his pocket and shows me one of his specially programmed thumb drives. It will read "empty" when it is plugged in to a computer, just in case it falls into the hands of a border guard. When the savvy (or unsuspecting) user double-clicks on the logo, the program launches, and installs a file called "Welcome World" on his computer. (Some funders object to these surreptitious distribution techniques, fearing they might endanger innocent people.) Then there is the self-destruct option. "We set it to erase itself after a month, or after a certain number of downloads," Kim explains, holding up one of the thumb drives. "Even if you are caught reading the e-book, the national security police won't be able to trace it. After all, you can say that when *you* got it, you thought it was empty!"

Given the grip that the North Korean regime retains on information, the mission of these subversive organizations can seem quixotic—an act of faith as much as it is journalism. Of all the narrowcasters tenaciously targeting North Korea, the narrowest is Shiokaze ("sea breeze," in Japanese), a station created by the Investigation Commission on Missing Japanese Probably Related to North Korea, or COMJAN. In the late 1970s, North Korea began randomly abducting Japanese citizens from beaches and parks, and holding them captive in Pyongyang for the next quarter century. Their families assumed they had either eloped or died. Precisely why they were abducted has never been clear, although it most likely has to do with training spies. Even the exact number of abductees isn't known. At a 2002 summit with Japanese Prime Minister Junichiro Koizumi, Kim Jong Il confessed to having taken 13 Japanese, five of whom were still alive (and were soon returned to Japan). The Japanese government insists that at least 17 were kidnapped, and refuses to believe that the others have died. From the third floor of a less-than-spiffy apartment building near Tokyo's Iidabashi railway station, COMJAN advocates on behalf of abductees *not* officially recognized by the Japanese government, and hopes to reach them with its radio broadcasts.

On the day I visit, Araki Kazuhiro, a professor of Korean studies and COMJAN's chairman, is sitting in the tiny, make-shift plywood radio booth, reading news about recent nuclear-arms negotiations for one of Shiokaze's twice-daily shortwave broadcasts. After he finishes, we sit at a conference table and have some tea. Araki says he believes that more than 400 Japanese have been abducted, and that the kidnappings continue even today. As with many of the other shortwave broadcasts, North Korea often jams Shiokaze's signal. Shiokaze regularly switches frequencies, but the North quickly locates the new one, and jams it.

While the Daily NK and other outlets occasionally interact with their listeners, Shiokaze operates in a virtual void. Other than the five Japanese released in 2002, no abductee has ever been heard from. I reluctantly broach the subject: Does Araki have any evidence that anyone in North Korea—abductee or not—has ever heard the broadcast?

Araki and his producer consult with each other. "Well, we once heard about a high-school student who was able to pick up the program in Pyongyang, but we're not sure about that," he says. After more tea, Araki excuses himself and returns to the booth. It is almost noon, and he needs to finish one more Korean-language segment before the afternoon program is beamed across the sea and into North Korea.

Critical Thinking

1. Boynton writes, "In their surveys of North Korean refugees, Haggard and Nolan found a clear connection between 'consumption of foreign media' and 'more negative assessments of the regime and its intentions.'" How likely do you think it is that surveys of Americans would show the same findings?

2. Is it possible, in the modern world, for a government to control its national narrative?

ROBERT S. BOYNTON directs New York University's Literary Reportage concentration and is writing a book about the Cold War in Northeast Asia.

UNIT 3
Players and Guides

Unit Selections

Learning Outcomes

After reading this Unit, you should be able to

- Propose reasonable standards of "fair use" and "fair compensation" for Internet content.

- Develop a reasoned proposal regarding ways the government (through regulation and/or funding) should appropriately exert control over mass media ownership, content, and agendas.

- Articulate a viewpoint on the boundaries of free speech.

- Propose rules of ethical practice for publishing or posting graphic photographs and vetting politicians' truthfulness.

- Discuss the case for and against strict separation of information and advertising functions of media.

Student Website

www.mhhe.com/cls

Internet References

The Electronic Journalist
  www.spj.org
Federal Communications Commission (FCC)
  www.fcc.gov
Poynter Online: Research Center
  www.poynter.org
World Intellectual Property Organization (WIPO)
  www.wipo.org
Photo Ethics
  www.sree.net/teaching/photoethics.html
Ethics Case Studies
  http://journalism.indiana.edu/resources/ethics/#photos

The freedom of speech and of the press are regarded as fundamental American rights, protected under the United States. Constitution. These freedoms, however, are not without restrictions. The media are held accountable to legal and regulatory authorities whose involvement reflects a belief that the public sometimes requires protection.

Regulatory agencies, such as the Federal Communications Commission (FCC), exert influence over media access and content through their power to grant, regulate, and revoke licenses to operate. Ownership regulations have traditionally centered on radio and television because of the historically limited number of broadcast bands available in any community (called spectrum scarcity). The courts exert influence over media practice through hearing cases of alleged violation of legal principles such as the protection from libel and the right to privacy. Antitrust law has been summoned in attempts to break up media monopolies. Copyright laws protect an author's right to control distribution of her or his "intellectual property." Shield laws grant reporters the right to promise informants confidentiality. The courts have heard cases based on product liability law, in which plaintiffs have—sometimes successfully and sometimes not—sued media companies for harmful acts attributed to a perpetrator's exposure to violent media content. The Federal Trade Commission (FTC) and the United States. Food and Drug Administration (FDA) have regulatory controls that affect advertising.

The first three articles in this section deal with regulatory and access perspectives. "What's a Fair Share in the Age of Google?" describes tension regarding application of fair use and copyright law to the Internet, noting "there is a growing sense among the 'legacy' media, at least, that Google facilitates a corrosive move away from paying content providers for their work." When information is free (using either definition of "free") what rights do the creators have? "Long Live the Web: A Call for Continued Open Standards and Neutrality" makes a case for open access with regulatory presence: "A neutral communications medium is the basis of a fair, competitive market economy, of democracy, and of science. Debate has risen again in the past year about whether government legislation is needed to protect net neutrality. It is. Although the Internet and Web generally thrive on lack of regulation, some basic values have to be legally preserved." In "A Vaster Wasteland," former FCC Commissioner Newton Minow proposes six national policy priorities he believes should guide mass media regulatory decisions. Three are related to access, three to priority applications.

The next two articles address free speech. "Frenemies of Free Speech" offers differing historical and contemporary perspectives on boundaries enforced in the interest of civility and tolerance: "All censorship—particularly self-censorship driven by fear—creates hatred and contempt for the censor. How can they whose feelings we are trying not to hurt possibly regard us? Certainly as weaklings, but also as weaklings with a secret sense of our own superiority." Coming at the issue from a different angle, "The End of Secrecy" (using either definition of "end") explores WikiLeaks and the concept of secrecy as a form of media regulation.

© McGraw-Hill Companies, Inc./Jill Braaten, photographer

Beyond the reach of legal and regulatory sanction, there is a wide gray zone between an actionable offense and an error in judgment. For example, while legal precedence makes it difficult for public figures to prevail in either libel or invasion-of-privacy cases, it is not necessarily right to print information that might be hurtful to them. Nor is it necessarily wrong to do so. Sometimes a "good business decision" from one player's perspective impedes another's success. Sometimes being "truthful" is insensitive. Sometimes being "interesting" means being exploitive. Some media organizations seem to have a greater concern for ethical policy than do others; however, even with the best intentions, drawing the line is not always simple.

The remaining articles in this unit raise questions of judgment and ethical practice. "The Quality-Control Quandary" discusses immediacy versus accuracy as traditional journalists struggle with acceptable expectations for proofreading and fact-checking prior to online posting. "The Fact-Checking Explosion" is a different take on "fact-checking," exploring both utility and ethics of media truth squads dedicated to separating "truth from fiction in political claims." "Too Graphic?" is about news photos covering the January 2010 earthquake that devastated the island nation of Haiti. Technology such as Photoshop makes it easy to edit photos, and often photo editing is done for aesthetic reasons rather than with intent to deceive. What are the limits of acceptable practice? "A Porous Wall" addresses the traditional boundary between news and advertising copy in newspapers, and how newspapers come to terms with changing rules as they fight to sustain revenue. "What Would You Do?" ponders the ethics of investigative experimenters, who "step out of their customary role as observers and play with reality to see what will happen." "The Lives of Others" is about gatekeeping in the context of reality shows such as *America's Most Wanted*.

What rules of practice should be applied in balancing the public's right to know against potential effects on individuals and society at large? Which great photograph shouldn't run? Which facts shouldn't be printed? What are the appropriate boundaries of free speech? Who owns media channels and makes these decisions? Is it ethical for journalists to cover stories on issues about which they have strong personal views, or does such practice compromise objectivity? Is it fair to become a "friend" to win trust, then write a story that is not flattering or does not support the source's views or actions? Should the paparazzi be held legally responsible for causing harm to those they stalk, or should that responsibility be borne by consumers who buy their products? What about the well-intentioned story that attempts to right a social wrong, but hurts people in the process?

These are not easy questions, and they do not have easy answers. Media in the United States are grounded in a legacy of fiercely protected First Amendment rights and shaped by a code for conducting business with a strong sense of moral obligation to society. But no laws or codes of conduct can prescribe appropriate behavior for every possible situation. When people tell us something in face-to-face communication, we are often quick to "consider the source" to evaluate the message. Media-literate consumers do the same in evaluating media messages.

What's a Fair Share in the Age of Google?

How to Think about News in the Link Economy

Peter Osnos

The buzz inside Google is overwhelmingly positive about what the company does and how we will all benefit from the results—including the embattled denizens of newspapers and magazines who increasingly see Google as an enabler of their demise. Barely a decade ago, Google received its first $25 million investment, based on search technology developed by Sergey Brin and Larry Page, the company's co-founders. By the time it went public just five years later, "Google" was a verb. Today it is the dominant force in what has turned out to be the central organizing principle of the Internet's impact on our lives: the search function and the accompanying links, keywords, and advertising that make sense and commerce out of the vast universe of information and entertainment on the Web. Google is as important today as were Microsoft, IBM, and the original AT&T, linchpins of our culture and economy, in the development of modern computation and communications.

By contrast, the great twentieth-century print companies, such as Time Inc., Tribune, and The New York Times Company, are in a battle for survival, or at least reinvention, against considerable odds. Google has become a kind of metaphor for the link economy and the Internet's immense power to organize content. Yet as the global leader among Web-based enterprises, it has also become a subject of debate and controversy, even though its sense of itself is still as benign as the playful tenor of its Manhatttan offices, where the fittings include scooters for zipping around the halls and a lavish free cafeteria.

At lunch there, I was surrounded by an animated crowd that included Brin, Google's thirty-six-year-old co-founder, wearing jeans, a sweater, and a demeanor indistinguishable from the rest of his eager young crew. Google maintains that it is actively working to make journalism and literature truly democratic and, functionally, easier to do. Google's "Office of Content Partnerships" sent me a list of "free tools journalists could use today for nearly every aspect of their work," including Blogger, a platform for publishing online; Google Analytics, for measuring Web traffic; Google website Optimizer; and other tools. The publishers of newspapers, magazines, and books, recognize that Google and the link-referral service it represents have become

inextricable from their audiences' lives, and indispensable to reaching that audience in large numbers.

And yet there is a growing sense among the "legacy" media, at least, that Google facilitates a corrosive move away from paying content providers for their work. Proceeds go instead to those who sell advertising and other services while aggregating and/or lifting material they did not create. It is true that the content providers have submitted to the link economy of their own accord. Still, in a piece last winter, I wrote that the notion that "information wants to be free" is absurd when the referral mechanism makes a fortune and the creators get scraps. That position was excoriated by some bloggers, including one who, in a quote cited on *The New York Times*'s Opinionator blog, called it "sheer idiocy."

Maybe. But only two months later, the Associated Press (clearly acting on behalf of the news organizations that own it) made a similar point and initiated a process that could end in lawsuits. Addressing the Newspaper Association of America, the chairman of the AP's board of directors, William Dean Singleton, CEO of MediaNews, said: "We can no longer stand by and watch others walk off with our work under misguided legal theories."

The full quote from which "information wants to be free" was lifted, by the way, is more ambiguous and complicated than that widely-quoted excerpt. The line comes from the futurist Stewart Brand, who first said it at a programmer's convention in 1984 and elaborated in his book, *The Media Lab: Inventing the Future at MIT,* in 1987, where he wrote:

> Information Wants To Be Free. Information also wants to be expensive. Information wants to be free because it has become so cheap to distribute, copy, and recombine—too cheap to meter. It wants to be expensive because it can be immeasurably valuable to the recipient. That tension will not go away. It leads to endless wrenching debate about price, copyright, 'intellectual property,' the moral rightness of casual distribution, because each round of new devices makes the tension worse, not better.

Brand leaves out another factor—that valuable information is expensive to produce. But two decades later, the battles he foresaw are fully engaged.

An ecosystem in which all stakeholders in the content economy have a fair share. That is one media executive's succinct summary of what is necessary to redress the growing imbalance of power and resources between traditional content creators and those who provide links to or aggregate that material. But the effort to find that formula is complicated because it involves technologies upgrading at warp speed, sweeping changes in popular habits, collapsing and emerging business models, and one of the basic pillars of our democracy—what we have always called a free press.

As this century began, newspapers, especially those in metro areas with dominant positions, were reporting profits of 20, 30, and even 40 percent. *The New York Times* was selling over a billion dollars a year in advertising and *Time* magazine held its seventy-fifth-anniversary gala celebration at Radio City Music Hall, which had been specially redone for the occasion. Fortunes disappeared in the tech bust of 2000–01, which seemed to underscore the fact that Internet-based commerce was in its formative stages. The news products on the Web—CompuServe, Prodigy, and America Online—seemed, on the whole, complementary to newspapers and magazines rather than competitive against them.

Yet the unlimited expanse that the Internet provides and the amazing capacity of Google (and Yahoo and MSN, etc.) to search it, soon began to change everything. Vending services like eBay and Craigslist flourished; sensations like MySpace and YouTube, where users provide the content, were born at the intersection of creativity and engineering; audiences were suddenly huge for essentially brand-new Web news providers online, such as MSNBC and CNN. Sites like The Drudge Report showed the potential of aggregation and, later, The Huffington Post showed the potential for garnering large crowds partly by recycling material created elsewhere.

Significantly, most of the established news organizations reached the same conclusion about how to take advantage of what was happening on the Web. They went for the model that had supported network television for decades—mass audiences attracted by free access that would justify high advertising rates. Virtually overnight, Google et. al. were delivering hundreds of millions of readers to media companies which, in turn, believed they could monetize those visitors.

This approach contrasted with the one adopted in the 1980s by the emerging cable systems for television. Those companies negotiated subscription fees with the providers of their most popular programming, such as ESPN and dozens of other channels, including some that carried news. (The average cable subscriber, for example, pays 77 cents per month for Fox News, whether they watch it or not.) Most cable networks also have copious advertising, from inexpensive pitches for local establishments to national campaigns. This flow of subscription revenues, combined with advertising, made cable programming a lucrative business—which, ironically, resembles the way newspapers and magazines operated until they unilaterally decided they were better off giving content away. (There are differences, of course, especially since barriers to a cable system are high, while barriers to launching on the Web are low, even though moguls like Barry Diller at The Daily Beast and others have found themselves investing real money there to get started.)

As the scale of the global economic implosion became clear, accelerating negative trends in circulation and advertising already under way, it became increasingly obvious that the free-content model was not working. News audiences were huge. On September 29, 2008, the day the Bush administration's first bailout proposal was voted down by the House of Representatives and the Dow fell almost eight hundred points, nytimes.com had 10 million visitors and 42.7 million page views. But revenues for The New York Times Company were disappearing so fast that this respected gatherer of news had to beg and borrow just to meet its debt obligations and maintain its news operation while also sustaining morale for the myriad innovations necessary to stay extant. This spring it threatened to shut down *The Boston Globe,* another financially sick newspaper with healthy traffic on its website. Unless new ways of attracting and sharing revenue are devised with the same breathtaking speed with which they have disappeared, the gathering of news by reputable, experienced institutions that are cornerstones of their community and the nation will be irreversibly damaged.

Print journalism bought into the free-news online model. Still, it is hardly surprising that the winners in the transformation of news dissemination, the distributors and aggregators, would become the focus of grievances by those they have trounced, willfully or not. So what is to be done to manage the consequences of this inexorable transformation of news delivery? If there is a simple, all-encompassing answer to that question, I did not find it in discussions with practitioners and pundits on all sides of the problem. But in the haze, I did find a tripartite framework for understanding the major aspects of the issue—let's call them the doctrines of Fair Conduct, Fair Use, and Fair Compensation.

Fair Conduct

On Saturday afternoon, February 7, 2009, SI.com, the website of *Sports Illustrated,* broke a huge story: Alex Rodriguez, the mega-rich Yankees star, had taken performance-enhancing drugs while playing for the Texas Rangers. *Sports Illustrated* released the story on its website rather than in the magazine, according to the editors involved, in an effort to enhance SI.com's standing as a destination for fans increasingly conditioned to getting sports news online. Within hours the story was everywhere, but if you went through Google to find it, what you likely got instead were the pickups that appeared elsewhere, summaries or even rewrites, with attribution. Most galling was that The Huffington Post's use of an Associated Press version of *SI*'s report was initially tops on Google, which meant that it, and not SI.com, tended to be the place readers clicking through to get the gist of the breaking scandal would land.

Traffic on SI.com did go up on that Saturday and for days thereafter, but not nearly as much as the editors had projected.

As long as the value of advertising on the Web is measured by the number of visitors a site receives, driving those numbers is critical, and therein lies the dilemma. Why did The Huffington Post come up ahead of SI.com? Because, even Google insiders concede, Huffington is effective at implementing search optimization techniques, which means that its manipulation of keywords, search terms, and the dynamics of Web protocol give it an advantage over others scrambling to be the place readers are sent by search engines. What angered the people at *Sports Illustrated* and Time Inc. is that Google, acting as traffic conductor, seemed unmoved by their grievance over what had happened to their ownership of the story. An *SI* editor quoted to me Time Inc's editor-in-chief, John Huey, noting crisply that, "talking to Google is like trying to talk to a television."

The rules of the road for distributing traffic on the Internet need to include recognition, in simple terms, of who got the story. The algorithm needs human help; otherwise, valuable traffic goes to sites that didn't pay to create the content.

Fair Use

This has to do with how content is gathered, displayed, and monetized by aggregators, not how it is found and distributed. Fair use is a technical term for the standards one must meet in order to use copyrighted material without the permission of rights holders, as in excerpts, snippets, or reviews, and it turns out to be far more flexible than I long had thought. U.S. copyright law sets four main factors to consider in determining what is fair use: whether the quotation of the material is for commercial gain, the nature and scale of the work, the amount being used in relation to the whole, and the impact on the value of the material by its secondary use.

The definition of fair use was central in the lengthy negotiations among book publishers, the Authors Guild, and Google to settle litigation over Google's intention to digitize copyrighted books for search and distribution without paying for them. At the outset, in 2006, Google apparently believed that releasing only "snippets" of the books meant it would prevail in a court test. The publishers and authors argued that once Google had unrestricted access to the content, it would inevitably be widely used in full or large part.

Ultimately, the sides decided not to force the matter to resolution. Instead, in October 2008, Google agreed to pay $125 million to the plaintiffs and to establish a system to pay copyright holder, share advertising revenues that may result, and build a registry for all books that are available.

The book agreement—actually the settlement of several lawsuits—is nearly 150 pages, plus attachments, of excruciatingly complex detail. Debate over the terms ever since they were announced has been fierce and the court has already postponed final comments from interested parties until October 7. He will then look at the criticisms put forward by, among others, the Harvard librarian and lawyers funded by Microsoft who contend that Google is gaining what amounts to a monopoly in the digital book arena. Then, the judge will determine whether to approve the agreement as is, or send it back for further nego-

tiations to satisfy the objections of its critics. He cannot amend the terms himself.

How the logic of publisher-author-Google pact applies to the news business is not clear—except that Google has acknowledged that the right to scan and distribute information has value, which can be shared with the originators of that content. Google's licensing agreement with the AP and other wire services—in which it publishes some AP content on its own servers rather than merely linking to it—may be another illustration of the same idea: pay to play.

But what of the aggregation of links? The Google position is that a link with a sentence or two as a tease is fair use of the material, and the site that generated the content actually is a beneficiary of the traffic. With news, the argument becomes entangled in whether the aggregation enhances or detracts from the value of the original content, and also in determining what amounts to fair use when an aggregator surrounds those links with its own summaries, blogs, and other interpretative embellishments, as some aggregators do. The news organizations also argue that aggregators should pay for that right to aggregate when they sell advertising around the links and snippets.

It would take a mind-bending interpretation of fair use to work these issues out, especially if the case went to trial. Many news providers don't have the time that a case would take (years, probably). And Google, again, may not want to force a final determination of the matter, as in the books case. As the controversy over Google's role in news intensified in the spring, executives from The New York Times Company, The Washington Post Company, and presumably others, met with Google in search of formulas that might balance their respective interests. Every one involved has signed nondisclosure agreements. If progress has been made in these discussions, it has not become public.

Fair Compensation

All of this still leaves the considerable question of monetizing the reading of material on the free-to-access sites that newspapers and magazines offer, now that it seems that online advertising alone will not be enough to support those operations. There are many ideas around for micropayments or subscriptions, memberships or paid sections within a free site, out of which may come a viable business solution or solutions. Based on my own reporting, the answer could be in some combination of individual payments or cable and telephone fees. Americans routinely pay telecom providers (Verizon, Optimum, and AT&T are the ones in my house) to deliver information and entertainment by television, computer, and wireless devices. The goal would be to extend those payments to the originators of news content. Google, it seems to me, might serve as a kind of meter, helping determine what percentage should go to the content originators. Complicated? Yes, but that is the kind of challenge that computers and the engineers who master them are meant to meet.

One of the best statements on this subject came from Jonathan Rosenberg, president for product management at Google, who wrote on a company blog, "We need to make it easier for the experts, journalists, and editors that we actually trust to publish their work under an authorship model that is authenticated and extensible, and then to monetize it in a meaningful way." The book publishers and authors agreement with Google recognized that goal, acknowledging that all information is not equal and cannot be free and endure.

These fairness goals for the internet age are plainly arguable. However, this is not a debate that will end in a vote that determines the outcome by majority rule, which is why predicting where things will go next is so hard. Still, what is known, earnestly but correctly, as accountability journalism—news that orders and monitors the world—is indispensable, and paying for it is vital to society. We now know conclusively that digital delivery is going to be a (or perhaps the) main way people find out what is happening around them, so the burden of responsibility on those who frame the way news is presented is incalculable.

Google is in its adolescence as a company. Cycles in the digital era tend to be short, but Google and the enterprises and services it encompasses are at the pinnacle now. What the company will do with that power is unknown in large part because, like most big institutions, Google limits transparency and is defensive when it comes to criticism.

There is a message in history for Google's leaders: nothing in the realms of business, information, entertainment, or technology remains as it is. Brin and Page stand on the shoulders of Gates and Jobs who followed Watson, Sarnoff, and Paley, who came after Luce and Disney and succeeded Hearst, Edison, and Bell. The next breakthrough innovators are doubtless at work somewhere. Will they help meet society's fundamental demand for news that supports itself in a way that Google and the rest of the digital generation say they want to do, but have not yet done?

Google is an extraordinary company with a nonpareil record of creativity. What a wondrous thing it would be for newsgathering, in a time of mounting crisis, if Google turned out to be as much a source of solutions as it is a part of the problem.

Critical Thinking

1. Summarize Stewart Brand's well-known "Information wants to be free . . ." description in your own words. Is it accurate?

2. What are reasonable standards of "fair use" applied to information distributed on the internet?

PETER OSNOS, *CJR*'S vice-chairman, is the founder and editor-at-large of PublicAffairs Books and a senior fellow for media at The Century Foundation. His previous *CJR* piece was about the future of books.

Long Live the Web: A Call for Continued Open Standards and Neutrality

The Web is critical not merely to the digital revolution but to our continued prosperity—and even our liberty. Like democracy itself, it needs defending

TIM BERNERS-LEE

The world wide web went live, on my physical desktop in Geneva, Switzerland, in December 1990. It consisted of one website and one browser, which happened to be on the same computer. The simple setup demonstrated a profound concept: that any person could share information with anyone else, anywhere. In this spirit, the Web spread quickly from the grassroots up. Today, at its 20th anniversary, the Web is thoroughly integrated into our daily lives. We take it for granted, expecting it to "be there" at any instant, like electricity.

The Web evolved into a powerful, ubiquitous tool because it was built on egalitarian principles and because thousands of individuals, universities and companies have worked, both independently and together as part of the World Wide Web Consortium, to expand its capabilities based on those principles.

The Web as we know it, however, is being threatened in different ways. Some of its most successful inhabitants have begun to chip away at its principles. Large social-networking sites are walling off information posted by their users from the rest of the Web. Wireless Internet providers are being tempted to slow traffic to sites with which they have not made deals. Governments—totalitarian and democratic alike—are monitoring people's online habits, endangering important human rights.

If we, the Web's users, allow these and other trends to proceed unchecked, the Web could be broken into fragmented islands. We could lose the freedom to connect with whichever websites we want. The ill effects could extend to smartphones and pads, which are also portals to the extensive information that the Web provides.

Why should you care? Because the Web is yours. It is a public resource on which you, your business, your community and your government depend. The Web is also vital to democracy, a communications channel that makes possible a continuous worldwide conversation. The Web is now more critical to free speech than any other medium. It brings principles established in the United States. Constitution, the British Magna Carta and other important documents into the network age: freedom from being snooped on, filtered, censored and disconnected.

Yet people seem to think the Web is some sort of piece of nature, and if it starts to wither, well, that's just one of those unfortunate things we can't help. Not so. We create the Web, by designing computer protocols and software; this process is completely under our control. We choose what properties we want it to have and not have. It is by no means finished (and it's certainly not dead). If we want to track what government is doing, see what companies are doing, understand the true state of the planet, find a cure for Alzheimer's disease, not to mention easily share our photos with our friends, we the public, the scientific community and the press must make sure the Web's principles remain intact—not just to preserve what we have gained but to benefit from the great advances that are still to come.

Universality Is the Foundation

Several principles are key to assuring that the Web becomes ever more valuable. The primary design principle underlying the Web's usefulness and growth is universality. When you make a link, you can link to anything. That means people must be able to put anything on the Web, no matter what computer they have, software they use or human language they speak and regardless of whether they have a wired or wireless Internet connection. The Web should be usable by people with disabilities. It must work with any form of information, be it a document or a point of data, and information of any quality—from a silly tweet to a scholarly paper. And it should be accessible from any kind of hardware that can connect to the Internet: stationary or mobile, small screen or large.

These characteristics can seem obvious, self-maintaining or just unimportant, but they are why the next blockbuster website or the new homepage for your kid's local soccer team will just appear on the Web without any difficulty. Universality is a big demand, for any system.

Decentralization is another important design feature. You do not have to get approval from any central authority to add a page or make a link. All you have to do is use three simple, standard protocols: write a page in the HTML (hypertext markup language) format, name it with the URI naming convention, and serve it up on the Internet using HTTP (hypertext transfer protocol). Decentralization has made widespread innovation possible and will continue to do so in the future.

The URI is the key to universality. (I originally called the naming scheme URI, for universal resource identifier; it has come to be known as URL, for uniform resource locator.) The URI allows you to follow any link, regardless of the content it leads to or who publishes that content. Links turn the Web's content into something of greater value: an interconnected information space.

Several threats to the Web's universality have arisen recently. Cable television companies that sell Internet connectivity are considering whether to limit their Internet users to downloading only the company's mix of entertainment. Social-networking sites present a different kind of problem. Facebook, LinkedIn, Friendster and others typically provide value by capturing information as you enter it: your birthday, your e-mail address, your likes, and links indicating who is friends with whom and who is in which photograph. The sites assemble these bits of data into brilliant databases and reuse the information to provide value-added service—but only within their sites. Once you enter your data into one of these services, you cannot easily use them on another site. Each site is a silo, walled off from the others. Yes, your site's pages are on the Web, but your data are not. You can access a Web page about a list of people you have created in one site, but you cannot send that list, or items from it, to another site.

The isolation occurs because each piece of information does not have a URI. Connections among data exist only within a site. So the more you enter, the more you become locked in. Your social-networking site becomes a central platform—a closed silo of content, and one that does not give you full control over your information in it. The more this kind of architecture gains widespread use, the more the Web becomes fragmented, and the less we enjoy a single, universal information space.

A related danger is that one social-networking site—or one search engine or one browser—gets so big that it becomes a monopoly, which tends to limit innovation. As has been the case since the Web began, continued grassroots innovation may be the best check and balance against any one company

or government that tries to undermine universality. GnuSocial and Diaspora are projects on the Web that allow anyone to create their own social network from their own server, connecting to anyone on any other site. The Status.net project, which runs sites such as identi.ca, allows you to operate your own Twitter-like network without the Twitter-like centralization.

Open Standards Drive Innovation

Allowing any site to link to any other site is necessary but not sufficient for a robust Web. The basic Web technologies that individuals and companies need to develop powerful services must be available for free, with no royalties. Amazon.com, for example, grew into a huge online bookstore, then music store, then store for all kinds of goods because it had open, free access to the technical standards on which the Web operates. Amazon, like any other Web user, could use HTML, URI and HTTP without asking anyone's permission and without having to pay. It could also use improvements to those standards developed by the World Wide Web Consortium, allowing customers to fill out a virtual order form, pay online, rate the goods they had purchased, and so on.

By "open standards" I mean standards that can have any committed expert involved in the design, that have been widely reviewed as acceptable, that are available for free on the Web, and that are royalty-free (no need to pay) for developers and users. Open, royalty-free standards that are easy to use create the diverse richness of websites, from the big names such as Amazon, Craigslist and Wikipedia to obscure blogs written by adult hobbyists and to homegrown videos posted by teenagers.

Openness also means you can build your own website or company without anyone's approval. When the Web began, I did not have to obtain permission or pay royalties to use the Internet's own open standards, such as the well-known transmission control protocol (TCP) and Internet protocol (IP). Similarly, the Web Consortium's royalty-free patent policy says that the companies, universities and individuals who contribute to the development of a standard must agree they will not charge royalties to anyone who may use the standard.

Open, royalty-free standards do not mean that a company or individual cannot devise a blog or photo-sharing program and charge you to use it. They can. And you might want to pay for it if you think it is "better" than others. The point is that open standards allow for many options, free and not.

Indeed, many companies spend money to develop extraordinary applications precisely because they are confident the applications will work for anyone, regardless of the computer hardware, operating system or Internet service provider (ISP) they are using—all made possible by the Web's open standards. The same confidence encourages scientists to spend thousands of hours devising incredible databases that can share information about proteins, say, in hopes of curing disease. The confidence encourages governments such as those of the United States. and the U.K. to put more and more data online so citizens can inspect them, making government increasingly transparent. Open standards also foster serendipitous creation: someone may use them in ways no one imagined. We discover that on the Web every day.

In contrast, not using open standards creates closed worlds. Apple's iTunes system, for example, identifies songs and videos using URIs that are open. But instead of "http:" the addresses begin with "itunes:," which is proprietary. You can access an "itunes:" link only using Apple's proprietary iTunes program. You can't make a link to any information in the iTunes world—a song or information about a band. You can't send that link to someone else to see. You are no longer on the Web. The iTunes world is centralized and walled off. You are trapped in a single store, rather than being on the open marketplace. For all the store's wonderful features, its evolution is limited to what one company thinks up.

Other companies are also creating closed worlds. The tendency for magazines, for example, to produce smartphone "apps" rather than Web apps is disturbing, because that material is off the Web. You can't bookmark it or e-mail a link to a page within it. You can't tweet it. It is better to build a Web app that will also run on smartphone browsers, and the techniques for doing so are getting better all the time.

Some people may think that closed worlds are just fine. The worlds are easy to use and may seem to give those people what they want. But as we saw in the 1990s with the America Online dial-up information system that gave you a restricted subset of the Web, these closed, "walled gardens," no matter how pleasing, can never compete in diversity, richness and innovation with the mad, throbbing Web market outside their gates. If a walled garden has too tight a hold on a market, however, it can delay that outside growth.

Keep the Web Separate from the Internet

Keeping the web universal and keeping its standards open help people invent new services. But a third principle—the separation of layers—partitions the design of the Web from that of the Internet.

This separation is fundamental. The Web is an application that runs on the Internet, which is an electronic network that transmits packets of information among millions of computers according to a few open protocols. An analogy is that the Web is like a household appliance that runs on the electricity network. A refrigerator or printer can function as long as it uses a few standard protocols—in the United States., things like operating at 120 volts and 60 hertz. Similarly, any application—among them the Web, e-mail or instant messaging—can run on the Internet as long as it uses a few standard Internet protocols, such as TCP and IP.

Manufacturers can improve refrigerators and printers without altering how electricity functions, and utility companies can improve the electrical network without altering how appliances function. The two layers of technology work together but can advance independently. The same is true for the Web and the Internet. The separation of layers is crucial for innovation. In 1990 the Web rolled out over the Internet without any changes to the Internet itself, as have all improvements since. And in that time, Internet connections have sped up from 300 bits per second to 300 million bits per second (Mbps) without the Web having to be redesigned to take advantage of the upgrades.

Electronic Human Rights

Although internet and web designs are separate, a Web user is also an Internet user and therefore relies on an Internet that is free from interference. In the early Web days it was too technically difficult for a company or country to manipulate the Internet to interfere with an individual Web user. Technology for interference has become more powerful, however. In 2007 BitTorrent, a company whose "peer-to-peer" network protocol allows people to share music, video and other files directly over the Internet, complained to the Federal Communications Commission that the ISP giant Comcast was blocking or slowing traffic to subscribers who were using the BitTorrent application. The FCC told Comcast to stop the practice, but in April 2010 a federal court ruled the FCC could not require Comcast to do so. A good ISP will often manage traffic so that when bandwidth is short, less crucial traffic is dropped, in a transparent way, so users are aware of it. An important line exists between that action and using the same power to discriminate.

This distinction highlights the principle of net neutrality. Net neutrality maintains that if I have paid for an Internet connection at a certain quality, say, 300 Mbps, and you have paid for that quality, then our communications should take place at that quality. Protecting this concept would prevent a big ISP from sending you video from a media company it may own at 300 Mbps but sending video from a competing media company at a slower rate. That amounts to commercial discrimination. Other complications could arise. What if your ISP made it easier for you to connect to a particular online shoe store and harder to reach others? That would be powerful control. What if the ISP made it difficult for you to go to websites about certain political parties, or religions, or sites about evolution?

Unfortunately, in August, Google and Verizon for some reason suggested that net neutrality should not apply to mobile phone–based connections. Many people in rural areas from Utah to Uganda have access to the Internet only via mobile phones; exempting wireless from net neutrality would leave these users open to discrimination of service. It is also bizarre to imagine that my fundamental right to access the information source of my choice should apply when I am on my WiFi-connected computer at home but not when I use my cell phone.

A neutral communications medium is the basis of a fair, competitive market economy, of democracy, and of science. Debate has risen again in the past year about whether government legislation is needed to protect net neutrality. It is.

Although the Internet and Web generally thrive on lack of regulation, some basic values have to be legally preserved.

No Snooping

Other threats to the Web result from meddling with the Internet, including snooping. In 2008 one company, Phorm, devised a way for an ISP to peek inside the packets of information it was sending. The ISP could determine every URI that any customer was browsing. The ISP could then create a profile of the sites the user went to in order to produce targeted advertising.

Accessing the information within an Internet packet is equivalent to wiretapping a phone or opening postal mail. The URIs that people use reveal a good deal about them. A company that bought URI profiles of job applicants could use them to discriminate in hiring people with certain political views, for example. Life insurance companies could discriminate against people who have looked up cardiac symptoms on the Web. Predators could use the profiles to stalk individuals. We would all use the Web very differently if we knew that our clicks can be monitored and the data shared with third parties.

Free speech should be protected, too. The Web should be like a white sheet of paper: ready to be written on, with no control over what is written. Earlier this year Google accused the Chinese government of hacking into its databases to retrieve the e-mails of dissidents. The alleged break-ins occurred after Google resisted the government's demand that the company censor certain documents on its Chinese-language search engine.

Totalitarian governments aren't the only ones violating the network rights of their citizens. In France a law created in 2009, named Hadopi, allowed a new agency by the same name to disconnect a household from the Internet for a year if someone in the household was *alleged* by a media company to have ripped off music or video. After much opposition, in October the Constitutional Council of France required a judge to review a case before access was revoked, but if approved, the household could be disconnected without due process. In the U.K., the Digital Economy Act, hastily passed in April, allows the government to order an ISP to terminate the Internet connection of anyone who appears on a list of individuals suspected of copyright infringement. In September the United States. Senate introduced the Combating Online Infringement and Counterfeits Act, which would allow the government to create a blacklist of websites—hosted on or off United States soil—that are accused of infringement and to pressure or require all ISPs to block access to those sites.

In these cases, no due process of law protects people before they are disconnected or their sites are blocked. Given the many ways the Web is crucial to our lives and our work, disconnection is a form of deprivation of liberty. Looking back to the Magna Carta, we should perhaps now affirm: "No person or organization shall be deprived of the ability to connect to others without due process of law and the presumption of innocence."

When your network rights are violated, public outcry is crucial. Citizens worldwide objected to China's demands on Google, so much so that Secretary of State Hillary Clinton said the United States. government supported Google's defiance and that Internet freedom—and with it, Web freedom—should become a formal plank in American foreign policy. In October, Finland made broadband access, at 1 Mbps, a legal right for all its citizens.

Linking to the Future

As long as the Web's basic principles are upheld, its ongoing evolution is not in the hands of any one person or organization—neither mine nor anyone else's. If we can preserve the principles, the Web promises some fantastic future capabilities.

For example, the latest version of HTML, called HTML5, is not just a markup language but a computing platform that will make Web apps even more powerful than they are now. The proliferation of smartphones will make the Web even more central to our lives. Wireless access will be a particular boon to developing countries, where many people do not have connectivity by wire or cable but do have it wirelessly. Much more needs to be done, of course, including accessibility for people with disabilities and devising pages that work well on all screens, from huge 3-D displays that cover a wall to wristwatch-size windows.

A great example of future promise, which leverages the strengths of all the principles, is linked data. Today's Web is quite effective at helping people publish and discover documents, but our computer programs cannot read or manipulate the actual data within those documents. As this problem is solved, the Web will become much more useful, because data about nearly every aspect of our lives are being created at an astonishing rate. Locked within all these data is knowledge about how to cure diseases, foster business value and govern our world more effectively.

Scientists are actually at the forefront of some of the largest efforts to put linked data on the Web. Researchers, for example, are realizing that in many cases no single lab or online data repository is sufficient to discover new drugs. The information necessary to understand the complex interactions between diseases, biological processes in the human body, and the vast array of chemical agents is spread across the world in a myriad of databases, spreadsheets and documents.

One success relates to drug discovery to combat Alzheimer's disease. A number of corporate and government research labs dropped their usual refusal to open their data and created the Alzheimer's Disease Neuroimaging Initiative. They posted a massive amount of patient information and brain scans as linked data, which they have dipped into many times to advance their research. In a demonstration I witnessed, a scientist asked the question, "What proteins are involved in signal transduction and are related to pyramidal neurons?"[1] When put into Google, the question got 233,000 hits—and not one single answer. Put into the linked databases world, however, it returned a small number of specific proteins that have those properties.

The investment and finance sectors can benefit from linked data, too. Profit is generated, in large part, from finding patterns in an increasingly diverse set of information sources. Data are all over our personal lives as well. When you go onto your social-networking site and indicate that a newcomer is your friend, that establishes a relationship. And that relationship is data.

Linked data raise certain issues that we will have to confront. For example, new data-integration capabilities could pose privacy challenges that are hardly addressed by today's privacy laws. We should examine legal, cultural and technical options that will preserve privacy without stifling beneficial data-sharing capabilities.

Now is an exciting time. Web developers, companies, governments and citizens should work together openly and cooperatively, as we have done thus far, to preserve the Web's fundamental principles, as well as those of the Internet, ensuring that the technological protocols and social conventions we set up respect basic human values. The goal of the Web is to serve humanity. We build it now so that those who come to it later will be able to create things that we cannot ourselves imagine.

Note

1. Clarification (2/17/11): This sentence as written creates the impression that the demonstration was linked to the Alzheimer's Initiative. Rather, it refers to a separate undertaking and should read: In a different project, which I saw demonstrated, researchers at the University of Amsterdam asked the question, "What proteins are involved in signal transduction and are related to pyramidal neurons?"

Critical Thinking

1. Describe the distinction between the Internet and the Web. What are "open standards"?

2. What counterargument might "closed world" companies make against open standards? From your perspective, which argument is more compelling?

A Vaster Wasteland

Fifty years after his landmark speech declaring television programming a "vast wasteland," the author surveys the reshaped media landscape and lays out a plan to keep television and the Internet vibrant, democratic forces for the next half century.

NEWTON N. MINOW

Fifty Years Ago next month, I stood before the annual convention of the National Association of Broadcasters for my inaugural public address as President Kennedy's chairman of the Federal Communications Commission. My first objective in the job was to clean up the agency and the industry, which before I arrived had been embroiled in quiz-show, payola, and agency scandals. My second was to expand choice for viewers, by advancing new technologies in the belief that more choice would result in more and better content.

My objective at the convention was to tell broadcasters that the FCC would enforce the law's requirement that they serve the public interest in return for their free and exclusive use of the publicly owned airwaves. Too much existing programming, I said, was little more than "a procession of game shows . . . violence, sadism, murder, Western bad men, Western good men, private eyes, gangsters, more violence, and cartoons." Television, I said, was too often a "vast wasteland."

I knew broadcasters would not be happy. My favorite response was from the Hollywood producer Sherwood Schwartz, who named the sinking ship in *Gilligan's Island* after me. The "vast wasteland" was a metaphor for a particular time in our nation's communications history, and to my surprise it became part of the American lexicon. It has come to identify me. My daughters threaten to engrave on my tombstone: ON TO A VASTER WASTELAND. But those were not the two words I intended to be remembered. The two words I wanted to endure were *public interest*. To me that meant, as it still means, that we should constantly ask: What can communications do for our country? For the common good? For the American people?

We did some great things, to be sure. We expanded choice with public broadcasting, cable, and satellites. *Sesame Street* became one of the most-watched television programs in the world. Our televised presidential debates, once groundbreaking and then abandoned until 1976, became the most substantive view of our presidential campaigns. We launched the first communications satellite in 1962. On a visit to the space program, President Kennedy asked me about the satellite. I told him that it would be more important than sending a man into space. "Why?" he asked.

"Because," I said, "this satellite will send ideas into space, and ideas last longer than men."

But our failures were equally dramatic, particularly in using television to serve our children and to improve our politics. For 50 years, we have bombarded our children with commercials disguised as programs and with endless displays of violence and sexual exploitation. We are nearly alone in the democratic world in not providing our candidates with public-service television time. Instead we make them buy it—and so money consumes and corrupts our political discourse.

The past 50 years have seen sizzling and explosive advances in technology. Fifty years ago, the FCC regulated telephone service that came by wire, and television service that came through the air. Today, as MIT's Nicholas Negroponte predicted, these services are mostly reversed. The next 50 years will see even more technological miracles, including the marriage of computers, television, telephony, and the Internet. What we need, to accompany these changes, are critical choices about the values we want to build into our 21st-century communications system—and the public policies to support them. I believe we should commit to six goals in the next 50 years.

Our first must be to expand freedom, in order to strengthen editorial independence in news and information. Freedom of thought is the foundation of our national character, and at its best the Internet represents the full flowering of that freedom. The Internet itself is the result of an open system that has encouraged technological innovation and creative energy we could never have dreamed of—and, happily, the FCC, under its talented chairman, Julius Genachowski, is leading public-interest advocates and industry groups to both meet the practical needs and uphold the democratic values at stake.

Our second commitment should be to use new communications technologies to improve and extend the benefits of education at all levels, preschool through postgraduate. In the midst of a bloody civil war, the Land Grant College Act of 1862 made the United States world leader in higher education and established the foundation upon which the nation's defense, diplomacy, and economic competitiveness have relied for 150 years. But today it no longer makes sense to let television broadcasters use the largest and most valuable swath of our electromagnetic spectrum to send out signals that more than 80 percent of American households don't need because they receive their television service through cable or satellite. We should auction off this precious real estate and use the money to invest in education. It's time for a new land grant act—a Land Grant of the Airwaves.

Our third commitment should be to use new technologies to improve and extend the reach of our health-care system. Other developed countries are far ahead of us in telemedicine, using wireless communications and high-definition imaging to provide preventive health care at low cost. No organization in the world is a more sophisticated user than the United States. military, which provides primary care through telemedicine to many of its personnel around the world. Certainly we should commit to using telemedicine to serve Americans at home. Last year's telecommunications-policy proposal by the FCC wisely includes improved health care as a goal.

Fourth, the nation's communications infrastructure for public safety and local and national security is a dangerous disgrace. We learned that most vividly on September 11, 2001, when first responders could not communicate with one another, and the nation's commercial and emergency networks were virtually overwhelmed with traffic. Congress and the FCC must build and maintain a new and secure communications network as a national-security priority.

Fifth, we need to give greater support to public radio and public television. Both have been starved for funds for decades, and yet in many communities they are essential sources of local news and information—particularly public radio, which is relatively inexpensive to produce and distribute and is a valuable source of professionally reported news for millions of Americans. There is virtually nothing else like it on the air. Public-television stations, as I saw when I was the chairman of PBS, are overbuilt, sometimes with four competing in the same market. Where that is so, stations should be sold and the revenue dedicated to programming a national news and public-affairs service, built on the foundation of the splendid PBS *NewsHour.* And a crucial part of that service—as with public media around the world—should be to promote the country's arts and culture.

Finally and critically, if over-the-air television is to survive as a licensed service operating in the public interest, we must make better use of it in our politics. It is simply unconscionable that candidates for public office have to buy access to the airwaves—something the public itself owns—to talk to the public, unlike in most other major democratic countries.

The United States. Supreme Court has moved aggressively over the past decade to overturn congressional action to reform campaign finance. I believe the Court is wrong in thinking that money is speech and speech is money. A lawyer arguing a case before the Court is allowed 30 minutes for oral argument. The Supreme Court would laugh if a lawyer who wants more than 30 minutes went to the court clerk's office to buy it.

Put simply, candidates for public office have to raise huge amounts of money to buy access to the public airwaves so they can talk to us. And because airtime is so expensive, they talk to us in slogans and slurs, and only obliquely, if at all, about substance. Recent court decisions that it is constitutional to limit contributions but not expenditures seem to me to threaten the life of the democratic process. The logic of this arrangement reminds me of Justice Robert Jackson's warning, two generations ago, that the Constitution is not a "suicide pact."

Recent Supreme Court decisions remind me of Justice Robert Jackson's warning that the Constitution is not a "suicide pact."

Of course, any limitations on free speech are a concern in our constitutional system, and no one should suppose that the problem of cash in our campaigns has an easy First Amendment answer. But television is another matter. If broadcasters are to continue as the lone beneficiaries of their valuable spectrum assignments, it is not too much to require that, as a public service, they provide time to candidates for public office. That time is not for the candidates. It is for the voters.

As we think about the next 50 years, I remember a story President Kennedy told a week before he was killed. The story was about French Marshal Louis-Hubert-Gonzalve Lyautey, who walked one morning through his garden with his gardener. He stopped at a certain point and asked the gardener to plant a tree there the next morning. The gardener said, "But the tree will not bloom for 100 years." The marshal replied, "In that case, you had better plant it this afternoon."

Critical Thinking

1. Fifty years ago, as FCC Chairman, Newton Minow's platform was that the FCC must enforce the requirement that broadcasters serve the public interest in exchange for the privilege of access to the nation's publicly owned airwaves. What are your thoughts on his contemporary priorities for serving the public interest?

2. Is television a "vast wasteland"?

NEWTON N. MINOW is the former chairman of the Federal Communications Commission, PBS, the Rand Corporation, and the Carnegie Foundation, and is the Annenberg Professor Emeritus at Northwestern University.

Frenemies of Free Speech

The damage that benevolent censors do.

Sam Schulman

This weekend is the anniversary of the first truly liberal attempt to prevent hatred by restricting free speech. On March 15, 1939, Denmark made it a criminal act to spread "false rumors or accusations" in order to incite "hatred against a group of the Danish population because of its creed, race, or nationality"—with a fine for those who did so in speech and detention or prison for those who did so in print or broadcasts. The law was designed to hamper the activities of Danish Nazi sympathizers. On May 31 the same year, Denmark made itself even more secure against Nazism by signing a non-aggression pact with Germany. Less than a year later, Hitler initiated the six-hour conquest of Denmark by putting an armored battalion on the regular ferryboat from Rostock to Denmark. The treaty didn't stop him, nor did the fear of feloniously violating Section 266b of the Danish Penal Code by inciting hatred against Jews and Communists.

The German Army packed its bags in 1945, but Section 266b remains in force, much modernized (it now applies to hatred of any group, not just Danes, and prohibits insults to sexual identity), a standing rebuke to what Europeans call "the American version" of free speech: freedom to speak unconstrained by restrictions against "hate," against insulting or offending individuals or groups, and without special protection for specific religions (Islam), races, or historical facts. In 2011 so far, American-style free speech has been widely condemned (for the Tucson mass murder, notably), though it has also had moments of popularity, particularly since the Arab revolutions began in Tunisia, and again with the madcap activities of public employee unions in Wisconsin. Even Tom Friedman took a holiday from his admiration for Chinese autocracy to celebrate the Twitter revolutions.

But "the European version" of free speech, if we may call it that, soldiers on doggedly. Courts in Austria, Denmark, and France have this year convicted journalists and political volunteers (none of them neo-Nazis) of hate-speech crimes, which generally took the form of making observations about the frequency of certain violent crimes among immigrant groups in Denmark and France, and in Austria about the respectability of the historical Muhammad. Fashion designer John Galliano may soon go on trial in France for racial insults uttered in a Paris bar. There is no doubt among European liberals that "hate speech" must remain restricted in this fashion. After all, as a columnist in the Netherlands' *NRC Handelsblad* explained, "everyone knows it's wrong to insult someone's race or religion. So why shouldn't it be a crime as well?"

A special focus of the war against American-style free speech is the campaign to stigmatize critical discussion of Islam as Islamophobia. Anti-anti-Islamists, as Lee Smith terms Western apologists for Islamism, present a hydra-headed definition of Islamophobic speech. In New York, regarding it as in poor taste to build a mosque on the site of the 9/11 attacks is Islamophobia. In Sweden, Islamophobes betray themselves by suggesting that the suicide bomber who tried to commit mass murder in Stockholm was an Islamist. In Britain, Conservative party chief Baroness Warsi declared that the mark of Islamophobia is to distinguish between moderate and extremist Muslims (a distinction that she is famous for having made herself in a plucky BBC interview filmed just after she was egged by extremist Muslims in Novemer 2009).

The lesson is that believers in free speech should keep their opinions to themselves. Simon Jenkins wrote that freedom of speech itself, not the man who pulled the trigger, was the real culprit in the Tucson murders: "Language that might not disturb a balanced mind" can "clearly stimulate and legitimize an unbalanced one." Thinking at all about Islam, in its rich variety of cultural and religious expression, is not only an insult, but tantamount to shouting "pedophile" in a playground. As a Norwegian antiterror expert told the press, "Islamophobia leads to discrimination that may lead to terrorism."

It's no wonder that so many in Europe believe in the notion of "good censorship"—and are willing to prescribe it to us. The European chattering classes believe that it is easy to draft sensible limits on free speech in the interest of civility, tolerance, peace, and civilization. And it may seem to the publics in European countries that silencing and even imprisoning a few journalists and center-right politicians will be worth it if it attains social cohesion. They will never really know, since European national publics no longer have the power to decide on such matters—limitations on freedom of expression come increasingly from EU directives and court decisions. But the notion that speech could be limited in a benevolent way has a history that goes back a century before Denmark's 1939 experiment, and in two little known but dramatic instances failed in ways that are spectacularly ugly—and still have consequences today.

What did happen when "good censors" went to work in British India and antebellum America? Enormous political impact and dire consequences. These two little-known examples took place almost simultaneously, in the mid-1830s, at opposite ends of the world. And both were attempts to deal responsibly with horribly difficult questions of politics, race, and religion.

In 1837, the great liberal polymath Lord Macaulay and two colleagues in Calcutta drafted an entirely new Penal Code for British India. It was designed to replace at one stroke the existing criminal law, which was largely a hodgepodge of old laws from the previous Mughal regime, and was finally adopted in 1860. Macaulay's work not only survived the entire period of British rule, but has survived independence to become the penal code of India and Pakistan alike. One section in particular has become a cause of great strife in 21st-century Pakistan: Macaulay's decision to regulate and criminalize insults to religion became the core of Pakistan's notorious "blasphemy laws" (which politicians currying favor with religious parties made much more stringent beginning in the 1970s).

In January of this year, Salman Taseer, the governor of Pakistan's Punjab Province, was assassinated for proposing a humanitarian modification to the blasphemy laws—which might have spared the life of a Christian woman, Aasia Bibi, whose arrest had become an international cause célèbre. Last week, the controversy claimed another victim, Shahbaz Bhatti, the sole Christian member of the government and an advocate of reforming the blasphemy law. He was gunned down while driving in Islamabad. Much of Pakistan's population, major media figures, and most of the opposition parties celebrated Taseer's assassination and made or tolerated threats against anyone who would dare touch the laws. Bhatti knew he was courting his own death by accepting the dare.

Starting in 1835, another group of well-meaning liberals—politicians, intellectuals, and businessmen in Northern states—undertook a campaign against abolitionism in order to placate their Southern political and business partners. Hardly defenders of slavery, these "anti-antislavery agitators" are the true ancestors of the "anti-anti-Communists" of the 1950s and of today's "anti-anti-Islamists."

Macaulay was motivated by the need to promote tolerance in a country shared by a few thousand European Christians, millions of Muslims, and, as Macaulay put it, "tens of millions of Hindus strongly attached to doctrines and rites which Christians and Mahomedans join in reprobating." While Mughal law protected Islam alone against insult (and did so haphazardly), Macaulay's code gave people of any faith protection from having their "religious feelings" wounded—by words, gestures, trespass, and destruction of property. Macaulay was confident that magistrates would apply the law only to deliberate, malicious, and considered insults—not passing observations or anything said in the heat of religious dispute in defense of one's own religion. Good jurists would ensure that the subjective impression of the injured party would never define the crime of blasphemy (which is precisely how the modern-day European hate speech laws do operate).

The American experience was rather more complicated. Antislavery sentiment had been widespread in the South as well as the North as recently as the 1820s, when the South still had hundreds of antislavery committees. Southern authorities cracked down and eliminated these associations, and in 1835 began a concerted campaign on the Northern great and good. The campaign on the part of what abolitionists later called "the Slave Power" exerted "coercive pressure on freedom of expression in spite of the enshrinement, in the Constitution's First Amendment, of a foundational right to speak." It "used legislation and bullying to stifle agitation against the South's labor regime, portraying debate on the subject as a threat to the Union's survival. An ideological *cordon sanitaire* was erected along the Mason-Dixon line, but the campaign did not relent at the region's borders; it extended throughout the country. . . . Although the assault on free speech specifically targeted abolitionist protest, it was meant to have a chilling effect on all discourse," including "literary and speculative discourse"—and, according to Michael T. Gilmore, author of *The War on Words: Slavery, Race and Free Speech in American Literature,* from which these passages are drawn, it did.

Gilmore's astonishing book is not history but lit crit, and finds a strong current of self-censorship running through the literature of the 19th century. He argues that the North's appeasement of the Slave Power up to the eve of the Civil War, and of White Supremacy after Reconstruction, deformed even the greatest writers of the century, from Emerson and Hawthorne to Twain and Howells. (Gilmore's "Slave Power" theory has been argued by a line of historians which includes Russel B. Nye, Leonard L. Richards, David Grimsted, and Michael Kent Curtis—and disputed by a formidable antagonist, David Brion Davis.)

Gilmore's argument is *engagé,* and he writes with impeccable bien-pensant convictions. He says that the "perilous state of civil liberties under the Bush administration" helped to inspire *War on Words,* and its title is an homage to Pablo Neruda, the Chilean poet who played Walt Whitman to Stalin's Lincoln and refused to challenge the Soviet policy of silencing writers like Pasternak and Brodsky. Gilmore's academic New Left sensibility permits him the radical's pleasure of admiring energetic and vital slavery supporters like Senator John C. Calhoun of South Carolina and John Randolph of Roanoke, and sharing their contempt for the Northern liberals who tried to appease the South by silencing Northern abolitionists. The list of Northern appeasers includes surprising figures like the Unitarian minister William Ellery Channing, who "attacked abolitionists in graceful language without reading their work," deploring urbanely how the abolitionists "exaggerated slavery's evil and painted the master as monster" (in the words of David Grimsted), without bothering to learn very much either about slavery or abolitionism.

The campaign against freedom of speech by Northern antislavery activists began in 1835 with lawfare, violence, and what today would be called BDS: boycotts, divestment, and sanctions. Responding to Southern pressure,

Northern leaders held anti-abolitionist meetings in major cities from Portland, Maine, to Philadelphia; landlords who rented space to abolitionist meetings were boycotted. Pro-slavery mobs supported the lawfare campaign with threats and attacks, culminating in the mob murder of an Illinois editor. Arguably, the first victims of lynchings were not black slaves and freemen but white abolitionists. As a Richmond newspaper observed with contemptuous accuracy in 1836: "Depend upon it—the Northern people will never sacrifice their present lucrative trade with the South, so long as the hanging of a few thousands will prevent it."

The North bowed to economic pressure and the threat of violence from the South. Without actually legislating against the First Amendment (as many Southern states had done), authorities and civic leaders in the North made speaking out against slavery practically impossible. In 1836, the upstate New York abolitionist Alvan Stewart wrote that an abolitionist is perfectly free to denounce slavery "in the silent chambers of his own heart, but must not discuss it in public, as it may then provoke a syllogism of feathers, or a deduction of tar."

Southern states were ingenious wagers of lawfare, inventing many devices still used today against freedom of speech in Europe and Canada and advocated by improvers of freedom of speech elsewhere. It was Senator Calhoun, not an anti-imperialist student leader or a Church of England bishop, who argued that speech that hurt feelings should be banned. Anyone who criticized slavery "libeled the South and inflicted emotional injury" and made "reflections injurious to the feelings of himself, and those with whom he was connected" in "highly reprehensible" language. Speaking in favor of the infamous gag rule passed by the House in 1836, which would gut the constitutional right to petition the government if slavery was the subject of the petition, Calhoun (who wanted the same rule in the Senate) denounced hate speech with a passion that any NGO spokesperson might envy. Brandishing a petition that called slaveholders pirates dealing in human flesh, Calhoun denounced its blatant Carolinaphobia: "Strange language! Piracy and butchery? We must not permit those we represent to be thus insulted."

The war against free speech ebbed and flowed with other issues: the Missouri Compromise and the Kansas-Nebraska Act. But the high water mark came with John Brown's raid on Harper's Ferry in October 1859. Harper's Ferry inspired the Democrats to invent a strategy I wrongly thought Dick Morris had devised in 1995 after the Oklahoma City bombing: blame Republicans for the violent act of a madman with whom they had nothing to do. Illinois senator Stephen A. Douglas put it with a bluntness which anticipates a Paul Krugman column: "The Harpers Ferry crime was the natural, logical, inevitable result of the doctrines and the teachings of the Republican Party, as explained and enforced in their platform, their partisan presses, their pamphlets and books, and especially in the speeches of their leaders in and out of Congress."

John Brown was arrested, interrogated, tried, and executed (in a very efficient six weeks). But this did not satisfy the anti-hate speech crowd. Douglas insisted that those who thought slavery was wrong—and thus had created the atmosphere of violence that stimulated and disturbed Brown's mind—must "repudiate and denounce the doctrines and teachings which produced the act." Three months after Harper's Ferry, Douglas proposed a new Sedition Law that would not merely ban slaveholder-phobic speech, but criminalize antislavery sentiment.

Douglas's outrageous Sedition Law proposals provoked Lincoln's great Cooper Union speech (a speech so grand that Garry Wills thinks it comparable to candidate Obama's famous Philadelphia speech about race and Reverend Jeremiah Wright). Lincoln described how prudent restraint of speech easily leads to criminalization of thought. What did Douglas want, Lincoln asked? Opponents of slavery must

cease to call slavery wrong, and join [the Southern people] in calling it right. And this must be done thoroughly, done in acts as well as in words. Silence will not be tolerated; we must place ourselves avowedly with them. Senator Douglas' new sedition law must be enacted and enforced, suppressing all declarations that slavery is wrong, whether made in politics, in presses, in pulpits, or in private. We must arrest and return their fugitive slaves with greedy pleasure. We must pull down our free-state constitutions. The whole atmosphere must be disinfected from all taint of opposition to slavery, before they will cease to believe that all their troubles proceed from us. . . . They will continue to accuse us of *doing*, until we cease *saying*.

The lesson is that when ideas are truly in conflict, the effort to soften the stark disputes by preventing antagonists even from describing their ideas with candor and honesty is hopeless—and makes things worse. The effort to make Northern speech conform to Southern feelings did not succeed—it merely provoked the South and its supporters to raise their standard for civil speech, until speech and the ideas behind it had to conform exactly with their own belief in slavery. Controlling speech did not control the conflict, as the proponents of hate speech believed it would, any more than the Weimar Republic's constraints on the expression of anti-Semitism prevented the triumph of an anti-Semitic party in Germany—nor, as I argued in these pages recently, has banning Holocaust denial in Europe eradicated Holocaust denial or promoted philo-Semitism.

The fate of the blasphemy law in Pakistan, designed by a pioneer of modern thought specifically to promote tolerance, is similar. Pakistan's religious majority has adopted Salman Taseer's admitted assassin Qadri as a national hero. The Lahore bar, which two years ago engineered the "Black Revolution" that drove President Musharraf from office, showered the killer with flower petals, and—more shocking—offered him free legal representation. Magistrates and policemen dealing with him are threatened if they treat him as a suspect. The blasphemy law itself has become an idol. Some Pakistanis argue that reverence for the blasphemy law has enabled one strand of Islam to drive out all others: Although the occasional Christian or Hindu defendant gets the publicity, the overwhelming majority of victims of the extrajudicial punishments that take place in its name are themselves Muslim (like Taseer). As the Pakistani-American writer Omar Ali explains, the blasphemy laws are popular because they give

> the message that anything and everything can become blasphemy, and once the accusation is made, the accused is done for. It doesn't matter what happens in court. . . . Any court that lets off a blasphemer can itself be accused of blasphemy. Anyone who suggests the law is open to misuse is guilty of blasphemy. . . . With this weapon in place, anyone opposing the mullahs and their version of Islam can be accused of blasphemy. The law is there to intimidate and to take away the public space from liberal forces (and not just secular liberal forces, even a mildly liberal interpreter of very orthodox Islam like Javed Ghamdi has had to leave the country).

There is another point to be made here, an embarrassing one. When threatened by violence, cowards (like me) respond by throwing freedom of speech overboard. The South defended slavery with far greater passion and earnestness than the North disapproved of it. The freedom with which modern Westerners speak of various subjects has a direct relationship to the level of discomfort we feel. A cosmopolitan liberal like Ian Buruma feels perfectly comfortable teasing Ayaan Hirsi Ali about her naïve admiration for the Enlightenment; no one would advise him to give lectures about tolerance to the Islamists who tormented her physically in Africa and threatened her life in Holland. You may recognize Buruma's unpleasantly patronizing tone if you read his spiritual predecessor, William Ellery Channing, urbanely admonishing the abolitionist William Lloyd Garrison about the crudity of his antislavery rhetoric at a time when Garrison's neck was coveted by every lynch-gang on either side of the Mason-Dixon line.

Those in the West who want to limit free speech feel physically safe and morally superior. Professor Talal Asad of CUNY has published a book about the "supposed stand-off between Islam and liberal democratic values" which inquires "into the evaluative frameworks at stake" in understanding the conflict between blasphemy and free speech (*Is Critique Secular? Blasphemy, Injury & Free Speech*). Asad gets Omar Ali's goat, because he is "a Westernized postmodern thinker, safely ensconced in New York and thoroughly immersed in the categories and arguments of the Western academy." Intellectuals in Pakistan who care to inquire into the evaluative framework of the blasphemy regime don't have it so easy. Just after the Taseer assassination, the great physicist and peace advocate Pervez Hoodbhoy appeared on a popular Pakistani talk show, which was taped in front of a college-student audience. Hoodbhoy described the proceedings:

> Even as the mullahs frothed and screamed around me (and at me), I managed to say the obvious: that the culture of religious extremism was resulting in a bloodbath in which the majority of victims were Muslims; that non-Muslims were fleeing Pakistan; that the self-appointed

"*thaikaydars*" of Islam in Pakistan were deliberately ignoring the case of other Muslim countries like Indonesia which do not have the death penalty for blasphemy; that debating the details of Blasphemy Law 295-C did not constitute blasphemy; that American Muslims were very far from being the objects of persecution; that harping on drone attacks was an irrelevancy to the present discussion on blasphemy.

> The response? Not a single clap for me. Thunderous applause whenever my opponents called for death for blasphemers. And loud cheers for Qadri. When I directly addressed Sialvi [a moderate cleric from the Barelvi sect to which Qadri belongs] and said he had Salman Taseer's blood on his hands, he exclaimed "How I wish I had done it!"

Fear of violence—and the desire to limit violence to those already subject to it—is what really inspires the movement to restrict free speech. If we say nothing, then Islamists will concentrate their efforts on dissenting Muslims like Hirsi Ali; Southern slaveowners will cultivate their plantations. The *New York Times*'s Robert Wright admits this with admirable candor when he pleads for the suppression of "Islamophobia": "As Islamophobia grows, it alienates Muslims, raising the risk of homegrown terrorism—and homegrown terrorism heightens the Islamophobia, which alienates more Muslims, and so on: a vicious circle that could carry America into the abyss." If only avoiding the abyss were as easy as sustaining abysses in faraway countries. Unfortunately, history shows us the opposite. The efforts of Macaulay and the Northern moderates to avoid offensive speech led inexorably at least to the brink of tyranny, a brink over which many despairing Pakistani moderates think it will lead their country in no more than five or ten years.

Just as bad, these restrictions on free speech exacerbated conflict by forcing antagonists into dishonest positions. Because they were spared disagreement, the members of the injured party became ever more convinced of their righteousness, while those who suppressed the speech of their fellow-believers forgot their own convictions. The faults of each side were amplified, not moderated. Each side knew that the other was lying. Compromise or even peaceful coexistence became less, not more likely.

In suppressing speech, we begin, honestly enough, as cowards, but become falsely convinced of our own virtue. The poststructuralists and the NGOs tell us that through self-censorship of our real beliefs, we become better human beings than we really are. But to those for whose sake we self-censor, we begin to seem even worse than we really are. All censorship—particularly self-censorship driven by fear—creates hatred and contempt for the censors. How can they whose feelings we are trying not to hurt possibly regard us? Certainly as weaklings, but also as weaklings with a secret sense of our own superiority. We cherish our freedoms, but think they are too good for others.

An enthusiastic defender of slavery, John Randolph of Roanoke, showed us exactly how the self-censors deserve to be regarded in a wonderfully contemptuous description of the Northern Democrats who voted for the Southern interest on the Missouri bill of 1820. "They were scared at their own dough faces—we had them! . . . We could have had [any number of] these men, whose conscience, and morality, and religion, extend to thirty-six degrees and thirty minutes north latitude." Restricting free speech is no more than an attempt to draw a new Mason-Dixon line behind which we protect our own political virtue, while withholding it from others. And it will be about as useful a way to create social harmony as Section 266b was at keeping "denigrators of national origins" out of Denmark on April 9, 1940.

Critical Thinking

1. Define "good censorship."
2. Look up the wording of the First Amendment and the Supreme Court's interpretation of free speech in relation to libel, slander, and obscenity. Are these fundamentally different from the examples upon which Schulman builds his case?

The End of Secrecy

Micah L. Sifry

"In one direction we can reach out and touch the time when the leaders of the Soviet Union thought that the explosion at the nuclear reactor in Chernobyl could be kept secret from the rest of the world. In the other direction we can see a time—already upon us—when fourteen-year-old hackers in Australia or Newfoundland can make their way into the most sensitive areas of national security or international finance. The central concern of government in the future will not be information, but analysis. We need government agencies staffed with argumentative people who can live with ambiguity and look upon secrecy as a sign of insecurity."

—*Senator Daniel Patrick Moynihan,*
Report of the Commission on Protecting and
Reducing Government Secrecy, *1997*

"Three may keep a secret, if two of them are dead."
—*Benjamin Franklin*

For some time now, our leaders have been saying that they understand—nay, that they embrace—the disruptive potential of the Internet. Take President Obama, who used networked technology so adroitly in his 2008 election campaign. Here he is talking about the power of the Internet at a town hall meeting with students in Shanghai in 2009, where he memorably declared:

I am a big believer in technology, and I'm a big believer in openness when it comes to the flow of information. I think that the more freely information flows, the stronger the society becomes, because then citizens of countries around the world can hold their own governments accountable. They can begin to think for themselves. That generates new ideas. It encourages creativity.

Obama added, "The truth is that because in the United States information is free . . . I have a lot of critics in the United States who can say all kinds of things about me. I actually think that that makes our democracy stronger, and it makes me a better leader because it forces me to hear opinions that I don't want to hear."

Or take Secretary of State Hillary Clinton. No American official has been more eloquent in expressing support for the power of the Internet than Clinton, who gave a highly visible speech on "Internet freedom" on January 21, 2010, in Washington, where she waxed poetic about how "the spread of information networks is forming a new nervous system for our planet," adding:

The Internet is a network that magnifies the power and potential of all others. And that's why we believe it's critical that its users are assured certain basic freedoms. Freedom of expression is first among them. This freedom is no longer defined solely by whether citizens can go into the town square and criticize their government without fear of retribution. Blogs, e-mails, social networks and text messages have opened up new forums for exchanging ideas, and created new targets for censorship. . . .

Now, ultimately, this issue isn't just about information freedom; it is about what kind of world we want and what kind of world we will inhabit. It's about whether we live on a planet with one Internet, one global community and a common body of knowledge that benefits and unites us all, or a fragmented planet in which access to information and opportunity is dependent on where you live and the whims of censors.

The words are nice, but unfortunately theirs has been a kind of bloodless embrace, a rhetorical gesture to a changing culture without any real content and certainly no loss of control. Yes, as a candidate Obama allowed his supporters to use his online social network, my.BarackObama.com, to organize a 20,000-strong petition objecting to his flip-flopping on the issue of warrantless wiretapping. But after an e-mail response and a few hours of question-deflecting by his advisers on his blog, the issue was dropped. Most politicians, including Obama, have used the Internet to consolidate their power, not to empower others for any other purpose.

To be sure, they've been fascinated by the Internet's potential to challenge the status quo elsewhere. President Obama deftly used YouTube to address the Iranian people directly at the beginning of his administration, posting a message of friendship at the time of the Nowruz (springtime) celebrations that, according to YouTube's open tracking analytics, was indeed widely watched inside Iran. And administration officials like Clinton have spoken out often in defense of bloggers' free speech rights, and condemned countries like China, Egypt, Iran, Tunisia, Uzbekistan and Vietnam for clamping down on the Internet and cracking down on human rights activists using online social network platforms.

But the reason the recent confrontation between WikiLeaks and the United States government is a pivotal event is that, unlike these other applications of technology to politics, this time the free flow of information is threatening the establishment with difficult questions. And not by embarrassing one politician or bureaucrat but by exposing systemic details of how America conducts its foreign and military policies. Or, as writer Bruce Sterling memorably put it, "Julian Assange has hacked a superpower." The result is a series of deeply uncomfortable contradictions.

The idea that the wondrous "new nervous system" for the planet that Clinton saw being created by all this online freedom might want to turn its attention to the most powerful country on the planet shouldn't be a shock to leaders like her. But when the State Department cables started to leak, she fell back on a much older way of seeing the world. "The United States strongly condemns the illegal disclosure of classified information," she said in her prepared statement the day the news broke. "It puts people's lives in danger, threatens our national security and undermines our efforts to work with other countries to solve shared problems." She added later, "Disclosures like these tear at the fabric of the proper function of responsible government." The notion that lying to the American public, or the world, about the conduct of foreign or military policy might be more damaging to the fabric of international relations or to the functioning of responsible government was not addressed.

'You Can't Handle the Truth'?

Here is Clinton's problem: in the networked age, when the watched can also be the watchers, nothing less than the credibility of authority itself is at stake. Western governments presumably rest on the consent of the governed, but only if the governed trust the word of those who would govern them. In this changed environment, the people formerly known as the authorities can re-earn that trust only by being more transparent, and by eliminating the contradictions between what they say and what they do. Compounding this challenge, today when a crisis strikes, information moves faster than the "authorities" can know using their own, slower methods. WikiLeaks, and other channels for the unauthorized release and spread of information, are symptoms of this change, not its cause.

Unfortunately there is a large gap between what American officials have told the public about their actions and what they have actually done. Transparency may be the best medicine for a healthy democracy, but from the government's perspective, the problem with the WikiLeaks revelations from the Iraq and Afghanistan wars, plus the State Department cables, may well be that they expose too much. Not in the sense of giving away military secrets that endanger troops in the field or human rights workers; so far both the Pentagon and the State Department have explicitly admitted that no such harm has occurred (though the original release of the Afghanistan war records may have placed some civilian informants in danger from the Taliban).

Rather, the war logs and diplomatic cables show that the nine-year war in Afghanistan is doomed. And this is not something the governments fighting that war want to tell their public. As Javier Moreno, editor of *El País,* wrote in a long essay explaining why his paper decided to work with WikiLeaks in publishing the State Department cables,

> Tens of thousands of soldiers are fighting a war in Afghanistan that their respective leaders know is not winnable. Tens of thousands of soldiers are shoring up a government known around the world to be corrupt, but

which is tolerated by those who sent the soldiers there in the first place. The WikiLeaks cables show that none of the Western powers believes that Afghanistan can become a credible nation in the medium term, and much less become a viable democracy, despite the stated aims of those whose soldiers are fighting and dying there. Few people have been surprised to learn that the Afghan president has been salting away millions of dollars in overseas aid in foreign bank accounts with the full cognizance of his patrons.

He added, "We may have suspected our governments of underhand dealings, but we did not have the proof that WikiLeaks has provided. We now know that our governments were aware of the situations mentioned above, and, what is more, they have hidden the facts from us."

Instead of an honest discussion about what the war logs and cables tell us in toto, we have been treated to a bizarre and contradictory set of responses. Sometimes, what Julian Assange has done is portrayed as worse than what Al Qaeda has done. Former House Speaker Newt Gingrich: "He should be treated as an enemy combatant and WikiLeaks should be closed down permanently and decisively." And other times, we are told that the so-called revelations are actually pretty humdrum. Defense Secretary Robert Gates: "Is this embarrassing? Yes. Is it awkward? Yes. Consequences for United States foreign policy? I think fairly modest." Nothing to see here; move along please.

There is only one way to reconcile these seemingly contradictory messages coming from the government and its allies in Congress and the media. At some fundamental level, they probably understand that the conditions for maintaining their monopoly on critical information have been broken. But they apparently still hope that the next Bradley Manning, the alleged leaker, will be dissuaded from an act of conscience if he believes either that the personal cost will be too high or that his actions won't make a difference. Of course, neither approach will work, as long as millions of other government employees have access to the information the government is trying to hide. The Age of Transparency is here not because of one transnational online network dedicated to open information and whistleblowing named WikiLeaks but because the knowledge of how to build and maintain such networks is widespread.

The End of Secrecy

Let's posit that what Assange is doing is "radical transparency," i.e., publishing everything he can get his hands on. He has not, in fact, been doing that, though he is obviously publishing a great deal of raw material. Given that the Internet is a realm of abundance—not scarcity, like the old ink- and airtime-based media—this is a feature, not a bug. Raw-data dumps of previously private or secret information are now part of the media landscape. As Max Frankel, former executive editor of the *New York Times,* recently put it, "The threat of massive leaks will persist so long as there are massive secrets."

Security expert Bruce Schneier makes a similar point. "Secrets are only as secure as the least trusted person who knows them," he wrote on his blog a few weeks after Cablegate erupted. "The more people who know a secret, the more likely it is to be made public." Somewhere between 500,000 and 600,000 military and diplomatic personnel had access to the SIPRNet system that Bradley Manning is alleged to have tapped. The government doesn't know precisely how many people overall have security clearances to classified information. Based on reporting from the Government Accountability Office, Steven Aftergood, a secrecy expert, estimates that this number is 2.5 million.

In other words, since this kind of "radical transparency" is technologically feasible, like it or not, it is a given. Efforts to stop it will fail, just as efforts to stop file-sharing by killing Napster failed. As Schneier sagely points out, "Just as the music and movie industries are going to have to change their business models for the Internet era, governments are going to have to change their secrecy models. I don't know what those new models will be, but they will be different."

Fourteen years ago, Senator Daniel Patrick Moynihan led the bipartisan Commission on Protecting and Reducing Government Secrecy. Its recommendations are worth revisiting in light of WikiLeaks. "It is time for a new way of thinking about secrecy," the commission's report began. "Secrecy is a form of government regulation. Americans are familiar with the tendency to over-regulate in other areas. What is different with secrecy is that the public cannot know the extent or the content of the regulation." The Moynihan Commission was examining a condition not unlike that of the present day, where millions of people had security clearances and hundreds of thousands of new "top secret" documents, whose disclosure could presumably cause "exceptionally grave damage to the national security," were created each year. But the commission was convinced that the culture of secrecy was out of control and hurting the country:

> Excessive secrecy has significant consequences for the national interest when, as a result, policymakers are not fully informed, government is not held accountable for its actions, and the public cannot engage in informed debate. This remains a dangerous world; some secrecy is vital to save lives, bring miscreants to justice, protect national security, and engage in effective diplomacy. Yet as Justice Potter Stewart noted in his opinion in the Pentagon Papers case, when everything is secret, nothing is secret. Even as billions of dollars are spent each year on government secrecy, the classification and personnel security systems have not always succeeded at their core task of protecting those secrets most critical to the national security. The classification system, for example, is used too often to deny the public an understanding of the policymaking process, rather than for the necessary protection of intelligence activities and other highly sensitive matters.

Well before Facebook, YouTube, Twitter and thumb-size memory sticks, Moynihan foresaw that the information age would make the culture of government secrecy untenable, even picturing a time "when fourteen-year-old hackers in Australia or Newfoundland" could penetrate the government's most sensitive secrets. With his commission, mandated by an act of Congress, he tried to turn the paradigm on its head. "The great discovery of Western science, somewhere in the seventeenth century," he wrote, "was the principle of openness. A scientist who judged he had discovered something, published it. Often to great controversy, leading to rejection, acceptance, modification, whatever.

Which is to say, to knowledge. In this setting science advanced, as nowhere else and never before."

It is long past time for governments to embrace this paradigm. "Where you're open, things will not be WikiLeaked," says Christopher Graham, Britain's information minister. "Quite a lot of this is only exciting because we didn't know it." He adds, "The best form of defense is transparency—much more proactive publication of what organizations do. It's an attitude of, 'OK. You want to know? Here it is.'" Jeff Jarvis, a professor at the City University of New York Journalism School, argues that government should be transparent by default, and have to justify when it chooses to make something secret, not the reverse. And he, too, sees something positive in the impact of WikiLeaks. "Perhaps the lesson of WikiLeaks should be that the open air is less fearsome than we'd thought," he blogged. "That should lead to less secrecy. After all, the only sure defense against leaks is transparency."

People who think more transparency will lead only to the hiding of secrets deeper in the bureaucracy, or that it will prevent government officials from conducting any kind of meaningful business, and that as a result we will know less, not more, about the workings of government or the powerful should think again. By that logic, we should require less public disclosure, not more. Why ask campaign contributors or lobbyists to disclose any of their activities? In fact, when people think what they're doing is subject to public view, their behavior generally changes for the better. Thus Cablegate—which exposed many sovereign powers to a new level of public scrutiny, warning them that more such scrutiny is always a possibility in the future—should, on balance, lead to better behavior. Why? Because the cost of maintaining the contradictions between what you say in public and what you do really has just gone up another notch.

Carne Ross is a British diplomat who resigned his post at the United Nations over the dissimulation that his government practiced during the lead-up to the invasion of Iraq in 2003. "From now on, it will be ever more difficult for governments to claim one thing and do another," says Ross. "For in making such claims, they are making themselves vulnerable to WikiLeaks of their own." If all it takes is one person with a USB drive, the "least trusted person" whose conscience may be pricked by a contradiction in his or her government's behavior, that information can move into public view more easily than ever before. That is the reality of the twenty-first century. It would be far better for all of us if our governments and other powerful institutions got with the business of accepting that transparency will be a new fact of life, and take steps to align their words with their deeds. In that respect, Hillary Clinton should thank Julian Assange rather than apologize to world leaders for what he did.

Judging from another "Internet freedom" speech Clinton gave in the wake of the Tunisian and Egyptian revolutions, a new era of openness and candor is not upon us. She declared America's support for the "freedom to connect" online "to solve shared problems and expose public corruption," and she insisted that "governments also have a duty to be transparent," but insisted that WikiLeaks could somehow be walled off from these principles because it "began with an act of theft." "Government documents were stolen, just the same as if they had been smuggled out in a briefcase," she declared, as if that meant the information in those documents was somehow unfit for public consumption or discussion simply because they weren't leaked in the proper way, say to Bob Woodward. For someone who has tried to be an Internet progressive, it was a singularly ostrichlike move. And unfortunately for Clinton and all the other world leaders, burying your head in the sand doesn't make bottom-up transparency disappear.

Two, Three, Many Leaks

That's because the genie has escaped from the bottle. Whatever else you may say about Assange, his greatest contribution to global enlightenment is the idea of a viable "stateless news organization," to use Jay Rosen's phrase, beholden to no country's laws and dedicated to bringing government information into public view. Even if Assange—who has just lost round one of his fight to avoid extradition to Sweden to face rape charges—goes to jail and WikiLeaks is somehow shut down, others are already following in his footsteps. Or as futurist Mark Pesce nicely put it, "The failures of WikiLeaks provide the blueprint for the systems which will follow it."

Since Cablegate, several independent WikiLeaks-style projects have announced themselves, including: BrusselsLeaks.com (focused on the European Union); BalkanLeaks.eu (the Balkan countries); Indoleaks.org (Indonesia); Rospil.info (Russia); two competing environmental efforts, each claiming the name Green-Leaks; and the Al-Jazeera Transparency Unit, which in January began publishing (with the *Guardian*) a cache of documents from inside the Palestinian Authority that exposed the minutes of high-level PA negotiating sessions with Israel and the United States. Some recent graduates of the CUNY Journalism School launched a simple tool, Localeaks, for publishers interested in attracting whistleblowers. And even the *New York Times* announced it may create a special portal for would-be leakers.

Perhaps the most important of these fledgling efforts is Open Leaks.org, which is being built by Daniel Domscheit-Berg, Herbert Snorrason and other former WikiLeaks associates. Of all these efforts, OpenLeaks is most likely to have the technological and cryptographic skills needed to succeed in a world filled with shady actors opposed to transparency. And unlike WikiLeaks, it is designed to be decentralized.

In mid-December, Domscheit-Berg told me that OpenLeaks was trying to correct mistakes in the WikiLeaks approach. "I am not into being a leader, and I don't trust the whole concept of leaders either," he said, adding, "If you follow the debate around why we left the WL [WikiLeaks] project, you will find that a strikingly important detail." He described OpenLeaks as more of a technological service provider to many media organizations, as well as others with an interest in opening up information, like NGOs and labor unions. Instead of acting as

a central hub for leaks, it will provide a dedicated website for handling leaks to each entity. In his view, this approach has several advantages:

> Firstly, the system will scale better with each new participant. Secondly, the source is the one that will have a say in who should exclusively be granted first access to material, while also ensuring that material will be distributed to others in the system after a period of exclusive access. Thirdly, we will make use of existing resources, experience, manpower etc. [to] deal with submissions more efficiently. Fourthly, we will be able to deliver information more directly to where it matters and will be used, while remaining a neutral service ourselves. And last but not least, this approach will create a large union of shared interests in the defense of the rights to run an anonymous post-drop in the digital world.

Of course, we can't take for granted that the powers that be will let this happen without a fight. In that respect, the battle over WikiLeaks has had another salutary effect: it has delivered a wake-up call to everyone who thought the free and open Internet was a settled fact. Freedom of the press is no longer the exclusive province of those who own one, but while the Internet has drastically lowered the barriers to entry into the public sphere, it has not eliminated them. Right now, unpopular or disruptive speech online will probably exist in a twilight zone, semi-free, sometimes capable of threatening powerful institutions and other times subject to their whims. What's needed is much more robust discussion of how the Internet can become a genuinely free public arena, a global town square where anyone can speak. Or, to be more precise, an Internet whose underlying architecture is really free of government or corporate control, as decentralized and uncontrollable as life itself.

Critical Thinking

1. Senator Daniel Patrick Moynihan is quoted as saying, "Secrecy is a form of government regulation. Americans are familiar with the tendency to over-regulate in other areas. What is different with secrecy is that the public cannot know the extent or the context of the regulation." Is there any information that should be classified?

2. Should WikiLeaks be shut down? Explain your reasons why or why not.

Micah L. Sifry, a former Nation associate editor, is co-founder of the Personal Democracy Forum, editor of its techPresident.com blog and senior adviser to the Sunlight Foundation. This easy is adapted from his new book, *WikiLeaks and the Age of Transparency*.

The Quality-Control Quandary

As newspapers shed copy editors and post more and more unedited stories online, what's the impact on their content?

CARL SESSIONS STEPP

Sunrise approaches on a Friday morning, and the St. Louis Post-Dispatch website is being updated early—from Mandy St. Amand's bathroom.

St. Amand, the Post-Dispatch continuous news editor, has balanced her laptop on the toilet lid and, while drying her hair and prepping for the office, is reworking homepage headlines.

Not surprisingly, no copy editor is handy at 5:30 A.M., so St. Amand's work goes online unchecked by a colleague. She estimates that between 40 and 50 Post-Dispatch staffers can post directly to the site, often remotely and without a second read—a growing, troubling trend in these days of never-ending news cycles and ever-dwindling editing corps.

A similar if less dramatic effect follows on the print side, where buyouts and layoffs over several years have cut the number of Post-Dispatch copy editors from more than 40 to about 21. The inevitable result, not only at the Post-Dispatch but at newsrooms nationwide, is that fewer editors scrutinize copy, and they often spend less time per item than they would have just a few years ago.

Together, these developments raise unprecedented questions about the value—and the future—of editing itself. Already at many news organizations, journalists and readers alike have noticed flabbier writing, flatter headlines, more typos. How far can you cut editing without crippling credibility? How do you balance immediacy and accuracy? How much does fine-tuning matter to the work-in-progress online ethos?

"When you think about the assembly line that was a newsroom, it's changed," says Post-Dispatch Editor Arnie Robbins. "In the world we live in now, readers expect immediacy, and we have to deliver. But we also have to be careful."

At ground level, these concerns fuel another trend: developing ways to maintain reasonable quality control now that the end-of-the-line copy desk can no longer process everything. Interviews and visits by AJR make clear that newsrooms are lurching toward new ways, from "buddy editing" (where you ask the nearest person to read behind you) to "back editing" (where copy is edited after posting) to "previewing" (where

copy goes to a holding directory for an editor to check before live posting).

For now, though, progress is slow, and the risks seem scary.

Bill McClellan, a Post-Dispatch columnist since 1983, has one of the news organization's most familiar bylines. But he recently experienced a "brain cramp" and called Missouri a blue state, even though it has gone Democratic only twice in the past eight presidential races. The error zipped past editors and ended up in print.

McClellan won't blame the copy desk, which he says is "astoundingly good," and regularly calls to check things like song lyrics he's tangled. "Nine times out of 10 the copy desk catches things," he says, "and the red-blue error was the tenth."

But, he adds, "You never do more with less. You do less with less. You have fewer copy editors, more mistakes get through."

Reporter Adam Jadhav remembers writing that a woman had lost her right arm in a car crash. Six paragraphs later, he called it her left arm. Like McClellan, Jadhav takes full responsibility for his errors. Still, he says, "I'd like to think that a reasonably worked copy desk could catch them."

"Obviously in the future there are probably going to be fewer and fewer reads," Editor Robbins says. "There is concern there, and there is some risk there. However, I think it is manageable."

Can good editing endure amid all the changes?

Mandy St. Amand, by now operating from the newsroom rather than the bathroom, thinks about the question. "I really wish I had a wise-sounding, beard-stroking answer," she says. "But I don't."

Post-Dispatch Managing Editor Pam Maples is leading a newsroom tour, pointing out physical and operational alterations aimed toward Journalism 2.0.

In the center, a glass office has been dismantled, creating space for a 9:30 A.M. stand-up news huddle—earlier, faster-paced and more Web-oriented than before. A homepage editor presides. For the first agenda item, she turns to a dry-erase board where the phrase "top mods" appears in all caps. What should fill the modules atop the website?

The newsroom now has two early-morning reporters, often hustling on traffic and weather stories. Their goal is to start the process of moving at least 20 items a day through the top Web positions. The nine editors also discuss tomorrow's printed paper, but they project urgency to get moving online.

"Anything that happens, our assumption is it goes online," Maples says. "It puts a demand on editors and how they manage their people and how they think. Deadline is always."

Maples and Robbins have graciously let AJR into their newsroom at a bad time: the week after the paper laid off 14 people in the newsroom, including several editors. Four other rounds of layoffs or buyouts have taken place since 2005. A news staff of about 340 five years ago is about 210 today, Robbins calculates. Some 40 pages of space per week have been lost in the newspaper, which is introducing a narrower page width that could cost another 5 percent of newshole.

These challenges are not unique to St. Louis, but the Post-Dispatch seems a symbolic place to examine their impact on editing. It is a 241,000-circulation, middle-American, blue-collar institution, founded in 1878 by Joseph Pulitzer, the editing giant famous for preaching "accuracy, accuracy, accuracy."

Even today, four years after the Pulitzer family sold the paper to Lee Enterprises (see "Lee *Who?*" June/July 2005), a visitor is reverently shown a vacant but still furnished office, last occupied by a Pulitzer family member, where portraits of multiple generations of the family peer down. As you enter the paper's downtown lobby, the founder's words thunder from the front wall: "Always remain devoted to the public welfare."

The ghost of Joseph Pulitzer, it seems, haunts the Post-Dispatch, and perhaps newspaper journalism itself. Can "accuracy, accuracy, accuracy" survive "cuts, cuts, cuts"?

Post-Dispatch staffers warm to the challenge.

"We have a brand," says Deputy Metro Editor Alan Achkar. "People expect from the St. Louis Post-Dispatch a level of quality and accuracy. If we don't have good, responsible journalism that people can bank on, we don't have anything."

But maintaining quality takes more and more effort.

"For the Internet, speed is king," Achkar says. "You often worry that we're just slapping stuff online without properly vetting it. . . . It's added work. Sometimes you feel that no one wants to acknowledge that putting out a newspaper—even a thinner one—is a monumental task."

Top editors acknowledge that, by policy, cutbacks have fallen disproportionately on editors. Saving reporting jobs is the priority.

"People on the street, you try to protect as much as possible," Robbins says. "That's not to minimize the importance of editing and design at all. But ultimately you have to make tough decisions. Reporters on the street do separate us from other places."

So, the assigning editors and copy editors who are left adapt.

These days, says Frank Reust, a Post-Dispatch copy editor for 10 years, editors find themselves hovering somewhere between "comfortably rushed" and "always having to railroad stuff."

That means more rapid copy editing and sometimes, especially for wire stories, fewer reads. For online copy, says designer and Web producer Joan McKenna, "we are forgiven for mistakes. Speed is much more important than anything else."

The fallout so far seems noticeable but not calamitous. More than one reporter mentioned increased reaction from readers pointing out errors, mostly small. For example, a sportswriter's post confusing the names of two St. Louis Rams coaching prospects was flagged in the comments section and fixed within minutes.

Editors also express some larger concerns.

For instance, Reust sees less creative time applied to the "accuracy and tone" of headlines. He also worries that writers and editors brainstorm less. "The general time devoted to good writing is almost nonexistent now," he says.

Jean Buchanan, the paper's assistant managing editor for projects, sees that too. Writers sometimes can't get an editor's attention when they need it, and less time goes into those vital ingredients of enterprise and investigations, "rooting around for potential stories, requesting information that might lead to a story, meeting with small groups of reporters talking about what they are seeing."

Reid Laymance, the assistant managing editor for sports, spends more time on hands-on editing and less on planning. His editors have less time to develop "extras" like charts or breakout boxes. Down a copy editor since he took over last spring, "we're not as much editors as we used to be," he says. "Our guys have become processors. Getting the game in by 8 o'clock, making sure the headline fits, that's all we have time for."

Director of Photography Larry Coyne offers a good news/bad news example. With today's digital cameras, it isn't uncommon for photographers to shoot a thousand exposures on an assignment, many times more than they previously would have. Online galleries allow far more photos to run. But Coyne has three-and-a-half photo editors today instead of the five-and-a-half of about three years ago, so collaboration and editing can suffer. "There is more emphasis on quantity and getting them out," he says, "and less on feedback with photographers."

In fairness, it must be emphasized that not one of these editors comes across as whiny or bitter. They seem candid about their plight but determined to succeed. "Every time there's a reduction in staff," copy editor Reust says, "there is a period where you feel the load is just too much to handle. Then two months down the road you're thinking, 'We can handle things.'"

Patrick Gauen, the self-described "cops and courts editor" and a veteran police reporter, looks back over his 24 years at the paper and says, "A lot of what is changing—the platform stuff—really doesn't matter to me. It gets to the public one way or the other. . . . I feel like I still have the time I need. Our adequacy of editing is still good."

> **"There are so many balls in the air at once and some of them are going to drop. You try to understand which ones are breakable and try not to let those go."**
>
> —Patrick Gauen

He lives by something he once heard: "There are so many balls in the air at once and some of them are going to drop. You try to understand which ones are breakable and try not to let those go."

General assignment reporter David Hunn echoes that balanced sentiment. "The most serious stories I write" get attentive editing, he says, but the rush to post online is "kind of like the Wild West. . . . If anything is clear to me right now, it's that we are feeling our way as we go—and as a whole doing a pretty good job of it."

Editors being editors, though, they tend to see themselves in a code orange world, their equivalent of an earthquake zone or hurricane corridor, bracing for the Big One.

"What will wake us up," says Enterprise Editor Todd Stone, "is going to be the first big lawsuit where somebody really gets creamed. It's going to happen. And I'd bet you about 10 bucks it will be because of a lack of editing vigilance."

At the Washington Post, another paper that has lost editors, A-section copy desk chief Bill Walsh has the same worry.

"I keep fearing a disaster of some kind. I think it is only a matter of time," says Walsh, a nationally known blogger and author. "Doing more with less is always going to mean a compromise in quality. Three sets of eyes are always better than two."

Last year, the Post's ombudsman at the time, Deborah Howell, made a public pitch for editing. Reporting that the Post had lost 40 percent of its copy editors since 2005, Howell wrote that they are "the last stop before disaster."

On Walsh's combined national-foreign copy desk, seven editors now work where 12 once did. Where a typical piece of copy formerly got careful reading from an assigning editor, copy editor, slot editor and an editor looking at page proofs, today there tends to be one less layer, with the slot editor just taking a "glance," Walsh says.

Front-page and other sensitive stories still get extra edits, but Walsh acknowledges, "We're probably spending on average less time with stories, although that is not universally the case. I can't say we are doing as good a job with a rim read and a half-assed slot read as we were with more people looking at every story."

To help compensate, Walsh adds, the Post has succeeded in improving flow so copy reaches his desk earlier. It is also stressing that assigning desks must polish stories as much as possible before moving them.

Forty miles up I-95, the Baltimore Sun offers its version of the same tale.

The Sun, too, features its founder's words on the lobby wall, A.S. Abell's 1837 exhortation to serve "the common good."

But like other newsrooms, the Sun has fewer editors' eyes trained on that common good. John E. McIntyre, the director of the copy desk since 1995, counted about 54 copy editors several years ago, 48 about a year ago and 34 as of January, for news, features and sports.

However, McIntyre points out a "grim advantage" for the Sun and other papers. For print, at least, there is less copy to edit. The paper, he says, has lost about a third of its staff in the past few years and almost that much newshole.

"The size of the paper has been cut back to the point at which we have just about enough copy editors to manage it," he says. "It's the only reason we are not slapping basically unread copy into print."

Still, McIntyre sees worrisome signs, like "minor errors in fact and slack writing," fewer minutes for making headlines shine and, of course, less attention to online postings.

"That scares the bejeezus out of me," says McIntyre, who writes a blog about language called You Don't Say (http://weblogs.baltimoresun.com/news/mcintyre/blog). "I would rather have people on the staff catch my errors than readers."

Like editors elsewhere, McIntyre pledges to maintain quality. "The Sun has a reputation for the accuracy and clarity of what it publishes, and we are going to find a way to uphold the paper's standards."

McIntyre, a charter member and former president of the American Copy Editors Society (ACES), believes in documenting to management the vital contributions editors make.

A man given to unusually natty dress for a newsroom, who sips tea from a real cup during an interview, he offers an earthy defense of the editor's role. It is, he says, "to save the paper's ass."

He keeps a file of great prepublication catches by editors. Not long ago, he says, a veteran reporter and an assigning editor let through a piece of libelous work. "Were it not for the copy editor," McIntyre declares, "the biggest decision on the afternoon after publication would have been how many zeroes to put on the settlement check."

ACES and its current president, Chris Wienandt, have boosted efforts to promote and defend editing.

"Everyone is trying to cut costs, and editors and copy editors are relatively invisible jobs," says Wienandt, the business copy chief of the Dallas Morning News. "There is still this perception that we are proofreading drones.

"But the work of the copy editor involves the most-read work in the paper—the headlines. Editors are guardians of credibility, and without credibility we really haven't got a leg to stand on. Imagine a manufacturing company that didn't have a quality-control department. They would be in hot water pretty quick if things started going out defective."

> **"Imagine a manufacturing company that didn't have a quality-control department. They would be in hot water pretty quick if things started going out defective."**
>
> —Chris Wienandt

Wienandt and other ACES board members have collaborated on several editorials on the organization's website (www.copydesk.org), scolding those like Tribune Co. owner Sam Zell, who complained that layers of editing delay publication.

If stories are posted too quickly, the ACES editorial countered, they are "more likely to contain errors . . . be unethical, or present an actual legal problem. . . . If credibility evaporates, so will sales."

ACES also attacked the idea of outsourcing editing. "You simply can't duplicate the collective wisdom of a locally based copy desk," another editorial argued. To diminish local editing would jeopardize quality and undermine "the key selling point to an industry that more than ever needs selling points."

What then is the future of editing? Will Sullivan, the Post-Dispatch's 28-year-old interactive director, appreciates the concerns of veteran colleagues but also welcomes a future of new thinking and tools.

He envisions that editing will become "more of a barn-raising . . . an everyone-is-an-editor model," where "the concept of news is a wiki" and a story becomes "a kind of rolling document" moving through a continuous editing process.

Better training can spread editing skills to writers and producers, he says. New tools, from automated step-savers like spell-check to simplified photo-editing software, can add speed and quality. Merging staffs can promote efficiency, for example, by assigning the same section editor to manage features on the Web and in print.

During this time of transition, several practices seem increasingly common:

- bringing copy editors in earlier to help with online copy and to expedite flow
- using floating, "quick-hit" editors to handle stories as they break
- expecting writers and assigning desks to move copy earlier
- enforcing the perhaps neglected principle that writers should be better self-editors
- encouraging "buddy editing," where a writer or poster doesn't wait for the copy desk but asks a colleague for a second read
- using "preview" directories as a holding point for material about to go live online, so an editor can look over it first

- creating protocols for Web editing, such as posting a note whenever something new goes onto the Web, to trigger an editor's check
- systematizing "back editing," so that even after being posted, all copy gets edited as soon as possible

Repeatedly, Post-Dispatch editors and reporters underline the importance of constant coaching and communicating to help solve problems early rather than dump them on editors late.

"The shift in responsibility has moved to the front end with the reporter and the originating editor more than ever," says Adam Goodman, deputy managing editor for metro and business news. "You can't rely on somebody catching things down the road as much as we used to. . . . It needs to be camera-ready when the reporter sends it."

Deputy Managing Editor for News Steve Parker tracks every published correction. ("It's kind of like being a prison guard," he jokes.) From 2002 to 2005, the annual number sat in the 800s. Then it began drifting downward, to 771 in 2006, 636 in 2007, and 546 last year.

Partly, Parker acknowledges, the drop reflects a declining newshole and volume of copy. But in 2006, the paper also developed a set of "verification guidelines" to reduce errors and spread accountability. They range from the basics ("Ask the subject to spell his/her name. . . . Just before ending the interview, recheck the spelling") to avoiding hoaxes ("Remember that IDs can be faked") to double-checking graphics ("A finished copy . . . must be provided to the reporter or originating editor before it is published").

In addition, Managing Editor Maples says, it becomes essential to recognize when you truly must take your time.

She cites high-profile breaking stories where the newsroom delayed or withheld postings while discussing thorny issues. When area police made a surprise discovery of two missing teenage boys, one of whom had been gone for four-and-a-half years, the Post-Dispatch held an early report because it was based on only one source. A television news operation broke the story, beating the paper by a few minutes. The Post-Dispatch also withheld other information because a reporter's online research was putting it in doubt. It turned out to be incorrect, but other outlets used it.

Last year, a Post-Dispatch stringer witnessed a shooting at a Kirkwood, Missouri, city council meeting. The stringer saw two people get shot, by someone whose voice she recognized, before she took cover under a chair. Reached on her cell phone, she identified both victims and the shooter. After a quick, intense debate involving key editors, the paper's website went with the names but not their conditions or other sensitive details.

By contrast, the paper last year apologized for a "journalistic breakdown" over a feel-good Easter story about a woman's past of "victimization . . . followed by recovery." Multiple details—including the woman's name, marriage, children and various dramatic incidents—were challenged after publication.

To Maples, the broad lesson is that "we have to keep talking about the balance between immediacy and standards . . . We can't slow down, but it should not be 'publish at all costs.'"

Reporters want the help. "If we have to wait six more minutes," says 24-year veteran reporter Tim O'Neil, "let's get it out correctly. The number of times I might grouse about being edited is outweighed by the times people have saved my tail."

Mandy St. Amand, the continuous news editor, once worked at the Associated Press and still believes, "Get it first, but first get it right."

But she recognizes, too, that changing times will test that venerable credo.

"I think there is a trade-off," she concludes. "The editing overall in terms of polishing has waned, but the sense of urgency and excitement has increased. I guess whether that's a fair trade-off will be decided by the readers."

Critical Thinking

1. To what degree do you assume fact-checking and accuracy in news stories you read online? In hard copy publications? Does it matter?

2. What are the implications of "the shift in responsibility [moving] to the front end with the reporter and the originating editor [unable to] rely on someone catching things down the road as much as we used to."?

CARL SESSIONS STEPP (cstepp@jmail.umd.edu), AJR's senior contributing editor, teaches at the Philip Merrill College of Journalism at the University of Maryland.

From *American Journalism Review,* April/May 2009, pp. 42–47. Copyright © 2009 by the Philip Merrill College of Journalism at the University of Maryland, College Park, MD 20742-7111. Reprinted with permission.

The Fact-Checking Explosion

In a bitter political landscape marked by rampant allegations of questionable credibility, more and more news outlets are launching truth-squad operations.

CARY SPIVAK

Gib Heinz was clearly annoyed when the Seattle Times launched its Truth Needle, a fact-checking initiative that seeks to separate truth from fiction in political claims.

"I'm absolutely stunned by the introduction of this new feature," the Freeland, Washington, resident wrote in a letter published by the paper on August 22. "This 'Truth Needle' is going to decide whether the claims are true or false? News reporting is reporting the news and facts and letting me decide what is true or false."

Sorry, Mr. Heinz, but you'd better get used to it. Not only does it appear that fact-checking operations are here to stay, but they are growing rapidly. Just this year, at least two dozen media organizations or universities launched or joined fact-checking operations. Some are flying solo; some are joining the St. Petersburg Times' PolitiFact network; and others are forming new cooperatives, such as AZ Fact Check, a partnership announced in August that includes the Arizona Republic, Phoenix's 12 News and the Walter Cronkite School of Journalism and Mass Communication at Arizona State University.

In each case reporters are leaving the comfort of the press box, where they watch and report on the action, and are getting onto the field to play referee.

"It's a complete reversal of traditional journalism" says Jim Tharpe, editor of the Atlanta Journal-Constitution's PolitiFact Georgia.

The fact-checking explosion may have begun in 2004 after the media's initially flat-footed response to the attacks on Sen. John Kerry by the group that called itself Swift Boat Veterans for Truth. But the just-completed 2010 election featured fact-checking on steroids. A bitterly divided electorate and a political landscape replete with high-decibel claims and counterclaims on cable television and echoing throughout the blogosphere have made neutral arbiters more crucial than ever.

"I never thought journalism would be like this," says Bill Adair, the St. Petersburg Times' Washington, D.C., bureau chief and editor of PolitiFact, the Pulitzer Prize-winning fact-checking operation that is exporting its approach to local news

operations across the country. "It's just the right formula for the new era."

PolitiFact and other fact-checking ventures are filling a void in political reporting, says longtime Washington Post political reporter and columnist David Broder. "So often in the past, the voters have been left with nothing but a 'he said, she said'—there was no third source with an objective view," Broder says, asserting that reporters are the people best equipped to serve as the arbiters of truth.

"'Who are the alternatives?' is the question," says Broder, who has covered politics for the Post since Lyndon Johnson was in the White House. "In this respect, the press is becoming a little more aggressive, and that's good."

Politicians, many of whom may despise the idea of having their every word—not to mention every advertisement—scrutinized by reporters, are taking notice of the fact-checking teams. "The candidates hate these," says Rick Wiley, a national political consultant. "It's hard for them, because they see it as people coming out and attacking them personally."

Especially when they're called liars—a charge that could easily be picked up and ballyhooed by an opponent in an attack ad.

"What I've heard from folks running for office is that they don't want a 'Pants on Fire,'" says Ken Goldstein, a professor of political science at the University of Wisconsin-Madison who specializes in political advertising. "Pants on Fire" is the worst rating doled out by PolitiFact, reserved for assertions that make a ridiculous claim and are clearly false. Goldstein admits being surprised that some politicians have even changed the wording of statements in response to criticism from a fact-checker. "If you had asked me before, I would have been dismissive about the impact of these," Goldstein says. "But I have been hearing some anecdotal evidence that some politicians know that it's in place and are reacting."

In September, the Milwaukee Journal Sentinel's PolitiFact Wisconsin gave Tom Barrett, the Milwaukee mayor and Democratic gubernatorial candidate, a "Pants on Fire" rating for erroneously boasting on his campaign website that violent crime had fallen 20 percent during his tenure. The following day, Barrett, who went on to lose the governor's race, corrected the claim. "If I had read it I would have caught it," the mayor told the paper. The Journal Sentinel, where I work, is one of eight newspapers to buy the PolitiFact license for use in their home markets.

In June, Markos Moulitsas, the founder and publisher of the liberal blog Daily Kos, was nailed when he erroneously said Turkey is an Arab country. The comment came during a roundtable discussion on ABC's "This Week" show, which is fact-checked weekly by PolitiFact. Moulitsas quickly tweeted a correction after the show, but it wasn't enough to avoid being hit with a "False" rating on the Truth-O-Meter.

"There's a hunger for this," says Richard Wagoner, deputy metro editor who oversees the paper's Truth Needle, which launched in August. "There's so much noise in these political campaigns. People have to know what is true out there and what isn't."

Still, reporters should not think that their incisive research will compel politicians to clean up their acts, cautions Brooks Jackson, director of FactCheck.org, the 7-year-old site that serves as the template for modern fact-checking initiatives. A project of the Annenberg Public Policy Center of the University of Pennsylvania, FactCheck.org operated on a budget of more than $900,000 in fiscal year 2010.

"Ever since the Greeks invented the word 'demagogue,' politicians have been acting like this," Jackson says, referring to their propensity to do or say whatever they deem necessary to grab and keep power. "It's not going to change."

Jackson points to former New York Mayor Rudy Giuliani as proof. The one-time Republican presidential hopeful repeatedly makes erroneous statements, even after being corrected by fact-checkers and others, Jackson says. He notes that Giuliani has often said that men with prostate cancer have a 44 percent survival rate under England's health care system—a lowball figure that has been contradicted by FactCheck.org, other news outlets and a host of experts.

Yet, Jackson says, Giuliani used to ignore the evidence and criticism and kept repeating the falsehood. "He's incorrigible," Jackson says. "Just incorrigible." (Giuliani did not respond to requests for comment.)

What was up with that? I asked Wiley, who was deputy political director for Giuliani's 2008 campaign for the GOP presidential nomination. "There are some politicians who, if they believe something, they're going to say it," Wiley says. "That's just the way they are. . . . There are some battles you're not going to win."

Despite the best efforts of the fact-checking outfits, many people continue to cling to canards like the "death panels" supposedly in the health care reform bill and President Barack Obama's alleged lack of a valid U.S. birth certificate.

So why bother spending all this time holding politicians accountable? The 68-year-old Jackson, who is frequently referred to as the father of fact-checking, doesn't hesitate before answering. "It's a First Amendment thing," he says. "It's what we do." It's necessary for the electorate to have somebody separating fact from fiction, Jackson says, regardless of what

people choose to do with the information. "Our audience—the citizens and voters—need to know this. . . . [They're] awash in all sorts of unverified, false, misleading information."

Teams of reporters are scouring the airwaves, speeches, brochures, websites and legislative sessions weighing the accuracy of virtually every word uttered by politicians and TV talking heads. PolitiFact and FactCheck.org focus on national politicians, while scores of reporters are doing local checks, either through independent operations or PolitiFact spinoffs.

"We could do this on the national level," Jackson says, "but what about the guy running for governor or the guy running for dogcatcher?"

Local reporters at a variety of news operations are taking the challenge. Among them are PoliGraph, a partnership between Minnesota Public Radio and the Humphrey Institute of Public Affairs at the University of Minnesota; the Denver Post's Political Polygraph; the Tacoma, Washington, Tribune's Political Smell Test; the Voice of San Diego's fact-check blog; and BamaFactCheck.com, launched in September by the Anniston Star, the Decatur Daily, the Dothan Eagle, the Opelika-Auburn News, the Times Daily of Florence, the Tuscaloosa News and NBC 13 WVTM-TV of Birmingham. Unlike PolitiFact and FactCheck.org, both of which post new items year-round, some local fact-checking services may publish only during election season or as needed. Others, however, hope to keep an eye on the politicians on a continuing basis.

Each site uses different categories for rating the veracity of comments. For example, Caesar Meter, an initiative of the News Journal in Wilmington, Delaware, dubs true statements "Tall in the Saddle" while pegging false ones as "Horse Puckey."

Says Adair, who hopes that PolitiFact eventually has a partnership with media outlets in all 50 states: "My ultimate goal is that every politician in America ought to face the Truth-O-Meter," the trademarked graphic that ranks political claims on a scale ranging from "True" to "Pants on Fire." The flashy online version features a meter engulfed in flames, making it easy for a political opponent to play off the name and the graphic in a campaign attack ad.

To reach his ambitious goal, Adair, the creator of and an enthusiastic evangelist for PolitiFact, is traveling the country signing up media outlets to join his network. Each one that does pays between $25,000 and $30,000 for the first year, says Neil Brown, editor of the St. Petersburg Times. Then the tab drops to $1,000 per month.

Demand for the Truth-O-Meter, or the various independent versions of it that are springing up, is an outgrowth of the increasingly bitter rhetoric and name-calling on the campaign trail. Despite the reservations of Seattle Times reader Gib Heinz, reader response to fact-checking has been extremely positive, editors and reporters agree.

"The politicians hate it and the readers love it," says Atlanta's Tharpe. "And that's fine."

The politicians hate it and the readers love it. And that's fine.

Tharpe and Martin Kaiser, editor of the Milwaukee Journal Sentinel, report they receive complaints from both sides of the political spectrum. "I love it because it confuses the partisans on both sides," says Kaiser, who sees ideas like fact-checking as a key to industry survival, a thought embraced by Jackson and others.

"The function of the press, if we're going to survive, has got to evolve from being a gatekeeper [for information] to a referee or an arbitrator or some sort of adjudicator," Jackson says. "That's the audience that we need to figure out how to serve. . . . You don't serve it by just printing all the news that's fit to print. You have to address the false and misleading stuff."

And that's just what many in the fact-checking movement are doing. Topics that have been placed under the truth squad microscope include:

The serious: Did President Obama in 2009 exaggerate the number of people who would be covered by his health care proposal? (He did, according to FactCheck.org.)

The silly: In 2007, PolitiFact reviewed a music video in which the so-called "Obama girl" declares during a faux debate; "At least Obama didn't marry his cousin" as Giuliani did. (PolitiFact's ruling: True.)

The subjective: TBD.com's The Facts Machine in September looked into whether Washington, D.C., Mayor Adrian Fenty was a jerk. (The fledgling website's conclusion: Mostly On Point. Fenty later lost his bid for re-election.)

"We pushed the limit of the format with that one," says Kevin Robillard, the first-year reporter who does the bulk of the reporting for The Facts Machine. "We backed it up with a lot of reporting. You can't make three phone calls and declare Adrian Fenty a jerk."

Even unnamed bloggers or chain e-mailers are considered fair game for scrutiny. Brown, the St. Petersburg Times editor, bragged in his paper's 2009 submission to the Pulitzer Prize committee that PolitiFact shot down outlandish claims involving Obama.

"PolitiFact sorted out the truth about global e-mail attacks on Barack Obama, including that he used a Koran instead of a Bible when he was sworn into the U.S. Senate ("Pants on Fire"/False) and that his middle name was Muhammed (also "Pants on Fire"/False)," Brown wrote in his letter to the committee.

Jackson, who worked as a reporter at the Associated Press, the Wall Street Journal and CNN before launching FactCheck.org, says there is plenty of room for more players in the fact-checking game. He is especially open to those who can try out some gimmicks and add a little flash to enhance the format's appeal to the public. He says of the Penn-affiliated FactCheck.org, "We have to maintain a pretense of Ivy League respectability. As much as I admire what Bill [Adair] is doing [at PolitiFact], we can't get away with that ourselves."

Among the gimmicks that Jackson must eschew are pictures of Pinocchio, which the Washington Post used in its The Fact Checker feature in 2008, or the graphics in the Seattle Times that show the city's iconic Space Needle building with flags that indicate the truthfulness of a statement. And, of course, Jackson isn't going to put a match to a politician's trousers.

"It's a gimmick, but it's a hell of a good gimmick," Brown says of the Truth-O-Meter. "We've taken it beyond the academics . . . so this could be part of a mainstream, solid newsroom."

Though not particularly gaudy, the FactCheck.org website provides readers with an array of graphics and links. It also attracts significant attention, drawing 455,370 unique visitors in September compared to 407,164 for PolitiFact, according to Compete Inc., a company that tracks Web traffic.

If Jackson is the father of political fact-checking, then Brown and Adair are like the children of a successful entrepreneur who are trying to take Dad's single grocery store and turn it into a national chain.

Brown and Adair quickly realized that they had something they might be able to take national. Fact-checking ventures were popping up, the public seemed to enjoy them and the media were fascinated by PolitiFact, which ran its first item on August 22, 2007.

Adair made more than 200 media appearances in 2008 to discuss PolitiFact and its judgments, "including regular stops on MSNBC, NPR and CNN," Brown told the Pulitzer judges.

"We knew that people were going to come to us and want to do it," Adair says. "So we knew we had to design a business around it."

The eight newspapers that have bought the PolitiFact licensing rights and entered into partnerships with it are allowed to sell advertising on their own PolitiFact sites and to offer PolitiFact through print syndication to others in their state. When stories written by state sites are posted on the national PolitiFact site, the local newspaper gets credit for the pageviews its item receives.

In return, the media outlet agrees to produce several PolitiFact items each week—there is no quota, but Adair hopes to see about five per week—and to assign qualified reporters capable of meeting PolitiFact standards to research and write the stories. Reporters are given training as well as a manual detailing how to research and write a PolitiFact story.

For help in designing a game plan for expansion, Adair looked at two successful franchise operations: McDonald's and Subway. "They had a lot of good lessons," Adair says. "Both places rely heavily on training manuals and standardized procedures. Both do lots and lots of training, periodic quality control."

Adair keeps a close watch on what the local operations are producing. In one case, he says, a reporter who was not meeting PolitiFact standards was reassigned after Adair questioned the reporter's work. "We license our brand and our methods to our partners, and they agree to follow our methods," Adair says. "They are required to follow our standards for journalism."

When a media outlet buys into PolitiFact, editors and reporters receive about three days of training that includes explaining the formula for writing a PolitiFact story. Instead of the traditional inverted pyramid style, the PolitiFact stories follow a pyramid model, with the most important fact—the verdict—coming last. A dose of irreverence is encouraged. All sources are cited and comments from anonymous sources are forbidden.

The reporter who researches and writes the story recommends a Truth-O-Meter rating, but it is a panel—generally consisting of two or three editors—that makes the final judgment. Local editors decide which items should be investigated.

Though local news operations are often fiercely independent, the success of PolitiFact is persuading some editors to sign up for the program. The savings that come from joining a group as opposed to launching an independent operation also help make PolitiFact attractive to cash-strapped editors.

"I don't think this would have happened if everybody was rolling in the dough," Brown says. "Things have changed."

Indeed, he says, his paper and other regional media could follow suit and look for other ideas that could be shared with, or sold to, other newsrooms. "We should all be looking at things that are points of distinction," he says.

Some papers, however, prefer to go it alone.

Editors at the Seattle Times, for example, liked the idea of launching an in-house truth squad. "It was the kind of reporting that we want to do and want to do more of" Wagoner says. Times representatives met with Adair but decided the paper was not willing to devote the resources that would be required to join the PolitiFact network. "The commitment of personnel was pretty big" and would have cut into the paper's ability to do in-depth reporting on other topics, Wagoner says. "Something has to give at some point," he says, adding that PolitiFact is a year-round operation. The Times is continuing its popular Truth Needle, though Wagoner isn't sure how often it will appear. "It depends on the flow of the news," he said.

Newspaper consultant and AJR columnist John Morton says PolitiFact's unusual national licensing effort appears to be off to a good start, as its affiliates already include "fairly substantial newspapers." In addition to the Atlanta Journal-Constitution and Milwaukee Journal Sentinel, other newspapers in the PolitiFact network are the Austin American-Statesman, the Miami Herald, Cleveland's Plain Dealer, Portland's Oregonian, the Providence Journal and the Richmond Times-Dispatch.

"With the reduced staff that almost all newspapers are struggling with, they don't have the manpower to devise a good system," Morton says.

"We could have reinvented the wheel," says Julia Wallace, editor of the Journal-Constitution, which joined PolitiFact in June. "I didn't understand why we would want to."

The Journal Sentinel's Kaiser, which launched PolitiFact Wisconsin in September, says he was impressed with the PolitiFact style and the light touch it often uses. "One of the strengths of it is the consistency," Kaiser says. He says he decided to join the network as he watched yet another campaign season featuring politicians exchanging charges with nobody stepping in to separate truth from fiction.

"This is a revolutionary way to cover politics," Kaiser says.

Politicians on both sides of the aisle praise the concept of fact-checking enterprises but criticize the way they operate. Political staffers say they don't mind having their bosses' words scrutinized but object to what they view as subjective decisions sometimes based on ridiculous levels of word parsing.

"They have a very, very clear objective not to say that politicians are telling the truth," says Edward Chapman, a Democratic consultant who worked on the unsuccessful gubernatorial campaign of outgoing Georgia Attorney General Thurbert Baker. Chapman complains that he once spent an hour arguing with PolitiFact Georgia over whether a ranking of No. 47 on college entrance exams placed Georgia "right at the bottom," as Baker had said.

"It was a surreal experience," Chapman says. "If we had said 'near the bottom' they would have given us a true." Instead, the statement scored a rating of "half-true."

The dislike of having fact-checkers study the meaning of every word is, in fact, producing some bipartisan agreement among political staffers in a climate where that commodity is rare indeed. "The analysis of a single word or phrase misses the larger scope of what the candidate is saying," says Jill Bader, a Republican who has worked on campaigns in the District of Columbia and two states, most recently Wisconsin. "That fact that you guys get to choose which part of an ad you're going to highlight isn't really objective."

After Roy Barnes, the unsuccessful Democratic candidate for governor in Georgia, said, "If we have to scrape the gold off the gold dome, you make sure that education comes first," PolitiFact Georgia gave him a "Pants on Fire" rating. The reason: The cost of scraping the gold would exceed the value of the precious metal. That ruling made even some journalists cringe.

"I wondered why are they even doing that one; people know he wouldn't go up there and scrape the gold off the dome," says Lori Geary, a reporter with WSB in Atlanta. "They take it verbatim. . . . Sometimes, I'm like, 'Well, what he said and what he implied are different.'"

But PolitiFact Georgia remains unapologetic. "We have every right to check hyperbole," says Tharpe, who wrote the Georgia dome item that ran in February. "It's fair game."

Overall, Geary says, she supports PolitiFact because it provides a service to readers and viewers. WSB is the sister station of the Journal-Constitution, and Geary does a weekly report during which she confronts a politician who is the subject of an upcoming PolitiFact Georgia report. She tells the politician the verdict PolitiFact Georgia has reached about a statement the political figure had made and solicits his or her reaction.

"I've had some of them cuss at me. . . . I've had to bleep out a few candidates," she says. "The viewers love it."

Political consultant Wiley says fact-checkers would be more effective if they skipped the nitpicking and focused instead on the overarching message. Instead of using journalists to make all the calls, Wiley suggests news outlets hire former campaign staffers who understand how messages are being spun by candidates. "Now [fact-checkers] are choosing black and white statements. But if you had some political hacks, they would look at an ad and say, 'C'mon guys, this is what they're really saying.'"

Though not endorsing hiring old pols, TBD's Robillard sees Wiley's point about the limitations of fact-checkers. "You could fact-check the little lie, but you can't fact-check the big lies," he says. "If somebody says health care reform will make the country a better place, you can't fact-check that."

Regardless, politicians and their staffers are learning to adapt to the growth of truth squads. "It certainly becomes part of the overall picture, not the determining factor in how deci-sions will be made, but we have to be aware of this stuff," says Patrick Curley, a longtime Wisconsin Democrat and political confidant to Barrett, the Milwaukee mayor. Politicians are learning to use the ratings as a weapon to either promote them-selves or attack their opponents, says Curley, who is Barrett's chief of staff.

"Everybody is kind of getting into the game. . . . All over the country, you're going to see Truth-O-Meters," Curley says. "It's already entered the calculus. It didn't take long."

Everybody is kind of getting into the game. . . . All over the country, you're going to see Truth-O-Meters.

Critical Thinking

1. Bill Adair, of the *St. Petersburg Times* and PolitiFact, is quoted as saying, "I never thought journalism would be like this. It's just the right formula for the new era." From your perspective, is the fact-checking explosion ethically responsible practice? A good gimmick or good reporting?

2. Brooks Jackson, director of FactCheck.org, says, "The function of the press, if we're going to survive, has got to evolve from being a gatekeeper [for information] to a referee or an arbitator or some sort of adjudicator." Do you agree?

CARY SPIVAK (cspivak01@gmail.com) is an investigative reporter for the Milwaukee Journal Sentinel, focusing on business issues, and an occasional contributor to PolitiFact Wisconsin. He wrote about inves-tigative websites funded by short-selling stocks in AJR's Fall issue.

Too Graphic?

American newspapers, often squeamish when it comes to running disturbing images, overcame their inhibitions after the Haitian earthquake. Journalists say powerful, graphic photographs made clear the depth of the tragedy and fostered support for rebuilding the devastated island nation. But to some, the deluge of images of naked corpses and severed body parts was insensitive and dehumanizing.

ARIELLE EMMETT

One by one the photos trickled in; then they came in torrents. On a piece of cardboard draped over a makeshift stretcher, the corpse of a Haitian man lay caked in dust like a powdered doll, a woman's dark legs in capri pants striding past him. In another image, a young man was digging his way out of a collapsed school building after the quake. As he picked his way through the rubble with hand tools, trying to rescue a teacher trapped inside, he looked up at the camera, seemingly unaware that he was flanked by a schoolgirl kneeling lifeless at her desk, her head and neck pinned by blocks of collapsed concrete.

The photos displayed by dozens of U.S. newspapers and websites showed tiny Haitian orphans crawling and playing in tent cities. There were hundreds and then thousands of photos of dazed, poorly bandaged victims; of nude or partially nude bodies falling out of pushcarts; of men in surgical masks dragging by legs and arms the bloated dead to parking lot morgues. The cinderblock houses and government palaces had been leveled by a seismic blast; there were images of body parts and screaming people, collapsed grocery stores and looters shot in the act.

It was hell, a 7.0 magnitude earthquake that struck Haiti on January 12, killing an estimated 230,000 people, leaving perhaps 3 million injured or homeless.

American news photographers with digital cameras and satellite phones rushed to the scene. This was not like Afghanistan or Iraq, with countless rules of embedding and the continual threats of bullets and roadside bombs. And editors generally loath to publish graphic and disturbing images saw justification for doing so in the case of the catastrophe in Haiti. This time, photographers and videographers went all out, loading their digital cameras with as much grief, hope and horror as they could bear.

"One of the reasons the pictures were more graphic in Haiti was that the Haitian people wanted the journalists to photograph the dead bodies and tell their stories. They wanted the world to see, to know how horrible it was," says Michele McNally, assistant managing editor for photography at the New York Times, which initially sent five photographers, including Pulitzer Prize-winner Damon Winter, to cover the disaster.

But Valérie Payen-Jean Baptiste, a Haitian elementary school principal who lost every possession, her home and school, and nearly her family in the quake, was sickened by the images. "I'm tired of it; the photos are too much," she says. "I know that [news outlets] took pictures, and that enabled people to raise money. But what I see is that people in Haiti are really upset. Some view the photos as an insult, a disaster, since we have already suffered so much."

"I'm not criticizing journalists [who] talk about the facts of the earthquake," she wrote in a follow-up e-mail. "But my critique is about the tone of unnecessary pictures and videos that show pieces of bodies, dying people, the nudity of people, or the misery/tragedy of people in line for food and water. Seriously, is this cruelty really necessary to mobilize massive humanitarian action?"

Photojournalists and their editors thought publishing the photos was an essential aspect of covering the news. "At the Herald, and at most publications, I suspect, we try to strike a balance, delivering not only what readers want to see but also what they need to see. We must act with sensitivity but, more importantly, our mission is to create a complete and accurate visual report. In this story in particular, images of death were inescapable. Death was everywhere," says David Walters, the Miami Herald's deputy editor-photos and video. He says the more graphic images made up "only a small portion of what we publish."

Walters works with Patrick Farrell, who won a Pulitzer for his stunningly poignant black-and-white images of the Haitian survivors of Hurricane Ike and other storms in 2008. Farrell once again was dispatched to Port-au-Prince right after the earthquake to document fresh heartache. "I thought [the quake] was the worst thing I'd ever seen. I was thinking if it gets worse than this, it's the end of the world," he says. "You can't tune it out; until you're looking at your pictures on the computer, you're thinking this is a movie, it isn't real."

And he adds emphatically, the Haitian photographs are essential. "I'd say there were not enough images of Haiti; I would say you can never have enough," Farrell says. "People need to know that the suffering continues; they're suffering just living a normal life. They get slammed with four storms, and now this. It's cruel and unlucky."

From the Miami Herald to the Palm Beach Post, the Birmingham News to the San Jose Mercury News, the Los Angeles Times to the Lincoln Journal Star, the New York Times and more, the verdict was the same. Unvarnished stories and images of Haiti's horrific loss and the rare, miraculous rescue of victims dominated A sections and front page real estate for several days—in some cases, a week to 10 days and more. Many journalistic boundaries were crossed on television. CNN's Sanjay Gupta, a neurosurgeon, was photographed performing brain surgery on an injured Haitian girl; Anderson Cooper of the same network interrupted his on-the-scene newscast to sweep up a boy in the midst of a violent looting incident. Other newscasters were filmed giving water to the trapped and weeping.

The more images of unimaginable suffering were published, the more international aid poured in.

Photo coverage of the quake touched off an intense debate about the role of the explicit photo—the iconic, bloody shot—in a media world of surprisingly delicate sensibilities. Did news outlets publish images that were too graphic, and too many of them? And what of stark depictions of other disasters, natural or man-made? Or U.S. military casualties? What about victims of terrorism or crimes of passion? Should all of them get the same treatment?

Readers and newspaper ombudsmen in January engaged in spirited exchanges about whether the media had gone too far. And if the public was surprised by the tone and volume of the photography, that shouldn't come as a shock. Because in recent years, for a variety of reasons, powerful, iconic images of national and international events have been harder to find in many American newspapers.

Many dailies have taken a hyperlocal approach to news coverage. News managers say that rather than publish national and international news that is widely available on the Internet, news organizations should heavily emphasize material that they are best suited to dominate: local news. Generally, newspapers with heavily local orientations avoid large-format foreign news photos and packages on their front pages and inside their A sections.

Another factor: Editors, troubled by sinking circulations, are wary of alienating their remaining readers by publishing images they may find troubling. In particular, many news outlets are reluctant to spotlight photos of dead or wounded U.S. troops or foreign civilian casualties.

Yet that doesn't mean compelling photography isn't widely available. News organizations publish powerful photographs by professional photojournalists and citizen journalists alike on their websites. The computer is considered a more private viewing arena than the newspaper. Online images may be edgier and more graphic than what appears in print, and they are viewed by millions of people who flock to photo galleries and slide shows.

"The Internet has become the saving grace of photojournalism," says Donald Winslow, editor of News Photographer magazine, a monthly publication of the National Press Photographers Association. "What you see in the daily newspaper today is the lowest common denominator of what a photographer is willing to print."

Tim Rasmussen, assistant managing editor for photography at the Denver Post, says the unlimited space online has greatly deepened photojournalism's ability to tell the story. "We put far more compelling, important news photos for the U.S. and the world on our website now than we ever put in the newspaper," he says. "We've built a good online audience for our photography with high-end photo blogs and galleries. . . . There is more emphasis online on national and international news than in the newspaper."

Despite the abundance of material on the Web, the timidity of many news organizations is a source of concern for some journalists. "The truth is that there is a lot of visual censorship that goes on," Washington Post picture editor Bonnie Jo Mount was quoted as saying in a column by Post Ombudsman Andrew Alexander. "We're in a culture that censors visuals very heavily. I think that sometimes works to our detriment because we don't run visuals that people need to see."

Haiti, though, was an exception. The country's rich culture and frequent natural disasters have spurred graphic coverage before—particularly photos of naked children who had been killed during the tropical storms of 2008. "In the past I've objected to this graphic coverage, particularly in regards to children," says Leonie Hermantin, a deputy director of Lambi Fund of Haiti, a Washington D.C.-based nonprofit that focuses on Haiti's economic development. "But the earthquake was of such apocalyptic, horrible dimensions that, in this case, it's OK to show what those who remain alive have to deal with. This is what children are seeing on a daily basis. The images afford an opportunity to be there vicariously, and at that level I do not object."

But, she adds, some images did go too far and showed no respect for the dead. "There has always been a sense among photographers that everything goes in Haiti," she says. "You can take whatever shot you want, because the people are poor and the government never reacts with outrage when these images are displayed." Hermantin does not fault the photojournalists, though. The news and photo editors who decide what gets published "should think they are not dealing with animals, but with people who care very much about dying with dignity. People from Haiti want to be buried clothed."

Hermantin and Farrell agree that Haiti's nightmare was beyond anyone's imagining. "You could write a million times that there are 100,000 people dead in the streets," Farrell says. "But if you don't see it for yourself, or in pictures, you won't believe it. It just won't register."

But it did register. It registered with billions, and for some the light it cast on the country and its multiple catastrophes was unnatural. Payen-Jean Baptiste, the Haitian elementary school principal who was trapped with her husband and two small daughters in a car during the earthquake, says she and her extended family needed no more graphic reminders of falling buildings or crushed bodies. "We lived through it," she says. "I have nightmares, and I am fighting these images. I just can't imagine what this is like for my two little girls, who are also dealing with nightmares. Two or three days after the quake, my four-year-old fell down because she was running, and she started crying nervously, thinking that she will die. So I can't understand the purpose of publishing such pictures or watching such horrifying things on TV for entertainment."

Payen-Jean Baptiste doubts that media coverage of the disaster will provide any more than a temporary Band-Aid. "As for helping Haiti," she says, "Haiti has been 'helped' by nations for 25 years. . . . The country is becoming poorer and poorer all the time. Thanks to the media, who will be motivated to go to Haiti in the next decade after seeing how 'ugly,' 'poor' or 'insecure' it can be?"

Many American news consumers wondered the same thing. Christa Robbins of Chicago wrote a letter to the New York Times protesting the graphic images of corpses and destruction published by the paper. The letter was quoted in a column by Times Public Editor Clark Hoyt. Robbins wrote, "I feel that the people who have suffered the most are being spectacularized by your blood-and-gore photographs, which do not at all inform me of the relief efforts, the political stability of the region or the extent of damage to families or infrastructure."

Robbins and other readers suggested that Haiti was considered fair game because it was *other*—black, poor and foreign. "If this had happened in California, I cannot imagine a similar depiction of half-clothed bodies splayed out for the camera," Robbins wrote. "What are you thinking?" A Washington Post reader wrote to Ombudsman Alexander: "I wonder if the editors of the Washington Post would run pictures of charred smoldering bodies or of a young girl crushed to death if those bodies had been of a 12-year-old girl from Chevy Chase or a 45-year-old father of three from Cleveland Park," referring to two largely white, well-off local communities.

At the same time, some readers defended the use of graphic images. One of them, Mary Louise Thomas of Palatka, Florida, wrote to Hoyt that a photo of a dead baby lying on her dead mother impelled her to cry for an hour. "But run from it? Never," Hoyt quoting her as saying. She added that those repelled by such images "should really try staring truth in the face occasionally and try to understand it."

While Alexander and Hoyt defended their papers' Haitian imagery, arguing it underscored the gravity and urgency of the situation, both also acknowledged that there are multiple standards for choosing photographs. One standard—proximity to readership—prevents most newspapers from publishing pictures of dead bodies with local stories because of the "likelihood that readers may be connected to the deceased," Alexander wrote.

The sheer magnitude of a disaster also influences editors' willingness to publish images of pain, according to Hoyt. During the 2004 Indian Ocean tsunami, for example, "The Times ran a dramatic front-page photo of a woman overcome with grief amid rows of dead children, including her own," he wrote. Though some readers protested, Hoyt continued, "the newspaper's first public editor, Daniel Okrent, concluded the paper was right to publish the picture. It told the story of the tsunami, he said."

National newspapers like the Times, however, do not have the same strictures as many local and regional dailies, which readily invoke reader demographics to help winnow out certain disturbing images. "It's weird what offends people, what actually bothers people over breakfast," says Torry Bruno, associate managing editor for photography at the Chicago Tribune. At his newspaper, he says, decisions about graphic photos depend on the circumstances: "In each case, we have long, thoughtful conversations about whether or not publishing is the right thing to do," he says. After the quake, for example, "We published an image of an arm coming out of some rubble with a weeping person behind it," Bruno recalls. It was a decision that Tribune editors felt was warranted, given the depth of the catastrophe.

Haiti aside, there is widespread agreement among those who practice and monitor photojournalism that America's newsrooms have become far more cautious when it comes to choosing photographs. "The kind of enlightened editor I used to have at the Palm Beach Post doesn't exist anymore," says Winslow, the NPPA photojournalist. News editors "today don't want to offend readers, and they don't want to piss people off, and they don't want to take the phone calls [from irate readers] the next day."

Kenny Irby, visual journalism group leader and director of diversity at the Poynter Institute, says the shift in newspaper photojournalism is a byproduct of economic flux. "There is a declining commitment to quality photojournalism today in mainstream media," he says. "But it's not part of a sinister plan. It's the reality of an industry . . . where print publications are all struggling. Photography is an expensive endeavor; it costs to deploy and support photographers in remote locations."

Another factor: "There is less training and less of the intellectual photo editor thinking about the assignment," says Michel du Cille, the Washington Post's director of photo/multimedia/video. At some, though not all, newspapers, he continues, "the editors are going for the gimmicky photograph over a storytelling photograph. Yes, that's happening around the country, and we are fighting it in the newsroom."

The transformation of American photojournalism didn't happen overnight. "I started to see the change in photo editing after I retired in 1990," says James Atherton, a former Washington Post photographer who took many iconic photographs of U.S. and world leaders, from President Truman to Martin Luther King Jr. to Pope John Paul II to Jimmy Carter. "Newspaper photos are less high quality than they used to be because they're [mostly] feature pictures, not breaking news pictures," he says.

Moreover, Atherton says, the U.S. military has often handcuffed the press by restricting access to citizen casualties in foreign wars in which U.S. troops are involved. An exception: an April 29, 2008, Associated Press photo of the death of a 2-year-old Iraqi child, Ali Hussein, who died in Baghdad during a U.S. bombing raid. The image of a suffocated child appeared on the front page of the Washington Post. Although the photograph was beautifully framed and shot—a potential icon—a survey of U.S. newspapers suggests that Ali Hussein's image was rarely used. The photograph, on the other hand, was commonly distributed and published in foreign media.

"It's taken a long time for us to suddenly realize that when we lose soldiers over there that civilians are dying too," Atherton says. "Civilians should be counted."

But even if news organizations wanted to publish such pictures, it's become increasingly difficult for their journalists to get access to them. During Vietnam, for example, "U.S. photojournalists had virtual carte blanche to photograph whatever they wanted," Winslow says. Journalist Malcolm Browne recorded the Buddhist monk Thich Quang Duc setting himself on fire on a Saigon street in 1963 to protest the corruption in the Diem regime. The image ended up on the front page of the Washington Post.

Photographer Eddie Adams produced the chilling, split-second capture of Gen. Nguyen Ngoc Loan executing a suspected Viet Cong prisoner in 1968. These images, along with Nick Ut's iconic 1972 photo of a young South Vietnamese girl fleeing after a napalm attack, were published and helped change the course of the war.

But the U.S. military altered rules of journalistic access after Vietnam. "The first [Persian] Gulf War had 100 percent photographic censorship; the military kept you on boats," Winslow recalls. "Then the military came up with the idea of 'embedding' in Iraq." Today, journalists who embed with U.S. troops in Afghanistan or Iraq are governed by military regulation limiting where they can go.

U.S. photojournalists went to Haiti to document the enormity of the battered island nation's misery.

For Haitian citizens who wanted their privacy respected, and who seek a long-term international commitment rather than charity, the graphic photography may have a tarnishing effect. "People in Haiti are strong," Payen-Jean Baptiste says. "There are people [here] fighting alone to recover and try to get back on their feet. They are used to dealing with such unfairness. But if there is a way we can stop humiliating them by taking away their dignity while they are suffering, that would be the best help forever we can bring to this nation."

The Miami Herald's Walters sees a broader issue. "Some people, both readers and journalists, find some of the images from Haiti to be gut-wrenching and undignified. These graphic, hard-hitting photos always spawn debate in our newsroom . . . careful debate. But the fact remains that the devastation in Haiti is gut-wrenching and in many instances, tragic circumstances *have* stripped away the dignity of victims who were so mercilessly affected by this disaster. That part of the story must be acknowledged in both words and pictures or the story is incomplete."

Critical Thinking

1. How would you define *ethical practice* in publishing graphic photographs of death? Where is the line between *graphic* and *too graphic?*

2. Should the rules differ online vs. on television?

ARIELLE EMMETT, a former Temple University journalism professor, is studying for a PhD at the Philip Merrill College of Journalism at the University of Maryland. She wrote about journalism and social networking in AJR's December 2008/January 2009 issue.

A Porous Wall

As news organizations, in their struggle to survive, blur the line between editorial and advertising, does credibility take a hit?

Natalie Pompilio

The latest fissure in the wall between editorial and advertising came in April, when the Los Angeles Times ran a front-page advertisement that could easily have been confused for an actual news article. Placed prominently in the left-hand column below the fold, an ad for the police drama "Southland" carried NBC's peacock logo and was labeled "advertisement," but it was written in story form as if a reporter had accompanied the police officer who is the show's main character on a ride-along.

Many in the Times' newsroom balked, including Editor Russ Stanton. A circulated petition decried the ad as deceptive and said it made "a mockery of our integrity and our journalistic standards."

The newspaper's publisher responded that the ad netted a premium rate and was part of the effort to ensure the survival of his publication, which has cut hundreds of jobs in the last year and whose parent company, Tribune Co., has filed for bankruptcy.

Is this a sign of things to come or simply a misstep as newspapers seek to redefine themselves as economically viable?

"There's so much economic pressure, it seems everything is on the table," says Andy Schotz, chairman of the Society of Professional Journalists' ethics committee and a general assignment reporter for the Herald-Mail in Hagerstown, Maryland. But "we have to be vigilant about maintaining the integrity of the news side. A struggling economy is not a reason to loosen the standards."

There was a time when advertisements on the front page of a newspaper were anathema, when the separation between marketing and editorial was as vigorously defended as the separation between church and state. "We were all so pristine," recalls Geneva Overholser, director of the School of Journalism at the USC Annenberg School for Communication and former editor of the Des Moines Register. The attitude, she says, was "no one from advertising should ever darken the newsroom."

Those days seem to be gone, as remote as newsrooms thick with cigarette smoke and loud with the clatter of typewriter keys. Even Overholser says, "I long ago gave up the idea of front-page ads as sin."

Front-page and section-front advertisements are more common, with even the most respected publications putting prime news real estate up for sale (see "No Longer Taboo," June/July 2007). Sponsored content, online and in print, is growing. Advertisers are crossing lines with their marketing techniques, packaging selling points as news to increase their product's credibility while possibly hurting journalists'.

While many experts agree the beleaguered news industry has to change its ways in order to survive, the question is how to do so while maintaining credibility and standards.

"Now, when newspapers are desperately trying to figure out what their future is, it's time to figure out what the principles are," Overholser says. "The rule is you don't try to deceive or fool readers. That's deeply offensive and breaks the bond with readers. That's not about the wall breaking down. That's about principles. It's about credibility."

Bob Steele, the Poynter Institute's Nelson Poynter Scholar for Journalism Values, says the idea of a solid Berlin Wall-type structure between advertising and editorial is outdated. He's long seen it as more of a picket fence: Each side has clearly delineated roles and principles, but "you can talk over the picket fence. If there's a gate, you can go back and forth," he says.

Skip Foster, former editor and now publisher of the Star in Shelby, North Carolina, says a different game is afoot when marketing and advertising decisions directly affect the number of newsroom bodies left to cover the news. While the L.A. Times ad may have stirred up a controversy, he says, at least it took a chance with something new.

"If we're not goofing up occasionally, we're probably not testing that line as we should," he says. If "we don't start trying some crazy things and [won't] be willing to fail and look stupid, I don't think we're going to make it."

He believes it's time to question those who simply want to maintain the status quo when talk comes to the dividing line between news and ads: "Did we have the line in the right place in the first place?" he asks. "How movable is that line? Is the line in a different place online and a different place in print?"

This is not the first time print organizations have made short-term news decisions that may not be in the long-term interest of the publication, he says. Some papers, his included, used to mock the old TV adage "If it bleeds, it leads." Now he finds his front page playing to the idea. "And not feeling bad about it, either. If it's what people want and we can benefit from it, there aren't many win-wins out there," he says. "Having a long-term view is a lot harder when you don't know what the long term's going to be or if the long term includes your presence as a news organization."

The Star hasn't dabbled in much front-page advertising—"we're probably holding out for too high a price," Foster says—but he's willing to consider it. The "right" advertisements will be clearly labeled with some design oversight so it's not messing up the page, but otherwise it's "'you know it when you see it' type stuff," he says.

"If somebody comes to us willing to pay the premium rate to do something that doesn't fit into my initial set of standards, I'll listen," he says. "We're not going to do anything that's masquerading as news, but the rest is gray."

The bottom line is not to deceive: One newspaper publisher, who didn't want to be quoted by name, so as not to alienate his marketing department, described how one major local business not only wanted to sponsor a column related to its industry but also have one of its own writers produce it. Why not, the business argued, as another nearby newspaper is already doing the same thing? The publisher declined the column—and the ad revenue.

Kelly McBride, ethics group leader at Poynter, says she constantly gets questions on this issue. "Every major metro market is debuting new products meant to generate more revenue, and there's questions about all of it," she says.

She's written about one TV station that put a fast-food company's cup in prominent places on its anchors' desks during newscasts, and she participated in a panel discussion with bloggers whose independence was marred by the many handouts they received. She recently took a call from someone who knew of a newspaper that has a nightlife column that is editorially driven in print but is an advertisement online.

> ## "It's going to become increasingly murky what is independent journalistic judgment and what is influenced by an advertiser with an ulterior motive."
>
> —Kelly McBride

"I see the business imperative to find new sources of revenue and new ways to make money. What worries me is the cost to credibility," she says. "You can't tell me that people are not confused. I believe the audience is savvy, but I also believe the more things we throw at them, the more confusing it gets. The ultimate result of all of this is in the audience's mind. It's

going to become increasingly murky what is independent journalistic judgment and what is influenced by an advertiser with an ulterior motive."

More than one person interviewed for this article noted the growing number of advertisements packaged as news copy and wondered if publications should accept them. Weekend newspaper inserts have featured an advertisement for the so-called "Amish fireplace," an electric heater. The full-page ad is designed to look like a news story, complete with bold headline, subheads, photos and a byline. The word "ADVERTISEMENT" appears in small print at the center of the top of the page.

SPJ's Schotz notes that ad designers will "push as far as they can" unless pushed back. In one case, a reader called Schotz's newsroom about an ad, wondering if reporters knew whether its claims were true. "I put him in touch with our advertising department," Schotz says. "We're used to how a newspaper is put together and what is what, but many people aren't necessarily as sophisticated."

At his own newspaper in Hagerstown, Schotz dislikes the placement of so-called "sticky ads"—the removable promo stickers that are now appearing on front pages. When, after a long illness, a local politician died, his name was stripped across the front—but the sticky ad was stuck over the all-important verb in the headline—"DIES".

"You can't have two pieces of information in the same physical spot," Schotz says. "You can't have a news headline and an ad and expect they won't interfere with each other."

Sponsored content is another vexing issue facing journalists in the 21st century. For the last two years, Citizens Bank has sponsored a column in the Philadelphia Inquirer. The bank's trademark green outlines the column and its logo appears prominently on the front page of the business section. The column is written by veteran business reporter Mike Armstrong.

Inquirer Editor William K. Marimow says the sponsorship brings in "a significant amount of revenue" but his only real complaint about the advertising element of it is that it takes away from the newshole.

"It's probably symbolically annoying to some of us, but in my view it has no effect on what Mike Armstrong writes or doesn't write," Marimow says. "When Citizens Bank does something great, we're going to report it, and if they do something awful, we're going to report it."

Could other columns receive sponsorship? "As long as something does not intrude with the news, it's something I'll consider," Marimow says.

Armstrong says that while it may sometimes be awkward—"who else has a column that has an ad wrapped around it in this country?"—the sponsorship has no effect on what he writes. He still addresses banking issues, as do other reporters in the business section. In some ways, he says, the choice of sponsor may have made the project easier on him: Citizens Bank is owned by the Royal Bank of Scotland and doesn't make much news in Philadelphia.

"If they were a bailout bank, it would be a little uncomfortable," Armstrong says, "but I would need to be writing about it."

He doesn't even notice the ad anymore. "It's like wallpaper," he says. But readers notice it, and sometimes they are confused. "I've gotten calls from readers asking for the name of the branch manager in their neighborhoods," he says. "I say, 'I don't work for the bank.'"

In some ways, allowing the bank to put its logo on the business page is simply a placement issue, similar to the way a clothing store might ask that its ad go in the features section or a law firm might want its ad near the legal notices, says Robert Niles, editor of Online Journalism Review and a blogger for Knight Digital Media Center.

"If a sponsor wants to say, 'I want my ad to appear every day on page A2,' and it runs opposite someone else's column, we've given them placement," Niles says. "It's only a baby step to say, 'This column is presented by.' It's not 'produced by.' It's not 'created by.' It's just 'sponsored by.'"

> "For the advertiser, control of the day-to-day coverage isn't as important as there being coverage of the thing that is important to them."
>
> —Robert Niles

When Niles worked at the Rocky Mountain News, the online weather page was sponsored by the outdoor gear company REI. There's little doubt that REI wasn't able to control what temperatures were reported. "For the advertiser, control of the day-to-day coverage isn't as important as there being coverage of the thing that is important to them," Niles says. "They're smart enough to know that if they control the everyday coverage, the public will know and ignore it. It's no good to publish something that nobody reads."

Dallas Mavericks owner Mark Cuban said as much last year in a post on blogmaverick.com. In the December missive, Cuban proposed creating a "beat writer cooperative." Funded by major sports leagues, the cooperative would employ at least two writers in each sports market. The owners would benefit with increased, in-depth coverage of their teams. The newspapers would benefit because the writers would answer only to the editors they were writing for.

In an e-mail interview with AJR, Cuban explained that control of content wasn't what mattered.

"Newspaper coverage helps build awareness and commitment to a team. Whether it's positive or negative," he wrote. "The suggestion that there is a theme of control means that you believe that there cannot be any trust or contractual agreement between media and teams. That is just not the case. It would be incredibly easy to do a document of understanding saying, 'you write what you want to write. We won't have any say in the matter. Even if we get mad at you over what you wrote, we won't interfere. On the flip side, since we are contributing financially to your survival and hoped for success, we expect that you cover the team at minimum, on a daily basis during our season, and at least x times per week in the off season.'"

Such an agreement could improve sports coverage, according to Cuban.

Reporters and columnists in today's climate are so worried about keeping their jobs that they might hold back negative coverage so as not to affect their access to their teams. A cooperative would "provide some level of stability to the business of sports reporting [and] it could actually open the door for better reporting. Regardless of whether that coverage is positive or negative," Cuban wrote.

> "Either you trust your reporters to do their job and for editors and publishers to attempt to be impartial in the stories they choose, regardless of pressure from any outside source, or you don't."
>
> —Mark Cuban

"Either you trust your reporters to do their job and for editors and publishers to attempt to be impartial in the stories they choose, regardless of pressure from any outside source," he concluded, "or you don't."

Given all the entanglements, transparency may be the best way for news organizations to stay credible. "Anything that is sponsored by anything needs to be clearly labeled," Overholser says. "To me, transparency is the last strong ethic standing."

Readers have to know an organization's ethics policies—and be reminded of them again and again and again. McBride says that if she were editor of the Inquirer, for example, she might end each Citizens Bank-sponsored column with a tagline like, "Our standards for editorial independence can be found here," with an accompanying link.

"Full disclosure is a bare minimum," McBride says. "You also need to write policy and best-practices issues for your public and let them comment upon it."

What's worrisome, she says, is the fact that not everyone will hold to the same high standards. And that, she adds, "will undermine everything that we do. Their stink will wash off on us."

Fred Brown, a former SPJ president and vice chair of the organization's ethics committee, believes one of the mistakes the L.A. Times made with its front-page ad was not discussing the placement with everyone involved and invested in the product's credibility.

"If you're going to have standards that apply to your particular media outlet, everyone should have a say in what those standards are," Brown says. "That discussion needs to happen in the newsroom. Let the marketers in on the discussion, too. The problem is, reporters don't understand the marketing side, and the marketers don't understand the reporting side. Their goal should be the same, but their methods are different."

Brown recently worked to revise SPJ's ethics handbook. Someone asked about including the L.A. Times case as an example. He didn't think that was such a good idea.

"If you're going to have a good ethics case study, there ought to be two sides to that," he says. "In this case, one side would be, 'We have to survive,' but that's not an ethics question."

Critical Thinking

1. How would you define the rules of *ethical practice* regarding separation of editorial and advertising content and personnel in news media?

2. How do you respond to product placement in news media? Do you notice it? Do you have objections to it? To what degree do you think it affects consumer behavior? Are your thoughts any different regarding product placement in entertainment media?

NATALIE POMPILIO (nataliepompilio@yahoo.com), a former reporter for the Philadelphia Inquirer and New Orleans' Times-Picayune, is a Philadelphia-based writer.

From *American Journalism Review,* June/July 2009, pp. 32–37. Copyright © 2009 by the Philip Merrill College of Journalism at the University of Maryland, College Park, MD 20742-7111. Reprinted with permission.

What Would You Do?

The Journalism That Tweaks Reality, Then Reports What Happens

DANIEL WEISS

On a Friday morning last January, a group of Washington, D.C., commuters played an unwitting role in an experiment. As they emerged from the L'Enfant Plaza metro station, they passed a man playing a violin. Dressed in a long-sleeved T-shirt, baseball cap, and jeans, an open case for donations at his feet, he looked like an ordinary busker. In reality, he was Joshua Bell, an internationally renowned musician. The idea was to gauge whether Bell's virtuosic playing would entice the rushing commuters to stop and listen.

The experiment's mastermind was *Washington Post* staff writer Gene Weingarten, who had dreamed it up after seeing a talented keyboardist be completely ignored as he played outside another metro station. "I bet Yo-Yo Ma himself, if he were in disguise, couldn't get through to these deadheads," Weingarten says he thought at the time. Ma wasn't available to test the hypothesis, but Bell was.

For three-quarters of an hour, Bell played six pieces, including some of the most difficult and celebrated in the classical canon. Of 1,097 passersby, twenty-seven made donations totaling just over $30. Seven stopped for more than a minute. The remaining 1,070 breezed by, barely aware of the supremely talented violinist in their midst.

When Weingarten's account of the experiment ran in the *Post's* magazine three months later, readers followed the narrative with rapt attention that contrasted starkly with the indifference of the commuters. The article was discussed on blogs and other forums devoted to classical music, pop culture, politics, and social science. Weingarten said he received more feedback from readers than he had for any other article he had written in his thirty-five-year career. Many were taken with the chutzpah of disguising Joshua Bell as a mendicant just to see what would happen. Others were shocked that people could ignore a world-class musician. Still others argued that the results were insignificant: rerun the experiment outdoors on a sunny day, they said, and Bell would draw a massive crowd.

I was one of those rapt readers, but I wasn't quite sure what to make of the piece's appeal. Was it just a clever gimmick or was there something more profound going on? At the same time, the story felt familiar. Indeed, Weingarten's experiment was a recent entry in a journalistic genre with deep, quirky roots.

Working on a hunch that begs to be tested or simply struck with an idea for a good story, journalistic "experimenters," for lack of a better term, step out of their customary role as observers and play with reality to see what will happen. At their worst, these experiments are little more than variations on reality-TV operations that traffic in voyeurism and shame. At their best, they manage to deliver discussion-worthy insights into contemporary society and human nature. The very best, perhaps, serve up a bit of both. In any case, the growing number of journalists and news operations who do this sort of thing are heirs to a brand of social psychology practiced from the postwar years through the early seventies. During this period, considered by some the golden age of the discipline, experiments were bold and elaborately designed and frequently produced startling results. Many were conducted outside the laboratory and often placed subjects in stressful or disturbing situations.

These experiments also have roots in forms of investigative, immersion, and stunt journalism that have been practiced for more than a century. In 1887, while working on an exposé of asylum conditions, muckraker Nellie Bly demonstrated that one could feign insanity to gain admission to a madhouse—and when she began to insist that she was in fact perfectly sane, doctors interpreted her claims as delusions. In so doing, Bly anticipated psychologist David Rosenhan's classic 1972 experiment in which "pseudopatients" claiming to hear voices were admitted to psychiatric hospitals and then kept for an average of several weeks despite reverting to sane behavior.

It's difficult to pinpoint when the genre shifted, but by 1974, when New York City's WNBC-TV asked its viewers to call in and pick the perpetrator of a staged purse snatching from a lineup of suspects, the journalistic experiment had attained its modern form. The station was flooded with calls and, after fielding over 2,100, cut the experiment short. The results: respondents picked the correct assailant no more frequently than they would have by guessing.

Over the last decade, as best-sellers such as *The Tipping Point* and *Freakonomics* have lent social science a sheen of counterintuitive hipness and reality television has tapped into a cultural fascination with how people behave in contrived situations, journalistic experimentation has become increasingly common. In addition to *The Washington Post Magazine,* it has been featured in *The New York Times, Harper's,* and *Reader's Digest.* Its most regular home, however, has been on network-television newsmagazines.

ABC'S *Primetime* has staged a series of experiments in recent years under the rubric "What Would You Do?" which enact provocative scenarios while hidden cameras capture the reactions of the public. Chris Whipple, the producer who conceived the series, refers to it as a *"Candid Camera of ethics."* Starting with a nanny verbally abusing a child, the series has gone on to present similar scenarios: an eldercare attendant ruthlessly mocking an old man; a group of adolescents bullying a chubby kid; a man viciously berating his girlfriend, seeming on the verge of violence; etc.

The sequences tend to begin with the narrator pointing out that many pass right by the incident. Several witnesses are confronted and asked to explain why they didn't step in. One man, who gave the fighting couple a long look before continuing on his way, reveals that he is an off-duty cop and says he determined that no laws were being broken, so there was nothing for him to do. The focus shifts to those who did intervene, and the camera lingers over the confrontations, playing up the drama.

These experiments are, in a sense, the flip side of the reality-TV coin: rather than show how people act in manufactured situations when they *know* they're being watched, they show us how people act when they don't. And the experiments have clearly appealed to viewers. From the first minutes of its first hour, when its ratings doubled those of the previous week, "What Would You Do?" has been a success. After appearing periodically in 2005 and 2006, ABC ordered five new hours that were scheduled to air last November before the writers' strike put them on hold. It is, Whipple says, highly "watchable" television.

In the world of print, *Reader's Digest* has come closest to making such experiments a franchise. Over the last two years, the magazine has pitted cities around the world against each other in tests of helpfulness and courtesy, to determine which city is most hospitable. The first round used the following three gauges to separate the rude from the solicitous in thirty-five cities: the percentage of people who picked up papers dropped by an experimenter; the percentage who held the door for experimenters when entering buildings; and the percentage of clerks who said "Thank you" after a sale. When the scores were tallied, it was clear that *Reader's Digest* had hit the counterintuition jackpot: the winner was New York City. According to Simon Hemelryk, an editor with the UK edition of *Reader's Digest* who came up with the idea for the tests, the press response was "totally, totally mad." Hundreds of media outlets picked up the story. David Letterman presented a tongue-in-cheek, top-ten list of the "Signs New York City Is Becoming More Polite."

The notion that New Yorkers are more polite than commonly believed was also at the center of a 2004 experiment conducted by *The New York Times.* Reenacting an experiment originally performed by graduate students of social psychologist Stanley Milgram at the City University of New York in the early seventies, two *Times* reporters asked riders on crowded subway cars to relinquish their seats. Remarkably, thirteen of fifteen did

so. But the reporters found that crossing the unspoken social boundaries of the subway came at a cost: once seated, they grew tense, unable to make eye contact with their fellow passengers. Jennifer Medina, one of the reporters, says that she and Anthony Ramirez, her partner on the story, found the assignment ludicrous at first. "It was like, 'What? Really? You want me to do what?'" she says. "We made so much fun of it while we were doing it, but we got so much feedback. It was one of those stories that people really talked about." And papers around the world took notice: within weeks, reporters in London, Glasgow, Dublin, and Melbourne had repeated the experiment.

In these journalistic experiments, the prank always lurks just beneath the surface and is clearly part of the genre's appeal. During ABC *Primetime's* experiments, there always comes the moment when host John Quiñones enters and, with a soothing voice and congenial smile, ends the ruse. *These people are actors. You have been part of an experiment.* And in that moment, no matter how serious the scenario, there is always the hint of a practical joke revealed, a touch of "Smile, you're on *Candid Camera!"*

Sometimes the experiment is overwhelmed by the prank. Last year, *Radar Magazine* sent a reporter to snort confectioner's sugar in various New York City locales. The idea was to test anecdotal evidence from a *New York Times* article that cocaine use was growing more publicly acceptable. (The results: public snorting was actively discouraged at the New York Public Library's main reading room, but not at a Starbucks or *Vanity Fair* editor Graydon Carter's Waverly Inn.) Carter's own *Spy Magazine* pulled a classic prank/experiment in the late eighties when it sent checks of dwindling value to moguls in an attempt to determine who was the cheapest millionaire. (Donald Trump reportedly cashed one for just thirteen cents.) Even *Borat* was, in a sense, an extended experiment in the extremes to which a Kazakh "journalist" could push pliant Americans, and was anticipated by one of *Primetime's* "What Would You Do?" episodes in which a taxi driver goes off on racist or homophobic rants, baiting riders either to defy him or join in.

If Medina, the *Times* reporter, was made uneasy by the whiff of "stunt" in the subway experiment, she is not the only one. Even Weingarten, whose Joshua Bell experiment was a monumental success, looks at the genre slightly askance. Asked whether he plans to conduct similar experiments in the future, he replies: "If I can think of one this good, there's no reason I'd quail at it. But, you know, you also don't want to go off and be the stunt writer. I would need to feel as though the next thing I'm doing was of equal sociological importance. And this wasn't just a lark. We had something we wanted to examine, and it was the nature of the perception of beauty."

The appeal of the best journalistic experiments, indeed, runs much deeper than their entertainment value. Medina came to see her role in the subway experiment as that of a "street anthropologist or something, which is essentially what [reporters] are supposed to be doing every day." And Weingarten received over one hundred messages from people who said that his piece on the Bell experiment made them cry. (One testimonial from an online chat Weingarten had with readers: "I cried because I find it scary and depressing to think of how obliviously most people go through daily life, even smart and otherwise attentive people. Who knows what beautiful things I've missed by just hurrying along lost in my thoughts?") In essence, many readers imagined themselves as actors in the story. Weingarten set out to chronicle an experiment; he ended up writing a deeply effective profile of his own readers. "What Would You Do?" asks *Primetime*—and that, on some level, is the question that all such journalistic experiments ask. Would you walk by the famous violinist? Would you give up your seat on the subway? Would you protect a woman from an abusive boyfriend?

I n that quirky, postwar "golden age" of the discipline that informs today's journalistic experimenters, researchers captured the public imagination with bold, elaborately choreographed experiments that frequently drove subjects to extreme behavior or confronted them with seemingly life-or-death situations.

Stanley Milgram, the designer of the subway-seat experiment, was one of the most creative social psychologists of that era. His infamous obedience experiment, first performed in 1961, in which subjects were instructed to shock a man in a separate room every time he gave an incorrect answer on a memory test, showed that normal people were capable of great cruelty. Sixty-five percent of the subjects went to the maximum—450 volts—despite the test-taker's cries of pain and pleas to be released due to a heart condition. By the end, the test-taker no longer responded at all, having presumably passed out or died. (In reality, the test-taker was an actor and his protests tape-recorded.) Even more unsettling was Stanford professor Philip Zimbardo's 1971 prison experiment, in which college students randomly assigned to play the role of guards in a mock prison terrorized those playing inmates. Slated to run for two weeks, it was terminated after six days, during which several "prisoners" came close to nervous breakdown.

Given the dramatic nature of these experiments, it's little wonder they've provided such inspiration to journalists. Bill Wasik, an editor at *Harper's,* started the flash mobs trend in 2003 as an homage to Milgram, whom he considers as much performance artist as scientist. Flash mobs were spontaneous gatherings in which participants showed up at a given location for a brief period and did something absurd, such as drop to their knees en masse before a giant Tyrannosaurus Rex at Toys "R" Us. In a piece published in *Harper's,* Wasik explained that he saw the mobs as a Milgram-esque test of hipster conformity. Like a hot new indie band, he hypothesized, the mobs would rapidly gain popularity before being discarded as too mainstream and, ultimately, co-opted by marketers, which is more or less what happened.

Wasik argues that the popular resonance of experiments by Milgram and others of the golden age derives from the compelling narratives they created. "It's like a demonstration whose value is more in the extremes that you can push people to and the extremes of the story that you can get out of what people do or don't do," he says. "Milgram could have done an

authority experiment in which he got people to do all sorts of strange things that didn't seem to be simulating the death of the participant." Many contemporary social psychologists credit researchers from this fertile era with cleverly demonstrating how frequently human behavior defies expectations. But others, such as Joachim Krueger of Brown University, argue that the experiments were designed in ways that guaranteed unflattering results. "You could call it a 'gotcha psychology,'" he says.

Due in part to the rise of ethical concerns, contemporary social psychologists rarely do experiments that take place outside the laboratory or that involve deception or stressful situations. This has left journalistic experimenters as a sort of lost tribe of devotees of the golden-age social psychologists. Unlike investigative journalism, these experiments have largely flown under the ethical radar. This may be because of the fact that, while some journalistic experiments may be frivolous, they are on balance innocuous. However, as experimenters increasingly tackle sensitive topics, they have begun to draw some heat. In 2006, conservative bloggers accused *Dateline* of trying to manufacture a racist incident by bringing a group of Arab-looking men to a NASCAR race. And, last November, these same bloggers ripped an experiment by *Primetime* in which same-sex couples engaged in public displays of affection in Birmingham, Alabama, for attempting to provoke homophobic reactions. (As of press time, the same-sex segment had not yet aired, but according to the Fox affiliate in Birmingham, which broke the story, Birmingham police received several complaints from people disgusted by the sight of two men kissing in public.)

But what of the oft-cited "rule" that journalists should report the news rather than make it? Michael Kinsley, who conducted a 1985 experiment while at *The New Republic* to determine whether the Washington, D.C., elite actually read the books they act like they have, rejects the premise. "If you've got no other way to get a good story," he says, "and you're not being dishonest in what you write and publish, what's wrong with it?" Kinsley's experiment involved slipping notes deep into fashionable political books at several D.C. bookstores, offering $5 to anyone who called an intern at the magazine. In five months, not a single person claimed the reward.

J ournalistic experiments have been criticized far more consistently for their scientific, rather than ethical, shortcomings. Robert Cialdini, an Arizona State University social psychologist, believes strongly in the value of communicating psychological insights via the media, but he has found that journalists don't always value the same material that he does. For a 1997 *Dateline* segment on conformity, he conducted an experiment showing that the number of people who donated to a New York City subway musician multiplied eightfold when others donated before them. A fascinating result, but even more fascinating to Cialdini was that people explained their donations by saying that they liked the song, they had some spare change, or they felt sorry for the musician. These explanations did not end up in the finished program. "To me, that was the most interesting thing, the fact that people are susceptible to these social cues but don't recognize it," says Cialdini. "I think that's my bone to pick with journalists—they're frequently interested in the phenomenon rather than the cause of the phenomenon."

Others are frustrated by the premium journalists place on appealing to a mass audience. Duncan Watts, a Columbia University sociologist, designed an experiment for *Primetime* to test Milgram's small-world theory—commonly known as "six degrees of separation"—that people divided by great social or geographical distance are actually connected by a relatively small number of links. In the experiment, two white Manhattan residents competed to connect with a black boxer from the Bedford-Stuyvesant neighborhood of Brooklyn using the fewest links, then the boxer had to connect with a Broadway dancer. All three connections were made using at most six links. Watts says that after the segment aired in late 2006, he received an e-mail from its producer, Thomas Berman, saying that its ratings had been poor. (An ABC spokeswoman insists that the network was satisfied with the ratings.) "One of the limitations of this model is that it's crowd-driven, it's about entertainment," says Watts. "It's a bit of a Faustian bargain."

Another quibble that some social psychologists have with these journalistic experiments is the use of the word "experiment" to describe them in the first place. To a dyed-in-the-wool researcher, an experiment involves comparing a control group with an experimental one, in which a single condition has been varied so that any changes in the outcome can be clearly attributed. Practically no journalistic "experiment" meets this standard, but many golden-age experiments didn't either, strictly speaking. In addition, practically every journalistic experiment includes a disclaimer that its results are decidedly unscientific.

Wendell Jamieson, city editor at *The New York Times* who assigned the subway-experiment story, chafes at calling the exercise an "experiment," pointing out that it was conducted in connection with another article about the original experiment. "It's just a fun way to take a different approach to a story," Jamieson says, comparing it to when he was at the New York *Daily News* and sent a reporter to Yankee Stadium during a subway series dressed in Mets regalia. "It's tabloid trick two-hundred and fifty-two." Bill Wasik, the *Harper's* editor who started flash mobs, points out that using the word "experiment" is a way for journalists to appropriate the "alpha position" of science, lending their endeavors a sort of added legitimacy. "The piece is wearing a lab coat," Wasik says of his own article, which repeatedly describes flash mobs as an experiment, "but it's not entirely scientific by any means."

Perhaps no media outlet has tried harder to achieve uniformity in conducting its experiments than *Reader's Digest*. Detailed instructions for how to conduct its "studies" are distributed to researchers in more than thirty cities around the world to ensure that their results will be comparable. For the courtesy tests, researchers were told how long dropped papers were to be left on the ground, how far to walk behind people entering buildings to see whether they would hold the door, and what sort of demeanor to adopt when speaking with clerks who were being tested to see whether they would say "Thank you." Nonetheless, despite all the careful planning, New York City's courtesy title may need to be affixed with an asterisk. Robert Levine, a social psychologist at California State University, Fresno, did a series of helpfulness experiments in the early nineties in which New York City placed dead last out of thirty-six United States cities. While this doesn't necessarily contradict the *Reader's Digest* result, in which New York was the only U.S. city tested among a global selection of cities, Levine points out that all the *Reader's Digest* New York tests were carried out at Starbucks, yielding a potentially skewed sample. What if Starbucks employees and customers are simply more courteous than New Yorkers as a whole? "I'm not saying they screwed up," says Levine, "but that was certainly a flag that was raised for me."

So maybe journalists can and should be more careful in how they design experiments, but that debate, in many ways, is beside the point. The best examples of the genre are undeniably good journalism, and the lesser lights, for the most part, amount to innocuous entertainment. Indeed, my hope is that some enterprising reporter is even now hatching a plan to find out whether Joshua Bell really would draw such a big crowd outdoors on a sunny day in D.C.

Critical Thinking

1. What's the difference between ABC's "What Would You Do?" story set-ups and social psychology studies by Stanley Milgram and Philip Zimbardo?

2. How would you define *ethical practice* for mass media regarding journalistic "experimenters"?

DANIEL WEISS is a freelance writer based in New York City.

The Lives of Others
What Does It Mean to 'Tell Someone's Story'?

JULIA DAHL

On March 22, *America's Most Wanted* told my story. I wasn't the fugitive, or the victim, and it shouldn't have been my story. It should have been Tyeisha's. But as the producer from *AMW* told me, "Girls die in ditches every day. The reason Tyeisha stands out is because she was profiled in *Seventeen* magazine." I met Tyeisha Martin at a Red Cross shelter in Henry County, Georgia, on a sunny September afternoon in 2005. She was barefoot, wearing a tank top and Capri jeans, waiting in line to get a tetanus shot. I was living in a small town nearby called McDonough, south of Atlanta. I'd moved there a year earlier from New York City with my boyfriend. We were both writers, still thinking we might be able to publish the novels we'd written in grad school. I knew I wanted to write for a living, but I'd left my job at a women's magazine certain I'd never go back. I didn't like what I'd been able to write in that world. Every time I put together an article, it felt like I was building a little lie. Whether it was culled from quotes e-mailed through a publicist, like the cover story I did on the movie star; or built upon crude stereotypes, like the "profile" of the three beauty queens who lived together in Trump Place; or the time I followed the rules of a dating book and neatly concluded that it's better to just be yourself if you want to meet a guy. My instincts as a writer were nowhere in these stories. They weren't little windows on the human condition, they didn't wrestle with questions about the world; they passed the time on the Stair-Master, at the dentist, by the pool.

I justified it plenty. I told myself that Joan Didion had started at *Vogue*. I told myself it meant something that I could make it in the glossies. That I was successful. The problem was that I didn't feel successful. I decamped to Georgia, in part, to get some perspective on all this. But still, I wanted to write. So when *Seventeen* called and asked me to do a story for its Drama section about a young girl in Tennessee who'd been drugged and raped by her cousin, I said yes. Hell, yes. I did stories like this for two years. I went to Birmingham, Alabama, to learn about twelve-year-old Jasmine Archie, who died, according to police reports, after her mother poured bleach down her throat and sat on her chest until she stopped breathing. I went to Wythe County, Virginia, and knocked on the door of the home where fourteen-year-old Nakisha Waddell had stabbed her mother forty-three times and buried her in the backyard. I wrote about two teenage lesbians who murdered one's grandparents in Fayette County, Georgia. The stories were still formulaic, but instead of chasing publicists and trailing beauty queens, I got to read trial transcripts, track down family members, and hang out in county jails. Each story was an adventure, and, at least initially, the reporting felt like the kind of work I imagined a "journalist" would do.

Tyeisha was an accident. I was in Virginia reporting Nakisha's story when Hurricane Katrina hit, and my editor called to ask if I knew anybody in New Orleans. They wanted to profile a teenage evacuee. I said I might know someone—a girl I knew from the local coffee shop had been headed to Tulane—but I'd have to get back to her.

I promptly forgot about it. There was no easy way to find this girl, since I didn't even know her last name, and I was tired from the reporting trip. Sitting for hours with Nakisha's grandmother had been mentally exhausting. This was the second Drama piece I'd done, and I knew what *Seventeen* wanted was brief and uncomplicated. I wouldn't be able to tell how the old woman's hands shook, or how cigarette smoke was stitched into every fiber in her trailer. Or that hanging in the back hallway where Nakisha stuck a knife in her mother's throat was a plaque that read: "This house shall serve the Lord."

When I got home, I needed to get out of myself, so I went to the Red Cross shelter at the local church where my boyfriend's mom, a nurse, was helping tend to the hundreds of suddenly homeless people from New Orleans. That's when I saw Tyeisha, standing in the middle of a group of boys. Tall, bored, beautiful. I remembered the editor from *Seventeen* and I approached her. She agreed to be profiled. Over the next several days, as she waited for FEMA money in a Days Inn near Atlanta and tried to decide where to go next, Tyeisha told me about her life. She'd dropped out of school in the ninth grade and had a baby at seventeen (she was nineteen when we met). When Katrina hit, she had a GED, a job at a linen factory, and though she and her daughter, Daneisha, were living at her mother's house, Tyeisha dreamed of getting her own place.

On the evening of August 28, 2005, when residents were bracing for the storm, Tyeisha took her daughter to the little girl's father's apartment; he lived on the third floor and she thought two-year-old Daneisha would be safer there. Tyeisha spent the night with her sister, Quiana, and Quiana's boyfriend, Chuck. Before dawn, the water broke down their front door. Tyeisha was terrified as the water rose; she couldn't swim, and thought she was about to die. But Chuck and Quiana helped her, and the three of them climbed out a window and found a wooden door to float on. After several hours of paddling through the filthy water, they found a three-story house that had been abandoned, kicked in a window, and spent the night.

The next morning, the three refugees climbed up to the roof, and at the end of the day were lifted to safety by an Army helicopter. After several sweltering days in the gym at the University of New Orleans, they boarded a bus to Atlanta, where Quiana had friends. Through a series of fortunate coincidences, Tyeisha got in touch with her mother, who had Daneisha and was in Dallas. Her on-again, off-again boyfriend was in Texas, too. Tyeisha decided that's where she should be.

On Friday, September 16, 2005, I dropped Tyeisha off at the Atlanta Greyhound station. She bought a ticket to Dallas and set off for the fifteen-hour ride. Six months later, Tyeisha was dead. She was found in a ditch beside a rural road in Fort Bend County, Texas. She'd been shot in the back of the head.

I learned about Tyeisha's death from Quiana, who called me one night in March 2006 and whispered, "Tyeisha's gone." When she hung up, I went to my computer and found an article in the Texas paper: there was a sketch, and though her features were exaggerated, it was clearly Tyeisha. The article said the body they'd found had tattoos: *Daneisha, RIP Larry.* I remembered those tattoos. I'd asked about them as we sat on a bench outside the church. Larry was Tyeisha's father, who had died, she said, about a year before Katrina hit.

I called the number in the paper and asked to speak to the detective in charge. I explained that I hadn't seen or heard from Tyeisha in months, but I told him what I knew: that she'd survived Katrina, and that she'd apparently gone to Texas to be with her mother, daughter, and boyfriend. He asked me to fax him a copy of the article I wrote for *Seventeen.* He said they didn't have many leads. I gave him Quiana's number, and he promised to call me back. I called *Seventeen,* thinking that if the editors would allow me to write about her death, I could finance a trip to Texas. I could help find her killer. The impulse was a combination of personal outrage (I'd never known anyone who'd been murdered), curiosity, and ambition. I knew the victim and already had the family's trust. I began having visions of writing the *In Cold Blood* of the Katrina diaspora. But there was a new editor on the Drama section, and she didn't sound terribly excited about the idea. She said she'd talk to the editor-in-chief and get back to me.

Days passed. My editor called and said they might want to mention Tyeisha's death in the next issue, but that they didn't want a story about it. "It might be too morbid for the readers," she told me. In my three years covering crimes for *Seventeen,* I had written about four female murderers, about stabbings and suffocation and gunshots to the head. The editors I'd worked with talked a lot about what their readers "wanted." Those readers' attention spans were short, apparently, and their eyeballs had to be hijacked with big, red letters and shocking graphics. When my story about Nakisha ran, "She killed her mom" was

splashed in red letters across the first page; pictured below was a hunting knife "similar" to the one she'd used, and opposite was a grainy yearbook snapshot of Nakisha with stab marks Photoshopped all around her. I called to complain. My editor was polite, but said they knew what was needed to grab the readers' attention in this "media-saturated" environment.

Of course, I was as culpable as the editors at *Seventeen.* I did the reporting that revealed nuance and uncertainty, and then did what I was told and turned in simplistic, straightforward stories with immutable lines between cause and effect. So why didn't Tyeisha's unsolved death make the cut? It occurred to me that the story didn't fit the fiction of the magazine. The rigid code that dictated a certain number of pages be given to fashion, celebrities, and make-up also assured that lines didn't get crossed. Tyeisha's story had been one of triumph over tragedy. To have her escape Katrina and six months later be found by a roadside in rural Texas was just too complicated.

But I didn't push. I dashed off pitches to various other publications I thought might be interested in her story: *Texas Monthly,* the *Christian Science Monitor, The New York Times.* No one bit. So I let go. Quiana and I talked every few days, then every couple of weeks. The case went nowhere.

Six weeks later, I got a call from *America's Most Wanted.* Karen Daborowski, a producer, had read about Tyeisha in the *Houston Chronicle* and said they wanted to do a segment on her death. "Maybe we can find her killer," she said. I had not watched *America's Most Wanted* in years. In fact, had you asked me about the show the day before Karen called, I probably would have said it had been pulled by Fox a long time ago. But what I remembered as a mildly creepy combination of *Unsolved Mysteries* and *A Current Affair* had been airing nonstop every Saturday night since 1988. The show was still hosted by a man named John Walsh, who'd been thrust into the spotlight in 1981 when his son, Adam, was kidnapped and murdered. To date, it has helped catch a thousand fugitives.

So I agreed to the interview. But the interview turned into a request to travel with the producers and a crew to Texas. "We want the story to be about you," said Karen. "About your bond with Tyeisha and how you cared enough to find her killer." Calling my fleeting relationship with Tyeisha a bond was a stretch, but in my mind, Karen was asking how much I was willing to do to help Tyeisha. The story of her death deserved to be told, and if I couldn't convince *Seventeen* or any other publication of that, I figured I could get in front of a camera and help someone else tell it. I didn't think about what it meant, journalistically, to become an advocate for someone I'd written about. Having had no formal training in the craft I practiced, I navigated articles and the people involved by my gut, and I felt I owed Tyeisha this much. It also didn't occur to me that I'd become to Karen what Tyeisha had been to me: a subject. Just as I'd asked Tyeisha to relive Katrina beneath a magnolia tree so I could write an article about her for *Seventeen,* Karen was asking me to be a character in her own television report about Tyeisha.

On October 13, 2006, I met Karen and Sedgwick Tourison, another producer, at the American Airlines terminal at Baltimore's BWI. We landed in Dallas around noon and drove to a Whattaburger restaurant near the airport to meet Dave Barsotti and Tom Overstreet, the local camera and audio guys. We all said hello, then Dave dropped a mini-microphone down my blouse, tucked a battery pack into my pants, and told me to get in the driver's seat of the rented Jeep Cherokee. As I drove, Tom aimed his camera at me and Sedg prompted me to talk about what I was doing.

"I'm driving," I said, lamely.

"To . . ." steered Sedg.

"I'm driving to visit Tyeisha's mom, Cabrini, and her daughter Daneisha," I said.

We exited the freeway and made our way into Cabrini's apartment complex. As the crew unloaded the equipment, I wondered how I would greet Cabrini. The woman's daughter had been murdered not six months before, and here I was waltzing in with cameras and lights and four more strangers to poke at her pain. The point, obviously, was to find Tyeisha's killer. I hoped Cabrini knew that. Karen gave the word, and I walked down the outdoor hallway toward Tom, who had his camera positioned on his shoulder, and knocked on the door. Quiana opened it, looking gorgeous, just liked I remembered her. We hugged and I stepped toward Cabrini, who was wearing a T-shirt with a picture of Tyeisha on it. I wasn't sure if I should hug her or shake her hand, but she came toward me with her arms open, and I was glad. The crew flipped on the lights, wired everyone up, and we started talking on-camera, first about Katrina, then about what Cabrini remembered of Tyeisha's arrival in Texas. Tyeisha didn't want to stay in Dallas a day longer than she had to. "She was like, 'Mama, it's all old people around here,'" said Cabrini. So she took Daneisha and left for Houston, where her boyfriend lived. For the first time in her entire life, Tyeisha got her own apartment. Her own furniture. "She was so excited," said Cabrini. "She said, 'Mama, there's no rules. I can wake up when I want.' I said, 'Lord, I wouldn't want to live where there's no rules.'" In February, Tyeisha stopped calling. On March 9, 2006, six months to the day after I met her, her body was found in a grassy ditch at the bend of a county road.

We woke up early the next morning and met downstairs at the hotel for breakfast. Sedg laid out the day's schedule, which began with an hour of them filming me typing on my laptop in my room. Sedg wanted more shots of Quiana and me, so we picked her up and drove to a nearby park. Quiana was six years older than Tyeisha, and more articulate and outgoing. Life hasn't been easy for her. She is twenty-nine, and has four children. She had an emergency hysterectomy just a few months before Katrina hit. The storm washed away her home and separated her from her mother, sister, and children. She settled in Atlanta with her boyfriend, but they broke up. And then her sister was murdered.

When the cameras were ready, we said our lines. I asked her about the last time she talked to her sister, and she said it had been weeks and that she'd begun to worry. We repeated this sequence several times so they could film us from different angles. Quiana didn't seem to mind. I remembered what she said to me months ago, when she called and told me about the murder: "I don't want to see my sister on *Cold Case Files* in five years. I want somebody caught."

After we dropped off Quiana, Sedg and Karen told me they wanted some *Sex and the City* shots of me, so we stopped at an upscale strip mall to do more filming. Trailed by Tom and his camera, I dutifully walked into a boutique and gazed at racks of clothing I couldn't afford. Karen assured me that they needed shots like this to "set me up" as a former New York City magazine writer. They thought it important to play up the "fish out of water" angle: big-city girl gets caught up in a small-town murder. The whole thing was false, and I reminded Karen that I hadn't been on staff at a women's magazine since 2002. But in the language of reality television, three years of my life are boiled down to a shopping trip in order to facilitate a story arc.

That night we flew to Houston, and the next morning we showed up at the Fort Bend County sheriff's station. Inside, Detective Campbell—who Sedg had warned me was "all business"—opened his case file, and pulled out color photographs of the crime scene. There she was: lying in the grass, her skinny legs sticking out from under a yellow tarp. She had on the same blue jeans and belt she was wearing when I met her. The grass around her body was long and lush, green and damp. I wondered if it rained on her while she laid, eyes wide open, in the clover. She was found just a few feet off the road, and according to Campbell, had been shot there. There were minimal wounds other than the fatal bullet wound, which Campbell said suggested that she had been killed by someone she knew. Campbell told us that when he visited her apartment, "it was organized and homey. Like she was focused on raising a child." He showed us birth certificates and FEMA correspondence. She'd kept her papers in a shoebox. "She was doing all the things she should," he said. "She was setting up her future."

The big Texas sky was crowded with clouds in every shade of gray as we drove past fields of cows and ducks, past an old country homestead with a gated family cemetery in the front yard, past Trav's Roadhouse, to the bend in the road where Tyeisha was murdered. A house sat just a few hundred yards away, but Campbell interviewed the people there, and they didn't hear the gunshot. "The TV was probably on," he said. As Tom and Dave set up the shot, I stepped onto the grass, half expecting to feel some sort of ghostly presence. The sun shone through the clouds, but I tried to imagine the road at night. I tried to see her in her last moments. I tried to feel her fear. But I couldn't. All I could do was what I was doing, standing before the cameras to make sure she was not forgotten.

Months went by. And then a year. Occasionally, I would get a phone call from Karen, saying they were planning to air the show soon, but then she'd drop out of contact for a couple of months. At one point, it had apparently been slated to run as part of a special Hurricane Katrina hour in late 2007, but then she told me it was "so strong," they wanted it to anchor another episode. Tyeisha had been dead more than two years when the segment finally aired on March 22, 2008.

I was back in Georgia that weekend, visiting my boyfriend's family. We got take-out BBQ from a local rib shack and gathered in front of the TV. Before each commercial break, they teased my segment: "Coming up: a magazine writer leaves behind the glitzy New York fashion world in a quest for justice." I covered my face as they pasted my voice over clips of Sarah

Jessica Parker adjusting her skirt on the street and cringed at the reenactments. The "Julia" in the segment had a big apartment with leather couches, and the "Tyeisha" was much more conservative than the tattooed girl with messy, maroon-tinted hair extensions I'd met in Georgia. They flashed images of the real Tyeisha on the screen, but my face was the most prominent. The piece even ended with John Walsh giving me a "personal thanks" for being involved.

To me, the compelling story is still Tyeisha's. How, like thousands of her friends and neighbors in New Orleans, she was torn from her support system, separated from the people who looked out for her. She'd tried to rebuild a life for herself and her child in a new state and instead became the victim of a brutal murder. But no one else seemed particularly interested in that story. According to the Centers for Disease Control, homicide is the second leading cause of death for black women between ages fifteen and twenty-four, but even to *America's Most Wanted,* Tyeisha's tale was only worth telling in relation to me.

I suppose I knew that the press tends to illuminate the exceptions, the extremes. The plight of the family with septuplets instead of the more common burden of unexpected twins; the detained immigrant with the amputated penis instead of the thousands with untreated depression. The impulse is understandable, and certainly an oddball story can draw attention to a worthy issue, but what of the issues inside the more common stories? By their very nature, such issues—like mental illness in immigrant communities, or the high murder rate among young black women—are more intransigent, harder to untangle and fit into a facile narrative. I imagine that maybe Jill Leovy, a reporter at the *Los Angeles Times,* was thinking this way when she created The Homicide Report, a blog on the paper's website that attempts to report on every single homicide in Los Angeles County; last year, there were 324. As the explanatory page puts it, "only the most unusual and statistically marginal homicide cases receive press coverage, while those cases at the very eye of the storm—those which best expose the true statistical dimensions of the problem of deadly violence—remain hidden."

It remains to be seen whether my appearance on *America's Most Wanted* will lead to the capture of Tyeisha's killer. Two months after the show aired, there are no promising leads, but I believe I did the right thing, as a human being and as a journalist, when I realize that had I walked out of that Georgia church ten minutes later, or turned left instead of going straight out the door, Tyeisha Martin—not yet twenty years old, mother, sister, daughter, hurricane survivor—would have died not only too soon, but in silence.

Critical Thinking

1. How would you define the rules of *ethical practice* in "drama" pieces that personalize victims of tragedy? Who, besides the subject of a news story, is affected by such judgments?

2. Julia Dahl writes, "I suppose I knew that the press tends to illuminate the exceptions, the extremes." Do you find this to be true? To what effect?

JULIA DAHL is a writer who lives in Brooklyn.

Reprinted from *Columbia Journalism Review,* July/August 2008, pp. 32–36. Copyright © 2008 by Columbia Journalism Review, Columbia University.

UNIT 4

Paying the Bills

Unit Selections

Learning Outcomes

After reading this Unit, you should be able to

- Analyze similarities and differences in how bills are paid and profit is made across different kinds of media (e.g., movies, television, newspapers, Internet).

- Describe data mining and its place in Internet media business models.

- Define pros and cons of Comcast's acquisition of NBC Universal.

- Analyze the implications of tensions inherent in producing "free" media content.

- Describe the relationship between advertisers and mass media. Develop and support a reasoned prediction of how advertising dollars will be spent in 10 years.

Student Website
www.mhhe.com/cls

Internet References

Advertising Age
http://adage.com
Citizens Internet Empowerment Coalition (CIEC)
www.ciec.org
Media Literacy Clearing House
www.frankwbaker.com/default1.htm
Young Media Australia
www.youngmedia.org.au/mediachildren/03_advertising.htm

Mass advertising developed along with mass media; in fact, commercial media have been described by some as a system existing primarily for the purpose of delivering audiences to advertisers. Companies with products to sell use media as a means of presenting their goods and services in a positive light. They are willing to pay generously for the opportunity to reach mass audiences, but unwilling to support media that do not deliver the right kind of audience for their advertisements. While the people who produce media content can craft that content to reflect their own agendas and social/political viewpoints, they depend on distributors to communicate the messages. Whoever incurs costs, producer and/or distributor, relies at some level on financial backing from advertisers.

The price for selling commercial space is determined by statistical data on how many and what kinds of people are reached by the media in which the ad is to appear. Despite a tough economy, spending on TV grew 8 percent in 2010; $20 billion was spent on prime-time TV ads, a 6 percent increase. Fifty-three percent of prime-time ads were 30-second spots, though the number of shorter ads increased 12 percent. Nielsen research data indicate viewers are more likely to watch commercials during dramas than during comedies, resulting in higher brand recall. In the 2010–11 television season, a 30-second spot on *NCIS* sold for $150,708, on *House* $226,180, *Modern Family* $193,635, *The Big Bang Theory* $195,077, *60 Minutes* $98,126, *Dateline NBC* $50,048. *Sunday Night Football* spots sold for $415,000, *American Idol* spots for $467,617. A 30-second commercial during the 2011 Super Bowl ran $3 million. *Glee* commanded $272,694 for a 30-second ad spot in fall 2010 and $373,014 in spring 2011, when it aired after the *American Idol* results show. In a different kind of deal, Microsoft agreed to donate $2,500 to the Colbert Nation Gulf of America Fund each time Stephen Colbert said the word "Bing" on *The Colbert Report*. He did, and they did—about $100,000.

Super Bowl ads still draw a lot of attention, but changes in how consumers use and interact with media have had a significant effect on traditional advertiser–media relationships. Television rarely delivers the kind of mass–mass audience to advertisers upon which ad rate practices were built. According to a recent study by Marian Azzaro, professor of marketing at Roosevelt University in Chicago, advertisers would need to buy 42 percent more time on the three major networks than they did 10 years ago to reach the same number of consumers. DVRs and TiVo allow consumers to bypass traditional commercial messages. New media draw a lot of eyes, but counting consumers and assessing how they interact with advertising messages is a new science. Daily Google searches in 2000 numbered 100 million; in 2010, 2 billion. Active blogs in 2000 numbered 12,000; in 2010, 141 million. Video game revenue increased from $7.98 billion in 2000 to $19.66 billion in 2010. CD sales revenue decreased from $943 million in 2000 to $427.9 million in 2010. iTunes downloads increased from 0 in 2000 to 10 billion in 2010.

As the number of media choices increases and audiences diffuse, advertising agencies have adjusted their media-buying focus from quantity to quality of potential consumers who will be exposed to a single ad. The current focus of many agencies is

© The McGraw-Hill Companies, Inc./Christopher Kerrigan, photographer

niche advertising, with interest in data split by age, gender, ethnic background, and income factors that determine how a given consumer might respond to a product pitch. The outgrowth of niching is seen in media products from the Food Network and Home & Garden Television, to magazines targeted to narrowly defined interests (e.g., *Golf*), to ads on the Web, in video games, over cell phones, on "airport TV," and in classrooms on Channel One. Google reported revenues of $8.58 billion for the quarter ended March 31, 2011, an increase of 27 percent compared to the first quarter of 2010.

Sometimes, products are placed directly into entertainment media, where they can strike below the level of consumer awareness. Market research finds viewers 25 percent more likely to shop at Sears after viewing "Extreme Makeover: Home Edition," which features Sears Kenmore appliances and Craftsman tools. Coke is on the judges' desk on "American Idol," Doritos and Mountain Dew presented to challenge winners on "Survivor." Products or logos may also be inserted into already filmed movies and television programs—not a new practice, but one attracting new attention, as technological advances make it easier to do so.

The first article in this section, "Your Data, Yourself," is about data mining, the commerce associated with monitoring your Internet behavior: "Each of these pieces of information (and misinformation) about me is sold for about two-fifths of a cent to advertisers, which then deliver me an Internet ad, send me a catalog or mail me a credit card offer. . . . You know how everything has seemed free for the past few years? It wasn't. It's just that no one told you that instead of using money, you were paying with your personal information." "Multitasking Youth" reports on research about how young people consume offline and online media: "While young consumers' multitasking activity is not welcome news for marketers stuck in a mind-set of traditional approaches to advertising and media planning, this increasingly common approach to media consumption presents significant opportunities to companies seeking to engage their audiences in new and different ways."

"Unkind Unwind" is about paying the bills in the movie industry, where "some bold experiments are under way. Chaotically, but quickly, the studios are about to bulldoze conventional wisdom about how films should be sold." "A Television Deal for the Digital Age" discusses the Comcast-NBC Universal merger: "Because it will control not only what content gets produced but also how it is distributed, the powerhouse will be in an unrivaled position to . . . make Comcast–produced shows easier to watch on its online network than shows produced by others. It could also refuse to provide its content to online competitors—thus depriving them of any lifeblood—and it could extend its practice of requiring customers who want to watch popular shows online to prove they are subscribers to their local cable service."

"Tomorrow's Interactive Television" offers a proposal for direct pay-for-play Internet television, following an iTunes or eBay model. "Open for Business" takes a position that consumers will pay for niche-specific specialized information and the future of news media lies in "deciding what you can sell to those willing to pay . . . to underwrite the cost of producing original work that might remain free and be of interest to more than a select few."

"Pay to Play" continues this discussion. Blogger Alan Mutter suggests coverage of local sports, cultural activities, and specific companies or industries of targeted interest are areas a newspaper could specialize in and charge for.

From a media literacy standpoint, analyzing the truth and values communicated by advertisements themselves is only part of understanding advertising's impact. It is important to understand the gatekeeping role financial backers have in overall media content. Most advertising account executives admit their unwillingness to be associated with media that create negative publicity. All of them put a premium on reaching certain advertiser-desirable groups; media targeted to the interests of those audiences proliferate, while those attractive to other audiences do not. As William Powers wrote in *The Atlantic Monthly* ("The Massless Media," January/February 2005), "Although much changes in the media over time, there are some eternal truths. Most outlets crave two things, money and impact, and the easiest path to both is the old fashioned one: grow your audience. Ambitious niches will always seek to become larger, and in so doing attract a more diverse audience."

Your Data, Yourself

Every detail of your life—what you buy, where you go, whom you love—is being extracted from the Internet, bundled and traded by data-mining companies. What's in it for you?

JOEL STEIN

Three hours after I gave my name and e-mail address to Michael Fertik, the CEO of Reputation.com, he called me back and read my Social Security number to me. "We had it a couple of hours ago," he said. "I was just too busy to call."

In the past few months, I have been told many more-interesting facts about myself than my Social Security number. I've gathered a bit of the vast amount of data that's being collected both online and off by companies in stealth—taken from the websites I look at, the stuff I buy, my Facebook photos, my warranty cards, my customer-reward cards, the songs I listen to online, surveys I was guilted into filling out and magazines I subscribe to.

Google's Ads Preferences believes I'm a guy interested in politics, Asian food, perfume, celebrity gossip, animated movies and crime but who doesn't care about "books & literature" or "people & society." (So not true.) Yahoo! has me down as a 36-to-45-year-old male who uses a Mac computer and likes hockey, rap, rock, parenting, recipes, clothes and beauty products; it also thinks I live in New York, even though I moved to Los Angeles more than six years ago. Alliance Data, an enormous data-marketing firm in Texas, knows that I'm a 39-year-old college-educated Jewish male who takes in at least $125,000 a year, makes most of his purchases online and spends an average of only $25 per item. Specifically, it knows that on Jan. 24, 2004, I spent $46 on "low-ticket gifts and merchandise" and that on Oct. 10, 2010, I spent $180 on intimate apparel. It knows about more than 100 purchases in between. Alliance also knows I owe $854,000 on a house builtin 1939 that—get this—it thinks has stucco walls. They're mostly wood siding with a little stucco on the bottom! Idiots.

EXelate, a Manhattan company that acts as an exchange for the buying and selling of people's data, thinks I have a high net worth and dig green living and travel within the U.S. BlueKai, one of eXelate's competitors in Bellevue, Wash., believes I'm a "collegiate-minded" senior executive with a high net worth who rents sports cars (note to Time Inc. accounting: it's wrong unless the Toyota Yaris is a sports car). At one point BlueKai also believed, probably based on my $180 splurge for my wife Cassandra on HerRoom.com, that I was an 18-to-19-year-old woman.

RapLeaf, a data-mining company that was recently banned by Facebook because it mined people's user IDs, has me down as a 35-to-44-year-old married male with a graduate degree living in L.A. But RapLeaf thinks I have no kids, work as a medical professional and drive a truck. RapLeaf clearly does not read my column in *Time*.

Intellidyn, a company that buys and sells data, searched its file on me, which says I'm a writer at Time Inc. and a "highly assimilated" Jew. It knows that Cassandra and I like gardening, fashion, home decorating and exercise, though in my case the word *like* means "am forced to be involved in." We are pretty unlikely to buy car insurance by mail but extremely likely to go on a European river cruise, despite the fact that we are totally not going to go on a European river cruise. There are tons of other companies I could have called to learn more about myself, but in a result no one could have predicted, I got bored.

Each of these pieces of information (and misinformation) about me is sold for about two-fifths of a cent to advertisers, which then deliver me an Internet ad, send me a catalog or mail me a credit-card offer. This data is collected in lots of ways, such as tracking devices (like cookies) on websites that allow a company to identify you as you travel around the Web and apps you download on your cell that look at your contact list and location. You know how everything has seemed free for the past few years? It wasn't. It's just that no one told you that instead of using money, you were paying with your personal information.

> **You know how everything has seemed free for the past few years? It wasn't. You're paying with your personal information.**

The Creep Factor

There is now an enormous multibillion-dollar industry based on the collection and sale of this personal and behavioral data, an industry that Senator John Kerry, chair of the Subcommittee on Communications, Technology and the Internet, is hoping to rein in. Kerry is about to introduce a bill that would require companies to make sure all the stuff they know about you is secured from hackers and to let you inspect everything they have on you, correct any mistakes and opt out of being tracked. He is doing this because, he argues, "There's no code of conduct. There's no standard. There's nothing that safeguards privacy and establishes rules of the road."

At Senate hearings on privacy beginning March 16, the Federal Trade Commission (FTC) will be weighing in on how to protect consumers. It has already issued a report that calls upon the major browsers to come up with a do-not-track mechanism that allows people to choose not to have their information collected by companies they aren't directly doing business with. Under any such plan, it would likely still be O.K. for Amazon to remember your past orders and make purchase suggestions or for American Express to figure your card was stolen because a recent purchase doesn't fit your precise buying patterns. But it wouldn't be cool if they gave another company that information without your permission.

Taking your information without asking and then profiting from it isn't new: it's the idea behind the phone book, junk mail and telemarketing. Worrying about it is just as old: in 1890, Louis Brandeis argued that printing a photograph without the subject's permission inflicts "mental pain and distress, far greater than could be inflicted by mere bodily harm." Once again, new technology is making us weigh what we're sacrificing in privacy against what we're gaining in instant access to information. Some facts about you were always public—the price of your home, some divorce papers, your criminal records, your political donations—but they were held in different buildings, accessible only by those who filled out annoying forms; now they can be clicked on. Other information was not possible to compile pre-Internet because it would have required sending a person to follow each of us around the mall, listen to our conversations and watch what we read in the newspaper. Now all of those activities happen online—and can be tracked instantaneously.

Part of the problem people have with data mining is that it seems so creepy. Right after I e-mailed a friend in Texas that I might be coming to town, a suggestion for a restaurant in Houston popped up as a one-line all-text ad above my Gmail inbox. But it's not a barbecue-pit master stalking me, which would indeed be creepy; it's an algorithm designed to give me more useful, specific ads. And while that doesn't sound like all that good a deal in exchange for my private data, if it means that I get to learn when the next Paul Thomas Anderson movie is coming out, when Wilco is playing near my house and when Tom Colicchio is opening a restaurant close by, maybe that's not such a bad return.

Since targeted ads are so much more effective than nontargeted ones, websites can charge much more for them. This is why—compared with the old banners and pop-ups—online ads have become smaller and less invasive, and why websites have been able to provide better content and still be free. Besides, the fact that I'm going to Houston is bundled with the information that 999 other people are Houston-bound and is auctioned by a computer; no actual person looks at my name or my Houston-boundness. Advertisers are interested only in tiny chunks of information about my behavior, not my whole profile, which is one of the reasons M. Ryan Calo, a Stanford Law School professor who is director of the school's Consumer Privacy Project, argues that data mining does no actual damage.

Since targeted ads are so much more effective, websites can get away with charging more for them

"We have this feeling of being dogged that's uncomfortable," Calo says, "but the risk of privacy harm isn't necessarily harmful. Let's get serious and talk about what harm really is." The real problem with data mining, Calo and others believe, arises when the data is wrong. "It's one thing to see bad ads because of bad information about you. It's another thing if you're not getting a credit card or a job because of bad information," says Justin Brookman, the former chief of the Internet bureau of the New York attorney general's office, who is now the director of the Center for Democracy and Technology, a nonprofit group in Washington.

Russell Glass, the CEO of Bizo—which mines the fact that people are business executives and sells that info to hundreds of advertisers such as American Express, Monster.com, Citibank, Sprint and Google—says the newness of his industry is what scares people. "It's the monster-under-the-bed syndrome," Glass says. "People are afraid of what they really don't understand. They don't understand that companies like us have no idea who they are. And we really don't give as—. I just want a little information that will help me sell you an ad." Not many people, he notes, seem to be creeped out by all the junk mail they still get from direct-marketing campaigns, which buy the same information from data-mining companies. "I have a 2-year-old daughter who is getting mail at my home address," he says. "That freaks me out."

Why That Ad Is Following You

Junk mail is a familiar evil that's barely changed over the decades. Data mining and the advertising it supports get more refined every month. The latest trick to freak people out is retargeting—when you look at an item in an online store and then an ad for that item follows you around to other sites.

Last year, Zappos was the most prominent company in the U.S. to go all out in behavioral retargeting. And people got pissed off. One of the company's mistakes was running ads too frequently and coming off as an annoying, persistent salesman. "We took that brick-and-mortar pet peeve and implied it online," says Darrin Shamo, Zappos' director of direct marketing. Shamo learned, the hard way, that people get upset when their computer shows lingerie ads, even if they had been recently shopping for G-strings, since people share computers and use them in front of their kids. He also learned that ads that reveal potential Christmas gifts are bad for business.

Since then, Zappos has been experimenting with new ads that people will see no more than five times and for no longer than eight days. Zappos has also dumbed the ads down, showing items that aren't the ones you considered buying but are sort of close, which people greatly prefer.

And much like Amazon's "Customers who bought 1984 also bought *Brave New World*"–style recommendation engine, the new ads tell people what Zappos knows about them and how they got that information ("a company called Criteo helps Zappos to create these kinds of personalized ads"). It also tells them how they can opt out of seeing them ("Some people prefer rainbows. And others prefer unicorns. If you prefer not to see personalized ads, we totally get it").

If that calms the angry 15 percent of the people who saw these ads, Zappos will stick with them. Otherwise, it plans on quitting the retargeting business. Shamo thinks he'll just need to wait until the newness wears off and people are used to ads tailored for them. "Sometimes things don't move as fast as you think," he says.

They're not even moving that much faster with the generation that grew up with the Internet. While young people expect more of their data to be mined and used, that doesn't mean they don't care about privacy. "In my research, I found that teenagers live with this underlying anxiety of not knowing the rules of who can look at their information on the Internet. They think schools look at it, they think the government looks at it, they think colleges can look at it, they think employers can look at it, they think Facebook can see everything," says Sherry Turkle, a professor at MIT who is the director of the Initiative on Technology and Self and the author of *Alone Together: Why We Expect More from Technology and Less From Each Other.* "It's the opposite of the mental state I grew up in. My grandmother took me down to the mailbox in Brooklyn every morning, and she would say, 'It's a federal offense for anyone to look at your mail. That's what makes this country great.' In the old country they'd open your mail, and that's how they knew about you."

Data mining, Turkle argues, is a panopticon: the circular prison invented by 18th century philosopher Jeremy Bentham where you can't tell if you're being observed, so you assume that you always are. "The practical concern is loss of control and loss of identity," says Marc Rotenberg, executive director of the Electronic Privacy Information Center. "It's a little abstract, but that's part of what's taking place."

The Facebook and Google Troves

Our identities, however, were never completely within our control: our friends keep letters we've forgotten writing, our enemies tell stories about us we remember differently, our yearbook photos are in way too many people's houses. Opting out of all those interactions is opting out of society. Which is why Facebook is such a confusing privacy hub point. Many data-mining companies made this argument to me: How can I complain about having my Houston trip data-mined when I'm posting photos of myself with a giant mullet and a gold chain on Facebook and writing columns about how I want a second kid and my wife doesn't? Because, unlike when my data is secretly mined, I get to control what I share. Even narcissists want privacy. "It's the difference between sharing and tracking," says Bret Taylor, Facebook's chief technology officer.

To get into the Facebook office in Palo Alto, Calif., I have to sign a piece of physical paper: a Single-Party Non-Disclosure Agreement, which legally prevents me from writing the last paragraph. But your privacy on Facebook—that's up to you. You choose what to share and what circle of friends gets to see it, and you can untag yourself from any photos of you that other people put up. However, from a miner's point of view, Facebook has the most valuable trove of data ever assembled: not only have you told it everything you like, but it also knows what your friends like, which is an amazing predictor of what you'll like.

Facebook doesn't sell any of your data, partly because it doesn't have to—23.1 percent of all online ads not on search engines, video or e-mail run on Facebook. But data-mining companies are "scraping" all your personal data that's not set to private and selling it

---

Lengthy Disclaimers

Most sites tell you what they do with your data If you check their privacy policy, but It might take a while to read

Number of words in privacy statement

- **8,999—WebMD**
  Monthly visitors (unique): 22.6 million

- **5,861—facebook**
  Monthly visitors: 153.0 million

- **2,510—PayPal**
  Monthly visitors: 21.0 million

- **2,408—Bank of America**
  Monthly visitors: 24.6 million

- **1,845—TIME**
  Monthly visitors: 12.1 million

Sources: Individual websites; ComScore Inc. January estimates

---

to any outside party that's interested. So that information is being bought and sold unless you squeeze your Facebook privacy settings tight, which keeps you from a lot of the social interaction that drew you to the site in the first place.

The only company that might have an even better dossier on you than Facebook is Google. In a conference room on the Google campus, I sit through a long privacy-policy PowerPoint presentation. Summary: Google cares! Specifically, Google keeps the data it has about you from various parts of its company separate. One category is the personally identifiable account data it can attach to your name, age, gender, e-mail address and ZIP code when you signed up for services like Gmail, YouTube, Blogger, Picasa, iGoogle, Google Voice or Calendar. The other is log data associated with your computer, which it "anonymizes" after nine months: your search history, Chrome browser data, Google Maps requests and all the info its myriad data trackers and ad agencies (Doubleclick, AdSense, AdMob) collect when you're on other sites and Android phone apps. You can change your settings on the former at Google Dashboard and the latter at Google Ads Preferences—where you can opt out of having your data mined or change the company's guesses about what you're into.

Nicole Wong, deputy general counsel at Google, says the company created these tools to try to reassure people who have no idea how all this information is being collected and used. "When I go to TIME.com as a user, I think only TIME.com is collecting my data. What I don't realize is that for every ad on that page, a company is also dropping a code and collecting my data. It's a black box—and we've tried to open up the box. Sometimes you're not even sure who the advertisers are. It's just a bunch of jumping monkeys or something." Google really does want to protect your privacy, but it's got issues. First, it's profit-driven and it's huge. But those aren't the main reasons privacy advocates get so upset about Google. They get upset because the company's guiding philosophy conflicts with the notion of privacy. As the PowerPoint says

Into the Mines Joel Explains How His Browser Comes to Know So Much about Him

1. I visit lots of sports websites instead of writing my column
2. A tracking company drops a unique piece of code (a cookie) in my browser that logs the sites I visit and identifies me as a sports fan. The company can also tell where I live and what time I go to these sites
3. The Los Angeles Kings want to sell hockey tickets. They ask an Internet ad network (all of which own or employ tracking companies) to hook them up with some L.A. sports fans
4. A minute later, I go to TIME.com to read this great data-mining article. TIME.com has sold space on its site to the ad network, so I see an ad suggesting I go see the Kings. I buy tickets. I still haven't written the column

right up top: "Google's mission: to organize the world's information and make it universally accessible and useful." Which is awesome, except for the fact that my information is part of the world's information.

Tracking the Trackers

To see just what information is being gathered about me, I downloaded Ghostery, a browser extension that lets you watch the watchers watching you. Each time you go to a new website, up pops a little bubble that lists all the data trackers checking you out. This is what I discovered: the very few companies that actually charge you for services tend not to data mine much. When you visit TIME.com, several dozen tracking companies, with names such as Eyeblaster, Bluestreak, Doubleclick and Factor TG, could be collecting data at any given time.

If you're reading this in print as a subscriber, *Time* has probably "rented" your name and address many times to various companies for a one-time use. This is also true if you subscribe to *Vanity Fair, Cosmopolitan* or just about any other publication.

This being America, I don't have to wait for the government to give me an opt-out option; I can pay for one right now. Michael Fertik, the CEO and founder of Reputation.com, who nabbed my Social Security number, will do it for me for just $8.25 a month. His company will also, for a lot more money, make Google searches of your name come up with more flattering results—because when everyone is famous, everyone needs a public relations department. Fertik, who clerked for the chief judge of the Sixth Circuit after graduating from Harvard Law School, believes that if data mining isn't regulated, everyone will soon be assigned scores for attractiveness and a social-prowess index and a complainer index, so companies can avoid serving you—just as you now have a credit score that they can easily check before deciding to do business with you. "What happens when those data sets are used for life transactions: health insurance, employment, dating and education? It's inevitable that all of these decisions will be

made based on machine conclusions. Your FICO score is already an all-but-decisional fact about you. ABD, dude! All but decisional," says Fertik.

Even if I were to use the services of Reputation.com, there's still all the public information about me that I can't suppress. Last year, thousands of people sent their friends a Facebook message telling them to opt out of being listed on Spokeo.com, which they described as the creepiest paparazzo of all, giving out your age, profession, address and a photo of your house.

Spokeo, a tiny company in Pasadena, Calif., is run by 28-year-old Stanford grad Harrison Tang. He was surprised at the outcry. "Some people don't know what Google Street View is, so they think this is magic," Tang says of the photos of people's homes that his site shows. The info on Spokeo isn't even all that revealing—he purposely leaves off criminal records and previous marriages—but Tang thinks society is still learning about data mining and will soon become inured to it. "Back in the 1990s, if you said, 'I'm going to put pictures on the Internet for everyone to see,' it would have been hard to believe. Now everyone does it. The Internet is becoming more and more open. This world will become more connected, and the distance between you and me will be a lot closer. If everybody is a walled garden, there won't be an Internet."

I deeply believe that, but it's still too easy to find our gardens. Your political donations, home value and address have always been public, but you used to have to actually go to all these different places—courthouses, libraries, property-tax assessors' offices—and request documents. "You were private by default and public by effort. Nowadays, you're public by default and private by effort," says Lee Tien, a senior staff attorney for the Electronic Frontier Foundation, an advocacy group for digital rights. "There are all sorts of inferences that can be made about you from the websites you visit, what you buy, who you talk to. What if your employer had access to information about you that shows you have a particular kind of health condition or a woman is pregnant or thinking about it?" Tien worries that political dissidents in other countries, battered women and other groups that need anonymity are vulnerable to data mining. At the very least, he argues, we're responsible to protect special groups, just as Google Street View allows users to request that a particular location, like an abused-women's shelter, not be photographed.

Other democratic countries have taken much stronger stands than the U.S. has on regulating data mining. Google Street View has been banned by the Czech Republic. Germany—after protests and much debate—decided at the end of last year to allow it but to let people request that their houses not be shown, which nearly 250,000 people had done as of last November. E.U. Justice Commissioner Viviane Reding is about to present a proposal to allow people to correct and erase information about themselves on the Web. "Everyone should have the right to be forgotten," she says. "Due to their painful history in the 20th century, Europeans are naturally more sensitive to the collection and use of their data by public authorities."

After 9/11, not many Americans protested when concerns about security seemed to trump privacy. Now that privacy issues are being pushed in Congress, companies are making last-ditch efforts to become more transparent. New tools released in February for Firefox and Google Chrome browsers let users block data collecting, though Firefox and Chrome depend on the data miners to respect the users' request, which won't stop unscrupulous companies. In addition to the new browser options, an increasing number of ads have a little *i* (an Advertising Option Icon), which you can click on to find out exactly which companies are tracking you and what they do. The technology behind the icon is managed by Evidon, the company that provides the Ghostery download. Evidon has gotten more than 500 data-collecting companies to provide their info.

It takes a lot of work to find out about this tiny little *i* and even more to click on it and read the information. But it also took people a while to learn what the recycling symbol meant. And reading the info behind the *i* icon isn't necessarily the point, says Evidon CEO Scott Meyer, who used to be CEO of About.com and managed the *New York Times* website. "Do I look at nutritional labeling? No. But would I buy a food product that didn't have one? Absolutely not. I would be really concerned. It's accountability."

FTC chairman Jon Leibowitz has been pleased by how effective he's been at using the threat of legislation to scare companies into taking action and dropping their excuse that they don't know anything about you personally, just data associated with your computer. "We used to have a distinction 10 years ago between personally identifiable information and non-PII. Now those distinctions have broken down." In November, Leibowitz hired Edward Felten, the Princeton computer-science professor famous for uncovering weaknesses in electronic-voting machines and digital-music protection, to serve as the FTC's chief technologist for the next year. Felten has found that the online-advertising industry is as eager as the government is for improved privacy protections. "There's a lot of fear that holds people back from doing things they would otherwise do online. This is part of the cost of privacy uncertainty. People are a little wary of trying out some new site or service if they're worried about giving their information," Felten says.

He's right: oddly, the more I learned about data mining, the less concerned I was. Sure, I was surprised that all these companies are actually keeping permanent files on me. But I don't think they will do anything with them that does me any harm. There should be protections for vulnerable groups, and a government-enforced opt-out mechanism would be great for accountability. But I'm pretty sure that, like me, most people won't use that option. Of the people who actually find the Ads Preferences page—and these must be people pretty into privacy—only 1 in 8 asks to opt out of being tracked. The rest, apparently, just like to read privacy rules.

We're quickly figuring out how to navigate our trail of data—don't say anything private on a Facebook wall, keep your secrets out of e-mail, use cash for illicit purchases. The vast majority of it, though, is worthless to us and a pretty good exchange for frequent-flier miles, better search results, a fast system to qualify for credit, finding out if our babysitter has a criminal record and ads we find more useful than annoying. Especially because no human being

---

Track Back

Use These Sites to Protect Yourself and Your Information

- **REPUTATION.COM**
  For $8.25 a month, the site, founded by CEO Fertik, will work to keep trackers off your browser. For more, It'll massage the results of a Google self-search Into something more flattering

- **PRIVACYCHOICE**
  PrlvacyChoice.org

  This site tells you only what Google, Yahoo, BlueKai, Bizo and eXelate know, but it also lists more than 300 tracking companies and helps you opt out of being tracked by them

- **GHOSTERY**
  Ghostery.com

  With this free download, every time you go to a web-site, a pop-up window tells you all the companies that are grabbing your data

- **YOUR BROWSER**
  Forget your browser's "privacy" option; that just prevents people borrowing your computer from seeing what sites you've been to. New features on Firefox and Chrome allow you to request that companies not mine your data

- **ADVERTISING INDUSTRY**
  NetworkAdvertising.org and *AboutAds.Info*

  There's no one clearinghouse where you can put yourself on a "do not track" list, but you can opt out of data mining by all members of these two Industry associations

---

ever reads your files. As I learned by trying to find out all my data, we're not all that interesting.—With Reporting by Eben Harrell/LONDON

Critical Thinking

1. Based on information in this article, propose five principles for maximizing the effectiveness of Internet ads.

2. From your perspective, is there a need for government regulation to protect privacy from data-mining? Why or why not?

Multitasking Youth

To engage youth consumers, you must understand the paradox of their media consumption.

ANDREW J. ROHM, FAREENA SULTAN, AND FLEURA BARDHI

The ways in which consumers attend to and process information from commercial media has begun to change. Advertisers can no longer depend on consumers to attend to commercial media (TV, magazines and radio) in the same ways that previous generations did when there were minimal media alternatives. Today's technology-and information-rich environment enables individuals to consume large amounts of media as we view, read and surf across offline and online media—simultaneously. While watching the latest episode of Grey's Anatomy on television, we also might surf the Internet for deals on hotels for that much-needed vacation, check out various blogs for the latest in celebrity gossip and flip through Vanity Fair magazine all at the same time. In this way, we are more apt to consume media in a feeding frenzy that is fueled by the myriad media vehicles available to us 24/7.

We define media multitasking as the practice of participating in multiple exposures to two or more commercial media at a single point in time. Media multitasking has attracted the attention of advertisers and marketers because of the increasing challenges of engaging young consumers. Media multitasking is a particularly entrenched practice among Generation Y (Gen Y) consumers. Also known as "the Millennials," they are a specific cohort of individuals born from 1983 to 1997. Research demonstrates that the more media individuals consume, the more likely they will access several media types at once. For example, Nielsen Media estimates that almost one-third of all household Internet activity takes place while watching television. A 2006 Kaiser Family Foundation study illustrated a time-compression phenomenon where young consumers were able to compress eight hours of media consumption into 20 percent less time. How? By multitasking and overlapping their media consumption.

The implications of multitasking behavior on how consumers function in the marketplace are significant. For advertisers, Gen Y overlaps the 18-year-old to 34-year-old demographic coveted by marketers. Often referred to as the "digital generation," because they have grown up with the Internet and are the most active consumer group online, Gen Y represents more

than 70 million consumers in the U.S. and their spending power totals approximately \$200 billion. While young consumers' multitasking activity is not welcome news for marketers stuck in a mind-set of traditional approaches to advertising and media planning, this increasingly common approach to media consumption presents significant opportunities to companies seeking to engage their audiences in new and different ways.

In this article, we report on research we conducted with Gen Ys on their media consumption practices and experiences. Specifically, our research was guided by three questions:

1. How do Gen Y consumers multitask with media? What are their experiences related to media multitasking, and how has multitasking shaped Gen Y's media consumption?

2. What are the personal outcomes (benefits and challenges) of media multitasking among Gen Ys? How do Gen Y consumers cope with these challenges?

3. What are the implications of media multitasking behavior on the development of marketing communications strategy?

The purpose of this article is to highlight this multitasking phenomenon related to media consumption and what it means

Executive Briefing

Today's youth are media multitaskers who can watch TV, surf the Internet and read at the same time. This has a significant impact on the consumer marketplace. And while this can give them feelings of control, efficiency, engagement and assimilation, the paradox is that inefficiency, chaos, disengagement and enslavement also can occur. The authors propose that task-specific campaigns can help the positives outweigh the negatives in this paradox.

for marketers. Our findings are at the same time comforting and disturbing. On one hand, study participants reported feelings of empowerment, control, productivity and efficiency as a result of their self-described "mastery" of media access and multitasking. On the other hand, our study illustrates feelings of enslavement, chaos, disengagement and inefficiency on the part of participants with respect to their media consumption practices.

Media Multitasking

Today's media universe, consisting of both online and offline media, is as diverse as it is fragmented. Exhibit 1, a collage developed by one of the participants in our study depicting a "portfolio" of media vehicles and technologies, illustrates how media multitasking involves multiple communication technologies such as a TV, a magazine and a computer. Multi-tasking can also take place around a single technology, such as a laptop, on which one can simultaneously shop, read the New York Times and instant message with friends. This multitasking capability has been extended to mobile devices: Apple's iPhone and the Blackberry Storm both have facilitated single-platform multitasking. These devices are of growing interest to advertisers because of the location-based features that distinguish them from other media. In this way, the "three screens" (TV, personal computer and mobile phones) all facilitate media multitasking behavior.

Interestingly, research on multitasking outcomes is mixed. Studies on multitasking in the workplace have shown that employees benefit from the increases in work efficiency resulting from multitasking activity. A dominant conclusion in cognitive psychology research, however, is that multitasking behaviors inhibit or diminish task performance. In our study, we found that some level of multitasking can be beneficial for individuals in terms of their processing of media and commercial information.

The Multitasking Experience

We found that media multitasking is a normal, even ritualistic, activity among our study participants. They reported spending between 3 and 10 hours a day with media in a multitasking mode. Multitasking was portrayed as an integral practice within their daily routines of socializing with friends, accessing news, doing research and being entertained. Our findings suggest that young, media-savvy consumers craft what we call "personalized media portfolios"—a combination of old and new media through which they multitask. These media portfolios, consisting of online as well as offline media (primarily television) illustrate the way in which commercial media are increasingly consumed, simultaneously within established media portfolios that are consistent over time.

One important take-away from our research concerning the concept of media portfolios is that each media platform possesses relative strengths. The collage shown in Exhibit 1 illustrates the union of traditional media (such as TV and print) that provide significant audience reach with new digital media that provide richer levels of personalization and interactivity. This illustrates how traditional media can be used to drive traffic and usage of these new media platforms, whereas digital media can supplement and add richness to the offline experience.

The Good and the Bad

We also uncovered a "love-hate relationship" related to our participants' media consumption. As shown in the exhibit we found four positive and four negative consequences relating to commercial media consumption.

Positive Consequences

1. **Control.** We found that study participants multitasked as a way of exerting greater control over their media consumption. Multitasking enabled them to filter and decide which media-related information and messages to process. We found that it also made them feel a part of the marketing communication process. What this means to managers is that consumers will increasingly seek control as active participants within brand-consumer communications, rather than as passive recipients of commercial messages. Advertisers should seek to tap into consumers' desire for control over their media environment by delivering themes, stories and games (or other "tasks") that are of interest to them and that can be accessed simultaneously across different media.

2. **Efficiency.** We found that multitasking can enable individuals to become more efficient in their media consumption, resulting in "greater convenience," "time savings," "constant connectivity" and "greater access to information." It is also an integral part of individuals' pursuits of instant gratification, enabling them to participate simultaneously in multiple worlds outside their private spaces. It is important for marketers to recognize the in-and-out nature of consumers' access and attention to media. Brand and advertising content that does not provide an immediate "hook" or some form of instant gratification will risk being bypassed or ignored by these consumers.

3. **Engagement.** In addition to fostering greater control and efficiency, media multitasking also was seen as a fun and enjoyable activity. Compared to passive media, such as TV, media consumption while multitasking was viewed as more engaging because it involves the viewer more actively in the communications process. What this means to advertising and media strategy is that different media platforms that work together to enable convergence on a single topic, objective or "mission" may be an effective strategy for fostering consumer engagement.

4. **Assimilation.** Media multitasking enables individuals to connect with friends and family, as well as with their surrounding culture. Collages illustrated that a benefit of media multitasking was the connectedness it enabled.

Study participants were motivated to use media in order to strengthen their social networks and generate social capital.

Negative Consequences

1. **Inefficiency.** While media multitasking provided a greater sense of control, efficiency, engagement and assimilation, it also led to feelings of inefficiency. It was described as distracting, leading to procrastination and reduced attention. Participants reported that they paid less attention to important tasks and needed much more time to decode media content during multitasking, since they were continuously dividing their attention among various media and secondary tasks.
2. **Chaos.** Multitasking also led to feelings of disorder and upheaval. Moreover, participants were not only aware of

their inability to process effectively during multitasking; they also expressed negative emotions, such as stress and guilt, associated with the chaotic experience of multitasking.

3. **Disengagement.** Media multitasking led participants to feel less engaged with commercial media, because the multitasking process challenged their ability to process and decode advertising messages. Disengagement was related to whether their media consumption was strategic or passive in nature. In a passive mode, media multitasking fulfilled the participants' need for constant stimulation and was therefore more suitable for peripheral or surface-level processing of advertising content. Strategic, task-oriented multitasking, however, helped participants to integrate multiple sources of information in a complementary and constructive fashion.
4. **Enslavement.** Media consumption was also seen as addictive. Participants spoke of their dependency on

Exhibit 1 The Good and the Bad

Positive consequences		Negative consequences	
Factor	**Illustrative quote**	**Factor**	**Illustrative quote**
1. Control Multitasking enables consumers to filter and process communication content.	"When multitasking I feel like I am the operator of a mission impossible and in control. I have all the information at my reach . . . I feel like I have a handle on all of the different media." (Alex, 20 years old)	**1. Chaos** Media multitasking can lead to an experience of disorder and upheaval.	"Multitasking is stressful because you are doing so many things, but at the same time, you are efficient. There's so much going on at once that you are not taking it all in. It's pretty chaotic. You become bombarded with information and ads. You have to be efficient in order to manage it all." (Bill, 22 years old)
2. Efficiency Media multitasking enables consumers to carry out tasks and process content.	"Multitasking is exciting and fast paced. For instance, I got the TV on mute, and I'm listening to my favorite band, and I turn around and the TV catches my eye and I see my favorite band is coming to the area and then I go online to check for tickets. Instant gratification!" (Amanda, 23 years old)	**2. Inefficiency** Media multitasking can lead to distractions and procrastination.	"When I'm watching TV and talking on the phone, I don't pay attention to the phone call. After I hang up I'm still behind in the show or game or whatever. Although I'm doing two things, afterwards it's like neither of them happened. (David, 21 years old)
3. Engagement Media consumption through multitasking constitutes a hedonic experience.	All pictures convey emotions of happiness or up-beat feelings. Noise and eyes illustrate consumption between mediums. This might seem counter-intuitive (with the word noise), but my eyes and ears almost need the different mediums to stay intrigued." (Steve, 22 years old)	**3. Disengagement** Media multitasking can reduce consumers' involvement with particular messages.	"Dazed; confused; not paying attention to anything really. When I'm watching TV, I'm always doing something else. So I don't really pay attention to the TV. But at the same time I'm also not really paying attention to the other thing I'm doing." (Rich, 21 years old)
4. Assimilation Media multitasking enables individuals to connect with friends, family and cultural influences.	"One major advantage of media multitasking for me is the feeling of being 'connected.' If I am watching the news on TV while talking on my cell phone and checking out Myspace. com, I feel in synch with what is happening in today's world." (Tom, 22 years old)	**4. Enslavement** Media multitasking can be an addictive experience.	"I think I am probably A.D.D. undiagnosed. The cell phone buzzes and you get that text message and you just want to jump into it. And then you get an IM and you jump away from whatever you are doing." (Brandon, 20 years old)

media and technology, as well as their need to multitask to manage the vast array of media content available and stay "in touch" and "in the know." Participants expressed having a form of "attention deficit disorder," characterized by short attention spans and a need for ongoing stimulation from various media.

Media Overload

. . . [W]e found four strategies that participants employed for coping with their multitasking and media consumption behaviors:

1. **Restrict number of media platforms.** This strategy involves restricting the number of media used at one single point in time. For example, a situation where one is watching TV, reading a magazine, shopping online and listening to the radio involves four different media. Switching among these four media requires more cognitive resources than switching within one device. What this means to marketers is that marketing communications and advertising efforts should attempt to leverage the specific media their particular target audience accesses most readily.

2. **Restrict number of media topics.** This strategy involved restricting the number of topics across various media platforms. Participants sought to complement and add depth to their media experience by focusing on one topic area, yet also by accessing information on this topic across multiple media—for instance, by searching for results of a sporting event online while watching the same event on television. The implication for marketing communications strategy is that advertising campaigns can be developed to focus on a specific topic or task.

3. **Create media hierarchies.** The third coping strategy was to create media hierarchies. Traditional media were often consumed as background media; new digital media were primarily consumed in the foreground. Participants often watched television with the sound off, yet it remained a central part of their media hierarchy. Participants also expressed that they paid less attention to background media and used them to fill the voids in their social environment. They strategically created media hierarchies as a way to enhance the processing of interesting content. Consumption of background media helped to enhance consumer engagement, and hence increased motivation to process media content. What this means to marketers is that foreground and background media serve different roles: digital, and particularly interactive media, are the most effective for delivering primary messages and content, while background media helps to stimulate initial engagement and maintain consumers' motivation to remain involved with advertising messages.

4. **Create media synergies.** The fourth coping strategy was to create synergies. Participants paired media strategically to reduce complexity. Recognizing the strengths and limitations of one medium over another,

they developed combinations of media that worked together in synergy, such as by complementing resource-dependent media (media requiring greater cognitive resources) with resource-independent media. As a segmentation strategy, marketers should recognize the formation of media hierarchies and develop strategies of their own, based on media synergies.

Five Lessons for Managers

Our study shows that media multitasking is a prevalent and growing phenomenon among younger consumers. Because it is important for managers to consider the multitasking experience from the perspective of this consumer segment, we frame our findings with five lessons for marketers interested in reaching these media-savvy consumers:

1. **Gen Y processes information differently.** Managers must recognize that young consumers attend to and process communications differently than have previous generations.

2. **Leverage the behavior.** Our findings show that there are positive consequences resulting from the multitasking experience. Some level of media intensity and multitasking can be beneficial to attention and comprehension, but at the same time multitasking can be detrimental to consumers' ability and motivation to process content.

3. **Develop media strategies to address multitasking.** One strategy to counter the challenges and leverage the positive consequences associated with multitasking is to develop marketing communications that enable consumers to actively manage and control their media consumption. It will be increasingly important for managers to package commercial content and programming across multiple platforms. We refer to this as the "American Idol model," by which consumers become engaged with a single topic (e.g., choosing the number one amateur singer in America) via multiple media (TV, the Internet, and mobile marketing). This leads to lesson number four.

4. **Segment markets by media portfolios.** Running counter to existing assumptions about the reduced role of traditional media among young consumers is that while they concentrate their attention on foreground media (typically digital), they then use what they derive from the foreground media to elaborate on the content conveyed by traditional media. Although we found that TV often took on a background role, we also found that because Gen Y has grown up in a culture defined by television programming, as well as a culture where social interactions and entertainment tends to evolve around this medium, TV remained a central part of their media portfolios.

5. **Promote consumer control, rather than chaos.** Finally, advertising and brand managers must develop strategies that focus on a central, ongoing theme with

specific and engaging tasks that foster perceptions of consumer control—rather than perceptions of chaos. Further, when targeting consumer groups such as Gen Y, planners should develop message content in multi-platform campaigns that simultaneously employ both foreground and background media. Following a segmentation approach, campaigns could be structured around media portfolios that are identified as optimal in reaching specific target audiences.

> **Advertising and brand managers must develop strategies that focus on a central, ongoing theme with specific and engaging tasks that foster perceptions of consumer control.**

To address challenges to attention and comprehension that participants expressed regarding their media consumption, we propose that task-specific campaigns can foster greater consumer engagement, greater perceived control within the brand-consumer communication process and more effective message decoding and comprehension. Such strategies would satisfy the consumer's desire for control, while helping to align the consumer's coping strategies with those of marketing and advertising. Marketers would thus take an active role in facilitating consumers' multitasking by reducing the intensity of concentration required by a message or interaction, or by utilizing other strategies that facilitate decoding and comprehension.

Critical Thinking

1. What are the personal outcomes (benefits and challenges) of media multitasking?
2. What are the implications of media multitasking on marketing communications strategies?

ANDREW ROHM is the Denise and Robert DiCenso Associate Professor of Marketing at the College of Business Administration at Northeastern University in Boston. He may be reached at a.rohm@neu.edu. **FAREENA SULTAN** is a professor of marketing and the Robert Morrison Fellow at the College of Business Administration at Northeastern University. She may be reached at f.sultan@neu.edu. **FLEURA BARDHI** is an assistant professor of marketing at the College of Business Administration at Northeastern University. She may be reached at f.bardhi@neu.edu.

Unkind Unwind

The film industry tries to revive the ailing home-entertainment business.

"Be kind rewind", a 2008 comedy about the travails of a small New Jersey video store, is not the best film ever made about the film business. But it may be one of the most honest. Whereas most entries in this navel-gazing genre are about the making of movies—the scheming actors, the lying moguls—"Be Kind Rewind" is about the unglamorous but vital business of getting them into customers' hands. It is accurate in another way, too: it ends with the video store about to close, crushed by technological change.

Films open on big screens but make money on small ones. After a four-month exclusive run in cinemas (a "window", in Hollywood jargon) they become available as DVDs and Blu-ray discs—and, often, as on-demand videos and digital downloads. In 2010 Americans spent $18.5 billion on such things. Just $10.6 billion was spent on cinema tickets in North America. Another window opens about six months later, when films are sold to cable- and satellite-television companies. Perhaps two years after that they will be sold to free broadcast channels. Like cars, films become cheaper as they age.

Yet the once lucrative home-entertainment market is ailing. A steep decline in DVD sales has more than cancelled out growth in high-definition Blu-ray discs and electronic downloads. The overall home-entertainment market stands at 78 percent of its peak level, even before adjusting for inflation (see Figure 1). Few think the drop is over. And nobody appears to believe that the market will recover the heights of five years ago. "In retrospect, that was a bubble," says Tom Adams of IHS Screen Digest, a leading analyst of the market.

Mid-budget films of the kind that tend to be nominated for awards were the first to be caught in the downdraft. Partly as a result, studios have pruned their output. They are concentrating on big-budget spectaculars that will draw people to cinemas around the world. In 2006 the members of the Motion Picture Association of America released 204 films, including 80 from their subsidiaries—partly independent outfits like Miramax and New Line. Last year the studios released 141 films, including just 37 from subsidiaries. Truly independent filmmakers, who have lost not just home-entertainment revenues but also outside financing, are struggling even more than usual. If you think there are fewer thoughtful, well-crafted films around these days, you're right.

The DVD slump has also divided Hollywood. Film executives, though they eat in the same few restaurants and attend the same parties, cannot agree on the best way of reviving the home-entertainment market, or even on what has caused it to slump. But so perilous is their position that some bold experiments are under way. Chaotically, but quickly, the studios are about to bulldoze conventional wisdom about how films should be sold.

About one thing the studios are fairly sure. Piracy, which was widely viewed as the greatest danger facing the film business a few years ago, has been eclipsed as a threat. Illicit streaming and downloading are certainly rampant in countries like Russia and China. But such places never had much of a home-entertainment market. They

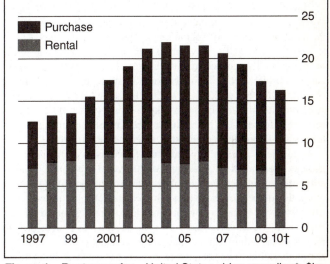

Figure 1   Rent asunder   United States video spending*, $bn
Source: IHS screen Digest   *Excludes digital   †Estimate

have simply moved on from pirate DVDs to illegal streaming. Piracy there represents growth forgone rather than losses.

In developed countries, particularly America (by far the biggest home-entertainment market), people have switched from buying to borrowing. Since 2007 the number of films rented in America has grown by 10 percent even as spending on home entertainment has steadily declined. People still go shopping for animated films that will keep their children quiet, and for beloved blockbusters: more than 30m DVDs and Blu-ray discs of "Avatar" have been sold worldwide. For everything else they are turning to a range of innovative, legal and—best of all—cheap alternatives.

One of the new entrants that worries the studios can be seen in a shopping mall in Crenshaw, at the smart end of south-central Los Angeles. The Walmart that anchors Crenshaw Plaza carries a good selection of DVDs and Blu-ray discs. On a recent visit "Red" could be had for $15 plus sales tax and "Toy Story 3" for $19.96. A triple pack containing a DVD, a Blu-ray disc and a digital copy of "Despicable Me" was going for $24.96.

On their way to the DVD section, however, many of Walmart's customers pass a cheaper option. In the entrance foyer, next to a fizzy-drinks machine, sits a red kiosk that rents films by the day. "Red", "Despicable Me" and "Toy Story 3" are all available on DVD for just $1 plus tax. Blu-ray discs cost only a shade more at $1.50 a day.

Rise of the Machines

This "Redbox" is owned by Coinstar, a firm that also builds change-counting machines. It is one of almost 30,000 that have been installed since 2006, many of them in the same Walmart stores that together represent the single most important retail outlet for film discs. A few years ago Hollywood and incumbent video stores like Blockbuster were focused on the threat from piracy and video streaming. Instead they have been undercut by a device that resembles a cross between a cash machine and a 1950s jukebox.

A studio would almost always rather sell a film than rent it. But if someone is determined to rent, the studio would rather he did it somewhere other than a kiosk. Last year Warner Bros estimated the average amount it received from various transactions (Figure 2). At the top of the list is an electronic download, a high-margin sale that earns $17.50 for the studio. The most profitable form of rental is a video-on-demand delivered through a cable or satellite set-top box, which is worth $3.50. Video-store rentals are worth $1.45. At the bottom of the scale are kiosk rentals. They are worth just $1 each to the studio, and would be worth even less if people were more punctual about returning their DVDs.

If Redbox worries the studios, Netflix terrifies them. That firm sends DVDs through the post to subscribers, who pay a monthly fee based on the number of films they want to keep at one time. It also allows them to stream films and TV shows at no extra charge. Viewers can watch on laptops or TVs connected to the internet, either directly or through games consoles. Netflix has more than 20m subscribers—up from just over 9m at the end of 2008. Its success has attracted rivals, including Amazon: the e-retailer bought lovefilm (a similar but inferior European service) in January. But Netflix has a terrific reputation among its customers and a considerable head start. It will be hard to catch.

Sandvine, a firm that helps internet-service providers manage their networks, reckons Netflix accounts for 20 percent of non-mobile internet traffic in America during the evenings. Yet the humdrum business of sending discs through the post is still crucial. Thanks to a legal doctrine developed in the days when most video stores resembled the tiny business in "Be Kind Rewind", discs can be rented as soon as they go on sale to the public. Netflix must agree on terms with the studios to stream their films over the internet, and tends to get them about a year after they appear in cinemas, if then. But it can send anything through

the post. The combination of old stuff available instantly and newer stuff by mail has proved immensely appealing.

The explosive growth of Netflix and Redbox has crippled video stores (see Figure 3), including the once mighty Blockbuster chain. Loaded with debt, it filed for bankruptcy last year. Similar pressures are building elsewhere. Other countries have not seen such disruptive change as America, partly because their laws do not favour rental outfits so strongly. But Japan, which also has streaming and film-rental kiosks, has seen video purchases decline twice as fast as rentals. Netflix has expanded into Canada and may well spread further. Not surprisingly, the media companies are digging in against the threat.

"I have nothing against $1 rentals—at some point," explains Kevin Tsujihara, head of home entertainment at Warner Bros. He just doesn't want cheap rentals competing with disc sales. So last year Warner Bros, Fox and Universal Studios struck deals with Netflix. The service would keep its hands off their movies for 28 days, to give them a chance to sell in shops and in high-street video stores—in effect creating a new window. In return, the studios allow Netflix to stream more old films and television shows. Sony keeps big-budget films out of Netflix's hands for 28 days but not smaller films. Attempts to impose similar terms on Redbox have been more fraught: the firm took the studios to court while attempting to fill its boxes with DVDs bought from retailers.

Shattered Glass

Fox and Warner Bros. claim that holding films back from cheap rental services has resulted in a modest bump not just in DVD sales but also in rentals from shops like Blockbuster, which continues to rent films as soon as they are released. Others believe the effect has been small or non-existent. "The consumer is not as sensitive to the window as we are," suggests David Bishop, head of home entertainment at Sony. Some hint the window should be longer than 28 days.

It may be that many consumers have learned to wait an extra month to see a film cheaply. Or they may simply be confused. Independent distributors, which are usually grateful for all the money and eyeballs they can get, have generally been happy to let Netflix and Redbox have

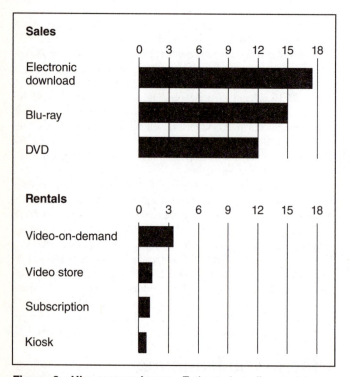

Figure 2 Hire means lower Estimated studio receipts per United States transaction, December 2009, $

Source: Warner Bros

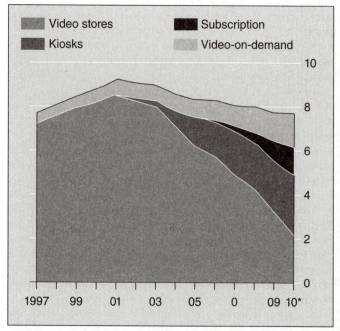

Figure 3 Going to the flix United States video-rental spending, $bn

Source: IHS screen Digest

*Estimate

their films. So has Disney. That company has a large consumer-products division, which brings in about as much as home entertainment. It is in Disney's interest to make sure that as many people as possible see "Cars 2", so that it can sell them Lightning McQueen toothbrushes.

Disney's stance irritates executives at other leading studios, who believe it is undermining the value not just of its own content but of everyone else's too. Netflix concurs that differences among studios have puzzled consumers. "If all the studios had moved towards a 28-day window, it would have influenced behaviour," says Ted Sarandos, chief content officer of Netflix. "But if you tell people that some movies are going to be accessible in some places, it's not going to change."

Having failed to erect a united front against cheap rentals, the studios are now muttering darkly about price increases. Netflix cut some deals to allow it to stream films and television shows when its business was small. The next round of negotiations will be tougher. The firm may be faced with a choice between reduced streaming rights or a cut in its hefty profit margin. But Netflix does not need to have every film and television programme. So large is its library, so superior is its software and so widespread is its distribution on devices that the loss of some content is unlikely to dent its appeal greatly.

Even if Netflix could somehow be brought down, the studios would still face a threat from television. Partly as a response to the rise of Netflix, pay-TV firms are making more films and programmes available to subscribers at no extra charge, often on mobile phones and tablet computers. Digital video recorders are becoming big enough to store hundreds of films. The latest set-top boxes from TiVo can search for films and television programmes across broadcast programme guides, video-on-demand menus and digital video recorders all at once. They can even suggest things to watch. People sometimes reach for a DVD when they cannot find anything to watch on TV. They may do so less and less.

For a Few Dollars More

The studios' next step will be to do something that was unthinkable just a few years ago: they will break the convention that cinemas have films to themselves for four months. As early as next month, several big studios (Disney, Fox, Sony and Warner Bros) are likely to begin renting films through pay-television boxes just two months after they appear in cinemas. The price will be steep—almost certainly more than that of two cinema tickets. The film will probably disappear from video-on-demand menus after a couple of weeks, before reappearing at a less eye-watering price at the usual time. For technical reasons few households will be able to receive them at first. But the principle will have been established.

The cinemas are furious. The National Association of Theatre Owners points out that box-office spending has held up well in the past few years—much better than home-entertainment sales, particularly when booming cinemas abroad are taken into account. Why would the studios hazard the one bit of the business that seems to be healthy?

Not all will: Brad Grey, the head of Paramount, says he has no desire to gamble on products that may cost $250m to produce and advertise. (Paramount is part of Viacom, controlled by Sumner Redstone, who also owns cinemas.) But the others will go ahead because they believe releasing films early on video-on-demand will not dent the popcorn market. "People go to the movies because they like to go to the movies," says Rob Friedman, head of Summit Entertainment. The most likely renters of premium on-demand videos, executives believe, are parents of young children, for whom a trip to the cinema costs $60 or $70 including the babysitter.

One hope is that offering newish films through set-top boxes will encourage people to rent more films that way. Video-on-demand has been slow to catch on, partly because couch potatoes dislike wading through alphabetical lists of titles. Mr. Adams of IHS reckons the average American household spent just $17 on video-on-demand in 2010. But there is some cause for optimism. Independent distributors such as IFC Films and Magnolia Pictures are miles ahead of the big studios; they often release low-budget movies to homes even before they appear in cinemas. As a result, video-on-demand is now an important sales channel for independent film.

The second thing the studios will do this year is to try to ginger up electronic sales. Film downloads through Apple's iTunes and other digital stores have not been popular so far. They are expensive, often costing more than DVDs. They are also inflexible, points out Mitch Singer of Sony Pictures, who also leads an industry consortium known as DECE. You can take a DVD to a friend's house, pop it into a portable player or a laptop and even play it in your sport-utility vehicle. None of which is possible at present with a digital download. "People don't want to buy something that won't work on a device they might want to buy in two years' time," says Mr. Singer.

All the big studios apart from Disney (once again going its own way) will start offering electronic copies of films that conform to a single format later this year. Buy a film, either as a download or as a Blu-ray disc that comes with digital rights, and a token will be stored in your account. In theory, you should then be able to play the film on television through your existing set-top box, download it to your laptop and your smartphone, and perhaps burn an extra copy to a DVD. Buying a film should begin to seem more appealing than renting it or downloading it illegally.

This method has another potential advantage for the studios: it should allow them to market their films more precisely. At present, whenever a studio launches a film it must create a marketing plan almost from scratch. Not only do the studios know much less about individual tastes than firms such as Netflix or Amazon. They are likely to know less than a shampoo-maker. But when people download films they leave clues about their tastes—clues that could be assembled into databases and used to target people who might be interested in the next release.

Some studios are beginning to think along these lines. On March 8th Warner Bros announced that it would start renting films through Facebook. It will hope that fans will do some of the marketing for it on the social network. But there is an uncomfortable caveat. In order for digital distribution to take off, the studios will probably have to bring prices down from their current heights. Internet shoppers have learned to expect bargains. If they don't get them, many will find illegal ways of getting hold of films without paying. Some Hollywood executives hope that digital downloading can shore up profit margins eroded by the collapse of DVD sales. That may well prove forlorn.

It will not be easy for an old industry to develop an entirely new set of muscles. But Hollywood must become more consumer-oriented. The alternative is watching the most lucrative part of its business slacken, slur and fail, like an old, worn-out VHS tape.

Critical Thinking

1. About how many movies do you see in a year? At what point in the distribution chain do you most often access a movie? How important is cost in your decision of how long to wait?

2. Describe the source of tension between Disney and other studios. Why does Disney play by different rules?

A Television Deal for the Digital Age

How to worry about the Comcast-NBC Universal merger.

JOHN DUNBAR

Those in the know say you don't need a television to watch TV anymore. All you need is an Internet connection and a screen. Missed last night's episode of *30 Rock*? No worries. Log on to Hulu and watch it on your laptop. Once you've done that, it's just a small step to drop your cable or satellite subscription and save a bunch of money, right? Not so fast. Watching your fill of free TV online isn't so easy, especially if you want to see this week's episode of *Glee* at the same time as your cable-connected friends or view special events like the Super Bowl. And Comcast's plan to acquire a majority stake in NBC Universal—marrying the king of distribution with a household name in programming—is likely to make free Internet TV trickier, not easier.

The Federal Communications Commission and the Department of Justice are closely reviewing the proposed merger because the combined company could play a major role in shaping the future of Internet TV competition.

Brian Roberts, Comcast's chairman and chief executive, told Wall Street analysts when the deal was announced in December 2009 that the venture would make Comcast "strategically complete." He said the transaction is pro-consumer because it will allow the company to "become a leader in the development and distribution of multiplatform 'anytime, anywhere' media that American consumers are demanding."

Not everyone believes that Comcast's prime motivation is to make its customers happy.

Where's the Competition?

Comcast's roots are firmly intertwined with its cable brethren, a tight-knit, largely interdependent group of companies that own and distribute content. Cable and satellite companies, like Comcast and DirecTV, make their money by charging subscribers for access to their distribution networks. They then take a big chunk of that money and use it to negotiate with content companies, including ABC network owner Walt Disney Company, Time Warner, and Viacom, for the rights to carry the programmers' broadcast and cable channels. The content creators make money by collecting these fees from cable companies and also from advertising.

It is a largely closed system that has been difficult for competitors to break into—more competition would hopefully mean lower prices for subscribers and better service in an industry that is not exactly known for it.

Some had hoped that the Internet would give rise to companies that would challenge the all-powerful cable industry, following in the footsteps of online avengers who took down record companies and news media empires.

Logic dictates that if viewers can watch what they want via their Internet connection, it makes no sense to keep paying for both broadband and cable or satellite service. But Comcast in 2009 collected more than $19 billion in revenue from cable TV service and nearly $8 billion in revenue on its broadband service. It is number one in both categories, with more than twenty-two million TV subscribers and more than sixteen million Internet subscribers. The company wants to keep both revenue streams, and to grow them.

One way to do that is to keep competition in check. Comcast would be in a unique position to do just that, especially because, by adding NBC Universal to its holdings, Comcast will become one of the nation's largest television programmers, too—the only company to have such a large position in programming, cable, and Internet distribution. Because it will control not only what content gets produced but also how it is distributed, the powerhouse will be in an unrivaled position to resist competition from Internet TV wannabes. Merger opponents are concerned that the company could disrupt competitors' content flowing over its broadband connections, meaning it could make Comcast-produced shows easier to watch over its online network than shows produced by others. It could also refuse to provide its content to online competitors—thus depriving them of any lifeblood—and it could extend its practice of requiring customers who want to watch popular shows online to prove they are subscribers to their local cable service.

Federal regulators will undoubtedly attach conditions aimed at preserving competition and protecting the public interest in return for approval of the deal. Meanwhile, Comcast is conspicuously vague about its plans for Internet TV.

"Because this a very new business and neither we nor anyone else has figured out how best to deliver video online to consumers, it would be premature to set in stone any plans with respect to putting content online in any particular fashion," said Comcast spokeswoman Sena Fitzmaurice.

Translation: don't hold your breath waiting for Comcast to welcome an Internet Utopia of free-flowing, no-charge television content. "It's not that Comcast thinks it can kill online video. They're not stupid like the recording industry was," said Harold Feld, legal director with the Washington, D.C., digital advocacy group Public Knowledge. "What they want to do is manage the terms under which we're going to change so that they can continue to make the tons of money they're making right now selling their cable service."

The Wide World of Internet TV

Neither Comcast nor NBC is an Internet neophyte. They haven't waited for the online barbarians to reach their gates; rather, each controls a user-friendly path for its content to migrate to the Web.

In addition to shows available on its own NBC.com, NBC partnered with News Corp. to create Hulu in March 2007, with Disney joining in April 2009. The ad-supported website opened to the public in March 2008 and now dominates the free Internet TV world, allowing anyone with a broadband connection to choose from among 2,600 current prime-time television shows for viewing. Hulu's offerings are extensive, but not all shows are available on the site and, for many TV series, only a few recent episodes are available for free. Comcast will assume NBC Universal's 27 percent ownership in Hulu if the deal goes through unscathed by regulators.

Comcast, for its part, joined with Time Warner in June 2009 to create a system called "TV Everywhere" that streams television shows to customers over the Internet—as long as they keep paying their monthly cable bill. It started when Time Warner agreed to allow Comcast cable customers online access to shows from Time Warner networks TBS and TNT. Today, a Comcast subscriber enters a code into a website to access cable shows that are not available for free online. The selection of shows available to stream over the Internet corresponds with the subscriber's cable package, making sure one isn't able to access a program online that hasn't been paid for with cable subscription.

Although management has been guarded about what will happen with online video after the merger, "lots of broadcast content" would go to Hulu and "cable content" would go on TV Everywhere, said Steve Burke, a Comcast executive and the new chief of NBC Universal. Burke was addressing Wall Street analysts the day the deal was announced.

Critics say Comcast will make NBC content less accessible, not more available.

"Comcast will build extensive moats around their content," predicted Susan Crawford, former special assistant to President Obama for science, technology and innovation policy, who is writing a book about the deal. "I can tell you confidently in the future you will need a cable subscription from Comcast to access online any cable channels that would otherwise be bundled by Comcast."

Comcast's Fitzmaurice insisted that the deal "will not in any way limit competition in the fragmented and dynamic marketplace

for online video content." Comcast's goal is to bring "more, not less" content to consumers across platforms.

Comcast has been buying full-page ads in *The Washington Post* trying to convince customers that the merger, and the TV Everywhere model, is good for them. Subscribers will be able to access a wide range of programming anywhere there is an Internet connection. Watching television will become a seamless experience as subscribers move from one device to another.

But that seamless experience starts to run into snags if viewers want to get their Internet TV from someone other than Comcast. Upstart Internet TV providers trying to compete with this juggernaut have already met with limited success—even some of the biggest companies in the country have been stymied in trying to break into the television business.

Google TV, for example, launched service in late 2010. Its programming partners include Turner Broadcasting, HBO and Netflix. But not one of the four major networks is available on the service.

Apple TV, a $99 device that delivers movies for as little as $3.99 and television shows for 99 cents apiece, has also met with resistance. NBC Universal does not make its content available to Apple TV customers, though ABC and Fox do. Steve Jobs, Apple's chief executive, hopes the rest of the networks will "see the light" and start offering their content.

Netflix has become extremely successful, first at streaming movies, but now also streaming broadcast television content—although its menu of available shows is somewhat limited. An Internet backbone company that distributes Netflix's online streams of television content, Level 3 Communications, launched a public battle against Comcast in December, accusing it of requiring Level 3 to pay unfair fees to Comcast to ensure its streams reach its customers. Comcast denies it is competing unfairly, but the battle is sensitive because federal regulators are grappling with how to craft rules to ensure all Internet content is treated fairly. This isn't the first time Comcast has been accused of disrupting the content of a competitor. (More on that later.)

At least some TV lovers are betting that despite Comcast and the cable industry's might, these new Internet TV ventures will allow them to cut their cable cords and save some money. Research firm SNL Kagan estimates that the number of households that will substitute online TV for traditional cable and satellite providers will grow from 1.5 million at the end of 2009 to 8.1 million households by 2014. Indeed, Comcast lost 275,000 cable TV subscribers in 2010's third quarter.

But others are not so sure that many will cut the cord. Susan Whiting, vice chair of Nielsen Company, the television rating service, told Congress in July that "at the present time" viewers appear to be using the Internet to add to rather than replace their usual viewing platforms. If she's right, that would make the family that runs Comcast very happy.

Keeping It in the Family

While Comcast is the nation's largest provider of cable TV and broadband services, it is still very much a family operation. It was founded by Ralph J. Roberts, now ninety, who, with two other investors in 1963, purchased a 1,200-subscriber cable television system in Tupelo, Mississippi. Today he carries the title of chairman emeritus.

His son, Brian Roberts, currently serves as chairman and chief executive, having joined the company in 1981, fresh out of the University of Pennsylvania's Wharton School of Finance. Roberts, fifty-one, has served as chief executive since November 2002 and chairman since May 2004 and is credited with building a mid-tier cable company into the titan it is today. Shares of the Fortune 100 company trade publicly, but Roberts owns a third of the company's voting stock, giving him by far the most control of any investor.

Roberts runs the Comcast empire from a sleek, glass-sheathed tower in downtown Philadelphia. In published profiles he is described as a polished and low-key dealmaker who is also a relentless, hard-ball negotiator, adept at sidestepping the spotlight. He has said NBC's *The Office* is one of his favorite TV shows.

An accomplished squash player, triathlete, and father of three, Roberts is active in Philadelphia philanthropy. He was paid more than $27 million in total compensation in 2009, ranking him forty-seventh on *Forbes*'s list of executive pay.

If he seals this deal, Roberts will step beyond the cable guys and into the flashier world of media titans.

Too Much Control?

Comcast's proposed deal unfolds in three stages. First, it calls for General Electric Company to buy the 20 percent of NBC Universal it doesn't already own. Comcast would then pay GE $6.5 billion for a 51 percent stake in a new joint venture containing NBC Universal and Comcast's cable networks and online properties. GE has an option to sell its stake in the venture to Comcast within seven years, giving Roberts 100 percent control.

Consumer advocates say the deal is bad because it will make it harder for new competitors to challenge cable and satellite television providers. Mark Cooper, research director at the Consumer Federation of America, told Congress in February that the cable industry is a "cartel" that will be "strengthened and extended to the Internet" if the merger is approved.

The merged company "touches every part of the media landscape," said Crawford, the former Obama adviser who questions the deal. If the deal is approved, Comcast will own the NBC affiliate and the dominant cable system in cities including Chicago, Philadelphia, Washington, Miami, Hartford, and San Jose. Owning a cable system and broadcast station in the same market was once against the rules, but such restrictions were abolished by a federal court ruling in 2001.

In addition to its broadcast and cable networks, NBC has 234 affiliated television stations that cover the nation. There's also Universal Pictures, theme parks, and fifteen owned-and-operated Telemundo Spanish-language stations.

Just as important as its distribution breadth, Comcast would be a heavyweight programmer, influencing what shows would be made available to online competitors. Merger opponents say it could not only withhold its programming, but also urge independent programmers to refuse to do business with Internet upstarts. Comcast paid more than $7 billion in 2009 for programming, a substantial sum that content providers would hate to jeopardize for fear of drawing Comcast's ire by selling programs to places Comcast doesn't like.

Indeed, some see NBC Universal's 27 percent ownership in Hulu as problematic. The concern is that Comcast will look at Hulu as a competitor for its television distribution business and pull NBC Universal programming off it.

Comcast's Fitzmaurice says the company's market power is overstated.

Comcast controls less than one quarter of national pay-TV market—one in three pay-television customers today is a satellite subscriber. "Our share is declining," she said. As for the Internet, Fitzmaurice said Comcast reaches less than 20 percent of the national broadband market. In programming, the combined company will control only 13 percent of the content market, trailing Disney, Viacom, and News Corp.

As to the Hulu stake, she said the deal "does not change NBCU's participation" in any way. That doesn't mean that all NBC Universal shows will be available on the Internet, however, due to uncertainty about whether online advertising alone can support the "creative infrastructure" needed to produce premium content.

Indeed, content sellers like Disney and Time Warner have expressed similar concerns that online advertising doesn't generate enough revenue to pay for quality programming—at least not yet. That means programmers are still reliant on cable and satellite distributors for the bulk of their revenue. So if those distributors frown on content sales to Internet companies, it's not hard to guess with whom the programmers will side.

The Dark Lord of Broadband

Indeed, there are few rules that require Comcast to play nice with Internet competitors and, well, its reputation for just the opposite is pretty well known. Comcast was awarded "The Worst Company in America" award for 2010 by The Consumerist, a blog published by Consumers Union, which opposes the merger. *Wired* once dubbed Roberts "The Dark Lord of Broadband." Its lengthy article described a bloody battle over Internet freedom, a fight that has some resonance with arguments being raised today by Netflix distributor Level 3 against the Comcast-NBC Universal merger.

In 2007, Comcast was accused of blocking file-sharing applications over its broadband Internet network, preventing users from sharing music and other content. The company denied it was playing Big Brother and shutting down so-called peer-to-peer traffic, but it later pledged to change how its network operated in managing bandwidth-sucking applications. The FCC at the time issued a scathing report that suggested the company was trying to kill a competing technology that threatened its own budding video-on-demand cable service. The federal agency did not fine Comcast but ruled that the company had violated the agency's Internet discrimination policy. Comcast appealed that finding and won its challenge in a federal appeals court.

Competitors worry that Comcast will block competitors both on its TV and its broadband systems.

A Media and Entertainment Titan

A combined Comcast-NBC Universal would be a powerful distributor and creator of news and entertainment

Comcast's Cable Television Networks[1]

El
Golf Channel
Style Network
Versus
G4
The Comcast Network
New England Cable News
CSN California
CSN Mid-Atlantic
CSN New England
CSN Northwest
CSN Philadelphia (85 percent)
CSN Bay Area (67 percent)
CSN MTN (50 percent)
CSS (81 percent)
Exercise TV (65 percent)

Comcast's Websites

fandango.com
movies.com
dailycandy.com
eonline.com
thegolfchannel.com
golfnow.com
style.com
versus.com
comcastsportsnet.com
g4tv.com
exercisetv.tv (65 percent)

Comcast's Other Entertainment Assets

Sports Teams
Philadelphia Flyers
Philadelphia 76ers
Other
Wells Fargo Center in Philadelphia
Flyers Skater Zone (community skating facilities)
Global Spectrum (public assembly management)
Ovations Food Services
Front Row Marketing Services
Paciolan (ticketing, fundraising, marketing)
New Era Tickets
Disson Skating (televised ice skating show producer)

NBC Universal's Cable Television Networks[2]

USA
Bravo
Syfy
Universal HD
CNBC
CNBC World
MSNBC
Chiller
mun2
Sleuth
Oxygen

NBC Universal's Websites

NBC.com
CNBC.com
ivillage.com
bravotv.com
usanetwork.com
oxygen.com
chillertv.com
syfy.com
holamun2.com
universalhd.com
sleuthchannel.com
accesshollywood.com
nbcsports.com
nbcolympics.com
televisionwithoutpity.com
msnbc.com (50 percent)
hulu.com (27 percent)

NBC Universal's Other Entertainment Assets

Movie Studios
Universal Pictures
Focus Features
Carnival
Cattleya (18.5 percent) not managed
Parks and Resorts
Universal Studios Hollywood
Universal Orlando Resort (50 percent)

Cable/Satellite Provider
Total universe among top twenty-five services is 96 million basic video subscribers

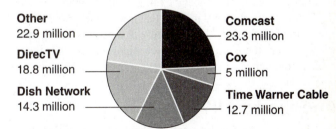

Other
22.9 million

DirecTV
18.8 million

Dish Network
14.3 million

Comcast
23.3 million

Cox
5 million

Time Warner Cable
12.7 million

Source: National Cable and Telecommunications Association

[1]Does not include five partially owned networks, such as TVOne, Sprout, and FearNet, in which Comcast owns a minority stake.
[2]Does not include fifteen partially owned networks, such as A&E, Lifetime, or The Weather Channel, in which NBC Universal owns a minority stake.

(Continued)

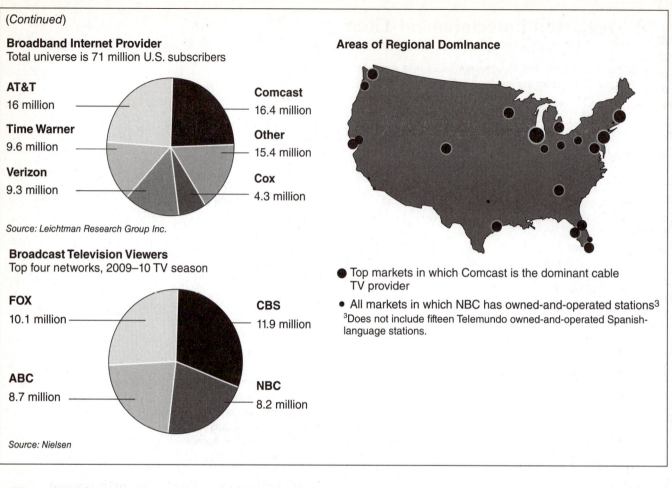

(Continued)

Broadband Internet Provider
Total universe is 71 million U.S. subscribers

AT&T — 16 million
Comcast — 16.4 million
Time Warner — 9.6 million
Other — 15.4 million
Verizon — 9.3 million
Cox — 4.3 million

Source: Leichtman Research Group Inc.

Broadcast Television Viewers
Top four networks, 2009–10 TV season

FOX — 10.1 million
CBS — 11.9 million
ABC — 8.7 million
NBC — 8.2 million

Source: Nielsen

Areas of Regional Dominance

● Top markets in which Comcast is the dominant cable TV provider

• All markets in which NBC has owned-and-operated stations[3]
[3]Does not include fifteen Telemundo owned-and-operated Spanish-language stations.

Bloomberg, LP owns BTV, a business news network that competes with CNBC, the NBC Universal-owned provider of financial news on cable. Its rival controls about 85 percent of the market for financial news, Bloomberg says in an FCC filing.

Comcast has "already demonstrated its ability to restrict or degrade service, to place restrictions on the online distribution of network programming as a condition of carriage," says the Bloomberg filing, referring to the fight over file-sharing networks.

Comcast will have "every incentive available to harm and discriminate against BTV to protect CNBC" as well as "the incentive and ability" to give CNBC the best channel position and to locate competing business channels far away. Comcast might even refuse to carry Bloomberg TV, the company wrote.

"There are already laws in place that govern these concerns," Fitzmaurice responded. "If Bloomberg or any other competitor has a concern, there are already mechanisms in place for them to file a complaint."

Access to All?

The chances of the development of a healthy, competitive, and profitable market of online competitors to cable are slim without some form of government intervention.

It took an act of Congress to make programming available to the direct broadcast satellite industry. DirecTV would have been a flop were it not for the Satellite Home Viewer Act of 1988 and the creation in 1992 of "program access" rules. The rules gave companies like DirecTV access to cable content on a non-discriminatory basis.

That protracted fight marked the last time there was a major new competitor brought into the pay-television business and it had a profound effect on the market. The second and third-largest providers of pay-TV service—DirecTV and Dish Network Corp.—are both satellite companies.

Today, the debate is about extending those "program access rules" to online content distributors—a condition that has been suggested for approval of the merger.

Comcast will "wield a powerful mechanism to retain its video services revenue stream by killing off emerging Internet-based competition before it can even get off the ground," reads a joint filing by the Consumer Federation of America, Consumers Union, Free Press, and the Media Access Project.

The filing points to Vuze, a company that tried to create an online TV company, "but lacked access to much premium content." After many years and more than $34 million in private equity, Vuze abandoned its first business model of competing with cable TV distributors, according to the filing.

When asked directly about whether Comcast would oppose extending program access rules to online providers, Fitzmaurice pointed to a footnote in a Comcast filing with the FCC that said that such a move "could stifle investment and innovation and would raise extremely complex issues involving a wide range of stakeholders."

The short answer: over this deal's dead body.

Roberts has warned analysts that if regulators attach conditions to their approval of the deal that he considers "material," he will walk away. Unlike many merger deals, this one requires no "breakup fee," so Roberts won't pay a penalty if he decides to break off the courtship because he doesn't like the way Washington winds are blowing.

Although the transaction has been scrutinized in numerous congressional hearings—four on Capitol Hill, one each in California and Chicago, plus a FCC public forum, also in Chicago—experts say few in Washington have the stomach for the kind of fight the satellite guys had over the program access rules.

Comcast, which counts seventy-eight former government employees as lobbyists, has spent heavily to convince members of Congress to support the deal. In the second quarter of 2010, the company spent $3.82 million on lobbying—the most it has spent in single quarter. Comcast has convinced a large number of lawmakers to support the deal. Bloomberg News reported that ninety-one House members and three Senators who received Comcast campaign contributions have written letters to the FCC supporting the merger.

Wisconsin Senator Herb Kohl, the Democratic chairman of the Senate Judiciary Committee's subcommittee on antitrust, has been a persistent pain in Comcast's neck regarding the merger. He has suggested rules akin to those that allowed the satellite industry to flourish be attached to this deal's approval.

Among Comcast's lobbying hires? Kohl's former long-time chief of staff, Paul Bock of Capitol Hill Strategies. Bock registered to lobby on behalf of the merger on September 1, 2009.

Despite Comcast's considerable political and financial might, the drift toward online television viewing is strong. Once upon a time, our grandparents couldn't see the sense in paying for cable, said Crawford. Now a younger generation has started an online revolution that threatens to upset the stability of the entire television industry.

"They can't avoid it forever," she said of Comcast. "And they know that. But they can stave it off."

Critical Thinking

1. Summarize the pros and cons of the Comcast-NBC Universal deal.

2. The FCC has been in a deregulatory mode for quite some time, arguing that spectrum scarcity no longer exists as an argument for curtailing free enterprise in media businesses. For example, restrictions on owning a cable system and broadcast station in the same market were abolished in 2001. Is this a good thing? Are there any media ownership regulations you think should be established or reinstated?

JOHN DUNBAR, a former reporter for The Associated Press and The Center for Public Integrity, is director of "Connected—The Media and Broadband Project," part of the Investigative Reporting Workshop at American University in Washington, D.C. This story is a joint project of CJR and the Workshop, and was jointly published. Workshop researcher Mia Steinle and graduate assistant Allison Terry contributed to this report.

Tomorrow's Interactive Television

The iPad and its successors could revolutionize television. But only if and when we choose this future.

JOHN M. SMART

The elephant in America's living room right now is that there is not nearly enough quality choice, specialization, and personalization on television. According to many social critics, 70 years of lowest-common-denominator, mass-produced, big-business-driven TV content and news has hobbled Americans' education and narrowed their worldview. It has stunted their social participation and increasingly distracted them with entertainments, as in decadent Roman times.

Those who want sustained, in-depth television coverage of any particular issue; who want more transparency, accountability, foresight, and the ability to measure progress (in their own or their party's terms) on an issue; who strive to see the United States in global context; and who desire collective action to fix a problem are today unable to use society's primary electronic medium. They can't use it. to interact with their fellow citizens or to produce programming worthy of their communities.

As the Internet advances, however, this is beginning to change.

In recent decades, many European arid Asian developed countries have become more equitably regulated in media ownership and transparency, and they are much further along in wired and wireless access to the Internet than the United States. Not co-incidentally, these countries also have superior educational performance, much stronger social safety nets, more-extensive personal rights, and greater citizen participation in governance. Many, including Germany, the Scandinavian countries, Japan, South Korea, Hong Kong, Taiwan, and Singapore, are centers for world-leading manufacturing run by high-paid workers.

The same can no longer be said for the United States, as demonstrated by the nation's persistent trade deficits and the 60-year collapse of steel, auto, and manufactured goods industries. Only 4 percent of all American firms and 15 percent of manufacturers do any exporting at all, according to Matthew Slaughter of Dartmouth College. The export economy has so little diversity that just 1 percent of U.S. firms account for 80 percent of exports.

But perhaps the deepest problem that the United States faces, as documented by the Gini coefficient, is that the rich-poor divide has grown so much in the last 40 years that it now rivals emerging nations, countries like Venezuela, Argentina, China, and Mauritania. Meanwhile, the developed countries mentioned earlier have all become more income equal over the same time period. Data-backed books like Richard Wilkinson and Kate Pickett's *The Spirit Level*

(Bloomsbury Press, 2009) document that income inequality leads to greater crime, educational failure, illiteracy, unemployment, poorer health, teen pregnancy, obesity, mental illness, homelessness, class warfare, and political deadlock.

Ingenuity and the right incentives can fix these problems, but the United States will first need new groups of citizens that recognize them as problems. U.S. leaders don't have the ability to change the system on their own. Furthermore, as the income gap data suggests, these leaders are increasingly among the ultra rich, so they may not be motivated to change the system.

To change this state of affairs, access to true Internet television, not the walled gardens that cable companies offer American consumers, will be a critical piece of social equity.

I argue that access to the Internet's media universe in our living rooms, with appropriate content controls for youth, should be the right of every citizen in a developed society. It's also something that the major telecommunications companies like Verizon and cable companies like Comcast want to slow down, according to testimony from public-interest groups like Public Knowledge, the Center for Public Integrity, and even industry groups like the Competitive Telecommunications Association.

How Television Could Rise from the Wasteland

Robert Putnam's perceptive book, *Bowling Alone: The Collapse and Revival of American Community* (Simon and Schuster, 2001), chronicles the loss of social identity and interpersonal relationship complexity that occurred in U.S. towns and communities from the nation's 1950s zenith to today's nadir. Putnam names a number of culprits for this, but principally blames television.

Network television steals our eyeballs out of complex, two-way, social interactions in human space. It focuses us instead on one-way electronic messages. In *The Assault on Reason* (Penguin, 2007), former U.S. Vice President Gore says that average American consumers have seen a steady loss of complexity in the political conversation in the last 50 years, and the quality of American media is directly to blame. Network television is, on average, a "vast wasteland," and has been so for decades, as then-newly appointed FCC chairman Newton N. Minow said in his famous speech in 1961.

TV production quality now rivals the movie studios, and programming choice has slowly expanded over the years (as noted in *The Economist*'s May 2010 report on the future of television, *Changing the Channel*). But compared with video on the Web, which includes user-created channels like YouTube's Disco project and peer-to-peer offerings, television is less competitive than it was. Cable television gave U.S. viewers first 50, then 90, then 150 channels of slightly more interesting wasteland.

I argue that access to tens of thousands of specialty channels, a variety of content-aggregation options, and collaborative filtering by peer and trusted expert rankings would better serve U.S. social needs. Such a system will enable all those who wish to do so to eliminate unpersonalized advertising. What we need is two-way communication: person-to-person and many-to-many, not one-to-many. What we need is an electronic re-creation of the interactivity of the 1950s communities that Putnam chronicles, but in digital space, with the modern world's collective intelligence and diversity. Social networks are a start, but not nearly enough. Web 3.0, comprising TV-quality peer-to-peer video delivered on the Web, will be the next major step in this progression.

Film and television remain among the least competitive and democratic of all media. They have historically high development costs (your average Hollywood movie costs more than $106 million). We've seen small cracks in the film distribution monopoly in the last decade, with all the new documentaries produced by "filmanthropists"—folks who mortgage their house and self-finance low-budget films with $100,000 of capital or less. Many of these filmmakers can now make their money back, plus a small profit, just by using the personalized Netflix content distribution and rating system ("you told me you liked this film, so you may also like this new film"), which surfaces such niche films for users to consider. Most of these films would never get on cable TV or the retail floor in any Blockbuster or Hollywood Video store. More recently we also have Netflix's Watch Instantly (streaming video), iTunes movies, and a few other Internet outlets for independently produced specialty content.

Imagine how much more important, entertaining, and educational video we will see once most of us have Internet televisions at home, managing our access to thousands of online video aggregation environments. Want to see a three-to five-minute public domain film summarizing a Wikipedia page? You'll be able to pay 25 cents for it through the iTV of tomorrow, and eventually someone will make that film for you (and all of us), and make a profit. The media marketplace will be forever splintered. The old media corporations, and their big federated ad clients, will have given up trying to keep the lid on our choice. The new video universe will finally have arrived for everyone.

The Future of the iPad: How the Television Will Be Revolutionized

Today, 17 years after the Apple "Newton" MessagePad debuted in 1993, tablet PCs like the iPad are poised to live up to the hype that first surrounded them and realize their promise. More than 3 million iPad units sold in its first three months. More-open and diverse Android tablets from more than 20 manufacturers, running software from Apple's rival Google, are also on the horizon. Uncomplicated and easy to use for brief tasks, tablets seduce us into even more online social interaction, eReading, eLearning,

gaming, and other activities, and bring us another step closer to wearable computing.

The iPad's blockbuster software application is also now evident. The tablet PC is an ideal platform to manage all of the video viewing we will be doing on the Internet televisions that are beginning to arrive in living rooms around the world. This "killer app" seems likely to sell tens of millions of tablets annually as media center computers and iTV roll out across the world in the 2010s. Consider the following facts:

- In 2009, 211 million TVs were sold worldwide. In 2010, 228 million are projected to sell, with 79 percent being digital-ready LCD TVs. There are now 2.3 billion TVs in the world, and 6.7 billion people.

- Fully 25 percent of U.S. TVs sold in January 2010 were connected by consumers to the Internet. About 10 percent of TVs sold came "Internet ready." The rest, and all our older TVs, are being Internet-connected via set-top boxes, media centers, DVRs, game consoles, and DVD players.

- Today there are 20,000+ streamable Internet TV channels, waiting to be connected to Internet-enabled TVs. With the accelerating popularity of YouTube, Metacafe, Vimeo, Viddler, etc., we can expect, and hope for, more than 100,000 specialized channels by 2015.

- A few companies, like Boxee, have had easy-to-use, open-source Internet media center software since 2008, and are now developing set-top boxes. The best of these include social networking, peer viewing, and chat-while-viewing features and deliver a far more rewarding and personalized viewing experience than cable or satellite TV.

- All media center devices currently use "dumb" remotes with unusable small keyboards, and display their viewing options in large characters, with low resolution, on a distant TV screen. Only one remote can be used at a time, so individual viewers can't search for or signal what they want to watch next, or multitask on the Internet with their remotes. None of these use the advanced voice command and search software we find on our phones. In short, the television is waiting to be revolutionized by next-generation media centers and tablet remotes.

With the right software, a tablet can rapidly organize the most relevant of 20,000 (or a million) potential channels for the viewer. It can deliver a highly personalized viewing and learning experience while we are in the same room with others who have their own tablets. It can allow social viewing options so rich that we haven't even fully visualized them yet.

Imagine a tablet that displays what's on your "top 50" favorite channels on the home screen, and with the next 50 channels or titles just a tap away. With key words, user rating, and community rating as filtering options, all of these video items would be fighting to get higher in your stack depending on your viewing habits, feedback, and interests. Imagine an extensive set of social viewing features (real-time chat, social network integration, video and audio conferencing, peer-to-peer video, etc.) allowing you to watch TV and videos with others, and see what your friends are watching right now. Imagine being able to use your tablet to check the Internet for more on any subject while watching the large screen, just as those with Wi-Fi enabled laptops do today.

The Road to iTV

To deliver Web 3.0 to the world, and release its full social value, the Internet television of the coming decade will need features like the following:

- **Voice search and command.** If you've tried Google voice search for iPhone and Android, you've seen part of the future of iTV. These systems get better every month the more people use them, just like Web search. With voice-enabled search, a universe of choice is just a spoken phrase away from every viewer.
- **Collaborative rating and filtering systems.** We need collective intelligence, like Netflix's recommendation engine, to help us find, rate, and comment on our favorite video for the time and context. In an iTV-enabled world, we could all watch the next State of the Union address with a real-time ratings and ranking screen to the right of our video, allowing us see our favorite pundit or NGO's thoughts on the truthfulness and value of what we are hearing, and to provide our own free-form or survey-based feedback. Forget the post-game talking heads. Let's move on to real-time analysis by the analysts of our choice.
- **Social viewing, social networks, and real-time chat.** We need the ability to do social viewing; that is, to see what our colleagues and friends are watching right now and have watched in the last few days, to see their ratings, to watch with them remotely, to share whatever we wish, to find others who rank the same way we do, and to form community viewing and discussion groups for all kinds of specialty content. Social networks with real-time chat will be the glue that binds the social viewing experience: think Facebook TV.
- **Real-time captions.** We need the option to run captions at the bottom of all our video, and a marketplace for caption types. Think of all the specialty analysis we could get for our favorite political, news, business, sports, science, technology, and other shows. Both push and pull content (captions, links, video, text, etc.) would come to our tablets, in context, as we are watching our videos. Tomorrow's videos simply need a standard, or a few competing standards, that will allow these captions to arrive in synch with the video stream.
- **Micropayments, better commercials, and per-click ads.** In the ideal iTV future, you can pay very small amounts, either to individual content providers or to channel and content aggregators, with a tap of the finger. There are hundreds of thousands Of eBay Power Sellers who make full-time incomes selling specialty products. Now we need hundreds of thousands of independent video producers and aggregators who make full-time incomes creating, curating, and remixing specialty video, audio, and other media on topics that we care about.

  We also need standards for controlling the commercials on these Internet video channels. Most critically, we need the ability to "like," "dislike," and give feedback to all the video advertisements (commercials) that come into our homes, and the option to ban (and easily unban, if we change our minds) ad content that doesn't fit our current interests.
- **An open video markup language (OVML).** Perhaps most importantly, we need an open-source semantic standard for tagging every bit of video, station ID, or advertisement, and embedding licensing information and time-coded content, so we can control when and how to display it in our homes and offices. As David Siegel describes in *Pull: The Power of the Semantic Web* (Portfolio, 2009), emerging semantic standards are empowering industries around the world today. At the base of iTV must be a rich standard for all online video media, developed by user-centric nonprofits.

—John M. Smart

In an Internet-enabled, transparent society, advanced content control could create many new communities of specialization. As Adam Smith said in *The Wealth of Nations,* specialization and hard work are the tried-and-true roads to understanding and mastery of our environment.

Youth today often multitask on the Web when they watch television, and audience share for network television has been falling for more than a decade as consumers' video options (DVD, DVR, Netflix, the Web) have grown. Nevertheless, according to the American Time Use Survey, in 2008 the average U.S. household still spent roughly 2.9 hours for men and 2.6 hours for women watching television each day. Television viewing remains the single largest discretionary activity that U.S. residents engage in daily, accounting for fully half of daily leisure time.

It is an easy thesis, therefore, that improving television's quality, diversity, and relevance is a uniquely important target for social progress. Opening up the idiot box and making it competitive is where we need to go next, if we truly care about American free enterprise, social diversity, and democracy. When a society's openness and diversity grow, the country gets less stable at first, and then much more stable and productive than it was before openness began, as Ian Bremmer notes in *The J-Curve* (Scribner, 2006).

Paying for the iTV Play

To maximize revenue for the hundreds of thousands of new iTV content creators (individuals, organizations, communities) who are currently shut out of the American living room, there will need to be a mix of payment options, including direct micropayments, personalized commercials, and click-through ads.

Micropayments can be used to purchase video content from a marketplace (like iTunes), or, more commonly, to purchase a subscription from a specialty channel producer, like today's magazines and newspapers, almost all of which may need iTV channels by the 2020s to survive. Programming on some channels will be monetized by more viewer-friendly versions of today's commercial

John Smart's Additional Recommended Media on Media

Books:

- *Breaking the News: Haw the Media Undermine American Democracy* by Jim Fallows (Vintage, 1996).
- *The Future of Media: Resistance and Reform in the 21st Century* by Robert McChesney et al. (Seven Stories Press, 2005).
- *The Problem of the Media* by Robert McChesney (Monthly Review Press, 2004).

Films:

- *Outfoxed,* 2004.
- *Weapons of Mass Deception,* 2005.
- *Manufacturing Consent,* 1993.
- *News War,* 1983.
- *Orwell Rolls in His Grave,* 2005. This last is my personal favorite. Be sure to watch all the special features on the DVD in order to get a gut understanding of how truly big-business-controlled, corrupt, and anticompetitive media access and policy are in the United States today.

—John M. Smart

breaks, commercials that we can automatically play captioned or at a much lower volume than the regular program, giving us back our conversation space, and a system that allows us to "like," "dislike," and permanently block commercials of any type.

Another form of payment, perhaps occurring in a hideable window adjacent to the video, will be context-based per-click revenue and advertising (like Google's AdSense), a revenue model that is already greatly broadening the availability of text-based content on the Web.

Prospects for iTV

Yochai Benkler's FCC-commissioned Berkman Center 2009 report, "Next Generation Connectivity," addresses America's lagging wired and wireless connectivity and affordability. Other leading developed economies, such as Japan, South Korea, Hong Kong, and parts of Europe, have many times more broadband (data transfer ability and speed) than the United States has today. The report urges a public-private partnership to make affordable, always-on broadband (1,000 Mbps or more, via fiber optic cable) into a public right. Such "gigabit broadband" is what will allow iTV to emerge in the United States, and the incumbent carriers will provide it as slowly as they can.

Another critical need is net neutrality—that is, the principle that all providers use the information superhighway at the same rates, without discrimination by content type. Some of the above countries, like Japan, have already passed net neutrality laws, while the United States has yet to even consider them in the courts.

I believe that it is the U.S. government's, not corporations', role to provide leadership to close the "fiber gap" that currently exists between the United States and leading Asian and European countries, to ensure that the poor have affordable access, and to develop the incentives for bringing broadband (via Wi-Max, LTE, satellite, and other routes) to rural areas. If the U.S. government mandated eminent domain of fiber access routes, and allowed any authorized firms to have access to fiber trunk cabinets, competitive delivery of fiber-to-the-premises (home or office) could be quickly achieved today in all U.S. cities and, a few years later, everywhere.

Americans have had a similar learning experience with the national highways in the early twentieth century, which were once networks of private roads. Road development is ideal to start privately, but once the cost of construction has been recovered plus a reasonable return on investment, private ownership is very inefficient to continue, with all those turnpikes and the constant need to "turn" a profit. U.S. leaders figured this out and nationalized the highway system. Today, the build-operate-transfer model—starting with private construction, a limited operating lease, and then transfer to public ownership—is the fastest-growing and most productive way to create new roads in any country.

I believe the same situation holds for wired and wireless communications channels, our information superhighways. These digital "roads" are great to build out privately, but once the corporations have made a reasonable profit, it's time to turn those data pipes into a publicly owned utility. Competitive private bidding would keep the public information superhighway maintained and free to all, and many new services and businesses would emerge, with far greater total market value than is possible in today's limited-connectivity world.

The big telecommunications and cable companies could then be freed to develop even faster and better communications technology, or, failing that, to become content providers. The government could grant them all one last five-year monopoly license before they started this in any state, to give them time to prepare for the rigors of the marketplace. In that setting, Comcast's recent purchase of NBC would be something we could champion (a move from carrier to content provider).

U.S. leaders may not act to fix the nation's growing connectivity gap anytime soon, as pundits and lobbyists will do their best to portray this as "inefficient governmental intervention." Yet, it is exactly such smart intervention that has allowed Asian countries like Japan and South Korea to leapfrog the United States in critical digital-infrastructure development and to develop profitable new businesses and exports around the high-bandwidth Internet, including several early versions of iTV.

Many Americans don't understand just how anticompetitive the nation's communications technology laws and regulatory agencies have become, and how much this diminishes the diversity and value of its digital economy. In an iTV world, we can imagine a lot of easily available quality media that would make this case. In the meantime, we do what we can.

John M. Smart is a futurist, president of the Acceleration Studies Foundation, and associate professor and Program Champion of the Master of Science in Emerging Technologies at the University of Advancing Technology in Tempe, Arizona. E-mail johnsmart@accelerating.org.

Originally published in the November/December 2010, pp. 41–46 issue of *The Futurist.* Copyright © 2010 by World Future Society, Bethesda, MD. Used with permission. www.wfs.org

Open for Business

**If you want readers to buy news, what, exactly, will you sell?
The case for a free/paid hybrid.**

Michael Shapiro

In the dark winter and spring of 2009, as dispatches from the news business grew ever more grim, as Jim Romenesko's posts took on the feel of casualty reports, newsrooms across the land began to feel like the Emerald City when the Wicked Witch soars overhead, trailing smoke and sending everyone scurrying not for cover, but for an answer, to the Wizard. So it was that in the midst of this gloomy time help appeared, and not merely the illusion of a wizardly hand. It came from Walter Isaacson and from Steven Brill, who were quickly joined by a determined chorus that, no longer willing to stand idly by as its trade died, took up a call that was clear, direct, and seemingly unassailable in its logic: *make the readers pay.*

They envisioned a happy time in which people so loved, or at least appreciated, what journalists did that they would pay to listen, watch, and read online. Excited by the prospect of compensation commensurate with their best efforts, news people raced to find evidence to support this encouraging talk. Suddenly, Peter Kann, dismissed as hopelessly un-Webby when he placed *The Wall Street Journal* behind a paywall in 1996, was being touted in retirement as a man so prescient about revenue streams that Rupert Murdoch, who had taken over Dow Jones with thoughts of bringing that wall down, was now preaching the wisdom of charging for access. People pointed to the money that came from subscribers to such sites as *Congressional Quarterly, Consumer Reports,* and *Cook's Illustrated* as evidence that Isaacson, who had made his case first at a speech this winter at the Aspen Institute and then on the cover of *Time,* had been right. Readers not only would pay, but were already paying. They paid for information and for access to newspaper websites, too—in places like Little Rock, Albuquerque, and Lewiston, Idaho. They paid by the year, the month, the week. Perhaps they might even pay by the story—a micropayment, like for a song on iTunes.

But then, as often happens when euphoria is built on hope born of despair, the good feelings began to recede. The readers-will-pay chorus was ever more drowned out by the voices of the doomsayers, the apostles of information-wants-to-be-free.

Paid content, they insisted, was an illusion. Take a closer look at the sites that charge, they argued, and you will see flaws in your logic: for one, many of them cater to audiences of narrow interest—lobbyists compelled to follow legislation through every subcommittee; business people whose firms cover the costs, so that they might make a buck at the expense of their competitors; lovers of the best, kitchen-tested recipe for Yankee pot roast. And as for those few newspapers that had gotten away with charging for Web access, note that almost all were small, or the sole purveyors of news for hundreds of miles around. These voices were joined by those who saw in the vanishing of the American newspaper a necessary death—much like the Israelites wandering the desert for forty years, waiting for those wed to the old ways to die out.

And so it went, variations on familiar themes that tended to leave little room for the clutter of a middle ground. The back and forth produced a stalemate on the difficult question of whether it was possible, or reasonable, to expect people to pay for news that they had come to believe should be free.

But it obscured the big questions that, logic suggested, would have to come next: If you were going to charge, what, precisely, were you going to sell? And if you sold something new, would that alter, or even revolutionize, the nature of the news?

One

In the beginning, there was the 900 number.

The service had been around for decades when, in 1987, AT&T allowed businesses leasing 900 numbers to charge for calls. People started to pay—for sports scores, news, weather, and stock quotes. Men also paid, sometimes quite a lot, to listen to women talk dirty. The change in dialing habits revolutionized the *idea* of the phone call. The telephone was no longer merely a device that allowed for remote conversation at minimal cost. It became a vehicle for running a business—you could make money with a phone, so long as you sold what people wanted to buy.

That lesson was not lost with the coming of the Internet. Even as people fretted about whether anyone would figure out a way to make a buck online, the pornographers, ever on the vanguard, shifted technologies and began charging not merely for a voice, but for a peek. Others took notice, with higher aspirations. Even as the early apostles of Web culture extolled the virtues of every-man-a-publisher, content did, in fact, go on sale.

Some of it sold. Much didn't—or at least not enough, in the news business, to make up for all the potential lost advertising revenue that has always been the financial backbone of the industry. Slate charged for access for about a year, only to reverse itself in 1999. The *Los Angeles Times* charged for CalenderLive, only to drop the fee in 2005, after twenty-one months of declining page views and modest revenue. *Variety* and Salon took down their paywalls, as did many of the handful of small newspapers that had charged—among them the *Creston* (Iowa) *News Advertiser,* the *Newton* (Iowa) *Daily News,* and the *Aiken* (South Carolina) *Standard,* whose page views tripled after its wall came down in 2007. The *New York Times* ended Times-Select in 2007, having calculated—at that time—that it could more than make up for the $10 million in lost revenue with the advertising generated by all the many new visitors to its site.

Still, there were holdouts, and the titan among the paid-content stalwarts was and remains *The Wall Street Journal,* which continues to charge subscribers $100 annually. While the number of subscribers has grown steadily to its present one million, they pale in comparison to the 20 million monthly unique visitors to The *New York Times,* which, for the moment, remains entirely free—but may not be for much longer.

The sense among the free-content advocates, though, is that the *Journal,* great as it is, is an outlier, a publication not written for a general audience but for the world of commerce. The same was being said of other specialized online publications that cater to people with a financial stake in the news they provided. The growing online presence of the trade press, in the view of the believers in free content, meant only that people already conditioned to spending hundreds or thousands of dollars a year for the brand of news that served their particular needs were now logging on, and not waiting for the newsletter to arrive.

Besides, walled-off content meant content that was not searchable, which meant that it did not draw the great flows of online traffic in a world where the hyperlink had become the coin of commerce and notice.

Sites like CQ.com—which boasted a multitude of databases, brought in about 43 percent of *CQ*'s annual revenue (somewhere between $50 million and $100 million; the company is privately held and will be no more precise about earnings), and had a large editorial staff (CQ Inc. employs more than 165 people)—while admired for the work they produced, were nonetheless relegated to the fringe because they were not part of the greater, link-driven conversation. And hadn't *CQ* subsequently started a free site, CQ Politics, which, while it generated less than 2 percent of the company's revenue, did attract an average of 450,000 uniques a month, ensuring that *CQ* was not left out of Washington's overheated political conversation?

The criticism was much the same for those sites that sold news whose value was not necessarily fungible—politically or financially, either in money earned (the business-to-business press) or in money well spent (*Consumer Reports*). These sites sold news that mattered only because everyone in particular slivers of the online world was talking about it. These were the sites that had occupied small pockets of Chris Anderson's Long

Tail, his theory about the rise of niche businesses online. Places like Orangebloods.com.

Orangebloods is a site that, depending on the time of year, has between eight thousand and ten thousand subscribers paying $9.99 a month, or $100 annually, for steady updates about all known thought regarding the University of Texas football team. The site covers practices and assesses the team's strengths and potential worries, but the least important thing it does is cover games. Everyone covers games, the reasoning went, and everyone *watches* games. So instead, Orangebloods found a niche within a niche: it reports and sells what no one else can provide, which is year-round coverage of Longhorns recruiting. Its reporters fan out across the state, and sometimes across the nation, meeting, observing, and collecting footage of leading high-school football players. They then pour all this into the Orangebloods site along with information about those potential Longhorns' size, speed, bench-pressing capacity, and GPAs, all the while offering interviews, commentary, starred rankings, and candid assessments of the Longhorns' chances of securing a commitment: *Solid verbal!*

Orangebloods is one of the 130 paid college-football sites that are part of Rivals.com, which Yahoo bought in 2007 for $100 million. Rivals is run by Bobby Burton, who in the early 1990s, as an undergraduate at Texas, worked in the football team's film library, converting film to video and then editing the footage so that coaches could study, say, tendencies on third and long. Burton took that passion—he uses the word often—to the *National Recruiting Advisor,* a newsletter that reported on recruiting and augmented its service with updates on, yes, a 900 number.

The business went through several iterations—free, then paid, then failing—before re-emerging in 2001. By then Burton had abandoned the idea of using citizen journalists to do his reporting for him, having determined that he needed professionals. In time, the combined editorial staff at Rivals grew to over three hundred and, as the site's reputation grew among the college-football cognoscenti, its subscriptions rose to its present 200,000; Orangebloods is among the most popular.

And that popularity, that desire to subscribe, says its editor, Geoff Ketchum, is as much about the news it reports as it is about the talking and ruminating with an audience that cares beyond all apparent reason about Longhorn football. They make full use of the site's message board, offering lengthy and deeply-felt opinions, and talk with one another with such familiarity that when one subscriber's child was diagnosed with cancer, his online friends raised money for treatment.

"We're like heroin for UT football fans. We've got all the nuts that exist. We cover what the people want to pay for."

—Geoff Ketchum

"We're like heroin for UT football fans," Ketchum says. "We've got all the nuts that exist." He says this with the affection of someone who recognizes his own. "We don't cover all the sports," he adds. "We cover what the people want to pay for."

Two

But would the people pay for news aimed not at the few but at the many? As zealots on either side of the pay divide duked it out, Nancy Wang ran the numbers. The news was not good. For either side.

Wang, who with her husband, Jeff Mignon, runs a Manhattan media consulting firm, crunched nine different scenarios for newspapers of two different approximate sizes—100,000 paid circulation and 50,000. (Here her base scenario was for a most typical American paper, which has 50,000 circulation, publishes seven days a week, charges $17 a month for print subscribers, has a website with 250,000 unique visitors, and online revenues of $700,000.) The analysis, Wang says, were based on real numbers, but were intended as projections of potential, not actual, revenue.

Her conclusions, which were reported in March 2009 by the Newspaper Association of America, essentially boiled down to this: once a newspaper put all its content behind a paywall, online subscriptions dropped dramatically and those subscriptions did not come close to making up lost advertising revenue. The advertising projections, she explains, were based on "very conservative," pre-recession numbers. "It's hard to say that putting in a paid model for content would pay on its own," she says.

But her results were not all that encouraging for the free-content crowd, either—those who advocate an advertising-only model despite the fact that revenue for online ads, though rising, is a fraction of what it is for print.

The online scenario that worked best, she concluded, was a compromise—combining free and paid content, at a percentage of 80 to 20, free to paid. But, she cautions, "there has to be something that people are willing to pay for."

Could that "something" be local news? Wang built her analysis on numbers from the NAA, the media buyers AdPerfect and Centro, as well as from Borrell Associates, a Virginia consulting firm whose president, Gordon Borrell, had for years preached that publishers were wrong if they continued to believe that local news as currently constituted would sell.

Borrell had begun his career as a reporter for *The Virginian-Pilot,* and so came to his conclusion with an understanding and empathy for the work reporters do. The problem, as he saw it, was that newspapers assumed they could continue to sell what he regarded as a tired and tedious product in a new medium simply because they had done so well selling it in an old one.

Borrell had issued his first comprehensive study on paid content shortly after the 9/11 attacks, a time when the public was devouring news, and so a moment when the prospect of online revenue would be running high. He surveyed nearly 1,900 online-newspaper readers and discovered that while people were willing to register for sites—a necessity in attracting advertisers—and might be willing to pay for some news, they were not about to start paying for general online news they had become accustomed to getting for free. He had thought at the time that they might, one day.

But now, eight years later, he saw no evidence of that happening. Readers simply did not value local news enough to pay for it. Borrell found only about 12 percent of most markets went to the Web for local news.

They still bought newspapers, though in diminishing numbers, and quite often not with the same imperative that drove Borrell's one-time newsroom colleagues. While journalists envision people tossing out the coupons to get to the news, many readers perform the ritual in reverse—tossing the news to get to the coupons, a practice confirmed by an NAA study that found that fully half of all readers bought local papers for the ads. Such, Borrell concluded, was the fate of a product that, in the eyes of its intended audience, was "not that compelling."

But wait. Hadn't the industry been pinning its hopes for well over a generation on local news, on bringing to suburban readers targeted versions of the traditional mix of local politics, cops, fires, courts, and the occasional strange doings that used to fill the big-city papers that everyone in town read? And hadn't the mix grown to include dispatches on schools and zoning and features of local interest? And hadn't some of that work been of consequence, hadn't it won awards and allowed publishers to speak of their "watchdog" role and to suggest, channeling Jefferson, that their work kept the citizenry informed and enlightened? *Not that compelling?*

Or did Borrell have a point? Was it possible that the self-satisfaction with which news organizations regarded themselves and their role had been undermined and diluted? The news purists had been warning for years of the danger of a culture in which publishers cheapened the value of their content with cutbacks intended to satisfy investors and media analysts. But no one had paid them much mind, because even in a diminished state the product still sold. If you could do it on the cheap, why not?

Lack of competition was good for profits but turned many dailies into vanilla approximations of themselves.

But it was not just the shareholders' fault. Competition, the catalyst that drove journalists, that fueled their anxiety, fear, ruthless streaks—qualities of personality that propelled them to succeed—had been vanishing for decades. Fewer newspapers in fewer towns found themselves in direct competition for stories, and while this helped make a good many papers very profitable (Exhibit A: Gannett), it also had the effect of rendering many newspapers into vanilla approximations of themselves. The papers weren't necessarily bad; they looked good and read well enough. But it was hard to imagine anyone standing on a street corner shouting, "Extra! Extra! Read all about it!" when the headline screamed ZONING DISPUTE.

The problem with the content, however, did not stop there. Stories were ever more routine, in the subject and in the way they were told—so much so that news, as defined and presented, had for years been an ongoing object of parody in, most famously, *The Onion.*

The pity of it was that in the decades that preceded the recent downsizing of content, newspapers had been stretching the definition of news in ways that made papers of the more distant past seem hopelessly narrow. *Front Page* romanticism aside, readers of, say, the *St. Louis Star* in 1942 would have had no sense of the dark and frightened mood in town in the first winter of World War II, because the paper did not consider such matters news. A generation later, everyone, it seemed, had an investigative team, as well as education, immigration, and health-care reporters, and a local columnist or two. The best writing was no longer necessarily on the sports pages and there was no shortage of FOIA requests. The definition of news expanded, as did the way news was told.

But then, over a stretch of years long enough that it was hard to notice, the reports that came back from once-proud-and-lively newsrooms were that it was getting very hard to, say, sniff out local corruption or capture the zeitgeist of a community when your beat had expanded from three towns to ten, and when the unspoken but well-understood directive from above was to feed the beast, in print and, in time, online. Newspapers still produced admirable work, but the appearance of another plaque on the newsroom wall tended to obscure the fact that while great work was still being accomplished, a good deal of what was otherwise being done was of diminishing value and allure.

So for Borrell, editors and publishers and owners who rallied to the cry of paid content were working under the misapprehension that what they had given away or sold very cheaply would suddenly be regarded as having value by readers whose needs had been sadly undervalued for a long time.

But Borrell still believed that there was money to be made in the news business—online and in print. Print was the place for display advertising, and for all those coupons and end-of-summer ads. Free online access brought the readers—the eyeballs—advertisers wanted. As for paid content, Nancy Wang and Jeff Mignon had for some time been preaching the virtues of a hybrid approach of mixing paid and free online content to the fifty or so news organizations of various sizes they consulted for, and the result, she says, was almost always the same: the young, Web-savvy people would get excited by the possibilities, and their older, more tradition-bound editors, she says, would scream, "NO!"

The resistance, she explains, was not a function of blind stubbornness, but rather a fear that that which they hold sacred was about to be diluted in the name of making a buck. And they were not altogether wrong.

It was at this moment in the conversation that publishers and editors were forced to confront a difficult choice: if a newsroom had a finite number of reporters, and if that newsroom needed a new revenue stream to make up for declining circulation and lower ad rates, it needed to report something that people wanted enough to pay for. Not all people. Just some, with the money and the willingness to pay.

That, in turn, meant *not* devoting the time, the staff, and the money to report on what was presumably of interest to everyone. It meant making the choice to provide content that was exclusive to paying customers. It meant satisfying the core readership at the expense of those unwilling, or perhaps unable, to prove their loyalty with a check or money order.

Something had to go, if you were going to stay in business. But if you were going to start selling news, you had decide what you could offer that people might buy.

And so once the conversation moved past the arguments about the *idea* of paying, and it became ever more apparent that news organizations would do well to charge for *something,* the word heard most often was "value."

Three

Peter Fader was such a fan of TimesSelect—the opinion-oriented section that *The New York Times* briefly put behind a paywall—that had the price doubled he would gladly have paid it. Times-Select represented value for Fader, a quality, he says, that always eclipses price when a purchase is being considered. Fader is a professor of marketing at the Wharton School at the University of Pennsylvania. He explains that pricing "is a trade-off attitude." Economists, Fader says, often make the mistake of building projections upon the supposition that people are rational beings. But people, he says, will perform the irrational act of paying for all kinds of things that they can otherwise get for nothing.

They will, for instance, pay 99 cents for songs on iTunes that can be downloaded for free because Apple makes the transactional experience not only legal, but easy, attractive, and accessible. People will also pay for subscriptions. They will, for example, willingly allow their bank accounts to be dunned $17 a month for Netflix even though weeks may pass without a rental or download. No matter, Fader says; those subscribers have fallen into an "electronic trance" in which they refuse to cancel because they anticipate renting one day, real soon.

Perhaps the best and most alluring analogy for selling news online is cable television. TV used to be free and in some places still is. But cable transformed the idea that the medium came without cost by making it into a medium that provided a wide choice of occasionally terrific content that was exclusive to those who paid for it.

The transformation did not come instantly, and despite all the new channels, the experience of watching cable TV is often as it was in the old five channels-plus-UHF days: *Nothing's on.* But cable offers lots of choices, on a sliding scale, and Fader says people will continue to pay for the promise of value because whatever disappointments they might have experienced—for instance, a weeper on Lifetime—have been outweighed by, say, *The Sopranos.*

New technologies arrive with lamentations for the institutions and traditions and old technologies sure to die out. It was that way with television—*the death of movie theaters!* And with FM radio—*the end of live concerts!* But new technologies do not replace the old, they merely take a place at their side. Grand and aging movie palaces became multiplexes, and owners did such a brisk business that people decided it was worth spending an extra $1.50 to pre-order tickets on Fandango. So it is that Fandango sells what once came without cost, but which now represents admission denied to someone else.

That, in a sense, is also the calculus for success at *Congressional Quarterly,* which sells information that is available elsewhere at no cost but at considerable hassle. If you are, for instance, a lobbyist who needs to know the status of a particularly worrisome piece of legislation, *CQ* can sell you, through its BillTrack database, the full text and an analysis of the bill, its status in committee, a profile of that committee, a district-by-district breakdown of the members of the committee, a dollar-by-dollar breakdown of those members' campaign contributors—in short, everything a clever lobbyist needs to know *before* that information comes to another clever lobbyist for the opposition. This is what Robert Merry, *CQ*'s president and editor-in-chief, calls "information paranoia," a particularly virulent affliction in Washington.

CQ sells access to thirty-five different databases. It has four niche verticals—homeland security, health, a budget tracker, and its political money line. It does give some information away for free. So do *The Wall Street Journal*—a story at a time—and the *Financial Times*—a limited number of stories each month, before the paywall goes up. But these are, from a marketing standpoint, the journalistic equivalent of movie trailers on Fandango: *If you loved our report on this stimulus package, you'll want to see . . .*

Merry thinks of *CQ* as a pyramid. At its base are the many visitors to CQPolitics who pay nothing but who do deliver eyeballs. At the top are those so ravenous for particular slices of news they can use that they will pay $10,000 or more a year for access. In other words, *CQ* sells various products for various media to audiences who differ not by geography or income but by need. It was doing so well before analysts like Wang and Mignon began preaching the virtues of the "hybrid" model to their sometimes-reluctant clients.

The Wall Street Journal will soon expand its existing free-for-a-single-story "hybrid" model into one that includes micropayments. The *New York Times* is considering such revenue streams as metered payments (like those at the *FT*) and premium content memberships that presumably would cater to the paper's most loyal readers. It is one thing for the *Times,* the *Journal,* and the *FT* to impose fees on some of their content because their content is so highly regarded by so many. But what of those general news publications that have done away with so much of their original coverage of anything that is not local, and have diminished even that? Are they doomed? Or can they save themselves by redefining their content, and by extension, news?

General news has long been predicated on the idea that people's primary interest in news was defined by where they lived. But that was never completely so. The ethnic press, for instance, is as much about where you are from as about where you landed. Similarly, magazines are now almost exclusively defined by the particular interests of their readers. (The demise of the general-interest magazine offers a powerful and emotional parallel to the fate of the general-interest newspaper: a generation ago it seemed impossible to envision an America without *The Saturday Evening Post, Life,* and *Look.*)

Yet most newspapers still represent a model defined by borders. This makes for a relatively easy business to run when most readers lived in one place—a small town or a city. With the post–World War II exodus to the suburbs, however, the urban newspaper model built on cops, courts, fires, and politics was essentially picked up and transplanted not to one locality but to many disparate places where, it was assumed, readers had little interest in the goings-on across the town line, and the ever more remote downtown. Gone was the big-city paper; in its place came the regional daily.

But now, *The Washington Post,* for one, has begun to embrace the idea of defining itself not as the newspaper of Washington, the physical entity, but as Washington, the idea—just as *The Wall Street Journal,* which the *Post*'s new editor, Marcus Brauchli, used to run, is not about Wall Street, a district in lower Manhattan. In a memo to her staff last December, the *Post*'s publisher, Katharine Weymouth, wrote of the paper as "being about Washington, for Washingtonians and those affected by it." The latter phrase is key. It suggests that the paper is both acknowledging the physical boundaries of a portion of its coverage—"the indispensable guide to Washington"—while expanding beyond them. It means that Washington is, in a sense, everywhere—in every tax dollar, FAA hearing, wherever Washington's institutions and influence reach. A new and different hyper-local.

If this succeeds, what's to stop, say, the *Detroit Free Press* from augmenting its definition of Detroit as a municipality with Detroit as an idea—say, all things automotive? There is news in cars, lots of it. And there are people who need to know it, not all of them residents of greater Detroit. One wonders what the denuded *San Jose Mercury News,* a paper that had been a model of the regional news organization, might have become had it positioned itself as the definitive source of tech news for a readership well beyond Silicon Valley.

Once a news organization sees itself as something more than in service of a place, it puts itself in a position to tap into one of the emotional imperatives that sustain the niche sites. Geoff Ketchum's Orangebloods, for instance, is not limited to resident Texans. Regardless of where they live, his core readers have proven themselves willing to pay for the knowledge his site offers so that they can remain a part of a conversation. "Newspapers can't entice us into small payment systems," argues the media thinker Clay Shirky, "because we care too much about our conversation with one another. . . ." Newspapers, as presently defined, cannot. But if Orangebloods can, why can't a vertical on what is otherwise a general news site?

Those conversations can be inclusive (pay $9.95 a month and become an Orangeblood) or exclusive (CQ BillTrack), but what they have in common is that each, in a sense, represents what might best be called a Community of Need. The need is for the news that fuels a particular conversation. So long as there is something new to report.

Niche sites succeed, in large measure, by staking out a line of coverage that represents precisely the kinds of stories that newspapers decided to abandon years ago because so many readers found them so tedious: process stories. The relentless journey of a bill through a legislative body—*cloture vote!* Tracking a running back as he decides between Baylor and Texas. But process stories are stories that, by their nature, offer an endless source of developments; there is always something new happening, even if to those on the outside of the conversation, it is news of little value. Robert Merry wonders, for instance, why so many newspapers abandoned their statehouse bureaus when those capital cities were awash in money, lobbyists, legislators, and eager-beaver aides who'd be willing to pay quite a lot for information that might give them an edge. They did so because most readers said the stories were boring—and that was true for most readers, but not all.

But there is an important caveat: such projects do not succeed if they're done on the cheap. They require reporters whose primary responsibility is to supply the endless news that feeds those relatively few readers' needs. The need is for news. Not opinion. (Bobby Burton is not alone in believing the *Times* erred in what it chose to place behind its TimesSelect paywall, which was not news but the opinions of its famous columnists.) The problem with opinion is that the Web has made everyone a columnist precisely because it costs nothing to offer a point of view. Nor does it cost very much, or sometimes nothing at all, to fill a site with well-intentioned work, and opinion, provided by citizen journalists. But as Burton discovered in the early days of Rivals, those amateur journalists may have wise and clever things to say, but when he wanted to regularly break news he went out and hired people who knew how to do it—and he pays them between $30,000 and more than $150,000 a year.

Orangebloods is only as good as its next scoop; because if its stories begin appearing with any frequency someplace else— and perhaps, for free—the compact that Ketchum has with his readers is in jeopardy. Which is why there is nothing passive or reactive about the site's approach to its work. That, however, has not always been the case for general news that has traditionally defined itself by default: it's news because it's always been news. This, in turn, has created a culture of news in which the operative verb, far too often, is *said,* a culture in which all a reporter needs to do is listen and record.

As a result, too much of what fills the news pages is, as is often said, stenography. And because it can be done quickly, and at great volume, and with relatively little effort, it endures. The timing could not be more dispiriting, given that the generation in power in journalism now came to the field with a sense of journalism's possibilities, and broadened the idea of what news could be. But this generation also came of age at a time of growing newsroom prosperity.

This expanded sense of what the content could be made newspapers fatter; new sections appeared; nothing had to go, save for those process stories that no one wanted to read. Not a tough choice. Not like now, when the redefinition of news may mean deciding what you can sell to those willing to pay, and, by extension, what you will give up in the rest of the day's report so that you can redeploy your shrinking staff.

Inevitably, this raises an existential issue: What are newspapers for? Do they exist to serve narrow bands of interest? Or are there issues that transcend the paying niches, journalistic responsibilities that we should worry might well be overlooked and ignored in the interests of satisfying those who foot the bill?

It is not enough to simply hope that editors and publishers will retain their nobler instincts, not when times are tough. But, at the risk of sounding cynical, there is every reason to believe that they might continue offering stories of consequence for a larger, and perhaps unpaying audience for another reason—because it might be good for business. There are stories that transcend demographic borders. They are stories that are universal in their appeal, and infectious in their presentation. Not all novels, after all, are written for niche audiences; some speak to people who, on the surface, have nothing in common with one another. And as it is with novels, and movies, and television shows that attract wide followings, there are stories that capture the eye and the imagination, and which lure readers who might stick around, or even come back, and bring advertisers with them. The burden rests on the news organization to do what news people have always done: find those stories.

Transform the everyday work of journalism from a reactive, money-losing proposition into a more selective enterprise.

So it is that journalism's crisis offers an opportunity to transform the everyday work of journalism from a reactive and money-losing proposition into a more selective enterprise of reporting things that no one else knows. And choosing, quite deliberately, to ignore much of what can be found elsewhere.

People will pay for news they deem essential, and depending on the depth and urgency of their need, they will pay a lot. Their subscriptions, in turn, might well help to underwrite the cost of producing original work that might remain free and be of interest to more than a select few.

Those subscriptions will not save newspapers. They alone will not pay for the cost of reporting. No one revenue stream will—not online or print advertising, or alerts on handheld devices, or new electronic readers that display stories handsomely. The hope is that they *all* will.

The means of distributing the news will change, but what is clear and unchanging is people's desire to know things, to be told a story, and to be able talk about it all with other people— for such things matter.

Extra! Extra! Read all about it!

Critical Thinking

1. Which do you predict is more likely: (a) Niche media will replace true mass-mass media; or (b) The most popular niche media formats will become the new mass-mass media (survival of the biggest sellers)? Why?

2. Construct your own survey to investigate what kinds of online content people you know would be willing to pay for, and how much they would be willing to pay for each hypothetical site. Summarize and analyze your results.

MICHAEL SHAPIRO, a contributing editor to *CJR*, teaches at Columbia's Graduate School of Journalism. His most recent book is *Bottom of the Ninth: Branch Rickey, Casey Stengel, and the Daring Scheme to Save Baseball From Itself.*

Pay to Play

As cash-strapped newspapers struggle to adapt to the Internet age, more and more are asking readers to pay for digital content. Is that a winning strategy for the future?

CARY SPIVAK

Newspaper publishers and executives these days can be divided into three groups:

First, there are those who charge readers to view at least some of their content on computers as well as smart phones or tablet devices like the iPad.

Second, there are those who are thinking about doing just that.

The third group? Executives who are watching the first two.

Proponents and critics alike agree that 2011 will see many revenue-starved newspapers begin charging for online news. Some will lock up much of their local content, while others will use a meter system in which readers get a handful of pageviews free but have to pony up if they want more. Still others will charge only for certain types of stories, say, news about a particular pro or college sports team or a specific industry. Most will continue to make some of their content available without charge.

With all the pressure that the Internet era and the economic downturn have placed on the beleaguered newspaper industry, it's hardly surprising that many news outlets are frantically searching for new revenue streams. Or that they are targeting customers who are enjoying their wares for free. The time has come, many in the business say, to stop talking and start charging.

"The only true failure in the time of adversity is the failure to take risks," says James Moroney III, publisher of the Dallas Morning News. "We are still in a time of great adversity."

Executives in Little Rock, where the Arkansas Democrat-Gazette in 2001 became one of the first metres in the nation to erect a paywall, say they are receiving more calls from counterparts in other cities who are getting ready to follow its 10-year lead. Many credit the paywall as a key reason the paper's daily circulation actually *increased* between 2000 and 2010.

"For a lot of papers, it's not if, but when," says Conan Gallaty, online director of the Democrat-Gazette. Gallaty readily acknowledges that the thought of a paywall—and the virtually guaranteed drop in pageviews once it goes up—"gives people in my position heartburn." He argues that although millions of hits on a free site may make reporters and editors feel good, lots of those hits bring very little money in the door. "Our motto is, 'only build what you could sell.'"

That's a view that's increasingly talked about by many, but for years it was embraced by very few. The prevailing wisdom was that all of those eyeballs would lead to a healthy influx of online advertising dollars. But while online ads have increased, they don't command nearly the rates of newspaper ads, and those retro print products continue to provide the overwhelming share of the revenue at most papers. But print advertising, not to mention print readership, keeps shrinking, and online ads haven't bridged the gap.

There are dozens of papers with paywalls already in operation, ranging from prestigious publications like the Wall Street Journal to a handful of regional dailies, among them the Daily Gazette of Schenectady, New York, and the Spectrum in St. George, Utah. In February, the Dallas Morning News joined their ranks, locking up the online incarnation of the paper as well as versions available on mobile devices.

In Philadelphia, access to philly.com, the Web Bite for the Inquirer and Daily News, is free. But Philadelphia Media Network, which owns the papers, this year began charging for its digital editions available on a variety of devices, including the Kindle, tablets and smart phones. "It's the newspaper, but it's a much more enhanced version," says Mark Block, vice president for external relations. For $2.99 a week, people who don't subscribe to the print version can get access to the e-edition of one of the daily papers plus links to other features, Block says. It costs $6.99 a week to subscribe to the print edition of the Inquirer and gain access to the digital version of the paper.

The Wall Street Journal paved the way for many others when it launched its paywall in 1997. (The company declined to break out how many of its subscribers are online only.) The jury is still out at the Times of London, which like the Journal is owned by Rupert Murdoch's News Corp. Almost immediately after it began charging for online and digital access in July, Web traffic declined sharply. In November, company officials expressed renewed confidence that the approach would work, saying the daily and Sunday papers had close to 200,000 paid subscribers for their digital products.

Those in the process of imposing or expanding pay-to-read plans run the gamut, from the small—such as the Intelligencer Journal-Lancaster New Era in Lancaster, Pennsylvania, which charges readers of Lancaster Online to view obituaries and is considering putting a price tag on local news—to the New York Times, which said last year it would start charging for content this year.

The Times, which is expected to release details of its pay-to-read plan in March, has said it will use a metered system.

"This process of rethinking our business model has also been driven by our desire to achieve additional revenue diversity that will make us less susceptible to the inevitable economic cycles," Janet L. Robinson, president and CEO of the New York Times Co., said in a press release last year announcing the decision. "We were also guided by the fact that our news and information are being featured in an increasingly broad range of end-user devices and services, and our pricing plans and policies must reflect this vision." L. Gordon Crovitz, a founder of Journalism Online, a service that helps publications charge for access to their digital content, predicts the Times will see an "$80 to $100 million revenue stream in the not too distant future" from the venture. Times officials declined to comment for this story.

Though the Times isn't saying much, its announcement alone was enough to get other newspapers moving in the same direction. As a result of fallout from the Times' decision, as well as what he's seeing throughout the industry, Crovitz predicts "2011 will be the year of many, many launches." Crovitz, a former publisher of the Wall Street Journal who led the move to erect the paywall around the paper, says that by the end of the year dozens of papers—possibly more than 100—will be charging readers through Journalism Online's Press+ service. In February, Google and Apple also jumped into the fray with digital subscription systems for newspapers and magazines.

Many papers will not use traditional paywalls—a term Journalism Online now eschews. "Paywalls are so last year," Crovitz says. "Our motto is, 'down with paywalls, up with freemium.'" That means the company is pushing the metered approach as well as bundling, in which newspapers sell package deals that include access to their print, online and mobile content. "Until very recently, technology was limited, so that publishers had to choose either a paywall, where everyone must pay, or fully free," Crovitz says. "Now technology lets publishers charge only their most engaged readers, who value unlimited access."

Ken Doctor, a former editor and media executive and author of "Newsonomics: Twelve New Trends That Will Shape the News You Get," preaches that the future may well belong to those who bundle. In fact, he says, the initial success of the iPad should give publishers the confidence to bundle and sell their different content offerings. "What the tablet does by accident is it gives the industry a do-over opportunity," Doctor says. Apple sold more than 13 million iPads last year and is expected to sell another 50 million in 2011, Doctor says, adding that an additional 20 million tablets made by other companies are also expected to be sold.

Dallas' Moroney agrees the iPad provides newspapers with an opportunity. "It's very friendly to people who enjoy reading a newspaper," he says. "It is a bit of a 'lean back' device, not unlike a newspaper."

The good news to Doctor is that users of digital devices are already accepting the idea of paying for content and services. "Readers are moving more quickly from print to digital," he says. "The earliest adapters [to mobile devices and tablets] are heavy news and information readers. If there is good, in-depth coverage, a serious focus on education and other issues I care about, I'm going to feel better about paying for that digital content."

> **If there is good, in-depth coverage, a serious focus on education and other issues I care about, I'm going to feel better about paying for that digital content.**

For editors and reporters this means a new obligation—writing and posting what people are willing to pay to read. "Editors for the first time will have direct responsibility for an increasingly important revenue stream," Crovitz says. He adds that in the much-missed days of booming ad sales, when advertising brought in 80 percent of a newspaper's revenue, there was less pressure to boost circulation revenue. "Now it's going to be at the top of their minds," Crovitz says. "Editors will be able to see what journalism they do makes people subscribe."

Alan Mutter, who writes the Reflections of a Newsosaur blog, predicts that most of the publishers who hope charging for content will be their financial salvation will be disappointed. "In the next 18 months, there will be more [paywalls] than there are today," says Mutter, a former editor and media executive turned consultant. Mutter's reason for pessimism: If newspapers charge for content, readers will have plenty of opportunity to find the same local news on other sites that don't charge, making it unlikely that many will ante up. "I don't think the typical reader will have any trouble finding lots of information for free."

Metros will have the toughest time with online tollbooths, says Rick Edmonds, media business analyst for the Poynter Institute. "It doesn't make sense for the typical metro," he says. "A moderately strong television station can just crank it up" and provide more news for free online, making it less likely people will buy access to the newspaper's website.

Besides, when a newspaper embraces a metering plan, that means it is putting a financial burden on its most loyal readers, says Steve Buttry, a former reporter and editor who is director of community engagement for TBD, a free local news website for metro Washington, D.C. "'Let's try to stick it to our best customers'—that doesn't sound like a good business plan to me," he says. Buttry doesn't rule out charging for online content, but he says publishers have to do it in a more creative way. As an example, he cites Politico, the free website and newspaper that feeds the habit of political junkies. (TBD and Politico are both owned by Allbritton Communications.) Politico this year launched Politico Pro, which offers $2,495-a-year subscriptions for in-depth coverage of subjects such as energy, technology and health care. True, only a small audience will spend that kind of money, but, Buttry argues, "at that price you don't need much more. You can build a base around a very small audience willing to pay."

That strategy may play well on K Street or with certain industries, but it's obviously not suited to the daily newspaper reader in Wichita or Fresno. To create online revenue for newspapers, Buttry says, publishers must look past paywalls and search for new ways to attract cash. That could mean helping advertisers make online sales or use digital technology to better target ads. "Does a local business want eyeballs or do they want sales?" Buttry asks. "We can help them make sales online. . . . Instead of this effort going into paywalls, they should be trying to make money off location-based news and commercial opportunities on mobile platforms."

Despite the naysayers, many editors are showing a willingness to charge for online content, albeit slowly and cautiously.

"People are simply learning how to do this. There isn't any model that's sure to work; you just try things and you learn," says Ernie Schreiber, online editor of Lancaster Online. The locally owned Intelligencer Journal-Lancaster New Era began, charging for access to its online obituaries last year and may soon start charging for other types of news or features, Schreiber says.

But why take the risk of losing audience share? "We're a newsroom, and like every other newsroom, we had to downsize," Schreiber says. "We need to have revenue to pay our employees." The paper allows readers to read seven obituaries for free each month before charging $1.99 per month or $19.99 annually for unlimited access. Schreiber says there is a small niche audience willing to pay to read obits. Included are those who have retired and moved out of the Lancaster area, as well as banks, stock brokerages and financial advisers—"anyone who has a fiduciary duty when somebody dies to take action or to close an account."

With more than six months' experience under his belt, Schreiber says that the audience has been OK with the pay-to-read plan. "Readers were amazingly understanding. They've read about the layoffs in the industry; they still generally like newspapers. They don't want them to disappear," Schreiber says. "Only two cursed me out." Schreiber declines to say how many people subscribe to the online obits; he says the number is growing and is giving the newspaper confidence to charge for other types of local news. "We feel certain that metered pay will open a new revenue stream and that fears of loss of readership have been vastly overstated," Schreiber says. He adds that six months after the site started charging for them, pageviews of obituaries went up 3.7 percent and unique visitors to the pages increased 6.8 percent. Average time on page more than doubled, from one minute to two-and-a-half minutes.

A lot has changed in the industry since Slate, a pioneering online magazine, started charging in 1998, an experiment it abandoned after a year, or even as recently as 2007, when the New York Times gave up on its two-year effort to charge for access to its star columnists. For one thing, Schreiber says, he thinks readers now accept that it costs money to produce the news. Others point out that technology has moved forward, giving newspapers more ways to deliver digital products to readers on the go.

"They'll pay reasonable amounts for quality news delivered when and how they want it," Schreiber says.

Technology is opening up new opportunities to papers that want to charge for content on smart phones and tablets—devices where consumers are already used to paying for services provided through apps—as well as online offerings. "The metered approach lets publishers have their cake and eat it, too, in a way that older paywalls did not," Crovitz said in a follow-up e-mail interview. "Publishers using the metered approach keep all their online ad revenues and all their online readers, whereas the older approach of a harsh paywall cuts off traffic dramatically and needlessly."

In Dallas, Publisher Moroney decided this was the year that the Dallas Morning News would follow the lead of the Arkansas Democrat-Gazette some 300 miles to the northeast and charge readers for online access. Readers of the Belo-owned Morning News now have to ante up whether they read the print version or tap into the newspaper's content via the Web, a smart phone or an iPad.

Moroney admits to a degree of anxiety. But, he says, newspapers have to act, because the old 80-20 business plan that for decades provided newspapers with handsome profits is dead. Sure, that now-quaint business model was great while it lasted. But, Moroney says, newspapers will never again be able to count on advertising for 80 percent of their revenue. "We just don't think the ability to drive ad revenue in the digital space is ever going to support the size of the newsroom that the Dallas Morning News employs," he says. So, he adds, leaders at the paper had to decide "what's the next logical way [to support a newspaper], and that is to look to the consumer directly and say, 'Will you pay for access?'"

Moroney is asking people to spend $33.95 a month to receive a seven-day home delivery subscription to the print edition plus full access to the paper's website. Monthly subscriptions to iPhone, iPad and e-editions of the paper can be bought for $9.99 each. Other packages offering different combinations of services are also available. Portions of the paper's site will stay free, particularly information that could readily be found else-where. Moroney believes metro newsrooms have something of value to sell. "It's the depth and breadth of reporting that we can do that nobody else could do," Moroney says. "That's what we believe gives us the opportunity. There is so much there that they can't get anyplace else."

And so the Morning News will continue to post breaking news for free. But if readers want to know more, they will have to pay. If a bank is robbed in downtown Dallas, that news might be free. But it's going to cost you to find out the status of the police investigation or the exclusive news that police believe the key suspect may have hit a half-dozen other banks in the Southwest. The same would be true for political and other news. Readers could find out for free the names of the candidates, but they'll have to pay to get an in-depth look into their backgrounds and campaigns.

That may not be enough.

Critics argue that most metros and regional papers, many of which have cut back sharply on their offerings in the face of financial reversals, simply don't have enough exclusive and valuable content that people will pay for. With aggregators, blogs and local websites in the mix, readers have plenty of other options to get their local news for free.

"The idea that the newspaper can charge for local content when other people are giving it away for free, I think, is a false hope," Mutter says. "It's not as though the newspaper publisher is master of his domain anymore."

The exception, Mutter says, may be the New York Times. "Most publications don't have as much compelling original content in a month as the New York Times puts out in a day," says Mutter, who has worked at the Chicago Sun-Times and the San Francisco Chronicle.

Ouch. To somebody like me—who has spent more than three decades in the newsrooms of regional papers—those words hurt. Is he saying we're not providing our readers anything worth paying for?

Not necessarily. Mutter says there are other things a newspaper can charge for—just not the daily local news. "A newspaper can be an expert on whatever it wants to be an expert on," Mutter says. Local sports teams, specific companies or industries or cultural activities, all are areas that a newspaper could specialize in and charge for, in his view. "Newspapers could use their unparalleled expertise on content that will be unique, and they could charge," Mutter says. "There's no reason they can't . . . except for lack of creativity."

Not every paper could, or should, be the New York Times. There are many markets out there willing to pay for local news, says Walter Hussman Jr., publisher of the Arkansas Democrat-Gazette. Like his. But it wasn't all that long ago, as I mention to him, that many in the industry brushed him off as kind of a nice Southern publisher with somewhat, shall we say, eccentric ideas.

"You're being kind," says Hussman, who erected his wall during a time when it was universally accepted that if the industry gave away the news online, it would recoup by selling ads. "Most people thought we were crazy," says Hussman of his decision to challenge conventional wisdom and charge non-subscribers for online access, a move he implemented to protect the printed paper. "They were saying, 'What on earth are those idiots doing in Arkansas?'" Today, some of those same people are calling Hussman for advice. But, he adds, he is still seeing confusion in the industry as many remain enamored with running up huge numbers of online views while keeping their fingers crossed that eventually the money will follow. Some don't want to risk losing the huge number of pageviews they now receive on free sites.

"I've had calls from fellows who are publishers of newspapers in large towns who want to do it but are saying, 'I don't know if the corporate office is going to let us do that,'" because executives fear losing pageviews. That thinking doesn't make sense to Hussman, whose WEHCO Media owns the paper. Lots of those online visitors are "out of the market. Those numbers don't really do our local advertisers any good," Hussman says. "It's just not going to generate a lot of revenue." One problem, according to Hussman, is newspaper politics, as those in online divisions don't want to do anything that will shrink the audience. "Any kind of traffic they get is traffic that helps to justify what they're doing or that they need another person."

I've had calls from fellows who are publishers of newspapers in large towns who want to [charge for content] but are saying, 'I don't know if the corporate office is going to let us do that.'

To Hussman, it's backward thinking. "They're letting the online portion of the paper kind of wag the dog," he says. "They're not looking at what really is best for the newspaper here."

The rap on the Democrat-Gazette approach is that it focuses too much on protecting the print version of the paper and too little on expanding the digital business—the future. Hussman brushes off the critics. "Our dinosaur print product still brings in 89 percent of our revenue," Hussman says. "I think it's a pretty good thing to protect."

Simple economics say it makes sense to emphasize advertising sales efforts on the print paper, where advertisers pay about $40 per 1,000 readers. Online ads typically bring in at most $10 per 1,000 readers, with most online ads paying only a couple of dollars—and often less than $1—per 1,000. (On the other hand, the number of those print readers is steadily eroding in most metro markets.) Hussman says his paper keeps plenty of news and features available for free, a move that helps keep pageviews up. Arkansas Online has seen its traffic steadily increase since 2006 and had 77 million pageviews last year, Gallaty says. He says the company saw its online revenue grow 17.7 percent over 2009. The site provides free access to breaking news, video, photos, local weather and other features. Print subscribers get free access beyond the paywall, while online-only subscribers are charged $15 a month.

In any case, publishers who do decide to charge have to be cautious before moving forward. Readers can be a fickle bunch. Just ask Tyler Patton, publisher of the Valley Morning Star in Harlingen, Texas, a Freedom Communications paper with a circulation in the 20,000 range.

Patton last year pulled the plug on the paper's experiment with a paywall just nine months after launching it. "It didn't go well," he says.

Surprisingly, he says, the objections didn't come from people who were charged $4.95 a month to read the online offerings. Rather, it was print subscribers, who were entitled to free access to the online product as long as they registered. "That was the most surprising thing by far," Patton says. "I guess people just don't like registering. . . . All they had to do is call in and get their account number."

So, what did Patton learn that could be shared with other publishers who are pondering whether they should set up online tollbooths? "Before you do it, you have to really, really research your online audience as much as you could," he says. "You could be surprised."

Critical Thinking

1. Ken Doctor, a former media executive and editor, offers this observation: "The earliest adapters [to mobile devices and tablets] are heavy news and information readers. If there is good, in-depth coverage, a serious focus on education and other issues I care about, I'm going to feel better about paying for that digital content." Do you agree?

2. If newspapers don't realize revenue from electronic distribution, what are their options for paying the bills?

CARY SPIVAK (cspivak01@gmail.com) is an investigative reporter for the Milwaukee Journal Sentinel, focusing on business issues. He wrote about the rise of political fact-checking by news outlets in AJR's Winter issue.

Test-Your-Knowledge Form

We encourage you to photocopy and use this page as a tool to assess how the articles in *Annual Editions* expand on the information in your textbook. By reflecting on the articles you will gain enhanced text information. You can also access this useful form on a product's book support website at www.mhhe.com/cls

NAME: DATE:

_____

TITLE AND NUMBER OF ARTICLE:

_____

BRIEFLY STATE THE MAIN IDEA OF THIS ARTICLE:

_____

LIST THREE IMPORTANT FACTS THAT THE AUTHOR USES TO SUPPORT THE MAIN IDEA:

_____

WHAT INFORMATION OR IDEAS DISCUSSED IN THIS ARTICLE ARE ALSO DISCUSSED IN YOUR TEXTBOOK OR OTHER READINGS THAT YOU HAVE DONE? LIST THE TEXTBOOK CHAPTERS AND PAGE NUMBERS:

_____

LIST ANY EXAMPLES OF BIAS OR FAULTY REASONING THAT YOU FOUND IN THE ARTICLE:

_____

LIST ANY NEW TERMS/CONCEPTS THAT WERE DISCUSSED IN THE ARTICLE, AND WRITE A SHORT DEFINITION:

NOTES

NOTES

4 1 16